SPANISH HISTORY SINCE 1808

SPANISH HISTORY SINCE 1808

Edited by

JOSÉ ALVAREZ JUNCO

Prince of Asturias Professor of Spanish History,
Tufts University, USA

and

ADRIAN SHUBERT

Professor of History, York University, Canada

A member of the Hodder Headline Group
LONDON
Co-published in the United States of America by
Oxford University Press Inc., New York

First published in Great Britain in 2000
This impression reprinted in 2002 by
Arnold, a member of the Hodder Headline Group,
338 Euston Road, London NW1 3BH

http://www.arnoldpublishers.com

Co-published in the United States of America by
Oxford University Press Inc.,
198 Madison Avenue, New York, NY10016

British Library Cataloguing in Publication Data
A catalogue record for this book is available from the British Library

Library of Congress Cataloging-in-Publication Data
A catalog record for this book is available from the Library of Congress

ISBN 0 340 66228 X (hb)
ISBN 0 340 66229 8 (pb)

2 3 4 5 6 7 8 9 10

Production Editor: Julie Delf
Production Controller: Fiona Byrne
Cover Design: T. Griffiths

Typeset in 10/12 pt Sabon by York House Typographic Ltd, Ealing, London
Printed and bound in India by Replika Press Pvt Ltd., 100% EOU,
Delhi-110 040

What do you think about this book? Or any other Arnold title?
Please send your comments to feedback.arnold@hodder.co.uk

Contents

Contributors

Paloma Aguilar is a Lecturer in Political Science at the UNED in Madrid and author of *Memoria y olvido de la Guerra Civil Española* (1996).

José Alvarez Junco is Prince of Asturias Professor of Spanish History at Tufts University. His books include *El emperador del paralelo: Lerroux y la demagogia populista* (1990) and *La ideología política del anarquismo español (1868–1910)* (1976).

Luis Arranz is Lecturer in the History of Political and Social Thought and Movements at the Universidad Complutense de Madrid. He is the author of a number of articles on nineteenth and twentieth century political history.

Edward Baker is Professor of Spanish at the University of Florida. His books include *Materiales para escribir Madrid* (1991) and *La biblioteca de Don Quijote* (1997).

Sebastian Balfour is Reader at the London School of Economics. He is author of *Dictatorship, Workers, and the City: Labour in Greater Barcelona Since 1939* (1989) and *The End of the Spanish Empire, 1898–1923* (1997).

Carolyn P. Boyd is Professor of History at the University of California at Irvine. She is author of *Praetorian Politics in Liberal Spain* (1979) and *Historia Patria* (1997).

Isabel Burdiel is Professor of Contemporary History of the Universidad de Valencia. She has written widely on the early nineteenth century and is author of *La política de los notables: moderados y avanzados durante el Régimen del Estatuto Real, (1834–36)* (1987) and 'Myths of Failure, Myths of Success: New Perspectives on Nineteenth Century Spanish Liberalism' in the *Journal of Modern History*, (Dec 1998), pp. 892–912.

Mercedes Cabrera is Professor of History at the Universidad Complutense de Madrid. She is author of *La patronal ante la II República: organizaciones y* *estrategia (1931–1936)* (1983) and *La industria, la prensa y la política: Nicolás Ma. de Urgoiti, 1869–1951* (1994).

William J. Callahan is Professor of History at the University of Toronto and Fellow of Victoria College. He is author of *Honor, Industry and Commerce in Eighteenth Century Spain, La Santa y Real Hermandad del Refugio y Piedad de Madrid, 1619–1832*, and *Church, Politics, and Society in Spain, 1750–1874*, (1984).

Demetrio Castro is Professor at the Public University of Navarra. He is author of *Los males de la imprenta: política y libertad de prensa en una sociedad dual* (1998).

Antonio Cazorla-Sánchez is currently a Research Fellow at the Universidad Complutense de Madrid. He is the author of *Desarrollo sin Reformistas* (1999) and of a number of articles on the origins of Francoism.

Jesús Cruz is Associate Professor of History at the University of Delaware. He is the author of *Gentlemen, Bourgeois and Revolutionaries: Political Change and Cultural Persistence among Spanish Dominant Groups, 1750–1850* (1996).

George Esenwein is Associate Professor of History at the University of Florida at Gainesville. He is the author of *Anarchist Ideology and the Working-Class Movement in Spain, 1868–1898* (1989) and co-author of *Spain at War: The Spanish Civil War in Context, 1931–1939* (1995).

Stephen Jacobson is Assistant Professor of History at the University of New Hampshire. He is the author of a number of articles on the legal profession in nineteenth century Catalonia.

Santos Juliá is Professor of History and Sociology at the Universidad Nacional de Educación a Distancia. His many books on modern Spanish history include *Madrid, 1931–1934: de la fiesta popular a la lucha de clases* (1984) and *Manuel Azaña: una biografía política: del Ateneo al Palacio Nacional* (1990).

Enrique Moradiellos teaches modern history at the Universidad de Extremadura. He is the author of a number books, including *Neutralidad benévola: el gobierno británico y la insurrección militar española de 1936* (Oviedo, 1990), *Las Caras de Clio: Introducción a la Historia* (Madrid, 1994) and *La Perfidia de Albión: el gobierno británico y la guerra civil española* (Madrid, 1996).

Javier Moreno Luzón is Lecturer in History at the Universidad Complutense, Madrid. He is author of *Romanones: Caciquismo y política liberal* (1998).

Mary Nash is Professor of Contemporary History at the Universidad de Barcelona. Her books include *Experiencias desiguales: conflictos sociales y* *respuestas colectivas* (1994) and *Defying Male Civilization: Women in the Spanish Civil War* (1995).

Xosé M. Núñez Seixas is Professor of History at the Universidad de Santiago de Compostela. He is author of *Historiographical Approaches to Nationalism in Spain* (1993) and co-editor of *O nacionalismo galego* (1995).

Leandro Prados de la Escosura is Professor of Economic History at the Universidad Carlos III in Madrid. He is author of *De imperio a nación: crecimiento y atraso económico en España (1780–1930)* (1988) and 'Growth and Macro-economic Performance in Spain 1939–93' in N. Crafts and G. Toriolo, (eds); *Economic Growth in Europe Since 1945* (1996).

Genoveva Queipo de Llano is Lecturer in Modern History at the Universidad Nacional de Educacíon a Distancia. She is the author of *Los Intelectuales y la Dictadura de Primo de Rivera* (1987).

Pamela Beth Radcliff is Associate Professor of History at the University of California at San Diego. Her monograph, *From Mobilization to Civil War: The Politics of Polarization in the Spanish City of Gijón (1900–1937)* (1996), was awarded the Sierra Book Prize for 1997 by the Western Association of Women Historians. She is co-editor of *Constructing Spanish Womanhood Female Identity in Northern Spain* (1999).

Fernando del Rey teaches the History of Social and Political Thoughts and Movements at the Universidad Complutense de Madrid. She is the author of *La Defense Contra la Revolucíon* (1995), and of *Proprietarios y patronos. La politica de las organizaciones economicas en la Espana de la Restauracíon*, Madrid (1992).

Adrian Shubert is Professor and Chair of History at York University. His books include *A Social History of Modern Spain* (1990) and *Death and Money in the Afternoon: A History of Spanish Bullfighting* (1999).

Nigel Townson teaches History at the Universidad Europea de Madrid. He is editor of *El republicanismo en España (1830–1977)* (1994).

Javier Tusell is Professor of Modern History at the Universidad Nacional de Educación a Distancia in Madrid. He is the author of numerous books on twentieth-century Spain, including *Antonio Maura: una biografía política* (1994) and *Franco, España y la II guerra mundial: entre el eje y la neutralidad* (1995).

Enric Ucelay Da Cal is Professor of History at the Universidad Autónoma de Barcelona. His books include *La Catalunya populista: imatge, cultura i política en l'etapa republicana (1931–1939)* (1982).

SUCH AS IT IS.

Spain - "I must uphold my national honor."
Detroit News.

Introduction

JOSÉ ALVAREZ JUNCO and ADRIAN SHUBERT

The Portuguese writer José Saramago based his novel, *The Stone Raft*, on the conceit that the Iberian peninsula became detached from the rest of Europe and floated into the mid-Atlantic. This metaphor is a perfect description of the way in which the histories of the two Iberian nations, Spain and Portugal, have been treated by historians of 'Europe', especially in the English-speaking world.

This detachment, the historians', not the peninsula's, derives from a number of causes. One is the way in which historians long defined what is important in history. So long as Clio suffered from tunnel vision, her gaze directed at power politics and high culture, the dismissal of these countries – and others – was explicable: they were not great powers and their thinkers and artists did not, by and large, form part of the continental canon. On the rare occasions when they served as the backdrop for the interests of their powerful neighbours, such as the Spaniards' resistance to Napoleon, they did at least come into view. Even then, the episode is generally referred to as the Peninsular War, a name which implies an external perspective and an external concern, rather than the War of Independence, which gives Spaniards' motivations and agency pride of place. Less immediately explicable is the absence of so imposing a figure as novelist Benito Pérez Galdós from the usual canon of nineteenth-century European literature.

The historians' shortcomings have been reinforced by trends emanating from the broader culture: a centuries-long tradition in which Spain has been both demonized and 'orientalized'. Such views have not been limited to the English-speaking world, but they have been unusually strong and persistent there. Moreover, with history written at the summit of the world-system of power, people at the lower levels often internalize such views and become obsessed with understanding what they are lacking. Both Spain and the Spaniards have long had to bear this burden of the stereotype.

The Islamic conquest of most of the Iberian Peninsula made it a borderland for Christian Europe, a kind of internal 'other'. In the later Middle Ages the Spanish kingdoms, and especially Aragón, assumed an active role in European affairs. With their mixture of mercantile deals, military aggression and outright piracy, Barcelona and Valencia differed little from Venice or Genoa but feelings of cultural superiority led Italian commentators to view their Spanish competitors as uneducated, cruel and ridiculously ceremonious rustics.

The consolidation of Aragonese dominance over Naples in the 1490s coincided with the ascendance to the Holy See of Alexander Borgia, a cardinal of Valencian origins. He exemplified the relaxed morality of the Italian Renaissance, but through a skillful process of 'projection', ascribing to others one's own unpleasant traits, his occupation of the throne of St Peter was interpreted as a symptom of Spanish 'corruption'.[1] Most significantly, the refined depravity of the Borgia family was explained as a consequence of the Oriental and African elements in Spanish blood, what the Florentine ambassador Francesco Guicciardini called the 'Jewish infection'.

Suspicion of a multi-cultural and multi-racial Spain was already present in the travel literature of the late Middle Ages. Baron Jaroslav Rosmithala, brother in law of the king of Bohemia, visited Castile in 1466 and complained that its people 'are infidels for the most part ... They look like the Gipsies who maraud our lands ... they live like them, stealing and committing mischief'. Twenty years later, the Polish nobleman Nicolaus von Poplau denounced Spaniards as 'crude ... they live with Saracen brutes, they deal with them, breathing their pagan air and imitating their customs'.[2]

Shortly thereafter the 'Catholic Kings' began the process of 'purifying' Spain of its Jewish and Islamic contaminants. They were given the choice of expulsion or conversion. Those who converted had their orthodoxy policed by the Inquisition and suffered discrimination under 'statutes of purity of blood'. This process coincided with the hegemony of the Spanish Habsburgs in Europe and with the acquisition of a massive empire in America. The enemies of the Spanish monarchy, especially Lutheran reformists, Dutch rebels and expelled Jews waged what was probably the first propaganda campaign in European history, launching the highly successful image of the Spaniard as intolerant priest–inquisitor, bloody *conquistador* of the Indies and brutal oppressor of valiant Dutch Protestants.

There was, of course, considerable truth to these images, but their power as propaganda lay in two corollaries, both of which were totally false: that Spaniards were immensely more cruel than the people who denounced them and that there was nothing more to Spain than cruelty and intolerance. This 'Black Legend', as it came to be called, had no room for the vitality and splendour of the Spanish Renaissance, the great mystics of the sixteenth century, or the poetry, drama and painting of the Golden Age. Above all, it could not admit to the relative freedom of political debate, the most significant example of which was that the most powerful arguments used by the enemies of the Spanish monarchy were provided by Spaniards such as

Bartolomé de las Casas, whose dissidence did not earn them punishment of any kind. That Samuel Johnson admitted that he learned of the cruelties of slavery from the theologians of the University of Salamanca says it all.

As this was the moment at which pre-national collective stereotypes were emerging in Europe, these negative portrayals became associated not only with Spanish policies but also with Spanish character and with the 'race' itself.[3] The image of Spain as the epitomy of absolutism and intolerance would remain fixed in the European collective mind for centuries.

The fate of Philip II is an outstanding example of this process of cultural construction. The son of a Portuguese mother and a Flemish father, Philip was made by the Anglo-Dutch propaganda machine into a monster, the embodiment of the 'immorality' coursing through Spanish veins. On the testimony of Antonio Pérez, Philip's former secretary become personal enemy, it was accepted that he had secretly murdered two of his wives and his son and heir, Don Carlos. Philip's policies are certainly debatable, but his personality was no worse than that of Henry VIII of England, whose public image was cleaned up so he could be a plausible champion of Protestantism. Don Carlos was an insane teenager whose death was almost certainly an accident, but the Black Legend would make him a martyr. The story became a favourite for writers, most famously Schiller, whose story Giuseppe Verdi later turned into a successful opera. The sombre Philip II and the Inquisition, labelled as Spanish, became popular ingredients of the Gothic novel.[4] As late as the 1840s, Théophile Gautier could see nothing in Philip's magnificent palace, the Escorial, but a gloomy pile dominated by 'an indefinable odour, icy and sickly, of holy water and sepulchral vaults'. And he could write without any trace of irony: 'Few people come back from the Escorial; they die of consumption two or three days later'.[5]

The Enlightenment added the idea of decadence to the negative image of Spain. For Montesquieu and Voltaire, the decline of Spanish power was proof of the damaging consequences of despotism and intolerance. Again, these charges were not baseless. Fear of new ideas, lack of political checks and balances and the prevalence of certain aristocratic attitudes certainly contributed to Spanish stagnation, but they were far from being a Spanish monopoly and certainly had nothing to do with inherited racial traits. Moreover, such a description was particularly inaccurate at a moment when the new Bourbon dynasty was undertaking major reforms. Charles III (1759–88) was a model of the 'enlightened' monarch of the period.

The eighteenth century also brought changes to the image. Travelling became popular among the British upper classes, and although Spain was not part of the Grand Tour that was *de rigeur* for young gentleman – itself a powerful comment on its presumed lack of cultural value – a number did go there. Their descriptions of the country faithfully reflected their prejudices: none failed to comment on the disrepair of the highways and inns, the bigotry and superstition of the people, the laziness and idleness of the aristocracy, the horrific spectacles of *auto de fe* and bullfighting.[6] At the same time, they began to notice the magnificence of decaying palaces, the chivalrous gesturing of the common folk and the shocking sensuality of the women dancing the fandango. For Henry Swinburne, visiting Spain in 1775, it 'exceeds in wantonness all the other dances I ever beheld'.[6] Once again, such lasciviousness was attributed to African or Oriental blood, but their curiosity foreshadowed a change in European sensibility and the emergence of Romanticism.

The real turnaround came with the war against Napoleon (1808–14). The conflict was a complex one, but at a time of growing romantic nationalism the Peninsular War became widely interpreted as the reappearance of an indomitable Spanish people, the same one that had resisted the Romans two thousand years before. It was at this moment that Lord Byron happened upon the scene. Byron saw the 'sons of Spain' heroically fighting for their freedom, inspired by the 'glorious tale' of Spanish history and by chivalry, their 'ancient goddess'. He was particularly impressed by the deeds of a woman named Agustina who, during the siege of Zaragoza, snatched a match from the hand of a dying artilleryman and fired off a canon. Her act earned this 'maid of Heaven' six full stanzas of Byronic verse: she embodied 'more than female grace ... form'd for all the witching arts of love' yet had the resolution to 'lead in Glory's fearful chase'.[7]

After the Napoleonic War hundreds of British and French veterans published memoirs of their experiences in Spain. Many openly exaggerated its dangers and exoticism. At the same time, Spanish artistic treasures arrived in London and Paris, in some cases the products of plunder, in others as gifts, such as those presented to the Duke of Wellington by the Spanish government. This 'discovery' of Murillo, Velázquez and El Greco triggered what E. Allison Peers called a 'Spanish revival'.[8] Even the picaresque novel, marked in its crudeness and realism, was enjoying a vogue, marketed as a tale of adventures and marvels.

One of the principal promoters of this worship of a romantic Spain was Victor Hugo, who was born in Madrid while his father was there as a general in the French army of occupation. Significantly, most of his references to Spain are in a work entitled *Orientales*. Many of these allusions contain geographic errors or outright fabrications, such as the minarets of Alicante, but this did not matter.[9] Spain was, he said, 'the homeland of his dreams', and his enormous popularity ensured that the image of Spain he chose to embrace would wield wide influence.

This was the genesis of a romantic view which would be refined by Washington Irving, Edgar Quinet, Gautier and many others. Spain became a land of gypsies, highwaymen, proud beggars, flamenco dancing, bullfighting, public executions by strangulation, monks acting as Carlist guerrilla fighters, passionate and dangerous women perfectly depicted by Merimée in his novel *Carmen* which Bizet later converted into an opera. The romantic re-evaluation of Spain did not alter the inherited stereotype, but approached it with a different sensibility. The characteristics now considered typically

'Spanish' were mere transpositions of those of the Black Legend. The anti-Napoleonic guerrilla is the Romantic's take on the soldier in Flanders or the New World *conquistador*. Instead of cruelty to be condemned there is audacity to celebrate. The proud beggar differs little from the idle and impoverished aristocrat whose uselessness had long been vilified. The Carlist monk is an updated inquisitor with religious fervour replacing fanaticism.

The change had little to do with Spain itself. Rather, it derived from s shift in the moral values and internal demands of the rest of Europe. Spain began to be valued positively because it offered an exoticism which satisfied the curiosity and the need to consume refined cultural products typical of the new middle classes which had reached a considerable level of well being. It was the moment when the daily press and the literary market place were emerging and the reading public demanded themes that attracted their attention. Romantic writers offered adventure, mystery and extreme emotion, and Spain provided the perfect backdrop, multi-coloured and sensational, even more so if one exaggerated the depiction as did Gustave Doré in his drawings of terrifying mountains, ruins and elaborate oriental garb.[10] At the same time, this exotic country was also close at hand and its people spoke a familiar language. Its exoticism was easy and superficial, a kind of costume jewellery.

Furthermore, Spain was seen as a pre-modern society and this was a second source of its magnetism. The effects of 'progress' were weighed more ambivalently in post-Revolutionary France or industrial England than they had been during the Enlightenment. Revolutionary terror, political instability, the empire of economic man all produced a critical reaction. In artistic and intellectual circles it became fashionable to distance oneself from the moral cynicism and aesthetic mediocrity of the 'bourgeois philistine'. In his *Conféssion d'un Enfant du Siècle* Alfred de Musset said it explicitly:

> we do not accept the inheritance of the past but we do not know how to build a new world. The only reasonable thing to do is to be tubercular, to be neurasthenic, to take drugs, to indulge in orgies or mysticism.[11]

There was another possibility: to escape, to Spain. But only after having idealized this nearby country as a paradise outside of history, untouched by industrialization, urbanization and capitalism. Thus Amédée Achard in 1847:

> it is still the old Spain. You can see, in the roads running along precipices, the same mules with ornaments, led by a *mulero* who sings a ballad, or the traveller with his gun hanging from the saddle; nothing has changed at the inn, not even the lamp, which comes from the Moors, or the chimney where you can see an eternally boiling pot full of peas. Here generations pass and habits remain.[12]

Where an eighteenth century observer would have condemned such a scene as a sign of 'backwardness' the Romantic saw it as loyalty to one's identity. That is why Quinet described Spain as 'aristocratic and proletarian', the opposites of the bourgeoisie that reigned in France. And that is why he ends his book with this exhortation:

> Close, Córdoba, your crenellated doors to the bourgeois spirit of this century! Is it possible that the Great Captain's cavalry will be replaced by the banking aristocracy? I willingly accept that the rest of human-kind is going to be dominated by greed and material values, but I hope that at least this garden of honour continues to be open to the dream-builders.[13]

Yet again foreigners' dreams mattered more than Spaniards' realities.

Spain's lack of modernity comprised three main aspects. One was openly political: the Spanish resistance against Napoleon was seen as a defence of Church and Crown. For French legitimists it was an example of loyalty to the legitimate monarch. In 1820 however, Spaniards were the first Europeans to fight for liberal freedom against reactionary absolutism. Spaniards had defended their king against foreign invaders but now they rose against him. Both liberals and conservatives praised Spain as a country of intense beliefs, sincerity and bravery. Custine saw in the Spaniard 'a man with a weapon and a faith [who] despises tolerance as a betrayal', while Quinet judged them superior to the rest of Europe 'because, even if they are in an abyss ... they still believe that dying for a cause is worthwhile'.[14]

This is nostalgia for a less politically developed society, based on personal relations rather than contact with an anonymous bureaucratic state. An even more telling example of such nostalgia was the attractiveness of brigands, who were seen to embody dignity, a spirit of adventure and an individual code of honour at odds with the law not very different from the American 'Wild West' a few decades later.

Spanish pre-modernity was also attractive in its social manifestations. Romantic travellers were particularly impressed by what they saw as the lower classes' disdain for material values. They praised the pronounced dignity found even among Spanish beggars who had the air of gentlemen, even if dressed in rags. Thus Merimée: 'Believe me, there are still values in this country, but only among the poor. The lower class which is corrupt in England, brutalized by the miseries of manufactures, is still good here'.[15] Such statements were less concerned with providing an accurate description of Spanish reality than in using Spain as a foil with which to criticize contemporary modernity: the effects of industrialization on the working classes and the fear of social revolution that haunted so many Europeans.

Finally, there was the moral and vital side to pre-modernity. Travellers to Spain went on endlessly about the spontaneity, the joy in living and the innate aesthetic sense of the Spaniards. When one reads that Spain is 'the country in which the heart still reigns' or that Spaniards are 'animated by a joy and vitality which have been lost here',[16] one understands that the commentators' concern is less with Spain than with the absence of these qualities and the conventionality and anonymity characteristic of urban mass societies 'here'.

Few, if any of these observers, were really interested in understanding Spain. The Spain that they sought and which – naturally enough – they found was an idealization, the counter-image to the quotidian reality they rejected and left behind. They were ambivalent about modernity; after all, Spain was an object to cherish but never a model to imitate. Hence the unease, even irritation felt by Spanish elites committed to modernizing their country when they heard such praise from foreign visitors whose own countries provided them with greater security and a higher standing of living than could Spain.

Washington Irving, Henry Wadsworth Longfellow, John Singer Sargent and a few other Americans contributed to this image, but it was the historian William H. Prescott who did the most to set the stereotype of Spain in the United States. His *History of the Reign of Ferdinand and Isabel*, published in 1837, 'shaped both the character and direction of historical research in Spanish studies for well over a century'. 'Prescott's paradigm' cast Spain's 'unhealthy combination of political despotism and religious bigotry' as the antithesis to the Protestant republicanism of the United States. Against the notion of 'American exceptionalism', that the United States 'possessed a unique history that destined it for greatness', Prescott described a Spanish exceptionalism that separated it 'from the European, that is Protestant mainstream and consequently [left it] bereft of the progress and prosperity that flowed in its wake'.[16]

Seen from the western edge of the Atlantic, Spain remained an imperial power – and a Catholic one to boot – which hemmed in the United States' own imperial ambitions, especially towards Cuba. (Of course, in 1835 and 1848 Americans had brutally seized over half of what had once been New Spain but which was by then independent Mexico.) Long after it had become a second- or third-rate power in European eyes, Spain remained a rival for the United States, and as a result the Black Legend had a longer life there. When the US finally engaged Spain in military conflict, in 1898, the Black Legend was trotted out in all its sixteenth-century fullness. A new edition of Bartolomé de las Casas' book on Spanish mistreatment of Native Americans was published in New York, and other works of propaganda carried the same message. Thus J.J. Ingalls' *America's War for Humanity*:

> Spain has been tried and convicted in the forum of history. Her religion has been bigotry, whose sacraments have been solemnized by the faggot and the rack. Her statesmanship has been infamy ... her wars massacres, her supremacy has been a blight and a curse, condemning continents to sterility and their inhabitants to death.[17]

Such views had even reached the remote and impoverished British colony of Newfoundland. D.W. Prowse's 1895 *History* of the island expressed relief that it had been 'discovered' by John Cabot and not by a Spanish explorer; if that had happened its history would have been one of 'chronic revolutions, disordered finances, *pronunciamientos*, half-breeds and fusillades'.[18]

The great American contribution to the image of Romantic Spain came between the 1920s and 1940s in the person of Ernest Hemingway. To Americans, who had long looked on Europeans as decadent, Hemingway described Spaniards as 'the only good people left in Europe' and Spain as 'the very best country of all. It's still unspoiled and unbelievably tough and wonderful'.[19] These are typically Romantic words of praise: for somewhere to be 'unspoiled' means that other places are already rotten. For Hemingway, the First World War had destroyed such values as dignity, honour, virility and a stoic acceptance of death; he thought he had found them alive and well in Spain, and above all in the bullfight, which he saw as a ritual of life and death that expressed the Spanish national soul.

These stereotypes had such power that they even affected interpretations of the Spanish Civil War. Given the marginality of Spain for so many years, world opinion had to explain the conflict in terms it could understand and so it reprised the existing stereotypes. The Republic embodied progress, education, tolerance and the rational humanist myth. Against that, Franco's Nationalists embodied the fanatical obscurantism of the Inquisition. But the Republic was also made to fit the Romantic stereotype, although in a slightly updated form to make it more appealing to left-leaning intellectuals of the 1930s: Spanish workers were the passionate people fighting against all odds for their freedom.

A perfect, yet tragic embodiment of the Spanish myth was the poet Federico García Lorca. An Andalucian, passionate, full of vitality and imagination, sympathetic to the gypsies and critical of the Civil Guard, he was brutally murdered in the prime of his life. The world was shocked, but if the impact of this brutality was so great it was because it matched the stereotype. Lorca was an exceptional poet, but there were other extraordinary poets in his generation, perhaps the greatest in Spain's literary history, but none of them achieved his international celebrity. But then they were not as easily understandable to the outside world.

Nor could the world understand the changes that occurred between the 1950s and the 1970s. With Francoism conceived as a relapse to the dark ages of the Counter-Reformation rather than as one more local version of the nationalistic and authoritarian reaction so common in inter-war Europe, the only conceivable outcome was stagnation, if not outright decline. The silence which fell over Spain after the Civil War also fitted the image of one of those dormant stages to which 'oriental' peoples are expected to succumb after their explosions of rage and orgy. Thus change was unlikely, but Spain did change. And with the death of the dictator in November 1975 the country experienced a smooth transition to democracy. Yet what was one of the great success stories of post-1945 Europe was a disappointment to some, for whom Spaniards were not following their script. Thus the French journalist who had expected something other than Spaniards' cold reaction to the attempted coup of 23 February 1981: 'Spaniards have lost their inclination to die for freedom'. That this 'inclination' had been another foreigners' dream never crossed his mind.

For their part, Spaniards decided that if they could not eliminate the stereotype they might as well profit from it. *Bienvenido Mr. Marshall*, an excellent film from the 1950s, provides an ironic account of Spain's exclusion from the Marshall Plan. Having heard that the US ambassador is about to visit, a Castilian village decides to please him by having all its residents dress up – as flamenco dancers! In the 1960s the entire country did more or less that in order to attract tourism. Across Spain towns with no tradition of flamenco or bullfighting hurried to build bullrings or gypsy caves to lure the American and European descendants of the Romantic travellers for whom 'Spain' was Andalucia. The government marketed the country under the slogan 'Spain is different' and the response of *Life* magazine to Spain's pavilion at the 1964 New York World's fair revealed the power of this construct:

> Spain gambled $7 million on being itself. Its pavilion lives up to everyone's romantic notion of Spain. Outside the almost religious hush in the museum alcoves, the pavilion comes noisily alive with flamenco wails, hand clapping, throbbing guitars and the sibilant undercurrents of Spanish accents.[20]

By the mid-1960s tourism was Spain's largest industry.

The successful modernization process seems to have finally eased Spaniards' anxieties. With a stable democracy and a high standard of living, as members of NATO and the European Union, there are no longer reasons for them to feel in any way 'different' or peripheral. Their self-presentation at Expo 92, which they hosted in Sevilla, made this perfectly clear:

> To show the reality of a modern, dynamic and open-minded country whose contributions to World History were often exceptional and even decisive, as with the incorporation of the American continent into European culture, which situates Spain in a privileged position of contact between the European Community and developing America. In practice, this must be done with the maximum of respect for our own pluralism and without triumphalism .... With our eyes on the present and the future, we want to underline essential aspects of our modern purpose, far from the past glories of empire, and more oriented towards international co-operation and integration, the product of the common will of the immense majority of contemporary Spaniards
> ....
> One of the objectives of the Spanish Section is the concern to modernize the stereotype which many citizens of other countries still hold in their cultural memory about the way of life, folklore and even

political and social structure of Spanish society . . . . It is very important that our foreign partners receive the image of the Spain of the 20th century: cultural diversity, tolerance, hard work and desire to modernize are the cliches of today.[21]

If Spaniards can now accept their country as part of Europe, it is time for scholars and their students to do so as well. Ideally, the broadening of Clio's gaze to include a much richer range of subjects will eventually undermine the 'league table' approach which valued national histories primarily by their diplomatic clout and military power or by the contribution of a handful of their citizens to European 'culture'. When historians concern themselves with topics such as international migration, gender relations and popular culture, among many others, there is no reason to assign the Spanish case less importance than those of Britain, France or Germany. In the longer run, the ongoing construction of the European Union may undermine national histories altogether. Put another way, as the narrative of modern European history changes, the idea of just what constitutes 'Europe' should change with it.

This book approaches the modern history of Spain in this spirit. Many of the authors are explicit in their assessment of Spain as one more variant of a richly diverse European story, but even those who are not share this basic assumption. The authors themselves are a diverse group. They come from England, the United States, Canada and Spain, and those from Spain are based in a number of that country's regions: Cataluña, Galicia, Madrid, and Valencia. The work of Spaniards all too rarely appears in English; we are particularly pleased at being able to include so much of it here, enriching in another way the historical perspectives available to the English-language reader.

Notes

1 Sverker Anoldsson, quoted by Philip W. Powell, *Tree of Hate: Propaganda and Prejudices Affecting US Relationships with the Hispanic World* (NY and London, Basic Books, 1971), p. 41.
2 Jose García Mercadal, *Viajes de extranjeros por España y Portugal* (Madrid, Aguilar, 1962), vol. I, pp. 298, 304 and 322.
3 See José Alvarez Junco, 'España: el peso del estereotipo', *Claves*, 48 (December 1994), pp. 2–10.
4 García Mercadal, *Viajes de extranjeros*, vol. I, p. 616.
5 See Philip Powell *Tree of Hate*; Sverker Anoldsson *La Leyenda Negra: Estudios sobre sus orìgenes*, Acta Universitatis Gothoburgensis, LXVI, 3 (1960); William S. Maltby *The Black Legend in England: The Development of Anti-Spanish Sentiment, 1558–1660* (Durham, NC, Duke University Press, 1971); and Charles Gibson, *The Black Legend, Anti-Spanish Attitudes in the Old World and the New* (NY, A. Knopf, 1971).
6 Lewis Hanke, *The Spanish Struggle for Justice in America*.

7 Gordon K. Thomas, *Lord Byron's Iberian Pilgrimage* (Provo, 1983) pp. 33–60.

8 E. Allison Peers, *A History of the Romantic Movement in Spain* (Cambridge, Cambridge University Press, 1940), vol. I, p. 159.

9 Léon-François Hoffmann, *Romantique Espagne: l'Image de l'Espagne en France entre 1800 et 1850* (New Jersey and Paris, University of Princeton/Presses Universitaires de France, 1961), pp. 36–7, 41.

10 Gustave Doré and Jean Charles, Baron de Davilliers, *Voyage en Espagne* (Paris, Le Tour du Monde, 1862–63).

11 See Hoffmann, *Romantique Espagne*, p. 148.

12 Amédée Achard, *Un mois en Espagne* (Paris, Ernest Bourdin, 1847), p. 19; quoted by Hoffmann, *Romantique Espagne*, pp. 153 and 158–9.

13 E. Quinet, *Mes Vacances en Espagne* (Paris, 1857) quoted by Hoffmann, *Romantique Espagne*, pp. 158–9.

14 Robert de Custine, *L'Espagne sous Ferdinand VII* (Brussels, Vahlen & Cie., 1838), vol. I, pp. 41–2; Quinet, *Mes Vacances*, p. 247; both quoted by Hoffmann, *Romantique Espagne*, p. 152.

15 Prosper Mérimée, *Lettres d'Espagne* (Paris, Revue de Paris, 1831–33); quoted by Hoffmann, *Romantique Espagne*, p. 158.

16 Richard Kagan, 'Prescott's Paradigm: American Historical Scholarship and the Decline of Spain', *American Historical Review*, April (1996), pp. 425, 429–31.

17 J.J. Ingalls, *America's War for Humanity* (New York, 1898).

18 Cited in Peter Pope, *The Many Landfalls of John Cabot* (Toronto, 1998) p. 109.

19 Edward F. Stanton, *Hemingway and Spain* (Seattle, 1989) p. xiv.

20 *Life*, August 7, 1964.

21 *Comunidades Autónomas* (Sevilla, 1992) p. 1.

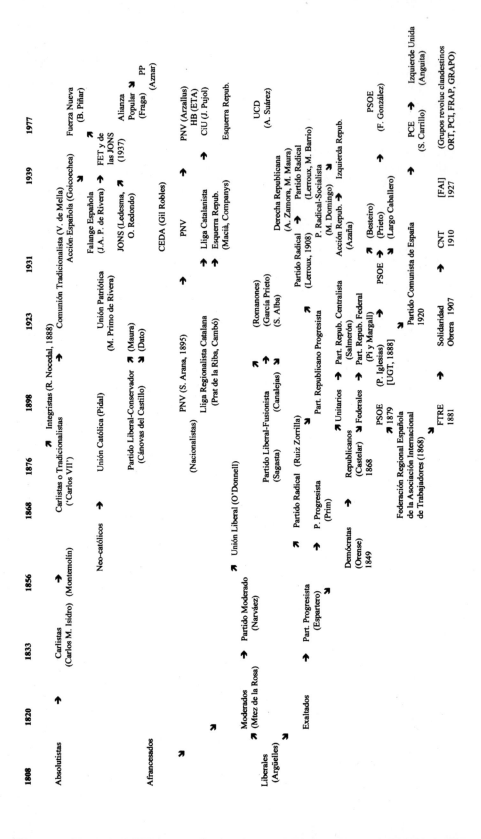

PART

I

THE TRAVAILS OF LIBERALISM, 1808–1874

The five essays in this section deal with the creation of a liberal-constitutional polity and some of the principal features of Spanish political life in the first three-quarters of the nineteenth century.

Isabel Burdiel tells the story of the difficult birth of that polity. During the reign of Charles IV (1789–1808), and particularly after the wars triggered by the French Revolution, Spain's Ancien Regime became increasingly unstable. The French invasion of Spain and the imposition of Napoleon's brother, Joseph, as king set in train a complex series of events that eventually brought that regime to an end. While some Spaniards collaborated with a French regime that promised significant reform, most resisted, although the motives behind their resistance were diverse and complex. Known in Spain as the 'War of Independence', the war against Napoleon (1808–14) also contained elements of a civil war. The struggle against the foreign enemy may have hidden this, but once that war had been won, Spaniards immediately plunged into a struggle between the absolutist supporters of the restored monarch, Ferdinand VII, and the Liberals who had given the country its first constitution, known as the Constitution of Cádiz or the Constitution of 1812. This conflict lasted twenty-five years, and was settled only after a seven-year long civil war, the First Carlist War (1833-1840), in which the Liberals defeated the supporters of the absolutist pretender, Ferdinand's brother Carlos.

But the Liberals were themselves divided into two principal groups, Moderates and Progressives, who fought each other to define the nature of the new constitutional system. The overthrow of the regency of the

Progressive general, Baldomero Espartero, brought the Moderates a victory that lasted until 1868. This quarter century of Moderate hegemony was underwritten by the control of political life by a narrow group of notables, reinforced by electoral fraud and tightening strictures on liberal freedoms, such as freedom of expression, as Jesús Cruz explains in his chapter. At the same time, as Cruz emphasizes, the Moderates were active builders and left Spain with an administrative and legal structure that long survived their own demise.

However limited they might look in retrospect, these changes constituted a real revolution, as Burdiel argues. The revolutionary nature of the period is perhaps nowhere more evident than in the experience of the Catholic Church, the subject of William Callahan's chapter. While neither Progressives nor Moderates questioned that Spain was and should remain a Catholic nation, they both shared a determination to reduce the wealth and power of the Church. Thus, the Inquisition was abolished; Church lands were disentailed and sold at auction; and limits placed on the number of religious orders and regular clergy, while the state began to challenge the Church's role in such key functions as education and welfare provision.

The main instrument of political change in this period, as Carolyn Boyd explains, was military force, and not just because there were two long wars, the War of Independence and the Carlist War. Between 1814 and 1820, the Liberals' struggle against Ferdinand's restored absolutism was carried on primarily through a series of military revolts known as *pronunciamientos*. Even after liberalism's victory in 1840, the turning points in the struggle between Moderates and Progressives came through military intervention. In particular, the Moderates' control of the political system left Progressives little choice but to turn to sympathetic generals if they wanted to come to power. Thus the political life of the period is strongly marked by the names of these military champions (*espadones*): Espartero, Narváez, O'Donnell, Prim, and such key events as the Revolution of 1854 and the 'Glorious Revolution' of 1868 began with *pronunciamientos*.

Moderates and Progressives were the most important groups within liberalism, but not the only ones. As Demetrio Castro describes, there very quickly emerged a left wing of liberalism, often bearing the features of earlier liberal secret societies. This political strand took institutional form in the Democratic Party, which was founded in 1849. Like the Liberals, Democrats had to deal with internal differences, especially the question of whether their programme was to be strictly political or also to include social objectives.

The shortcomings of the liberal system eventually brought revolution. The 'Gloriosa' of September 1868 chased Queen Isabella II from the throne she had occupied since 1843 and ushered in a tumultuous six-year period (*sexenio*), which saw the short-lived reign of Amadeo I, a king imported from Italy, followed by a short-lived Republic which dissolved into localist revolts (the Cantonalist movement) and another Carlist War, all set against the backdrop of a revolt in the economically crucial colony of Cuba (1868–78).

The *sexenio* was brought to an end in 1874 by a military coup. Its political backers wanted to return Spain to liberal constitutionalism; the challenge was to construct a system that was more open than that the Moderates had created, was able to reconcile the Church; and keep the military in the barracks.

1

The liberal revolution, 1808–1843

ISABEL BURDIEL

Between 1808 and 1843 the entire socio-economic order of the Spanish Ancien Regime was dismantled. The nobility and the clergy lost their legal privileges and the equality of all male citizens before the law was proclaimed. Entails, seigneurial rights and the tithe were abolished. The lands of the Church were disentailed and sold at public auction, the guilds were suppressed and economic freedom established. The Inquisition was dissolved and the Church's legal jurisdiction in civil affairs eliminated. The absolute power of the monarch was replaced by a parliamentary system based on popular sovereignty.

As in the other liberal countries in Europe, the new regime was constructed on the idea that access to active citizenship – the capacity to elect the nation's lawmakers or to be elected – must be limited to those who were capable of owning property and getting an education within the context of legal equality and the free market. Law and merit replaced privilege and honour as sources of political legitimation. Even so, as elsewhere in Europe, the liberal revolution did not automatically imply a transfer of political, economic or social power from the nobility and clergy to the middle class. Nor did it suppose the radical transformation of feudal economic relations into capitalist ones. What it did was to forge a new political arrangement of the mechanisms of social and economic power, and of the sources of cultural legitimacy, which had already undergone substantial change during the eighteenth century. The importance of those earlier changes, together with the impact of the crisis initiated by the Napoleonic invasion in 1808, is what defines the specific character of what contemporaries called 'the Spanish revolution'.

Liberalism was never the patrimony of a single class or social group. The crisis of the Ancien Regime provoked a profound convulsion that involved the nobility, the popular classes and the clergy as much as the middle classes. Nor did revolutionary liberalism constitute a systematic body of thought and action. It was the tactical outcome of circumstance rather than a programme.

As far as the majority of Spaniards were concerned, the reforms that were needed in the economic, and even in the political, sphere, could (and should) have been carried out without requiring a violent break with the Ancien Regime. Absolutism had to lose all credibility as an agent of change for liberalism to become a revolutionary ideology. Likewise, it took a bloody political struggle among groups which, despite their diversity, considered themselves to be liberals for the liberal state to take the conservative form it did after 1843. The liberal revolution was not anything other than the ongoing attempt to appropriate it and define it.

The crisis of the absolute monarchy

The fundamental breakdown of the mechanisms of power and legitimation of Spain's absolute monarchy took place during the reign of Charles IV (1788–1808). Ten years of lost wars, against the French from 1793 to 1795 and then against England from 1796 to 1802, demonstrated that the monarchy was incapable of even of guaranteeing the defence of its own territory, including the colonies. The French occupation of Catalonia and the Basque Country in 1794 was, in this sense, decisive in animating the rising against the French across the country in 1808.

The war effort fell on an economy that showed signs of exhaustion after a long period of expansion during the eighteenth century. In some areas the resistance against obligatory military levies and the numerous food riots ran together with urban protests and rural revolts against the payment of rents and seigneurial dues. This was the case, for example, in Valencia during the summer of 1801 when the farmers in the irrigated lands rebelled 'on the order of Pep del Orta that no one pay seigneurial dues on pain of death'. As was the case elsewhere, the antiseigneurial resistance included landowners and well-off tenant farmers and combined traditional ritual forms of protest with more modern symbols. One of the many local leaders who played the role of the Pep del Orta, a mythical popular leader analogous to Captain Swing or General Ludd, was said to 'wear a blue cap with a red stripe of the sort they call liberty caps'.

On the other hand, the instability of colonial shipping produced by the wars had a severe effect on Andalucian agriculture, Catalan and Valencian textiles and Castilian wool exports. While it is true that the definitive loss of the American colonies in the 1820s stimulated a reorientation to domestic and European markets, in the short run the political impact of the climate of uncertainty and massive economic losses cannot be underestimated.

In this context, the liquidation of the enlightened reforms of the reign of Charles III (1759–88) had left the monarchy politically rudderless and under the yoke of its endemic financial difficulties. Traditionally these had been alleviated by the sale of public debt backed up by the shipments of gold and silver from the colonies. When imperial income began to fail the Crown's room for fiscal manoeuvre became intolerably narrow. The ministers of Charles IV tried to deal with the situation by reducing the fiscal immunities of the privileged and selling some Church lands in 1798. In so doing, they infected them with the general sensation of precariousness and uncertainty. The court intrigues whose purpose was to put the Prince of Asturias (the title of the heir to the throne), the future Ferdinand VII, on the throne constituted a 'revolt of the privileged' which demonstrates the diversity of opposition to the traditional monarchy that was beginning to take shape.

The uprising in Aranjuez in March 1808 forced the dismissal of Charles' hated chief minister, Manuel de Godoy (1767–1851), and the abdication of the king himself. However, by then Napoleon's troops were already in the country by virtue of the Treaty of Fontainebleau (October 1807), which granted them right of passage to Portugal. With the Crown in dispute, Charles and Ferdinand went to Bayonne, on the French–Spanish border, where Napoleon forced them both to abdicate in favour of his brother, Joseph Bonaparte. In an attempt to attract support for the new king, Napoleon issued the Statute of Bayonne, which promised a number of reforms which had been sought by enlightened Spanish reformers. Some Spaniards, who became known as the *afrancesados*, rallied to the French cause.

The war against the French, 1808–1814

The vast majority of the country opposed the French presence and the transfer of the Crown to Joseph Bonaparte. This opposition led most spectacularly to the disorders in Madrid on 2 May 1808 which sought to prevent the departure of the last representative of the Royal family for France. One of Goya's most famous paintings depicts the mass executions of civilians by French soldiers the next day. The French thought that this would bring their troubles to an end; instead, they got a war that lasted six years.

What came to be known as the War of Independence (1808–14) was, in part, the response to a deep sense of crisis in Spanish society. It also became a powerful mechanism of political apprenticeship for the population as a whole, the lessons of which were not easily forgotten. Spanish liberalism would always look to 1808 as the moment of its birth. The independence movements in the American colonies only added to the general perception that it was indeed a kind of year zero.

Although it is likely that the events of 2 May 1808 were not entirely spontaneous, the spread of the risings across the entire country had an undeniable popular dimension. 'In all the cities, in all the villages' wrote the liberal Francisco Martínez de la Rosa (1787–1862), 'the movement began with the lower classes of society.' The result was the creation of the so-called Juntas, groups of local personalities selected through a process somewhere between election and self-appointment. Their purpose was to provide some structure to the rebellion against the French and the Spanish authorities who collaborated with them. Both in terms of their social composition and their powers the Juntas were highly diverse, although all of them followed a pattern of increasing concentration of power that led to the formation of regional Juntas Supremas which, from September 1808 on, were at least formally subordinate to a Junta Central. The process of 'centralization' brought tensions of its own. Behind the adjective 'patriotic' there lay a highly heterogeneous constellation of social interests and political positions, from absolutism through to radical liberalism, which shared only the desire to get rid of the French.

Although members of the elite classes worked to end the phase of popular revolt as soon as possible, for the first time the people had been the protagonists of a play that could not have been put on without their participation. The demands of war favoured forms of organization and expression that until then had been subject to the hierarchical structures of the Ancien Regime, as the proven resistance against joining the regular army and the clear preference for the almost autonomous and spontaneous formation of guerrilla bands show. But the guerrilla phenomenon was not driven solely by anti-French phobia and the pressure of ecclesiastical ideology; here too the diversity was very great. There were guerrilla bands commanded by priests, such as Father Merino who fought for 'God, fatherland and King', and others commanded by liberals such as 'El Empecinado'. Others mixed guerrilla activity with the traditional conflict against the owners of the land. The fact that much of the nobility collaborated with the French, at least initially, was a determining factor in this regard in Andalucia, Catalonia and Valencia. From the outset, resistance to paying many of the traditional obligations which bore on the land as well as the protests against a range of taxes in the cities were a significant part of the war.

The very existence of the Juntas was itself a revolutionary phenomenon. By rejecting the abdications at Bayonne and assuming power they had called into question the principal of the monarch's absolute sovereignty. In the view of the liberal priest Francisco Martínez Marina, Napoleon had 'done Spain a great favour' by breaking 'the ties that bound the nation to its Prince' thus permitting its 'effective regeneration. The nation', he said, 'does not dissolve or lose its political existence' but rather begins its recovery through 'the bodies and perfect communities' that antedated absolutism. In this way there emerged an unprecedented debate on the bases of sovereignty and the character of the traditional social contract which, in Spain as elsewhere in Europe, contained much 'invention of tradition'. In this context, in 1809 the Junta Central convoked the General Cortes of the Kingdom and consulted the country in a way that much resembled that which preceded the meeting of the French Estates General in 1789.

With the French occupying almost the entire country, the Cortes gathered in Cádiz in 1810 and in its inaugural session proclaimed that 'sovereignty resided in them'. In spite of the best efforts of royalist deputies pejoratively known as *serviles*, the Cortes carried out a frontal attack on the social, economic and political organization of the Ancien Regime. The abolition of seigneurial jurisdiction and the elimination of entail divided the nobility, among whom was a large group chiefly concerned to consolidate its right of land ownership. Thus, the Duke of Osuna reacted to the decree abolishing the seigneuries by saying: 'I was born a citizen before a grandee and I will be the first to sacrifice that useless tinsel when the nation removed it because it served the general good.'

Osuna, like many other former lords, assumed that he was renouncing only his right to administer justice in the king's name but many of his vassals gave the law a much more radical reading. Seigneurs had traditionally used their legal jurisdiction to create taxes on various things such as water, woods and scrublands as well as on commercial and artisanal activities such as milling and the baking of bread, and in many cases these had been a way for them to consolidate their property rights. For this reason, tenants saw the decree of 1811 abolishing seigneurial jurisdiction as an occasion to refuse to draw distinctions between income deriving from seigneurial rights and rents on land. The long battle for the land that began then, with refusals to pay any sort of dues, affected the very nature of the revolution and the possibility for the former seigneurs of establishing outright ownership of their lands.

The radicalism of the laws passed in Cádiz, including the Constitution of 1812 itself, hid the defensive nature of a political project that sought to fend off three dangers at once: the existence of an unpredictable king who would one day return and in whose name the revolution had been made; the unquestionable power of the old privileged groups and the influence of a reactionary ecclesiastical ideology on an overwhelmingly Catholic population and, finally, the power of attraction of the reforms of the pro-French government in a military situation whose outcome was far from clear.

In this context, the 'extraordinary Cortes' produced an extremely lengthy and detailed constitution which created a constitutional monarchy that found its legitimacy in the sovereignty of the people and was based on the division of powers, legal equality and personal liberty. Its defensive nature was most notable in the articles referring to the attributes of the Crown and in the inclusion of a number of aspects normally left to normal legislation, such as education policy and electoral laws. Its strict Catholic confessionality was due as much to tactical need as to the influence on the legislators of 1812 of one of the most national (and Rousseauian) streams of the criticism of absolutism. For writers such as Martínez Marina, Catholicism was the underpinning of Spanish society and, therefore, of its reform. Such reform required limiting the material wealth of the Church through the disentailment of its properties but also returning to the nation the source of basic legitimacy in religious matters. From this perspective, the confessionality of the Constitution was yet another way in which the nation could exercise its sovereignty by declaring *itself* Catholic.

However, the true social weight of liberalism, and absolutism, must be measured at the local and regional levels. Analyses that overemphasize the unrepresentantive nature of the liberalism of Cádiz ignore the fact that many of the measures passed there responded to the results of the consultation of 1809. Nor do they give sufficient weight to the intensive activity surrounding the displacement of established oligarchies. From 1808 on, merchants and liberal property owners paid for military expeditions against the French, tried to force out the most traditional elements within the Juntas, carried on an intense campaign for the convocation of the Cortes and controlled the town halls created by the new laws.

It was the activities of those groups that radicalized the absolutist reaction that accompanied the return of Ferdinand VII. The election campaign of the autumn of 1813 demonstrated the power of the *serviles* and their ability to create the atmosphere conducive to a counter-revolutionary coup. It is not by chance that the most virulent and organized push came from those places where liberal ideas had penetrated furthest. Valencia, an area with a strong anti-seigneurial movement and where municipal power had clearly changed hands, was the chosen locale for the plot that produced the Manifesto of the Persians that called on Ferdinand VII to restore the order that had existed prior to 1808. A royal decree issued in Valencia overturned the Constitution of Cádiz and all its works 'as if such things had never happened.' So began the first absolutist Restoration, which lasted from 1814 to 1820.

Restoration and revolution, 1814–1833

The relative ease with which the absolute monarchy was restored following the departure of Napoleon's armies says more about the precariousness of the liberal regime than it does about the strength of absolutism.

The resistance to paying seigneurial dues continued across the country, encouraged by the desire of the Crown to take back legal jurisdiction and the dues and income they produced. Thus, in 1816 the tenants in Villafranca de Penedès, in Catalonia, wrote to the king to denounce seigneurial rights as 'so harmful to agriculture' and state that recent events had led them to 'realize the injustice with which they have been collected for many centuries'.

At the other extreme, the aristocracy felt trapped between the radicalism of its vassals and the despotism of a king whose officials tried to take back rights and properties that seigneurial jurisdiction had usurped long before. The social consensus that underlay the monarchy was threatened from different directions at the very moment at which the economic crisis, exacerbated by the Napoleonic wars and the unstoppable process of emancipation of the American colonies, increasingly channelled these complaints into the language of liberalism. For the commercial and financial bourgeoisie and for the most dynamic landowners, noble or not, nothing could be more worrying than a rapacious absolutism that was incapable of guaranteeing trade and the collection of agrarian rents. The experience of 1808–14 had offered a set of possible solutions and found some social support which it had not enjoyed before.

While the restored Inquisition worked for 'the regeneration of customs' in politics as well as morality, masonic secret societies were being created and the formula of the conspiracy and the military coup (*pronunciamiento*) was taking shape. Between 1817 and 1819 there were attempts of this sort in Galicia, Barcelona, Valencia, Andalucia and Madrid, all forming part of a climate of insurrection which involved military officers, merchants, land-owners and even liberal priests and nobles. Finally, in 1820, uprisings in various Spanish cities allowed Rafael de Riego's *pronunciamiento* in Cádiz to succeed. On 9 July 1820, with the Cortes in session once again, Ferdinand VII took his oath to the Constitution of 1812.

The 'Liberal Triennium' of 1820–23 was the true proving ground of early Spanish liberalism. The fecklessness with which the absolute monarchy had confronted the economic crisis and the colonial question revived the hopes invested in the liberalization of the market for property and the circulation of goods. This explains the support the new regime enjoyed among the various bourgeois groups of northern Spain, Andalucia, Catalonia and Valencia. Their proposals were decisive for designing a project for agricultural, indus-trial and commercial reform that included the articulation of the domestic market and a new, post-colonial relationship with America and with Europe. On the other hand, the disentailment of ecclesiastical property attracted state employees, merchants, well-off tenant farmers and landowners, and even smallholders and small-scale tenants, to the liberal project.

From that point on one could no longer talk of liberalism as the party of a minority or the exclusive patrimony of a narrow elite. The press, the 'patriotic societies' and the circulation of a multitude of pamphlets and 'political catchecisms' significantly broadened the liberal public sphere. The utopian aspect of the first political liberalism, which was, in theory, univer-salist and all-inclusive, made it possible to be 'heard' and reinterpreted by many in the popular classes. In practice, however, this liberal ideal would produce innumerable conflicts. The situation was especially complex in the countryside. Some sectors of the peasantry, especially in Valencia, Catalonia, the Basque Country and Navarre, expressed their discontent with increasing taxes as well as with liberal land policy, and aligned themselves with the absolutist position of the clergy and the old local oligarchy. Others continued in the anti-absolutist bloc of peasants and wealthy farmers.

The social dimension of liberalism also provoked the first great division between Moderates (*moderados*) and radicals (*exaltados*). Two issues were decisive here. The first referred to the limits on, and even the very definition of, the 'sovereignty of the people'. The second issue was the possibility, or not, of an alliance with the privileged groups of the Ancien Regime.

For the Moderates, it was essential to revise and dilute the Constitution of 1812 to include the Crown in the definition of sovereignty of the nation through the concept of *shared sovereignty* between the Crown and the

Cortes that would include an upper house where the privileged class would be guaranteed representation. The Moderate programme was rounded out by control over the press, the patriotic societies and the National Militia. The Moderate minister Nicolás Garelly observed that

> The ideas of liberty injected superficially in the unprepared masses only serve to create unruly men who disobey legitimate authority .... The Constitution protects the freedom and rights of all Spaniards, but the equality of wealth and intelligence would be a nonsense.

Moderates supported the former seigneurs in their demands that villages be made to prove that the dues they were refusing to pay had their origin in seigneurial jurisdiction and not in the right of property ownership. The practical result was to foreclose any attempt at a radical abolition that favoured the tenants.

In contrast, the *exaltados* defended the integrity of the Constitution of 1812 while demanding freedom of expression and association and the right of all citizens to join the National Militia. On the subject of the seigneuries, the vast majority held to a radical interpretation of the 1811 decree of abolition which would have opened the way for tenants to become land-owners by questioning seigneurs' rights over lands they did not exploit directly. This difference also affected the articulation of civil society and political life through the greater or lesser participation of the people in shaping liberal legislation. This was not a trivial matter because the chances of significantly projecting the socio-economic advantages of the revolution downwards depended on the weight each group had in taking key political decisions.

In fact, the absolutist reaction took shape at the same time as the division of liberalism, and showed that the *exaltados* were correct when they insisted that 'not to call the people liberal is a danger for the revolution'. Even so, the royalists were unable to overthrow the regime on their own and had to call in French troops, the so-called '100 000 sons of St Louis', who invaded Spain in April 1823.

The second Restoration of Ferdinand VII (1823–33) began in a climate of official repression and vigilantism carried out by 'Royalist Volunteers', but even so, the last ten years of Ferdinand's reign did not simply amount to a turning back of the clock. On the contrary, these years were decisive in the reformulation of political attitudes by liberals and the Monarchy and broad sectors of the absolutist cause. The effort expended to stabilize the regime and prevent economic bankruptcy at times coincided with liberal aspirations. Proof can be found in the promulgation of the Commercial Code in 1829, the reform of the guilds, and measures to protect grain growers and assure free circulation of grain within the country.

In the end, this vacillating reformist programme failed for lack of financial resources and the absence of any social consensus. The loss of the colonies was followed by the division within absolutism itself, where one important sector was adamantly opposed to any reform that altered 'old customs'. The clergy and the most traditional local oligarchies had a strong presence in this 'apostolic opposition', and they quickly moved their support to Don Carlos, the king's brother and heir to the throne of the childless Ferdinand. In areas such as Catalonia, the Basque Country and Valencia they enjoyed significant support among the rural population and the small urban centres that serviced them which had been badly affected by rising taxes and falling prices for their products. These very heterogeneous social groups found common ground in their increasing difficulty in adapting themselves to the ongoing penetration of capital into their agricultural world. The tensest moment in this regard was the War of the Malcontents, a short-lived uprising in rural Catalonia in 1827.

Meanwhile, from exile and within the country itself, the liberal opposition was engaged in refining its positions and becoming even more divided. The failure of the Torrijos conspiracy in December 1831, one of a long series of similar failures, marked the decisive abandonment of Spanish liberalism's 'utopia of insurrection'. An important group of liberals felt it was possible to come to terms with absolutist reformers in a way that would 'finally make possible, without the dangers of a revolution, a stable constitution that would assure forever the persons and property of those who constitute society', as a document Ferdinand VII received from Paris in 1831 proclaimed. The author was Vicente Beltrán de Lis, a prosperous merchant, supporter of the liberalism of Cádiz and of the Triennium, purchaser of large quantities of disentailed lands and, by this time, creditor of a bankrupt monarchy. Two members of his family had died in the failed liberal insurrection of 1819.

The document could not have come at a better time. A pact between liberals and reformists had been blocked by the presence of Don Carlos as heir to the throne. However, in October 1830 something totally unexpected happened: Ferdinand's fourth wife, María Cristina de Borbón, gave birth to a daughter, the future Isabella II. During the pregnancy the king promulgated the Pragmatic Sanction, overriding the Salic Law of the House of Bourbon which prohibited women from acceding to the throne, and restored the Castilian laws which permitted female accession. After a number of attempts to annul Ferdinand's decree, the supporters of Don Carlos opted for violence. When Ferdinand died in September 1833 the First Carlist War (1833–40) began, and with it a new and definitive stage of the liberal revolution.

The Carlist War and the triumph of liberalism

Civil war and revolution marched hand in hand. It was apparent to everyone that the struggle between the Regent, María Cristina, and the pretender, Don Carlos, would affect much more than the dynastic question. The intransigence of the Carlists initially served as a moderating influence on liberals, while it also obliged the Crown to make concessions to them. The result was the Royal Statute, a pseudo-constitution that convoked a purely consultative assembly. Moderate liberals supported this initiative in the belief that they could use it, and the protection of the Crown, to realize a programme of 'legal and pacific reforms' that would lead to a union of the well-off classes against Carlism and, at the same time, avoid the political radicalization that had characterized the Triennium. For Prime Minister Martínez de la Rosa, the conundrum was 'how to combine liberty and order'. From this perspective, radical liberalism and Carlism were equally dangerous.

Inevitably, things were not that straightforward or that peaceful. The refusal of the Crown to approve the laws that would have made this balance possible undermined hopes that change would be sufficient and sufficiently rapid. And the tolerance that Carlists enjoyed from local authorities who vigorously persecuted the least sign of radical liberalism was obvious. The fear of a possible agreement between the Regent and Carlos left even Moderates disheartened and prevented the 'reform from above' that many liberals preferred to revolution.

In the summer of 1835 a Moderate newspaper described the situation in the following terms:

> If an inexplicable blindness . . . a long series of errors should lead us to the terrible crisis of having to choose between revolution and despotism, we have already too much suffered the errors of the latter to refuse to stand by the former.

Shortly thereafter there were insurrections across the country. Once again, Juntas were the method for channelling the revolutionary impulse and controlling the most radical elements. Army officers, merchants, property owners, professionals and former reformist officials took charge of municipal governments, a move which led to deepening divisions between the Moderates and those who soon called themselves Progressives because of their position on 'the degree and pace of reform'. Despite their differences, both groups shared a suspicion of popular violence and the conviction that it was necessary to return as quickly as possible to the respectability of parliamentary politics. If the Crown would accept the urgent need for a minimum social and economic programme, they could accept a reform of the Statute and forego raising the banner of the Constitution of 1812.

The appointment of Progressive businessman Juan Alvarez de Mendizábal (1790–1853) as prime minister in September 1835 appeared to mark the realization of this objective, but his dismissal in May 1836 once again blocked the possibility of a deal with the Crown. As one French diplomat put it, 'the situation has become extremely complicated, and a multitude of men of influence who had been calm until now have become most violently irritated'. It was these 'men of influence' who took charge of preparations for the definitive, nationwide uprising in the summer of 1836. A mutiny of the Royal Guard in the La Granja palace forced the Regent to accept the Constitution of 1812 and summon the Cortes.

The experience of revolution had taught many lessons, including the necessity of abandoning the radical spirit of 1812. The summer before, the liberal bourgeoisie had tolerated the burning of convents as a means of forcing the disentailment of Church lands 'from below'; what it could not tolerate were acts such the burning of the state-of-the-art Bonaplata textile factory in Barcelona. The social conflict that the revolution threatened to unleash had to be controlled. The collapse of the regime of the Royal Statute brought reform from above to an end. Control passed from the hands of moderate absolutists to those of the liberals, and when this happened the liberal rupture became a fact. This was not a popular revolution, nor was its objective to move from absolutism to democracy. It had been accomplished with the people but certainly not for the people. The convulsive history of the next ten years would derive from this tension between the respectable liberalism of Moderates and Progressives, who were anxious to rein in a revolution they had been forced to unleash, and a radical liberalism that sought to continue that revolution under the banner of the Constitution of 1812.

The pact between Moderates and Progressives was embodied in the new Constitution of 1837. It established a sovereignty that was shared between the Cortes and the Crown; left the Crown the power of vetoing legislation and dissolving parliament, and created a bicameral legislature. The almost universal male suffrage contained in the Constitution of Cádiz was replaced by a property-based suffrage that limited the right to vote to 4.5 to 5.5 per cent of the population. The pact of 1837 demonstrated the power of moderate liberalism in the construction of the new parliamentary monarchy of the 'middle classes' as well as its superior electoral organization: it controlled a parliamentary majority from the first elections of the new regime.

'Respectable liberalism's' moderation and will to compromise did not succeed in eliminating the revolutionary impulse that had given birth to the new regime. Although its popular wing had been controlled, the revolution had forced a definitive break with absolutism. It was in the local forum that the strength of the moderate liberalism declined most significantly. The war against the Carlists, which had been going on throughout these events, favoured local autonomy and political radicalization, especially in regions such as Catalonia and Valencia where the battle was most bitter. In those places the radicals found bastions in the Militia, in town councils and in the so-called Reprisals Committees, which terrorized the most moderate liberals as well as Carlists. This was possible thanks to the restoration of the local government legislation of the Cortes of Cádiz, which left broad powers to municipal governments while allowing all male citizens to participate in their election.

Table 1.1 Principal Liberal Legislation: 1834–1837

April 1834	Royal Statute
May 1834	Abolition of the Guilds Freedom of Cultivation of Land
July 1834	Abolition of the Inquisition
July 1835	Suppression of the Jesuits Closure of convents with fewer than 12 residents
September 1835	Return of disentailed lands to people who had purchased them in 1820–23
October 1835	Dissolution of all religious orders, except those involved in hospitals
February 1836	Disentailment of Church lands
March 1836	Suppression of male religious orders
August 1836	Abolition of the Mesta; freedom to enclose woodlands; end of price controls; restoration of local government laws of 1812 and 1823; abolition of primogeniture
September 1836	Abolition of prior censorship
December 1836	Abolition of the guilds; freedom of industry and commerce
June 1837	Constitution of 1837
July 1837	Property-based electoral law; abolition of female religious orders; abolition of the tithe; beginning of disentailment

This was the context in which the laws that killed the Ancien Regime were passed (see table 1.1). In those places where the local climate was most radicalized, tenants had the greatest success in confronting what they called the 'aristocratic reaction', by which they meant not the absolutists but their former seigneurs who had taken refuge in the moderation that underlay the constitutional pact of 1837. The struggle around the interpretation of the decree abolishing seigneurial jurisdiction is an excellent example of this sort of tension. In 1837 the Cortes tried to resolve the problem that had been created by the 1811 decree, which stated that in disputed cases it was the towns, and not the former seigneurs, who had to prove that the dues and obligations at issue derived from the lords' seigneurial jurisdiction and not their ownership of land. The overall result was that seigneurs consolidated their ownership of the land only in those regions where this had been accomplished earlier through a process of expropriation of peasant lands in which landowners who were not seigneurs also took part. Such cases were common in Extremadura, western Andalucia, and Castilla–La Mancha. Elsewhere, the seigneurs experienced significant losses.

As for disentailment itself, while it did not alter the structure of land ownership it did permit people with money or state bonds – merchants, government officials and army officers – to become landowners. In rural areas, a broad spectrum of large, middling and smallholders or tenants added to their properties while, for the most part, the nobility abstained from making purchases. Overall, about one quarter of the surface area of the country changed hands. For one sector of liberal opinion disentailment was the great lost opportunity to give the landless the chance to acquire property, but the demands of the war and pressure from the better-off wings of liberalism prevented this. Their goal was to find new resources for the army by reducing the public debt and restoring Spain's credit rating. The amount by which the debt was actually reduced was not significant but it is possible that it was sufficient to prevent national bankruptcy and, what was worse at that moment, the victory of Carlism.

In fact, the Constituent Cortes of 1836–37 did its work during the most tense moments of the war, when the Carlists were scoring decisive victories in Catalonia and Valencia and, in September 1837, managed to reach the gates of Madrid. The revolutionary impulse, modest assistance from Britain and France and the new resources found both within Spain and beyond underwrote the great liberal offensive of 1838–39 that ended victoriously in August 1839 with the signing of the Agreement of Vergara. The war continued in Valencia for nine more months, until it was brought to an end by the liberal capture of Morella in May 1840.

Moderates versus Progressives, 1840–1843

With the end of the war, the radicals lost one of the major conditions that had made it necessary for liberalism to secure popular support, and with the undisguised encouragement of the Crown, the Moderates began a large-scale political offensive to limit popular political participation in 1840. At the same time, they proposed reimposing the tithe, new electoral and press laws and purging the Militia.

For a monarchy whose ability to exercise political control over its territory was limited, the success of this offensive required the support of the army, the institution which had come out of the revolution and the war in best shape. The penetration of liberal ideas into the army, as well as its role as kingmaker, was made evident when the Regent went to Barcelona to secure the agreement of Baldomero Espartero (1792–1879), the commander in chief and a Progressive. His refusal to accept the proposed law on municipal governments, along with an uprising in Barcelona, forced the Regent to flee to Valencia where another insurrection forced her to renounce the regency and leave for France on 17 October 1840. Isabella, the future queen, was still only seven years old and until she came of age Espartero was the master of the situation. The Regency of Espartero (1840–43) marked the greatest and most spectacular expression of the liberal rupture. The ninth child of a wheelwright from an obscure village in La Mancha who had joined the army to fight against Napoleon and risen through the ranks to become a general, Espartero was the outstanding symbol of the imposition of popular sovereignty from below over the last remnants of absolutism. He was also, however, the first of a long series of soldiers who would shape the political life of modern Spain.

The Regency embodied Espartero's personal version of Progressive ideas, and this brought it into conflict not only with Moderates and radicals but even with many Progressives. The tremendously fluid and uncertain nature of the political space between those two enemies was the great tragedy of Espartero's regime, and that of Progressivism in general. In 1840 that space had been reduced to little more than a mild defence of the extension of the suffrage, civil liberties and municipal autonomy. In this context, the conflict over just what the term 'middle classes' meant took on an undeniable centrality.

From 1837 on Moderates and Progressives agreed that the right to political participation represented public recognition of the status achieved in the private sphere through education and property ownership. The difference between them lay in the fact that the Progressives tried to maintain the promise that the public sphere would be opened to 'those classes which are neither on the lowest rung of society nor situated at its head'. The restricted public sphere they had defended in 1837 included aspiring to broaden the middle classes through the elimination of 'the obstacles and shackles that prevent citizens who were born without a fortune from achieving it one day'. This would occur through the free play of the market and legislation designed to increase the opportunity for political participation. Thus, the revolution was a process open to the most characteristic social basis of progressivism: 'those enlightened and noble classes which are the ornament of nations in which ingenuity and talent, which are acquired through work, make up for the titles of birth and chance'. It was a narrow social constituency made up largely of members of the liberal professions who had acquired a political prominence far superior to their sociological strength and who, in 1840, sought to consolidate it by confronting what one Progressive paper called 'disorders, whether they are caused by the great or the small'.

Progressivism had already become little more than a timorous radicalism, continually bypassed by the democrats and republicans who considered themselves to be the authentic representatives of an as yet unrealized revolution. These were the groups who provided the most forceful response to the Moderates who, in 1841, tried to return to power through a military coup. There were radical movements from then on, and in 1842 one coincided with a series of strikes in the tobacco factories of Seville, on the docks of Valencia and in the printing shops of the capital. The artisans of Granada took to the streets demanding work. As one contemporary pamphlet put it, 'the government hears the R (for Republic) even in its dreams'. For radical liberals and the so-called 'pure' Progressives, it was essential to occupy the public sphere as a base from which to force the realization of the vague egalitarian utopia of early liberalism. This provided both their strength and weakness when confronting their opponents. For Moderates such as Martínez de la Rosa the liberal revolution was already complete and the only task remaining was to find 'a political solution to the practical problem of guaranteeing existing interests' while at the same time avoiding 'the storm of revolution' from below.

Once Carlism had ceased to threaten the basic achievements of liberalism, the fear of the 'people's' political activity left Espartero and his supporters without a substantive position, as his treatment of the Catalan uprising of November 1842 revealed. The uprising drew on the economic crisis, the discontent of the artisanate and the nascent working class over the increase in the consumption tax (*consumos*) and rumours of a commercial agreement with England that would harm the Catalan textile industry. It was this last element that led the bourgeoisie to participate in the rising. Espartero's response was to bombard Barcelona, impose a military occupation and carry out a severe repression.

There were attempts to follow the Catalan example in other cities, but the revolutionary impulse had already played itself out. Young Moderates helped organize a number of mob actions against Espartero which anticipated what would transpire a few months later when 'pure' Progressives and radicals allied with Moderates against the Regent. The result was the great revolt of the summer of 1843, which one nineteenth century historian has described as 'a gathering of cats and dogs for the purpose of catching the bone'. The common slogans of the rebels were the recognition of Isabella II and of the constitutional legality that had been violated by Espartero's dictatorial methods, overcoming the differences of the past, and the expulsion of Espartero from the country.

Progressives and radicals were removed from the leadership of the movement, that is from the Juntas, with relative speed and surprising efficiency. This had required that the army be in the hands of Moderate officers unhappy with Espartero. One of them, General Francisco Serrano (1810–85), was named head of the provisional government by the Catalan Junta and then entered Madrid, where he made it absolutely clear that the more progressive and federalist promises he had made in Catalonia were mere posturing. One final uprising, known as the Jamancia, failed to light the spark of revolution in the rest of the country. And, when in September 1843, the Catalan Junta refused to obey the new Moderate-dominated government, the desire of the Catalan bourgeoisie for political autonomy evaporated in the face of the intense social struggle that the movement had unleashed. Barcelona was bombarded once again, while the leading merchants, industrialists and property owners collaborated with the officers sent from Madrid. The conduct of the Barcelona bourgeoisie demonstrated what was true for the entire country: that the Moderates were the guarantors of order and security for the largest group of property owners of all types, and Barcelona the site where they could negotiate their place in the new liberal public sphere.

Conclusion

The speech of General Roncali to the troops who executed the last Progressive resisters in Alicante in 1844 embodied in all its crudeness the bloody end of the revolution and the beginning of the lengthy Moderate era: 'Woe to those who do not believe that the hour of revolution has passed. You have closed it in all of Spain with the keys of this conquered city.' The hour of revolution had passed because the passage from absolute monarchy to the liberal state had been completed and was irreversible.

The revolution had secured private property and the free market by means of disentailment and the abolition of seigneurialism. Trade and industry had been freed from the old shackles and the limited suffrage of the new parliamentary regime guaranteed the propertied a role in determining the budget and the general orientation of the government. The judiciary had been made independent; ministers were responsible to parliament and the Church put in its place. For the Moderates, nothing remained to be done.

The radical character of the Spanish liberal revolution was not diminished by the nature of its exhaustion. The way in which revolutions die, at whose hands and to whose benefit, is fundamental for understanding them, but it does not define them completely. 'The century in which we live contains the seed of all possible revolutions' said Martínez de la Rosa, but in the Spain of 1843 this was reduced to a single outcome. Its objectives included neither democracy nor an agrarian reform to benefit the peasants. But an agreement between the nobility and the bourgeoisie with the Crown as arbiter had not been possible either. The Crown was forced to accept a situation it had not created and which it had opposed on numerous occasions. Noble seigneurs did not escape unscathed, and the only ones who successfully adapted to the new situation were those who had been ready since the eighteenth century and who altered their social strategies accordingly. The revolution rearranged the possible relations between old and new property owners, and made the capacity of the former to adapt to the 'ways' of the latter the guarantee of their survival. The politically elitist and socially oligarchic liberal monarchy that was consolidated after 1845 was at one and the same time the outcome of a struggle against the old absolutist system and of a struggle over the definition of its liberal successor.

|2|

The Moderate ascendancy, 1843–1868

JESÚS CRUZ

With the coup against the Espartero Regency in 1843 the Moderates took control of the political process and their ascendancy lasted for most of what remained of the century. As José María Jover has persuasively argued, in the long term, the transformation of Spain into a liberal state was mainly the achievement of moderate liberalism. Radical liberals held power only during short intervals that were normally linked to revolutionary episodes. These were decisive moments in the process of the transformation of Spanish political and social structures, to be sure, but the long periods during which the liberal system matured were controlled by Moderates. Between 1843 and 1868 the Moderate party forged the political and administrative foundations of the liberal state. This hegemony, in the end, is the truly transcendent element of the period considered in this chapter.

These developments resulted from a reconfiguration of the factors that shaped the Spanish political scene: the Crown, the military, and the politicians. On the surface, the active participation of the military was the most evident, but we must probe further to examine the formation of the group that would dominate nineteenth century Spanish politics, leading the nation in the direction of an ordered process of negotiated adjustment instead of a revolutionary rupture with the past.

The power of the Notables: social foundations of the Moderate hegemony

Traditionally the years of the Moderate readjustment after 1843 have been interpreted as the definitive consolidation of a political system controlled by the middle classes. This system has represented, for many Spanish historians, the culmination of a process of bourgeois revolution. Although the bourgeois revolution model stems from a Marxist interpretation of the historical process, it was broadly accepted during the 1970s and 1980s by historians from diverse schools of thought. According to this interpretation, in Spain, as in the rest of Europe in the second half of the eighteenth century, an ascendant class of businessmen, landowners and professionals, all neglected by the forces that supported the Ancien Regime, pushed for a radical transformation of politics that would eventually change social relations and economic conditions. Liberalism was the ideology of this ascendant class and the revolution its main tool for defeating the dominant feudal aristocratic bloc that had kept absolutism and its unjust and dilapidated social system alive. On this view, the bourgeoisie drove the liberal gains of 1812, 1820, and especially the 1830s. However, these same historians need to explain the conservative shift of Spanish liberalism after 1843, as well as its lack of success in engendering long term political stability, large-scale industrialization, and social integration during the nineteenth century. The most extensive explanation that these historians offer sees these failures as stemming from the weakness of the Spanish bourgeoisie. Thus, they argue, between 1808 and 1843 the bourgeoisie sincerely embraced revolutionary ideology, but the increasing threat of a radical revolution led by rural and urban popular groups forced them into a tacit pact with the old landed aristocracy. The consequence was the creation of a socio-political bloc that, they contend, ended political democratization after 1843 and to some extent obstructed economic modernization.

Although this model has interpretive logic, it is based on a set of presuppositions that lacks empirical support. First, it is inconsistent with the assumption that liberalism and the bourgeoisie were complementary; that is, that liberalism was created exclusively by the bourgeoisie to serve its own social, political and economic interests: the promotion of capitalist development. Second, it assumes that there existed in Spain a defined bourgeois class strong enough to confront the forces of the Ancien Regime successfully. Finally, it asserts that there were two distinct periods in the history of nineteenth century Spain: one characterized by the ascendance of a revolutionary bourgeoisie that corresponded with the completion of the liberal revolution, the other characterized by the neutralization of that bourgeoisie which coincided with the domestication of the revolution and its conservative redefinition.

Historians are questioning all three of these assumptions, and helping to formulate a new understanding of the social forces behind nineteenth century Spanish liberalism. The notion that liberalism was the ideology of a single class has lost currency: rather, recent scholarship shows that all European liberal movements, including that of Spain, varied in social composition. Liberalism was thus formulated as an *instrumental* ideology not inherently attached to the interests of one single class. Because of its instrumental nature it accommodated the aspirations of a wide social spectrum that included bourgeois, nobles, and the popular classes. Moreover, due to its more precise explication of the nature and functioning of nineteenth century societies, this scholarship reveals that no country in Europe, with the exception of England, had a bourgeoisie strong enough to independently impose its own political agenda before 1850. Significantly, recent studies indicate that there was a great deal of continuity in the social composition among European elites between the second half of the eighteenth and the first half of the nineteenth century.

This continuity was also the case in Spain. Between 1812 and 1850 the bulk of the politically active class, including men who held high-ranking positions in the administration of the state, was composed of individuals from families of long-standing social position. Among these, landowning groups and dynasties of high administrators and elite professionals predominated, the majority of whom hailed from the various ranks of the old Spanish nobility. Most of them owned homes in Madrid, but they originally came from urban centres in provincial Spain where their families maintained strong ties to local life. Geographically, the agrarian provinces of Andalucia were better represented than industrial regions such as Catalonia. Of course, there were noticeable cases of politicians whose stories resemble the ideal of the bourgeois self-made man, but the humble origins of Espartero and the bourgeois background of Mendizábal were exceptions in a group mainly dominated by old elite families of landowners, bureaucrats, and professionals.

Hence, it is more accurate to see nineteenth century Spanish society as dominated by the old elites instead of the bourgeoisie. The ascendant bourgeoisie was only a portion, and not the most important one, of a dominant group made up primarily of traditional landowning and bureaucratic elites. What characterized this society was its oligarchic nature, in the sense that it was dominated by a powerful minority who controlled the government and exercised power by means of corrupt electoral practices. The notables – as the members of this oligarchy were called in the language of their time – possessed the political, economic, and social power within the community and managed to retain it by means of a social system based on patronage, loyalty and personal dependence. It is true that this group embraced many aspects of what we today consider the bourgeois tradition. By endorsing liberalism, for instance, they were committing themselves to the principles of equal opportunity and individual freedom. There is also enough evidence to suggest that these dominant notables adopted bourgeois values and bourgeois life-styles like their European counterparts. However, due to the oligarchic nature of the society of notables, none of these developments permeated large segments of Spanish society.

In sum, the Moderate readjustment after 1843 should not be interpreted as the result of the revolutionary bourgeoisie's concession to the forces of tradition; nor was it the culmination of a definitive consolidation of an ascendant middle class in Spain. There was no change in power relations in 1843, rather continuing hegemony of the traditionally dominant social classes. What happened can be better interpreted as the culmination of the process of political maturation of the dominant Spanish groups. After

Carlism's defeat there was a general conviction that the future of Spain could not be other than liberal. The question in 1843 and after was how to mould liberalism to the interests of this traditionally dominant sector of society from which the liberal political class derived. The answer at which they arrived was to set clear limits on the process of political and social reform, which is just what the Moderates did after engineering the fall of Espartero.

The taming of the revolution

The formal task of taming the radical liberal revolution was undertaken by what Raymond Carr has defined as the three internal forces that balanced Isabella II's constitutional monarchy: the Crown, the army, and the bulk of the dynastic parties. The Crown was unequivocally conservative, if not anti-liberal. Publicly, both Maria Cristina – the Queen Mother – and Queen Isabella herself were committed to liberal reforms, but they feared the liberal revolution because it represented a threat that would limit the power of the throne. The Crown conceived liberalism as a chronic disease with which one had to coexist and try to control in order to prevent its becoming a terminal illness. To do this, they gave steady support to the Moderates while ostracizing the Progressives. The strategy worked out well, although in the long run this partisan attitude damaged the mediating role of the monarchy, since it appeared to be unequivocally aligned with one of the sides in this struggle for power.

Partisan politics were even less propitious in the legal context, because the Crown still retained important portions of the executive power. The constitutionally-sanctioned Royal Prerogative gave the monarch the right to designate and dismiss ministers and to grant a decree to end the legislature and call for new elections. Isabella took advantage of this option whenever she felt threatened by liberal radicalism, a tendency that consistently favoured the Moderate Party. Thus, the Progressives felt that they were being deliberately neglected by a partisan monarch who was constantly challenging the liberal revolution, and little by little started to endorse the idea of finding a possible successor who would be willing to accept the rules of constitutional parliamentarism. In the beginning the idea appealed only to the radical wing of the Progressive Party and to the new left-wing, which had situated itself in the recently formed Democratic Party (see chapter 5). However, with the passage of time – especially after 1863 – the idea of replacing the monarch found support among all members of the Progressive Party and even among significant representatives of the Moderate centre.

The reasons for this shift were political and also related to the personal behaviour of the royal family. The court functioned not only as a cosy shelter but also as a powerful propeller of patronage, favouritism, and corruption. It is no exaggeration to say that Isabella's reign was one of the most corrupt periods in the nation's history. It was an era of economic and institutional experimentation in which a democratic ethos had not yet been forged. The opposition used allegations of corruption to diminish the prestige of the monarchy; they also drew attention to the disreputable private behaviour of the royal family. The Queen Mother had secretly married a supercilious official of the royal guard who, in spite of his plebeian background, was awarded the title of Duke of Riansares. Riansares assembled a clique of friends and favourites who became extremely influential in political life, which subsequently weakened Maria Cristina's reputation. None the less, Isabella, a sweet 13 year old blonde girl when she became Queen, and a gracious 16 year old adolescent when she married her cousin Francisco de Asis, was able to captivate the hearts of many Spaniards. The populist image she adopted was in many senses sincere and true to her personality. However, the populist queen performed much better in theatres, festivals, parties, and bullfights than in the council of ministers. The political, social, and economic precariousness of the period required something more; these were times for intelligent and cunning leaders. Isabella was not the latter, and after 1863 the opposition was able to transform her charismatic image of a popular Madonna into a portrait of a debauched woman and an irresponsible tyrant. Thus, the Crown that in 1843 had been an essential component of the concerted attempt to tame the liberal revolution gradually became its main obstacle.

The military formed the second internal force that worked for the control of radical liberalism. During the Carlist War the army started to play a decisive role in Spanish politics, a trend that lasted for more than a century, until the death of General Franco in 1975. The inclination of the military to actively intervene in politics in nineteenth century Spain is a phenomenon that can not be explained in simple terms. This interventionist propensity, which continued into the twentieth century in Spain as well as the greater Hispanic world, was not a manifestation of a 'distinctive' Spanish authoritarian tradition. Militarism, understood as the active intervention of the military in the process of political decision-making, was a common phenomenon in all of continental Europe in the past century, and is not an infrequent circumstance in the developing world today. In a general sense, modern militarism has resulted mainly from the weaknesses of civil society in countries in which political democratization is being guided by a political elite, but it also has to do with the different role assigned to the military in the context of the new liberal state.

Spain was no exception. Jaime Balmes, a representative of the conservative wing of the Moderate Party, wrote in 1846 that it

> is not that the civil power is weak because the military power is strong, but rather that the military power is strong because the civil is weak .... The political parties have alternated periods in power; but none

has succeeded in building a civil power; in the last instance all turned to the military to resolve their political differences.

Indeed, one of the major reasons for mid-nineteenth century Spanish praetorian parliamentarianism was the army's position as the only solid institution within the liberal state. The liberal political class was still in its formative stage, searching for the appropriate political programme that could create a lasting consensus. Though the Moderates provided the most durable platform for supporting a liberal programme, the consensus around it was always quite precarious, especially in the middle decades of the century. Part of the problem was the lack of leadership among civilian politicians, which provoked a continuous atmosphere of political instability and a sense of a lack of authority. Given all of these ingredients, it is not surprising that the military felt the seduction of playing the hero.

None the less, the mid-century military political protagonism of the military differed substantially from modern military dictatorship. In liberal states maturing around the mid-nineteenth century, functions and characteristics of both the civil and military branches of government were yet to be clearly defined. The military did not act as a specialized professional body with a special status within the state. It was aware of the historic function it played and the tremendous influence and power it had, but it did not consider its rights and duties toward the state different from those of civilians. On this understanding, it was perfectly legitimate for a military man not only to have political ideas but also to participate in the political process. In the long term this conception of the role of the military became a serious problem in Spanish politics, but it did not produce a military dictatorship until 1923. Political intervention was encouraged by politicians, often to defend civilian political programmes. Politicians accepted the *pronunciamiento* as a legitimate way to resolve political differences and seize power; likewise, elections and parliamentarism were for the military the only conceivable forms of politics. In short, both military and civilian politicians were committed to the general principles of liberalism and worked together for the construction of a constitutional monarchy.

After 1843 the military's political intervention increasingly abetted the conservative shift in liberal politics. The fall of the charismatic general Baldomero Espartero marked the beginning of a period of military realignment with the Moderate programme. Political positions for military officers resulted from personal relationships, not from corporate decisions; consequently, political alignments were as diverse as the number of available political options. It is true that the generals adopted independent styles of governing not always in tune with the civilian programmes they were supposed to represent. None the less, what generally prevailed were arrangements along the lines of the two major civilian political forces active in the Spanish political scene: the Moderates and the Progressives. Espartero was considered the candidate of the Progressives; however, his despotic style while governing in 1841 weakened his leadership. General Juan Prim, main sponsor of the internal Progressive opposition to Espartero, gradually won the leadership of the group, becoming the Progressive candidate around 1868. In spite of his exaggerated authoritarianism Ramón María Narváez and the more conciliatory Leopoldo O'Donnell became the sentinels of Moderate liberalism and the main leaders of the conservative reshaping of the liberal revolution. In the last instance, the military hierarchy was more attracted by the Moderate message of an ordered and controlled transition rather than the Progressive programme of democratic insurgence.

Along with the Crown and the military, the last and most important force in the process of political readjustment initiated after 1843 was the Moderate party. Contemporaries such as the Marquis of Miraflores pointed out that this group adopted this name only after 1845, in order to be distinguished from what were known as the Conservative or Constitutional parties. This observation is important in order to understand the meaning of the concept of a 'political party' in nineteenth century European politics. The Moderates, as well as the Progressives and the more radical Democrats, differed from parties of today. Led by a small and select number of individuals, they did not require of their followers the performance of duties nor did they provide the rights one associates with modern political affiliation. More than parties they were groups of notables aligned according to their commitment to a series of principles, attitudes, and ideas, as well as private interests that were attached to various positions of power at the national, regional or local levels. There was nothing like a normal membership. Alignments were formed on the basis of private commitments to these political groups during politically important moments, mainly elections. The idea of a party evolved as these political groups felt the need to achieve a higher level of articulation and visibility in order to win elections. The electoral process required the formation of a series of committees to select and present candidates, followed by the planning and running of political campaigns. Over the course of time, Spanish political life became more organized and visible, but remained controlled by an oligarchy that kept politics under the monopoly of the upper classes. Miguel Martínez Cuadrado has called the groups that ruled during this period the dynastic parties, since both Moderates and Progressives accepted the Bourbon monarchy as the proper framework for the liberalization of the state. Thus, what held together the conglomerate of peoples and interests that made up the Moderate and Progressive parties were not only ideas but also the concern of the elites to maintain positions of power.

The Moderates of the 1840s were the inheritors of two political traditions, one from eighteenth-century Enlightened Despotism, the other from an amalgam of the 1812 and 1820 Spanish versions of Burkean conservatism, seen most clearly in Royer-Collard's theory of the *just milieu*. Both ideological tendencies were a part of Martínez de la Rosa's failed experiment of the Royal Statute (1834), and they finally attained political maturity in the programme of the Moderate Party. The central principle that animated this political movement was the conviction that it was possible to build a liberal state by means of political reform. In other words, they contended that the transformation from an absolutist to a constitutional monarchy could occur as an ordered transition instead of through revolution. The Moderates envisioned a new state respectful of religious tradition, private property, and social hierarchy, but at the same time guardian of some level of individual freedom and equal opportunity. I use the qualifier 'some level' because the commitment of nineteenth century liberals to the principles of individual freedom and equal opportunity was limited by a restrictive conception of social hierarchy. Freedom of speech, for instance, was conceived as a universal right but in practice it was severely constrained by censorship laws. Likewise, theory spoke of legal equality, but participation in elections was limited to those males with prescribed levels of income and education. In such a context, the Moderates' pledge for an ordered transition meant the maintenance of religion as an essential instrument to assure the continuation of a common moral code. It also meant the preservation of a strong monarchy with enough power to both control the legislature and enforce order. Finally, it meant the defence of an organic conception of society in which social divisions were understood as natural and necessary for the stability of human coexistence.

The Moderates believed the most critical steps for the implantation of a liberal order had been taken in the 1830s. They argued that the years of Progressive radical politics had been a threat to the political, social, and economic stability that Spain needed in order to prosper. It was their task, they believed, to return politics to the path that would lead to the completion of the still unfinished task of constructing an authentic liberal order. 'The Spaniards are tired of alternatives and convulsions', claimed Narváez in his speech of investiture, in May 1844. 'They anxiously desire to enjoy tranquillity and peace under the empire of law and the custody of the Crown.'

However, the expected tranquillity never fully arrived, due to the persistence of political divisions among Moderates and within the Liberal family as a whole. The Moderates were divided into at least three different factions. There was a minority right wing led by the Marquis of Viluma and intellectually inspired by Jaime Balmes, who argued for a conciliatory approach with the Carlists in order to keep both the Crown and the Church prominent and strong. Up to 1854 the faction that dominated the party was led by Alejandro Mon and Pedro José Pidal, the designers and promoters of the most successful Moderate institutional policies during the decade after 1843. They succeeded in melding the larger population into the party and represented the most genuine version of Moderate philosophy and action. This can be described as a sort of 'closed centre', in the words of José Luis Comellas, less conciliatory toward absolutism than Viluma's followers believed they should be, but still quite conservative. But the true centre of Spanish politics during this time was located in what some historians have called the left wing of the Moderate movement, known as 'the puritans' and represented by Joaquin Francisco Pacheco. Their motto was that 'the political truth was not solely in the hands of a single party'; they were thus willing to foster greater pluralism, as well as willing to allow the political parties and the parliament to play leading roles, instead of the monarch. The puritans worked for rapprochement with the Progressives, a strategy which gave birth to the Liberal Union after 1858.

The Progressives were, according to Peter Janke, the Jacobins of Spain, but their programme was mainly influenced by English utilitarian liberalism, especially the ideas of Jeremy Bentham. Like the Moderates, the core of the group constituted a political clientele integrated by notables. However, the Progressive programme appealed to what Angel Bahamonde and Jesús Martínez have called 'the liberal populace' (*el pueblo liberal*), that segment of the lower middle classes and the working classes that actively supported the liberal revolution. The Progressives differed from the Moderates in defending higher levels of freedom of expression, a broader suffrage, more participation of the provincial and local powers in the political process, and a stronger parliament. They relied on the National Militia as the best vehicle to attain and sustain their political programme, and believed that revolution was a legitimate tool to gain power. They were willing to mitigate the influence of the Catholic Church in Spanish life, while still acknowledging that Spain was a Catholic country, and because of this they were determined to carry out the disentailment of Church lands, a process the Moderates had halted in 1843. Here we find the only aspect in which the Progressives' and Moderates' economic programmes differed even slightly; otherwise, both groups stood together in defence of economic freedom and private property.

Since 1840 the public leader of the Progressive Party had been General Espartero, but policy directives came from less popular politicians such as Pascual Madoz, Salustiano Olózaga, and Manuel Alonso Martínez. The Progressives were never called upon by the Crown to form a government; the only times they came to power were as a consequence of military *pronunciamientos* or popular rebellions. After 1843 the Moderates and the Crown worked together to exclude the Progressives from government, but that exclusion was also the result of the Progressives' misguided political strategies. They had decided to adopt a position of *retraimiento* (systematic electoral abstention) to protest against the favouritism that the Crown showed towards the Moderates. The strategy was a complete failure and only served to entrench the power of the Moderates.

The degree of division among Progressives was even greater than among Moderates. Espartero's leadership was contested from within the party precisely when the Moderates were succeeding in weakening established Progressive governments, as happened in both 1843 and 1856. The Progressives also always acted hesitantly, continually faced with the dilemma of finding a way to control the revolution and keep it from extreme radicalization. On the one hand they needed the help of the liberal mob to enact the revolution, but on the other hand they had to rather suddenly neutralize those same groups. The Progressives' reluctant policies resulted in the split of the Party and the rise of the Democrats as the new political force determined to bring an authentic democratic system to Spain.

The Moderates were able to maintain their hegemony up to the 1860s by implementing a programme aimed at limiting the presence of the opposition. If measured by their success in moving toward a true democracy, the Moderate years were a step backward. The Moderate programme rejected some of the more democratic achievements of previous Progressive legislatures. Because of the Moderate programme's restrictive nature political stability was precarious and the government was periodically challenged by revolutions. None the less, the Moderates created a legal and institutional apparatus that in the short run contributed to the unfinished task of building a liberal state, and in the long run succeeded in cementing that state's conservative nature.

Institutional instruments and political practice of the Moderate years

The main instrument that the Moderates used to tame the revolution was a 'reform' of the constitution that the Progressives had adopted in 1837 which ended in the proclamation of a new constitution in 1845. Despite the repetition of a large number of articles, this new body of laws differed so substantially in spirit from its Progressive predecessor, that it transformed the nature of the entire political system. Under the Progressive constitution national sovereignty had rested with the parliament, but the Moderates established a new form of sovereignty in which part of the Crown's traditional powers were restored. This was achieved by limiting the responsibilities of parliament and, subsequently, reinforcing the power of the monarch, the cabinet, and the senate in the decision-making process. There was a new senate whose members, undetermined in number, would be appointed exclusively by royal designation from among the notables of the kingdom. Along with this, the constitution suppressed the National Militia that had been a key instrument used by the Progressives to implement their revolutionary programme. In sum, the Constitution of 1845 established the foundations for a state in which the notables would continue building a liberal order on the basis of a combination of innovation and continuity instead of revolutionary rupture.

Once the constitution had established the framework for the new order, the Moderates embarked upon a feverish legislative programme in order to consolidate their rule. The main outcome of this process was the elaboration of new electoral laws and new norms for the regulation of freedom of speech. Both were, of course, restrictive. The 1846 electoral law restricted the franchise to a mere 1 per cent of the total population, 500 000 fewer voters than under the former Progressive law. Only some 100 000 male citizens fulfilled the requirements for age, income, and 'quality' that granted them the right to participate in the election of their parliamentarians. The law also changed the electoral unit from the province to a smaller region called the 'electoral district' that was easier to control. The rules for conducting elections were written in such a way that the party in power could rather easily control them. The political 'boss' – a provincial governor – was the key figure in the manipulation of the electoral game. He was in control of the process of voter registration, the creation of voting lists, the nominations of those who would supervise the polling places on election day, and the validation of the electoral results. Candidates had to meet restrictive requirements in terms of age, income, and status to be eligible for office, but their selection was strictly controlled by the political parties. In electoral periods a series of local and national committees nominated by the parties were in charge of the selection of candidates and the running of campaigns. On the surface the procedures appeared democratic, but the whole process was controlled by an elaborate system of power relations that connected the party oligarchies with the *caciques* (local patrons). The main figure in the electoral process was the local notable, who would have plenty of friends and especially subordinates in his electoral district. Local bosses – *caciques* – formed the backbone of this corrupt electoral system created to assure the perpetuation of Moderate hegemony.

But, as Comellas has pointed out, the Moderates were more than cunning political manipulators, they were also good administrators. The Moderate years bequeathed a set of institutions, laws, and practices that survived the turbulence of daily politics and helped to consolidate the liberal state. The Moderates reformed the old National Bank, converting it into the modern financial institution it is today. They also introduced the postage stamp and the use of the *peseta* as the national monetary unit, and took the first measures to create a state-supported education system. In the administration of justice and maintenance of public order the Moderates succeeded in formulating a new criminal code in tune with the spirit of rationalization that characterized liberal law; they advanced in the process of building a modern court system, and in 1844 created the controversial Civil Guard, a nationwide police force.

One of the Moderates' more lasting projects was the reform of the national treasury, carried out in 1845 by the minister Alejandro Mon and inspired by the economist Ramón de Santillán. Mon and Santillán had two main goals. First, they sought to rationalize the taxation system by reducing the large number of taxes mandated by the Ancien Regime to a few direct and indirect charges. The most profitable among those taxes was the *consumos* – sales tax charged on food and other basic necessities which bore most heavily on the less affluent – and which would be the cause of numerous riots in the future. *Consumos* represented the clearest example of the social unfairness that characterized this new taxation system. Second, the Moderates moved to reduce the huge deficit with the emission of new titles of public debt. Although this last goal was never achieved, these reforms definitively established a modern treasury for Spain. The Moderates also initiated a series of reforms of the state administration to make it more efficient. The intention was to professionalize its structures, to rationalize its procedures, and to centralize its management. Among the most important steps taken before 1848 was the creation of the new departments of Commerce, Education, and Public Works, the completion of the administrative division of Spanish territory in the provinces, and the approval of a bill to regulate municipal and regional powers that implied a tighter control of the central government over provincial life.

Moderate reformist activity reached its peak in 1851 during the Bravo Murillo administration. Bravo Murillo's general philosophy was that the administration's concerns and politics should run together, although under exceptional circumstances politics must be subordinated to administration. Bravo Murillo was the first of a long line of technocratic politicians in the recent history of Spain who were convinced that the stability of Spanish political life depended upon the improvement of the living standards of the Spanish people. During his short rule he designed and initiated ambitious plans of public works aimed at generating economic growth and attempted to create an administration staffed by competent professionals selected according to merit and efficiency instead of political loyalty. Bravo Murillo's aversion to conventional politics was the reason for his failure. He was unable to consolidate his own political support while the oligarchy of the Moderate party conspired effectively against him.

To some extent, Bravo Murillo's failure symbolizes in a more general sense the failure of Moderate attempts to build a framework for enduring political dialogue in Spain. The Moderates did succeed in taming the revolution and setting firm foundations for the liberal state, but they failed to sweep away the revolutionary threat. The Moderates did not turn to negotiation to implement their more conservative programme; rather, they preferred to impose it on others. The exclusion of the opposition gradually generated a sense of frustration, and in the end Spanish political life would not escape the vicious circle of revolutionary and counter-revolutionary thrusts. The days in which liberalism would be able to generate a system of enduring stability were still to come.

The Revolution of 1854 and the Liberal Union (1854–1868)

The first serious revolutionary attempt against Moderate rule occurred during the spring of 1848, when the Progressives tried to duplicate the revolutionary movements that were taking place across much of Europe in

Spain. However, the effort was a complete failure: Narváez acted rapidly and resolutely to repress the revolution while on the other side the Progressives were unable to mobilize the masses to man the barricades. They were divided regarding the goals of the revolution and there was a good deal of hesitation among those who feared that popular mobilization would end in social revolution. The result was the split in the Progressive forces that gave birth in 1849 to the Democratic Party, with its commitment to thorough democratization and social reform. Despite its failure, 1848 demonstrated that the seeds for revolution were nestled in Spanish soil and could germinate under more advantageous conditions.

This moment arrived in 1854. The political situation had so deteriorated that it was finally possible to create a broad consensus favouring change. The movement was composed of three different factions that pursued, in the words of Angel Bahamonde and Jesús Martínez, three different revolutions. First were the Moderate 'puritans,' who were willing to create a system in which the opposition could take part in a new democratic politics. Next were the Progressives, who actually sparked the revolution, believing it to be the only opportunity to reach power and implement their programme. Finally, the Democrats provided a great portion of the popular support. As usual, the military was the key to revolutionary success, as repeated *pronunciamientos* neutralized the government.

The movement attained its goals in July 1854 when General Espartero was called to take the presidency of a new cabinet. However, the Progressives were able to hold on to power for only two years, and in 1856 a new political movement inspired by the Moderates and called the 'Liberal Union' gained control of the government. The real winners of the revolution were not the radicals but rather a conglomerate formed among those at the centre of Moderate and Progressive liberalism. Espartero acted as a temporary charismatic leader, but the authentic head of the new situation was General Leopoldo O'Donnell.

Between 1854 and 1856 Espartero, with the Progressives' and O'Donnell's consent, tried to go back to the situation as it had been before 1843. The Progressive programme included the promulgation of a new constitution that would make it possible to expand freedom of speech, decentralize the state, reform the tax system, expand suffrage, continue disentailment, and restore the National Militia. The constitution was drafted and approved by the parliament in 1856, but it was never promulgated. The economic programmes, and more specifically the disentailing laws of Pascual Madoz, were the major achievements of the Progressive biennium. Rejecting protectionist trade policies, a series of new laws opened the Spanish markets to the flow of foreign capital, modernized the financial sector, and encouraged the creation of joint stock companies. Perhaps the most outstanding feature of this partial success was the creation of the Spanish railway network, containing about 3400 miles of line, in 1868. The disentailing laws of Madoz continued the process of liberalization and privatization of land and real property that had been interrupted after 1843. The goal was to complete the cycle of privatization of entailed properties, now focusing not only on the Church, but also on the common lands in the hands of the state, the military orders, and the municipalities.

Despite the positive impact of their economic policies, the two years of Progressive rule did not substantially alter the functioning of the state as it had been established by the Moderates. The 1854 revolution brought about more of a change of government personnel than a change of vision and policy; consequently, it was contested from the very beginning by those who dreamed of the coming of a new order. Now the voice of revolution was represented by the new Democratic Party, whose rhetoric and programme were even more radical than those of the Progressives. In fact, the more rebellious the Democrats seemed, the more hesitant and ambivalent appeared the Progressives. It was this combination of factors that brought to an end the Progressive biennium and the subsequent consolidation of the Liberal Union. The events of 1856 brought about the loss of confidence by liberal popular groups toward the Progressives' commitment to radical change. The two years of Progressive rule displayed the limits of the liberal revolution as it had been formulated by the Progressives in the 1830s.

The fourteen years that separate the 1854 revolutionary episode from the 'Glorious Revolution' of 1868 were marked by the attempt to build a liberal consensus. Bravo Murillo's technocratic liberalism had failed in this goal and thus opened the doors for a new political experiment, guided by the Moderates O'Donnell and Ríos Rosas, known as the Liberal Union. More a coalition than a party, the Liberal Union worked better as an experiment for the future than as a solution for the problems of the moment. The idea was promising, but in reality the experiment was sponsored by an alliance of notables with few popular links and strongly convinced that order should prevail over liberty. The Liberal Union brought about the longest period of stable government since 1833, but it finally failed in what was supposed to be its main goal: the unification of the entire liberal family in a common endeavour. Like the Moderates before 1854, the Unionist government ended up practising a policy of exclusion of its political rivals. The fear of a radical revolution was again the excuse to neglect and repress those who supported more democracy and social reform. In this, politicians were backed by the Crown, which was more and more identified as the main obstacle to democracy.

The coming of the 1868 upheaval shows the inability of Spanish liberals to achieve a stable political system. As we have seen, the years of the Moderate hegemony were decisive for the consolidation of a liberal state, but this state failed to provide the liberty and prosperity that many Spaniards would have expected from the early liberal project. Gabriel Tortella has pointed out that this political failure was in the last instance the consequence of the poor performance of Spanish economy and the persistence of traditional social structures. Indeed, in a society marked by deep social divisions, the margin available to traditional Spanish elites to establish political stability while maintaining their domination was very narrow. This explains the hesitations of the Progressives and the refusal of the Moderates and Liberal Unionists to open the political system to a greater degree of democratic participation. Under these circumstances, Spanish political life would continue to be marked by the menace of revolution, but now the social characteristics of that revolutionary potential threatened the traditional liberal elites more than ever. In the future, the maintenance of a stable political system would depend on the capacity of the elites to remain united, a condition that in the long run proved to be impossible amidst the turbulence of Spanish political life.

|3|

Church and State, 1808–1874

WILLIAM J. CALLAHAN

The political revolution accomplished by liberalism destroyed absolute monarchy. It also carried out an ecclesiastical revolution that transformed the place of the Church within state and society. The great Church of the eighteenth century, identified with the kingdom's traditional hierarchical society, the product of centuries of institutional development, possessor of immense riches and served by a numerous body of priests and the clergy, virtually collapsed as the result of the changes imposed by liberalism. The pace and timing of liberal policy towards the Church depended in large measure on an ongoing struggle between deputies favouring a gradualist approach and those supporting rapid and decisive action. During the most radical phase of the ecclesiastical revolution between 1835–36 and 1840–43, the state suppressed the male religious orders with few exceptions and ordered the sale of the regular and diocesan clergy's property. The tithe, bedrock of ecclesiastical finances for centuries, was abolished. A once impressive clerical establishment experienced accelerated demographic decline, while for a time the authorities arrested or exiled bishops and suspended new ordinations to the priesthood.

Clerical and lay critics of the time and since interpreted such measures as the result of corrosive, secular ideas bent on the destruction of Catholicism. The relationship between liberalism and the Church cannot be interpreted so simply. Even during the radical phase of the ecclesiastical revolution, the state remained officially Catholic. In fact, every constitution between 1812 and 1869 affirmed the confessionality of the state in one form or another. Prime Minister Juan Álvarez Mendizábal, author of the legislation suppressing the male religious orders, was a practising Catholic, as was the regent between 1840 and 1843, General Baldomero Espartero, whose government attempted a drastic administrative reorganization of the Church that would have substantially reduced papal authority over the Spanish Church.

The paradox of an officially Catholic state committed to dismantling the institutional and economic buttresses that had sustained the Church for centuries arose from several causes. The support of bishops and priests for absolutism between 1814 and 1820 and from 1823 to 1833, and their support for the Carlist rebellion of the 1830s hardened liberal attitudes towards the clergy. But the origins of liberal attitudes towards the Church were more complex. They were based on a civil–ecclesiastical model that reached its zenith during the second half of the eighteenth century. Liberalism's political programme broke decisively with the past. Its ecclesiastical policy sought to adapt the intricate and interdependent relations characteristic of the alliance between Throne and Altar identified with absolute monarchy to new circumstances.

Throne and Altar

Kings Carlos III and Carlos IV expanded royal control over ecclesiastical affairs. Although Spanish monarchs had struggled for centuries to extend their authority over clerical finances and patronage, the Bourbons aggressively promoted a regalist policy that created a Church with an internal administration resting for all practical purposes in royal hands. The concordat of 1753, wrested from the weak papacy of Pope Benedict XIV (1740–58), granted the king nearly complete control over ecclesiastical patronage, a right previously shared in tense relationship with Rome. Royal bureaucrats saw the concordat as equalling the conquest of the Moorish kingdom of Granada in 1492 in historic importance. Eighteenth-century regalism did not intend a break with the papacy, but it expressed the Crown's determination to exclude Rome as far as possible from participating in the administration of the Spanish Church.

Royal interventionism took many forms. The king named the kingdom's bishops whose credentials were carefully examined before appointment by a government body, the Council of Castile. The authority of the pope was limited to either approval or rejection of royal nominations. Carlos III expelled the Jesuits from his dominions in 1767 and secured the suppression of the Order from a reluctant papacy in 1773. Always suspicious of the autonomy of the Inquisition, in 1768 royal bureaucrats asserted the king's absolute right 'to watch over the use which the Inquisition makes of its jurisdiction, to enlighten it, reform its abuses, impose limitations on it and even to suppress it if this should by demanded by necessity and public utility'. Bishops expressing reservations about the extent of state control over the Church felt the full weight of official anger. In 1766, Bishop Carvajal y Lancaster of Cuenca was called to Madrid and subjected to a humiliating dressing-down by royal bureaucrats for questioning the extent royal power over the Church. Other prominent prelates were either forced to resign or eased from their positions for similar reasons. Nor did royal authorities feel any scruple about secretly opening the correspondence of clergymen whom they suspected of disagreeing with the prevailing regalist interpretation of civil–ecclesiastical relations.

Bourbon regalism concentrated on the practical objective of increasing royal control over ecclesiastical finances, patronage and administration. But regalism was also associated with a movement of religious reform arising from renovating currents within European Catholicism and an older tradition identified with the sixteenth-century Spanish followers of Erasmus. Although clerical advocates of change never produced a specific package of reforms on which they all agreed, their ideas focused on certain issues. Reformers sought to enhance the authority of the bishops with respect to the papacy and to exalt the role of the parish clergy over that of the religious orders in the name of a renewed Catholicism that looked back to the austerity and simplicity of the early Christian Church. Reformers did not question Catholic doctrine, but they called for the elimination of superstitious practices and extravagant popular devotions in favour of a more interior spirituality inspired by sacred scripture.

Despite papal hostility these ideas circulated widely within a cultivated ecclesiastical minority in Catholic Europe. The Spanish kingdom provided fertile ground for the development of the reforming movement through the emergence of a vital clerical culture. After 1750, advocates of reform, labelled 'Jansenists' by their detractors and 'enlightened Catholics' by later historiographical admirers, promoted changes within the Church that attracted the support of leading members of the hierarchy and a minority of clergy.

The cause of religious renovation appealed to regalists who maintained that the king derived his authority from God and was responsible, therefore, for the spiritual well-being of his subjects including the regulation of ecclesiastical discipline and religious practice. Regalists also wished to use the clergy to advance the Crown's secular policies, particularly in the area of economic improvement. Bishops and priests were expected to cooperate with the state's objectives by promoting the kingdom's material development, improving education, building public works, and, in general, advancing the Crown's utilitarian policies. 'Public utility', declared one advocate of a public spirited Church, 'is one of the objects of our religion. Its maxims lead to the good of souls and the tranquillity of peoples.' This practical emphasis caused royal officials to question the role of the religious orders. Critics argued that the number of monks and friars, 53 098 according to the census of 1797, was excessive for the kingdom's pastoral needs. The orders were accused of consuming their energies on promoting 'long prayers and the observance of certain exterior ceremonies' instead of deepening the spiritual content of religion and contributing to economic progress.

Royal bureaucrats were also concerned with the economic effects of the Church's extensive landholdings. In Castile alone, ecclesiastical institutions owned 15 per cent of the land and received 28 per cent of the gross income produced by the region's economy. Government officials and writers concerned with the kingdom's material condition saw the ownership of land by the 'dead hands' of religious institutions as an obstacle to agricultural progress which they believed could be advanced only through the creation of a robust peasantry possessing its own property. After 1790, these ideas became more influential, particularly after the publication of Gaspar de Jovellanos' proposal (1795) for a new agrarian law based on individual property ownership. Carlos III imposed limitations on the acquisition of new land by the Church and Carlos IV ordered the sale of the property of certain charitable and pious endowments in 1798, but the Bourbons did not directly attack the vast holdings of ecclesiastical institutions, although some clergymen viewed the 1798 initiative as a dangerous precedent.

Not all regalists were reformers, nor were all reformers regalists. But the idea that Crown and clergy should cooperate to eliminate abuses in the Church and purify religion became stronger among a minority of educated priests and some government officials after 1780. The decisions of a diocesan synod encouraged in 1786 by Grand Duke Leopold of Tuscany and directed by Bishop Scipione de' Ricci of Pistoia were received enthusiastically by Spanish reformers as an example of what might be achieved through the cooperation of an enlightened absolutist state and a reforming Church. The synod attempted to strengthen episcopal authority at the expense of the papacy, purify the liturgy of superstitious practices and limit the growth of the religious orders. The text of the synod's proceedings was quickly translated into Spanish and stimulated a wave of intellectual effervescence in the kingdom's universities during the 1790s, particularly in the University of Salamanca where some of the most prominent liberal deputies at the Cortes of Cádiz had been professors and students.

Carlos III and Carlos IV carried out some ecclesiastical reforms, but their effect was limited because of infighting within official circles and the opposition of some bishops and priests, especially after the outbreak of the French Revolution. The Church retained its vast property holdings. Widely expressed criticism of the religious orders did not lead to a general assault on the regular clergy beyond the suppression of the Jesuits and two small religious communities. No synod similar to Pistoia was ever held in Spain, although individual bishops campaigned against superstitious practices and sought to promote a more spiritual faith among clergy and laity.

The first liberal generation gathered in the Cortes of Cádiz inherited key principles from the regalist-reform tradition. Liberal deputies accepted without question the premise that Spain was officially Catholic and that Catholicism was essential for the nation's spiritual and moral welfare. They believed that religion, purified, simple and austere, was necessary for the orderly functioning of state and society. They maintained that responsibility for eliminating abuses within the Church fell to the government in cooperation with the clergy and not the papacy. They also expected the clergy to contribute to the political stability and economic prosperity of the new order. This mixture of secular and religious objectives sought to adapt the regalist-religious reform of the past to new circumstances. As far as the Church was concerned, the union of Throne and Altar reappeared in a new form through the alliance of Constitution and Altar. Whether the clergy would accept such a reformulation was another matter.

Constitution and Altar

Napoleon's intervention in Spanish affairs, beginning in 1807, threw the kingdom into political turmoil and provoked armed resistance against King Joseph Napoleon, placed on the throne by the emperor who unceremoniously deposed the Bourbon dynasty. By 1810 the new regime controlled all of peninsular Spain except for the city of Cádiz where its opponents gathered to deliberate in the kingdom's first modern parliamentary assembly. Despite the hostility between the Bonaparte monarchy and the Cortes of Cádiz, their policies coincided on important points. Both opposed the continued existence of a hierarchical society based on noble privilege. Each attempted to reform the archaic administrative reorganization of the old monarchy and to promote material development on the basis of prevailing views of economic liberalism that stood in sharp contrast to the mercantilist approach of the past. The methods employed by the two governments differed: the Bonapartist monarchy attempted to achieve its modernizing goals by decree, the Cortes of Cádiz through the legislation of an elected parliament.

Despite the accusations of impiety and irreligion directed against the Bonapartist monarchy by its opponents, its constitution, the Statute of Bayonne, declared without equivocation that Catholicism 'will be the religion of the King and the Nation and no other will be permitted'. The regime's ecclesiastical policy was inspired by the same regalist-reform ideas that inspired the liberal deputies at Cádiz. The Inquisition, long an object of criticism by eighteenth-century reformers, was abolished. To direct the energies of the parochial clergy towards pastoral work, the provision of thousands of benefices unconnected to the 'cure of souls' was forbidden. But Joseph Napoleon went further than the Cortes by suppressing the religious orders in 1809.

When the Cortes opened in 1810, its 308 deputies, including 97 clergymen, agreed in general terms on the necessity of ecclesiastical reform. Even the hierarchy supported the summoning of the assembly to remedy the highhanded regalism of Carlos IV's administration which some bishops believed had reduced them to being little more than 'deaf and dumb dogs'. The bishops accepted the idea shared by a majority of deputies that a national council of the Spanish Church should be called to undertake its reform. The possibility of a consensus was enhanced by the desire of the liberal majority to avoid extreme measures likely to alienate the hierarchy from the new political system. No comprehensive reform of either the secular or regular clergy ever occurred, although piecemeal measures were taken to reduce the number of religious houses and enhance the pastoral role of parish priests. Nor was there any serious attempt to interfere with the Church's extensive property holdings.

But these favourable circumstances disguised fundamental differences. The bishops expected the Cortes to free them from the regalist restraints of the past and to assign to the Church responsibility for implementing changes which they conceived in minimalist terms. Faithful to the regalist-reform tradition, the liberal majority believed that the state must assume direct responsibility for carrying out more far-reaching reforms, although political reality tempered their ambitions. Liberals wished to rationalize the Church's sprawling and sometimes chaotic organization of dioceses and parishes. They believed that the number of clergy should be reduced and redirected in accord with the kingdom's pastoral needs. They also sought to deepen the spiritual content of Spanish Catholicism by returning it to the simplicity and austerity of the early Church by eliminating what they saw as the excesses of popular piety.

This mingling of an unequivocal commitment to Catholicism with the liberal version of regalism appeared in Article 12 of the 1812 constitution. On the one hand, it declared that the religion of the nation 'is and will be perpetually the Catholic, Apostolic, Roman, the only true religion', while it prohibited religious toleration in no uncertain terms. On the other, it asserted that the nation would protect religion through 'wise and just laws'. Conservative clerical deputies quickly grasped the significance of this apparently innocent phrase. It provided, said one ecclesiastical critic, nothing more than an 'authorized pretext . . . for the Cortes to involve itself in the reform of the Church'. This is exactly what liberals had in mind. They saw the clause as legal justification for the government to implement changes in the Church inspired by the regalist-reform tradition of the eighteenth century.

A minority of clerical deputies, notably Joaquín Lorenzo Villanueva and Diego Muñoz Torrero, former professors at the University of Salamanca, were ardent defenders of the idea of ecclesiastical reform carried by the alliance of Constitution and Altar. But by 1812 the vast majority of bishops were becoming restless with liberal regalism's plans for the Church. The straw that broke the proverbial camel's back was the decision of the Cortes to abolish the Inquisition on 22 January 1813. Although the bishops once viewed the Inquisition with certain reservations because it infringed episcopal jurisdiction, they now deluged the Cortes with protests demanding the survival of the Holy Tribunal as necessary to defend religion. After fierce parliamentary debate, the Cortes decided upon abolition. Only 11 of the clerical deputies present in the chamber voted in favour but 32 voted against, a clear sign of diminishing ecclesiastical support for the regime.

On the eve of the Inquisition's suppression, the bishops issued a pastoral letter declaring that Spain was engaged both in a war against a foreign enemy and an 'internal war'. They identified their domestic enemies as 'ecclesiastics who presume themselves reformers' whom they described as 'rapacious wolves propagating perverse dogmas, false doctors promising liberty when they are the slaves of corruption'. At the same time, vitriolic denunciations of liberalism began to pour from clerical pens. Whatever their concerns about the past abuses of royal absolutism, most bishops and priests now desired the restoration of Fernando VII to full power. Still a prisoner of the French, the absent king appeared to the clergy as a providential figure who would deliver the Church from the hands of its enemies.

The rhetorical flights of the clerical campaign against liberalism far exceeded the reality of the Cortes of Cádiz's ecclesiastical policy, which was limited in scope and timid in application except for the suppression of the Inquisition. But certain issues discussed in parliamentary committees, although never producing legislation, show that important principles derived from the regalist-reform tradition were still alive. Liberal deputies talked about the necessity of reducing the size of the religious orders and diocesan clergy. They considered the important question of the state's ultimate rights over ecclesiastical property. They discussed the need to reorganize the Church's administration at the parish and diocesan levels. Although liberals took no decisive action on these matters, they did not forget them. All would resurface during the second liberal revolution between 1820 and 1823.

The absolutist regime installed by a military coup d'état in 1814 received the Church's enthusiastic support. Clerical authorities systematically removed from Church office priests who had supported ecclesiastical reform. But the unwavering commitment of the vast majority of bishops and clergy to the cause of Fernando VII came at a price. Although the former liberal deputies at Cádiz continued to believe in the alliance of Constitution and Altar, the repression of 1814–20 added an ingredient of resentment against the Church that was absent in 1810. It was unlikely that a second liberal government would deal with ecclesiastical reform as cautiously as the first.

The revolution of 1820 caught the Church by surprise. Fernando VII's decision to preserve his throne at any cost by accepting the 1812 constitution and the dominance in parliament of former moderate deputies at Cádiz dulled clerical responses to the revolution in its early stages. Pope Pius VII (1800–23) also urged prudence on the bishops before political reality. For a time it appeared that a compromise was possible between the ecclesiastical authorities and the regime. Bishops throughout the kingdom urged the faithful to live 'beneath the sweet empire of the Constitution'. In contrast to 1813, there were scarcely any clerical protests when the Cortes abolished the Inquisition in March 1820.

The relative calm of civil–ecclesiastical relations did not last. The Cortes of 1820 soon passed legislation inspired by the regalist-religious reform tradition that went beyond anything attempted at Cádiz. The liberal majority's decision to press further developed for several reasons. Unlike the situation in 1810, conservative defenders of the Church were weakly represented in parliament, while the 54 priests sitting in the chamber were for the most part supporters of ecclesiastical reform. As a result, the liberal majority had a freer hand to pursue its programme than had been the case at Cádiz. Legislation affecting the Church included measures to enhance the pastoral role of the diocesan clergy. A parliamentary committee dominated by reforming priests, among them Joaquín Lorenzo Villanueva and Diego Muñoz Torrero, proposed a reduction in the number of cathedral canons, the elimination of benefices unconnected to pastoral work, a reorganization of the country's parishes and a rational system of salaries for the parochial clergy. These proposals were moved by religious concerns. For example, the committee emphasized that the primary obligation of the parochial clergy was to teach knowledge of the faith.

With few exceptions the hierarchy viewed such proposals with suspicion. Episcopal unease deepened when the Cortes ordered the suppression of the Jesuits and the sale of their property for the benefit of the public treasury. Parliament then passed a law suppressing all monasteries, that is, the foundations of the strictly monastic orders, such as the Benedictines and Cistercians. The law also ordered a reduction in the personnel and number of houses of other religious communities such as the Franciscans and Dominicans. The property of the more than 800 monasteries and friaries falling under the terms of this legislation was sold at auction.

The ecclesiastical legislation of the Cortes of 1820 applied ideas discussed but never acted upon at Cádiz. But an important shift in liberal attitudes had taken place since 1810. The support of monks and friars for Fernando VII after 1814 deepened hostility against the regular clergy. For the first time the liberal state established its authority to sell the orders' property for a public purpose, namely the reduction of the national debt. The suppression of monasteries and friaries was justified on religious grounds, but to this was added a new dimension, the state's financial welfare. The Cortes of 1820 broke new ground in its policy towards the Church, but its legislation still reflected the idea that state and Church should cooperate to improve the kingdom's religious condition. As a result over 800 religious houses survived suppression, while the property of the diocesan clergy remained untouched. Although the clergy viewed liberal reforms with hostility, the deputies of 1812 dominating the parliament of 1820 attempted a compromise between an ascendant regalism in civil–ecclesiastical relations, the financial needs of the state and the Church's historic organization. But by mid-1821 a more extreme group of liberals, the *exaltados*, took power. Although they affirmed their commitment to Catholicism as the religion of the nation, they believed that the government should unilaterally force reform on the Church. The idea so dear to the liberals of 1812 that cooperation between Constitution and Altar would reconcile religion and liberty gave way to the concept that ecclesiastical reform should be imposed by the state alone.

Exaltado domination of the government in 1822 and 1823 failed to produce political stability. Moderate liberals objected to the extremism of official policy, while supporters of absolutism rose in revolt in the name of Fernando VII. The regime removed from office bishops whom it judged subversive. In Catalonia, where civil war raged, fifty priests, including the bishop of Vic, were assassinated by marauding liberal troops. The authorities accused the male religious orders in the region of supporting rebellion by word and deed and ordered their suppression. Even as these events unfolded in 1823, the *exaltado* Cortes named a parliamentary commission to consider ecclesiastical reform. The commission pushed the regalist-reform programme further than ever before. It proposed a radical diocesan reorganization based on provincial boundaries to replace the historic geographic distribution of dioceses. It called for the virtual elimination of the pope's role in episcopal appointments, the abolition of the tithe and the creation of a special tax to pay the secular clergy's salaries.

Chaotic political conditions prevented these proposals from becoming law, but they showed that the *exaltados* were prepared to abandon the compromise attempted by moderate deputies in 1820. Nor did the regime's officials feel any scruple about using force to attain their objectives. For example, soldiers were used to intimidate cathedral chapters who had been assigned the canonical responsibility of electing diocesan administrators to replace those bishops who had been forced to abandon their sees under government pressure.

Liberal ecclesiastical reform, whether in its moderate or *exaltado* version, was significant for the future. Reform was rejected by the vast majority of the hierarchy and clergy who looked again to the restoration of Fernando VII to absolute power. In some regions, priests participated actively in the revolt against liberalism. Of greater significance was the tendency of the bishops, whose eighteenth-century regalist predecessors were not averse to limiting papal authority, to turn to Rome to defend the interests of the Spanish Church. The repression and violence against priests and the clergy in 1822 and 1823 also undermined the credibility of reforming priests among the clergy. The reforming projects of the liberal period represented the last great surge of the regalist-reform tradition among a minority of priests, although a few figures survived to play a last act in 1834 and 1835 before being swept aside by events.

After recovering the absolute power he so dearly cherished, Fernando VII annulled liberal ecclesiastical legislation with one exception. The king refused to restore the Inquisition, fearing that the institution would be used against him by a new generation of clerical extremists intent on forcing the monarch to conform to their demands for the creation of a virtually theocratic society. But Fernando VII's second restoration allowed the Church to reestablish its traditional organization and recover its privileges and wealth. Political conditions following the king's death soon caused this centuries old structure to collapse. On its third appearance liberalism imposed changes on the Church that undermined its institutional foundations.

Ecclesiastical revolution

The moderate liberals dominating the government of Francisco Martínez de la Rosa (January 1834–June 1835) looked to the Cortes of 1820 for their model of ecclesiastical reform. The new government declared its intention to improve the status and economic situation of parish priests and reduce the size of the religious orders, but it did not wish to eliminate the regular clergy entirely. The government appointed a royal commission, the Real Junta Eclesiástica, on which ten reforming clerics sat, to produce a compromise package of reforms. An ecclesiastical policy based on limited reform might have succeeded in 1820. It was swept aside by events in 1834–35. Martínez de la Rosa's argument that reform of the regular clergy must be achieved through 'firm and measured steps, although they appeared slow', was rejected by *exaltado* politicians who subjected the religious orders to withering attacks. The regulars were compared to a 'robust plant which extends its branches through all Spain', a plant that could not be trimmed but must be deprived of 'the water that irrigates and feeds it'.

Resentment against the religious orders intensified because of the support given by some of them to the Carlist rebellion. Although a majority of the clergy sympathized with the cause of Don Carlos, there was no rush to back the pretender. Bishops and priests preferred to wait uneasily upon events. Carlism's commitment to save the Church from liberal reform appealed to the clergy, but most bishops and priests, aware of the uncertainty of the civil war's outcome, were cautious about lending active support to the rebellion. The clergy also realized that the Church's condition in regions controlled by Carlism was less than ideal. The Carlist kingdom in the north imposed heavy financial exactions on the Church. The Catholic press often complained of the depredations of Carlist troops who 'did not recognize any limits, any subordination or discipline' as they ravaged local populations.

But active support for Carlism on the part of some regulars deepened *exaltado* hostility against the religious orders. To this was added the appearance of a violent, popular anticlericalism focused on the regular clergy. The intense politicization of the urban masses, the identification of the religious orders with absolutism, deteriorating economic conditions in the cities and the mood of anger and terror created by the first appearance in Spain of cholera in 1834 formed an explosive combination which swirled around monks and friars, who provided a ready scapegoat for popular passions. Although episodic outbursts of violence against monks and friars occurred between 1820 and 1823, they bore no comparison to the savage assault of 17 July 1834 when rioting crowds in Madrid assassinated 78 Jesuits, Franciscans, Dominicans and Mercedarians. Similar scenes occurred in Zaragoza and Barcelona a year later. The government attempted to implement its plans for a limited closing of religious houses, but in many regions monasteries and friaries were already empty as their residents fled the popular fury which made a compromise solution to the question of the religious orders impossible.

In September 1835, a political crisis ousted moderate liberals from power. The new prime minister, Juan Álvarez Mendizábal, abandoned evolutionary reform in favour of rapid action on a number of fronts including the religious orders. Martínez de la Rosa hoped to resolve the problem of the regulars that had preoccupied liberals since the Cortes of Cádiz through a compromise that would have reduced the number of foundations while reducing the national debt through the sale of the property of suppressed religious houses. Mendizábal broke the connection between limited reform and partial disentailment. He proposed nothing less than the outright suppression of the male orders (with a few exceptions) and the sale of their property.

The decree of 11 October 1835 abolishing the male regulars nodded in the direction of the old regalist-reform tradition. Monasteries and friaries were 'useless and unnecessary ... for the spiritual assistance of the faithful'. But the motives behind suppression were primarily financial and economic. The religious orders' vast property holdings were 'prejudicial' to the kingdom's prosperity. Their sale would open 'a most abundant source of public felicity, giving new life to moribund wealth, removing obstacles to the channels of industry and the circulation [of wealth]'. The sale of the orders' property at public auction proceeded slowly at first, but by 1839 over 15 000 separate parcels had gone under the hammer.

The suppression of the male regulars opened a period that undermined the institutional bulwarks that had sustained the Church for centuries. Although the liberal parliamentary factions, now divided into the Progessive and Moderate parties, alternated in power in chaotic political circumstances, by 1843 the Church had seen the property of the diocesan clergy suffer the same fate as that of the religious orders. The tithe was abolished in favour of a system of government salaries for bishops and parish priests. Between 1835 and 1843 whatever vestiges remained of the idea of ecclesiastical reform carried out by the alliance of Constitution and Altar had vanished. By 1840 deaths, retirements and exile had reduced the hierarchy to a corporal's guard of 11 bishops, due in part to the refusal of Pope Gregory XVI (1831–46) to approve the government's episcopal nominations.

The few bishops occupying their dioceses scarcely knew where to turn. 'Observing the furious interference of the revolution, they were usually ignorant of how they could salvage the ship of the Church in the midst of such shocks,' declared one prelate. In fact, there was little the Church could do. The defeat of the Carlist rebellion in 1839 removed the faint hope of rescue from this source, while political upheaval in 1840 gave power to General Baldomero Espartero and the Progressives who were intent on forcing radical organizational changes on the Church. In May 1841 the government of the Espartero regency presented the most ambitious reform project yet advanced. The state intended to redraw an ecclesiastical map that had gone unchanged for centuries. Seventeen dioceses were to be suppressed and 13 new ones created. Over 3000 canonries in cathedral chapters were to be eliminated and 4000 of the country's 19 000 parishes closed. A later proposal planned to limit contacts between the papacy and the Spanish Church to the purely ceremonial.

This scheme for the creation of a national Church pushed the regalist-reform tradition to its extreme limit. The government proposed to act unilaterally without reference to either the papacy or the clergy, although it managed to find a few priests to cooperate with its plans. But events proved that a solution imposed by the state alone was impossible. The regalist currents that had once circulated widely among bishops and priests during the late eighteenth century and received support from a minority of reforming clergymen at Cádiz and during the Cortes of 1820 had largely dissipated. The clergy looked to the pope to save the Church in its moment of trial as the battle cry 'Rome is our end! Rome is our hope!' swept through clerical ranks. In practical terms, there was little Gregory XVI could do, but his vigorous attack (1 March 1841) on the Espartero regime's ecclesiastical policy inspired the lower clergy into a campaign of passive resistance against the government's schemes.

Towards a new settlement

In the end salvation came from another direction. The revolution of 1843 ousted Espartero and brought the Moderate party to power. For the Moderates, intent on excluding their opponents from power and yet determined to preserve for their supporters the gains made from the destruction of a hierarchical social order, including the sale of ecclesiastical property, an accommodation with the Church seemed tactically sound. A mutually acceptable arrangement promised to undercut the appeal of Carlism in the northern countryside, where it continued to enjoy popular support, and to win the backing of an institution fearful of another round of unilateral reform should the Progressives return to power. The Moderates remained faithful to liberal regalism in important respects. They insisted on retaining the state's rights over episcopal appointments and demanded extensive reform of diocesan and parish organization. Nor did they intend to restore the suppressed religious orders. But the Moderates were prepared to abandon liberalism's historic commitment to unilateral ecclesiastical reform in favour of a negotiated settlement with the papacy.

Years of difficult negotiations with Gregory XVI and his successor, Pope Pius IX (1846–78) finally produced the concordat of 1851. The concordat was a compromise between the kingdom's regalist tradition and the papacy's demand that any changes to the Church's traditional organization should be negotiated with Rome. The papacy accepted the sales of Church property already carried out, while the government promised to support the diocesan clergy financially. The concordat reaffirmed the Crown's patronage rights over episcopal appointments and endorsed the principle of diocesan and parish reorganization that liberals had sought since the Cortes of Cádiz. In turn, the government was willing to accept the restoration of a handful of male religious orders as part of the price required to reach agreement with the papacy. The concordat provided the basis for orderly relations between the Church and the liberal state, albeit in its most conservative version. The agreement opened a new period in civil–ecclesiastical relations, but it would not be an 'era of peace'. From the beginning, the concordat became a 'symbol of contradiction and polemic' in the turbulent world of liberal politics as the Progressives accused the Moderates of selling out to ecclesiastical interests.

Despite its recognition of the state's claims in certain areas, the 1851 settlement marked the effective end of a regalist-reform tradition according the government primary responsibility for imposing administrative changes on the Church. Such changes now had to be negotiated with the papacy. The concordat was significant for another reason. Although affirming that Catholicism 'to the exclusion of any other cult continues being the only religion of the Spanish nation', the concordat implicitly recognized that the state was no longer to play a role in promoting religious reform as liberals had attempted to do since the Cortes of Cádiz. No liberal government ever again attempted to impose on the Church ideas derived from the eighteenth century about the necessity of purifying Spanish Catholicism in its religious dimension. The concordat contained a regalist residue that would provoke ongoing controversy in civil–ecclesiastical relations, but it broke new ground by establishing a clear separation between purely religious activities, from which the state was excluded, and those limited areas of ecclesiastical patronage and finance in which the government still had an interest.

For this reason, civil–ecclesiastical conflicts during the period of Progressive rule (1854–56) and the democratic constitutional monarchy (1868–72) took on a different character from what they had been before 1843. The Progressive government brought to power by the revolution of 1854 refused to observe the concordat's terms and resumed the sale of the diocesan clergy's property. Although these measures provoked a hostile papal and episcopal reaction, they did not extend to the kind of sweeping programme of ecclesiastical reform identified with Mendizábal and Espartero. Nor did the government employ the tactics of exile and arrest once used to force recalcitrant bishops and priests into line. The revolutionary government also reaffirmed the confessionality of the state, although in more indirect form than the Moderate constitution of 1845. By this time, many Progressives accepted the principle of religious liberty, but despite their sympathy for toleration they drew back from endorsing it in their draft constitution, fearing that such a decision would strengthen Carlism which remained on the scene, a nagging danger for every liberal government.

By abandoning the extreme reforming projects of the past, the Progressives indirectly recognized that civil–ecclesiastical relations had entered a new phase. They had no desire to provoke the kind of fierce civil war between the government and the Church that had wracked the country during the 1830s and early 1840s. In any event, Progressive rule proved short-lived.

Church–State relations followed a smoother course between 1858 and 1863 during the government of the Liberal Union. The thorny question of the sale of the diocesan clergy's property was resolved in 1859, when Pius IX accepted the sales carried out until that time.

The 1851 concordat also introduced a significant change in the way that the Church sought to attain its objectives within the liberal system. By striking a deal with the papacy, the Moderates recognized the Church as a powerful interest group whose support they required to sustain their essentially oligarchic view of how the country should be governed. They were not prepared to give away all the eggs in their regalist basket, but their commitment to a negotiated settlement made it possible for the Church to seek to improve its position through distinctly modern lobbying efforts within the liberal system. Some laity and clergy continued to place their hopes in Carlism, but with shrewd practicality the ecclesiastical leadership realized that the possibility of restoring absolutism was remote and that effective lobbying with liberal politicians offered better prospects. During the semi-dictatorial government of the Moderate General Ramón Narváez between 1866 and 1868, intense clerical lobbying allowed the Church to expand its influence in education and secure a substantial increase in the government appropriation for the diocesan clergy's salaries.

The revolution of 1868 brought this satisfactory state of affairs from a clerical perspective to an abrupt end. At first glance, the legislation of the provisional government, dominated by Progressives and Moderates disgruntled with the excesses of General Narváez, and the ministries of the new king, Amadeo of Savoy, appeared to revive the extreme ecclesiastical policies of the past. The Jesuits were again suppressed, while the Church's role in education was severely limited. The constitution of 1869 broke with liberal tradition by recognizing religious liberty for the first time in the country's history. However it also reaffirmed the confessionality of the state, although in watered down language compared with earlier constitutional texts. These measures inevitably produced a hostile reaction on the part of the papacy and the hierarchy. The democratic monarchy was no more inclined than the Progressives to attempt radical ecclesiastical reform between 1854 and 1856. Governments sought to avoid a break with the papacy and, insofar as it was possible, maintain good relations with the bishops. They neither subjected their clerical opponents to the kind of official persecution that had occurred during the early 1820s, mid-1830s and early 1840s nor attempted to interfere with the Church's religious endeavours as earlier liberal regimes had done.

In fact, official policy between 1868 and 1872 conformed in broad outline to the new model of civil–ecclesiastical relations embodied in the 1851 concordat, although the authorities allowed the agreement to lapse. But they accepted the separation of function between purely religious activities, which were left to the clergy, and certain limited areas of competence, ecclesiastical patronage, Church finances and education, in which the state maintained an interest. Successive governments of the democratic monarchy attempted to adapt this model of Church–State relations by seeking a balance between the state's residual regalist rights, the confessionality of the state and the demands of an evolving public opinion committed to the principles of freedom of association, the press and religious liberty.

Achieving a workable balance among these objectives proved difficult. Carlists rejected the regime outright and rose in revolt in 1872. Bishops and clergy were more circumspect but expressed strong opposition to the introduction of religious liberty. On the other side of the spectrum, Republicans called for the complete separation of Church and State. But the modernizing liberalism in power between 1868 and 1872 followed a model of civil–ecclesiastical relations that in its essentials would endure until 1923. From the past it inherited liberalism's commitment to Catholicism as the religion of the state and retention of the government's regalist powers over episcopal appointments and ecclesiastical finances. To this inheritance it added concern with individual civil rights as a necessary condition for Spain to enter fully into what the regime's politicians saw as the increasingly secular, progressive and civilized world of Western Europe.

The formula of reconciling the existence of an established Church with the expanding content of the liberal political programme among Progressives and even some Moderates appeared contradictory to Republicans. During the brief history of the First Republic in 1873 they declared their intention to end the state's regalist tradition, government financial support for the Church and other ecclesiastical privileges. The Republic's solution, 'a free Church in a free state', failed to survive the regime's collapse. A military coup d'état in 1874 restored the Bourbon dynasty and opened the way to yet another version of liberal regalism in civil–ecclesiastical relations.

If the political coalition in power between 1868 and 1872 attempted an ecclesiastical balancing act inclining toward the left, the architect of the restored Bourbon monarchy, a former middle-of-the road Moderate politician, Antonio Cánovas del Castillo, tried a new balance inclining towards the right. The prime minister was a regalist who insisted on retaining the government's powers over episcopal appointments but he was willing to restore the 1851 concordat and make limited concessions to the Church. On the question of religious liberty recognized in the 1869 constitution, Cánovas proved an adept parliamentary tactician. He believed that a settlement with the Church was necessary to undercut the appeal of Carlism. Cánovas also wished to remove the issue of the Church as a source of division among liberals and realized that his objective of winning support for the new regime among former supporters of the democratic monarchy prevented restoration of the religious monopoly enjoyed by the Church before 1868.

The constitution of 1876 attempted to strike a balance between these contradictory objectives. Article 11 declared that the

Catholic, Apostolic, Roman religion is that of the state. The nation assumes the obligation to maintain the cult and its ministers. No one shall be disturbed in Spanish territory for his religious beliefs nor for the exercise of his own religion except for the respect due to Christian morality. However, ceremonies or public manifestations other than those of the religion of the state will not be permitted.

This ambiguous formula was designed both to satisfy the Church and win at least the grudging support of liberal politicians committed to religious liberty. Cánovas won his political gamble. The papacy and the hierarchy reluctantly accepted Article 11, as did most former Progressives.

Cánovas's ecclesiastical settlement proved no less controversial than earlier liberal attempts at compromise. The legal opposition in parliament, eventually gathered in the Liberal party, objected to restrictions on religious liberty and believed that Cánovas had conceded too much to the Church. By the turn of the century, a resurgent populist republicanism with strong anticlerical overtones began to attack the Church's constitutional and financial privileges with exceptional vehemence, while new social movements, particularly anarchism and socialism, saw Church and clergy as allies of an oppressive political and social system.

The hierarchy accepted the arrangements elaborated by Cánovas with some misgivings, but powerful currents of opposition to liberalism continued among Spanish Catholics. Carlists objected to the regime on both dynastic and philosophical grounds. They saw even the conservative liberalism of Cánovas as the embodiment of secular, intellectually corrosive values incompatible with their theocratic interpretation of human existence. After 1888, Catholic opposition to the liberal regime focused on the Integrist party founded by Ramón Nocedal, who shared the visceral hostility of Carlism towards liberalism without its dynastic entanglements. For Nocedal, no compromise was possible between liberalism and Catholicism. From the pages of the Integrist newspaper, *El Siglo Futuro*, Nocedal relentlessly attacked the liberal state and Catholics who cooperated with it. In the end, Cánovas' expectation that the role of Catholicism and the Church within Spanish society would be removed as a source of division and controversy proved illusory. The so-called religious question remained to divide Spaniards for generations to come.

|4|

The military and politics

CAROLYN P. BOYD

The army played a major role in Spain's liberal revolution. Military intervention in political life was not unique to Spain, of course; across post-Napoleonic Europe, defeated liberals vainly conspired with disillusioned and frustrated military officers to resurrect the political and social achievements of the revolutionary era. But in Spain, military intervention was more prolonged and its effects more profound. The military was integral to the evolution of Spanish political life after 1808. Not only did political groups enlist military support to effect alterations in the political direction of the state, but the army also collaborated in the articulation and administration of the liberal state as it developed during the course of the century. Spanish militarism, in other words, not only involved praetorianism – the direct use of military force, or the threat of it, against the established political order – but also a less direct, but pervasive, military influence on civilian institutions, policies, and priorities.

The sources of Spanish militarism were both external and internal to the military institution itself; they lay in the weakness of liberalism in a society where traditional values and interests remained strong, and in the internal tensions of a military organization radically altered by the pressure of war and political and social change. External and internal factors interacted to create a pattern of civil–military relations that made the assertion of civil supremacy increasingly problematic.

The army in the War of Independence

The war provoked a radical transformation of the army's structure and personnel. The army of the Ancien Regime had been a dynastic institution, owing personal allegiance to the monarchy. It was relatively modest in size, reflecting the restricted conduct of war in the eighteenth century, the limits of the Spanish treasury, and the equal weight assigned to the royal navy in the pursuit of Bourbon dynastic aims. Organized in 1704 along regimental lines, in imitation of French practice, the standing army was composed of professional soldiers recruited or conscripted from the lowest classes in society. Officers were trained in military academies or appointed as cadets in the regiments; after 1722, proof of nobility was required for both, so that by the end of the century, over 90 per cent of the officer corps was of aristocratic origin. The choicest command positions were reserved for the titled nobility, and most promotions were determined on the basis of seniority or status, rather than merit. Perhaps not surprisingly, desertion rates were high, discipline lax, and professional competence unevenly distributed.

Military training and leadership improved somewhat under the pressure of the wars that began in 1793. But the ingrained habit of absolute loyalty to the monarch made it difficult for the officer corps to support with unanimity or enthusiasm the popular revolt against the French invasion of 1808. As the Spanish state disintegrated, so too did its army. Some royalist units remained loyal to the collaborationist government in Madrid; others began serving the resistance at the orders of the local juntas. After an initial victory over inexperienced French troops at Bailén in July 1808, the demoralized Spanish army suffered a string of humiliating defeats as Napoleon expanded his forces to 250 000 seasoned veterans and began the systematic occupation of the peninsula from the centre outward.

The war did not conclude with an easy French victory for two reasons. The first was the arrival of approximately 50 000 British expeditionary troops led by the Duke of Wellington; after ousting the French from Portugal, Wellington organized sorties into Spain from a well fortified base of operations that kept constant pressure on the French forces until the tide turned in 1811. More important to the final victory, however, were the *guerrilla* forces organized to supplement the regular Spanish army. It was the Spanish War of Independence that gave the modern world the name and the successful model for guerrilla warfare. Numbering some 30 000 to 40 000 volunteers, partisan forces ranging in size from small bands to units approximating regular army regiments carried out brutal irregular warfare that pinned down a huge French army until the end of the conflict. Because they were recruited from and supported by civilians in the towns and villages of rural Spain, the guerrillas were difficult to capture and destroy. Their constant harassment forced Napoleon to maintain a large army of occupation in the peninsula, where it suffered a war of attrition that had a profound negative impact on the Emperor's continental strategy as a whole.

By 1814, the number of Spaniards under arms had risen to nearly 160 000, and the Spanish officer corps had expanded accordingly. In the process, the aristocratic monopoly on officer status was broken. Local juntas appointed and promoted officers in the regiments under their control on the basis of leadership and bravery in battle. To meet the demand for technically trained junior officers, the government opened the military academies to non-nobles for the first time. In the guerrilla units, farmers, friars, and labourers, many of them illiterate, rose to the top on the strength of talent and personality. The army thus became the first profession in which merit, rather than birth, determined entrance and advancement. As a corollary, the officer corps lost its internal homogeneity; its members were divided by social origin, age, training, and ideology. Those who had benefited from the new opportunities quite naturally sympathized with liberalism and its credo of freedom and equality, whereas aristocratic officers looked forward to the restoration of royal absolutism and caste privilege.

Partially offsetting these internal divisions was the tendency of officers to view themselves collectively as the highest expression of the national will. As self-styled military experts and patriots, they resisted civilian efforts to oversee the conduct of the war. Liberal politicians replied that the doctrine of popular sovereignty demanded civil supremacy over military policy. One result of this conflict was the creation in 1811 of the Central General Staff. Headed by the civilian Minister for War and composed of technically competent officers of liberal views, it served as the chief strategic planning organ of the army and the principal link between military professionals and civilian policy makers. While not totally resolving the tension between the military's desire for institutional autonomy and the state's demand for civil supremacy, the General Staff mediated between the two and contributed to the definition of the military career as a profession, rather than a birthright.

Further evidence of the liberal concern for civil supremacy appeared in the Constitution of 1812, which dedicated 10 articles to the nation's armed forces. These consisted of two parts: the permanent army and navy, entrusted with national defence and the 'conservation of internal order', and the National Militias, organized in the provincial capitals and composed of citizen volunteers serving when unspecified circumstances required. Partisans of the militias envisioned them as the bulwark of the constitutional order against the forces of reaction (including royalists in the permanent army).

The constitution divided responsibility for military decision-making between the king and the Cortes; the former, as commander in chief of the armed forces, was to declare war and confer ranks; the latter was to pass laws governing internal discipline, promotions, salaries, and training. In reserving for themselves responsibility for internal personnel matters, the deputies at Cádiz sought to ensure the fidelity of the officer corps to the new liberal order. In practice, however, reconciling the desire of civilian politicians for loyal subordinates with the desire of military officers for professional autonomy proved to be another source of tension. First of all, politicizing professional issues cast a shadow on the 'merit' promotions of those who benefited from them. Second, in an unstable political system, military personnel were at the mercy of the swings of the political pendulum. On the other hand, allowing the officer corps to establish institutional criteria independent of civilian control did not necessarily guarantee a depoliticized army because officers did not agree on what constituted 'merit'. Furthermore, even disinterested civilian efforts to regulate personnel matters were likely to provoke a defensive military response when career officers believed their livelihoods were at stake. That is, the professionalization of the officer corps fostered a bureaucratic mentality that predisposed officers to take political action against the state in defence of their corporate interests.

The rise of the *pronunciamiento* tradition

The Spanish officer corps was particularly sensitive about personnel issues because after the end of the war, there were too many officers for the country's peacetime needs – perhaps as many as 11 000 to 12 000. Competition among officers for scarce resources was exacerbated by class differences and ideological conflict. From 1814 onward, officers joined forces with civilians from whom they hoped to benefit professionally to alter the political situation in their favour. The precedent was set in 1814, when an offer of military backing from the Captain General of Valencia, General Elío, made possible Ferdinand's rejection of the constitution. Over the next six years, Ferdinand's partisan military policies provoked a series of military rebellions. Determined to restore the army's traditional social composition and royalist ideology, the King imprisoned or exiled leading liberal officers, derogated the liberal legislation that had opened the officer corps to non-nobles, dissolved the Central General Staff, and filled available posts with noble officers ideologically sympathetic to monarchical absolutism. To reduce costs, Ferdinand ordered the immediate dissolution of guerrilla units and a reduction in rank of their plebeian officers, who were then assigned to remote provincial garrisons or left without assignment at half pay. A similar fate awaited both academy-trained officers of bourgeois origin, and the 4000 junior officers who had been won over to liberalism while being held as prisoners of war in France. These professionally and politically discontented officers, many of them Freemasons, began to conspire actively to restore the liberal constitution of 1812. Five military rebellions between 1814 and 1820 ended in the exile or execution of their leaders before Major Rafael Riego rose successfully against the absolute monarchy in 1820.

Military intervention in this period took the form later known as the *pronunciamiento* – literally, a public 'pronouncement' of opposition to the existing government by a small network of military conspirators and their civilian allies. Often the *pronunciamiento* originated in a provincial garrison town at some remove from the capital; the intended objective was not to overthrow the government by force, but rather to test the general disposition of army opinion and the strength of the government's resolve. Success would be determined by the adherence of additional supporters, both military and civilian, and by the 'negative *pronunciamiento*' of the rest of the army – that is, by the refusal of neutral army units to support the government by actively suppressing the revolt. Risings that found no echo elsewhere could be easily isolated and crushed, but a government left defenceless by its own army might be compelled to seek an accommodation with the conspirators. The *pronunciamiento* was thus a form of psychological warfare that required self-confidence, patience, and nerves of steel.

More important than the morphology of the *pronunciamiento* were the structural reasons for its appearance and persistence throughout the first three-quarters of the nineteenth century. As a crude instrument of political change, the *pronunciamiento* reflected not only the discontent of the army, but also the lack of consensus on basic political values in Spanish society and the weakness of the social forces proposing political modernization. The only prospect for political change in a society with no consensus on political legitimacy and no legal mechanisms for peaceful political change lay in an alliance with the military. Claiming to represent a national will whose expression had been stifled by royal absolutism, liberals thus appealed to the army – the 'nation in arms' – to support their assertions of popular sovereignty. Bourgeois officers and former *guerrilleros*, who associated liberalism with the professional advancement and autonomy they had enjoyed during the War of Independence, were willing to lend their services to civilian conspirators in exchange for preferment in the event of victory.

Major Riego's *pronunciamiento* of 1820 owed its success to the unpopularity of service in the American colonies, where outnumbered, neglected, and unpaid conscripted troops fought a losing battle against insurgency and disease. Although the revolutions that had erupted across the American continent during the War of Independence had been temporarily suppressed, they had been rekindled after the restoration of the absolute monarchy. Financially strapped and lacking ships for transport, the King and his advisers had allowed the situation to deteriorate until 1820, when they made a final effort to assemble an expeditionary army. Liberal conspirators exploited the discontent among soldiers waiting to be shipped out from Cádiz by promising them back pay and a reduction in service. With these inducements before them, the rank and file seconded the rebellion of the junior officers who pronounced for the Constitution of 1812 in January 1820. Although most eventually deserted during the circuitous two-month journey through Andalucia that followed the failure of the revolt in Cádiz, as time passed, the advantage passed to Riego. Risings by civilian and military conspirators in the cities of the north and east, together with the 'negative *pronunciamiento*' of the rest of the army, which failed to take serious action against the rebels, finally convinced Ferdinand to endorse the constitution and to appoint a junta of liberal politicians to oversee its implementation.

The key role played by the army in the liberal triumph was reflected in the first measures of the new government. Liberal officers whose careers had suffered during the absolutist restoration were promoted; royalist regiments like the Royal Guards were dissolved; and the expeditionary army was discharged. The royalist faction in the officer corps, its career prospects dimmed by the liberal triumph, now turned to conspiracy to restore the status quo. The impact of the military plots and disorders that plagued the new regime from 1820 onward was magnified by the isolation of the liberals, who lacked popular support outside the large cities and who were themselves increasingly divided into *moderado* and *exaltado* factions. Too weak to govern alone, the moderate liberals in the government sought strength in the army.

Civilian reliance on military power during the Liberal Triennium set patterns that would endure well into the twentieth century. One development with far-reaching consequences was the expansion of military jurisdiction over civilians accused of political offences. When royalist judges blocked prosecution of anti-liberal conspirators in the civil courts, the Cortes passed a law giving military courts jurisdiction over anyone accused of disturbing public order or attacking constitutional principles. What began as an attempt to repress royalist conspiracy would later be applied indiscriminately to all political opponents of the established order. The expansion of the military *fuero* not only subverted the liberal goal of eliminating particularistic legal structures and privileges inherited from the Ancien Régime, it also reduced the stature of civil courts.

If justice was militarized, so were the state administration and the forces of order. In part, this was owing to the need to find employment for excess military personnel. For example, in 1822, the liberals created a system of provincial prefectures that was intended to establish the presence of the civil administration throughout the national territory. Over half of the newly appointed provincial political chiefs (*jefes políticos*), however, were unemployed army officers seeking placement in the emerging state bureaucracy.

In the absence of a civil police force, the liberals turned to the National Militias to maintain order. A revolt of Royal Guards against the government in July 1822 was foiled only after the National Militia was mobilized under the leadership of a former guerrilla leader, Colonel Evaristo San Miguel. The civil war subsequently initiated by royalist partisans in the rural north further cemented the Militias' role as the defender of the liberal order against its internal enemies. In Madrid, San Miguel was asked to form a ministry that was in effect a left-wing military dictatorship. The subsequent radicalization of government policy triggered the invasion by French troops, whose march toward the capital was unopposed both by the populace and by most officers, who hesitated to stake their careers on the defence of a doomed regime.

Thus, during the Liberal Triennium the chief role of the army was to defend the regime against internal enemies. In contrast, defence of the national interest abroad was given short shrift. Continued neglect of the colonial army, combined with a profound misunderstanding of the nature of the American revolutions, led to the definitive loss of most of the empire by 1824 (see chapter 7).

The restoration of the absolute monarchy in 1823 produced a round of military purges even more draconian than that of 1814. All members of the officer corps were stripped of their commissions and reinstated only after swearing personal fealty to the monarch. Military tribunals sentenced prominent liberal officers to prison or exile, liberal reforms were again repealed, and the National Militias were dissolved. Ultra-royalists advocated the abolition of the regular standing army altogether and its replacement with the Royalist Volunteers, provincial peasant militias armed and ready to defend traditional religion and absolute monarchy. As Ferdinand and his more moderate advisers soon perceived, however, a regular army led by professional officers was a more reliable tool of central authority than any militia; the Volunteers proved to be as fractious as the National Militias had been. Thus, after 1827 Ferdinand reconstituted the regular army. Former officers were reinstated after only a cursory review of their past records if they were willing to swear allegiance to the Crown. Given the choice, most officers – particularly those whose salaries were their chief source of income – were prepared to sacrifice political convictions in exchange for job security. By 1830 only extremists at both ends of the political spectrum were actively engaged in conspiracy against the monarchy. When the Carlists initiated an armed rebellion at the king's death, officers with a stake in the status quo opted to defend the Queen Regent and her infant daughter.

The Carlist War and the Regime of the Generals, 1833–1868

The Carlist war of 1833–39, like the War of Independence before it, made the army the political arbiter of Spain and established a new pattern of military intervention that persisted until 1875. The length of the war, extended to six years by the difficulties of suppressing a guerrilla war using conventional strategy and tactics, heightened the level of mutual frustration between the military and the civilian politicians, while at the same time intensifying their interdependence. Civilian efforts to dictate or even to criticize military policy met resistance from officers increasingly inclined to blame 'politicians' for their failures; at the same time, it encouraged dissatisfied officers to listen sympathetically to political groups eager to exploit military discontent for their own ends. Politicization of military affairs encouraged military intervention in politics, as well as professional rivalries among officers of disparate backgrounds and experience. By the end of the war, the stage was set for what has been called 'The Regime of the Generals'.

As before, military intervention was rooted in causes both external and internal to the institution itself. A fundamental problem was the narrow social base of the emerging liberal state. Although Carlism was confined to the countryside in the north and east, liberalism enjoyed active support among urban social groups – the aristocracy, the middle classes, and the urban working class – who comprised only a small fraction of the Spanish population. The so-called 'liberal revolution' was thus not a response to the demands of a growing and self-confident bourgeoisie, nor to a profound transformation of Spain's economic and social structures. Rather, it was the result of the military victory of a small, but politically significant, elite over its traditionalist opponents.

In a society weakened by war and political conflict, the army possessed considerable leverage. By refusing to fight, generals could dictate policy and insist on the dismissal of recalcitrant ministers. Subtle pressure from two leading generals, for example, convinced the Queen Regent to appoint the liberal Martínez de la Rosa as prime minister in 1833 and to grant the Royal Statute the following year. As the war dragged on, military discontent over unpaid troops and lack of supplies first prompted the appointment of the Progresista financier, Juan Alvarez Mendizábal, as prime minister in 1835 and later, his destitution after his disentailment policies failed to solve the financial crisis. Rival generals operating in different parts of the country cultivated friends at court in order to secure scarce resources for their armies. From pressuring ministers it was a short step to taking over the reins of government directly.

Internal divisions among its supporters further weakened the liberal state and encouraged political adversaries to court military allies. While old and new elites were beginning to pursue their common interests within the framework of Moderado liberalism, the Progresista party attracted *exaltados* favouring a more advanced democratic programme. Lacking the social homogeneity of the Moderados, the Progresista party was subject to constant fragmentation; furthermore, given the high property qualifications for voting under the Royal Statute of 1834 (and later, under the Moderado constitution of 1845), electoral results inevitably favoured the Moderados, even without the additional advantages conferred by electoral manipulation. Basic ideological disagreements meant that neither of the two major political groupings recognized the legitimacy of the other; the Crown, which might have mediated between the two, instead assumed a partisan role by showing a marked preference for the Moderados. Progresistas could only to hope to gain power through the use of force, or the threat of it – that is, through popular revolution and/or the *pronunciamiento*, justified in the name of a suppressed national sovereignty. The Moderados, in turn, cultivated their own military adherents, and were thus prepared to meet Progresista challenges with a display of counter-force.

Military intervention thus occurred at the invitation of civilian politicians and functioned as a moderating power within a party system that was both weak and exclusionary. From 1840 to 1868 Spain was governed almost continuously by generals – military politicians who used their political power not to militarize Spanish society, but to reward their political and military clients and allies and to deny the fruits of office to their opponents. Generals were political figures in a society in which war and political conflict had blurred the distinctions between military and civilian leadership and stimulated popular faith in messianic heroes. Both parties courted leading generals by appealing to their vanity and by exploiting their constant frustration with the financial and political obstacles to rapid victory. Rewards for military success and political loyalty might include pensions, decorations, promotions, and – most coveted of all – a title of nobility. Some generals, notably those who owed their professional careers to the guerrilla war of 1808–14, shared the radical politics of the Progresistas, but others were less ideologically motivated, although fundamentally committed to liberal constitutionalism. Neither General Narváez nor General Espartero, the *espadones* (literally, 'great swords'), respectively, of the Moderado and Progresista parties after 1840, was politically aligned during the Carlist war. When they did acquire a party affiliation, it was as individuals whose political and professional ambitions coincided with those of their civilian partners.

Although rule by generals was not identical to military dictatorship, the military possessed significant influence, as a pressure group and as a constituent element in the administration of the Spanish state. The line that separated the civilian and military spheres was not distinct. Not only did generals serve more or less continuously as heads of government and in the cabinet, but military heroes were also elected in large numbers to the lower house of the Cortes. Under the Constitution of 1845, captains general and lieutenants general in the army and navy were eligible for appointment as senators; once appointed, they held the seat for life. In the Cortes they comprised a powerful bloc that protected corporate as well as factional and personal interests.

The army continued to be heavily involved in the administration of the emerging Spanish state. Although the peninsula was reorganized in 1833 into a uniform system of 50 provinces governed by civil administrators appointed from Madrid, the *jefes políticos* were often army officers, as they had been during the Liberal Triennium. Furthermore, civil governors were often overshadowed by the 14 captaincies-general, the parallel politico-military territorial divisions inherited from the Ancien Regime, because of the Moderados' tendency to resort to martial law to maintain 'order'. Since the only recourse open to opponents of the status quo was public 'disorder', civil disturbances ranging from food riots to political and social protest triggered the declaration of martial law and the subsequent prosecution of the demonstrators by military tribunals. In response, antimilitarism became a central component of democratic and socialist ideology.

As an alternative to the army, the Progresistas championed the National Militias, which were revived in 1834. Initially recruited from among small and medium property holders in the cities, the Militias were intended to serve as both an army reserve and an urban police force. But they quickly became an instrument of political agitation at the service of the left wing of the Progresista party – a force of public disorder, rather than an agency of public order in the radical cities of the south and southeast. Militias were involved in the abortive Progresista *pronunciamiento* of 1835, in the sergeant's mutiny at La Granja in 1836, and in the *pronunciamiento* that elevated Espartero to the Regency in 1840. After the Moderado takeover in 1843–44, the government of General Narváez dissolved them and disarmed their members.

As a substitute, the Moderados created the Civil Guard. As its name implies, the Civil Guard was originally intended to strengthen the authority of the civil administration over the police functions of the state, particularly in rural areas. Expanding rapidly, the Civil Guard dominated the national territory through its posts established in the smallest towns and villages and along major transportation routes; by 1870, the number of posts had risen to 1609. Just ten years after its creation, the Civil Guard registered over 41 000 arrests nationwide. It thus served an important centralizing role in the articulation of the Spanish state.

Under the influence of Narváez, the Civil Guard was quickly militarized. Although not structurally part of the armed forces and deployed at the orders of the ministry of the Interior (*Gobernación*), its officers were seconded from the military list (and thus dependent on the War Ministry). Its distinctively uniformed troops were recognized and feared for their indiscriminately harsh treatment of criminals, political opponents, and rebellious farm workers. Institutionally self-contained and recruiting heavily from its own ranks, the Civil Guard soon developed a subculture whose values were inspired by those of the regular army. Its quasi-military status was formalized in 1878, when it was structurally integrated with the rest of the armed forces.

The armed forces thus comprised a powerful pressure group that limited the degrees of freedom enjoyed by Spanish governments, even when governments were headed by generals. Military or militarized forces maintained order; military courts decided the fate of those accused of political crimes or of disturbing the peace; and military politicians rewarded friends and clients by distributing promotions, choice appointments, and pensions. By one estimate, at mid-century the army and navy consumed over 27 per cent of the national budget, while over 88 per cent of Spanish functionaries were either military or militarized personnel, like the Civil Guard and the Carabineros (the Customs Police established in 1829). A weak state thus artificially bolstered its authority in return for the military colonization of the budget and the state administration.

The social structure of the Spanish army

The bloated size of the military bureaucracy was the product of thirty years of war and revolution. If large numbers of officers and troops could be justified during wartime, in peacetime many of them were superfluous and a burden on an already strained budget. The Treaty of Vergara, which concluded the Carlist war in 1839, exacerbated matters by incorporating all Carlist officers into the regular army list. The need to reward bravery in wartime and loyalty in an era of political upheaval led to frequent promotions; in 1840, there were 598 generals, two-thirds of whom were unnecessary. But although officers' salaries consumed approximately 60 per cent of the total army budget, salaries of individual officers, especially at the ranks below field officer, were low. Those with no posting received only half pay. Although economic stagnation kept prices stable or even falling until 1853, with economic expansion thereafter, inflation began to erode already inadequate salaries. Feeling underpaid and unappreciated, the officer corps became a dissatisfied and influential pressure group constantly demanding promotions and a greater share of the state budget.

To improve the professional situation of the officer corps, the first step was to reduce it in size, but this proved to be politically impossible, given the reliance of both political parties on the army, or a fraction of it, to stay in power. After a change of government, party supporters, whether civilian or military, expected to be rewarded with jobs, promotions, pay rises, and other preferment; disappointment predictably led to new conspiracies with opposition groups promising better treatment once in office. After seizing power in 1840, Espartero and the Progresistas reduced the size of the regular army by nearly 80000 men in order to expand the National Militia, their primary base of support, and openly discussed abolition of the standing army altogether. The result was the rallying of regular army officers behind the Moderado general, Narváez, who successfully toppled the Espartero Regency in 1843. Narváez quickly repaid his political debts; the following year the number of generals rose from 584 to 647, all officers were promoted to the next highest rank, the Militias were dissolved, and the regular army rose again in size to just over 100000. Only after Narváez had stabilized the political climate through a combination of harsh reprisals against his enemies and regular pay for the troops was he able to contemplate a slight reduction in military spending. A similar inflation of honours occurred after the Progresista *pronunciamiento* of Leopoldo O'Donnell in 1856, when all officers received promotion to the next highest rank and the troops saw their term of service reduced to two years.

Efforts to reduce the size of the military budget were thus constrained by the reality of a top-heavy, excessively large officer corps. Although some officers accepted occasional financial inducements to retire early, the lack of suitable alternative employment in a still largely agrarian economy meant that most officers elected to cling to their military careers, particularly those without other sources of income. Such reductions as were possible in the military budget had to come from the areas of discretionary expenditure – for example, in equipment and in training and maintenance of the troops. Obsolete equipment, inadequate training, and substandard sanitation, hospitals, housing, and food, produced appallingly high mortality rates among Spanish troops in peacetime and in war.

Diverse class backgrounds and professional interests meant that the officer corps could not always present a united front in pursuit of corporate aims, a reality that could be exploited by both military and civilian politicians seeking support for a *pronunciamiento*. By the 1840s approximately a third of the officers were of aristocratic origin, although fewer than 2 per cent were from the titled nobility. Especially in the Artillery Corps, a substantial fraction were sons of officers. Until 1842, aristocratic officers entered the officer corps as cadets, either by studying in an academy, as in the case of the technical branches like the Artillery and Engineers, or by entering a regiment for a brief period of training with a commission to follow. Such officers generally possessed independent sources of income, held moderate liberal views, and were less susceptible to political appeals from groups promising professional advancement. Indeed, officers in the technical branches made it a point of honour to refuse all promotions not based on seniority.

The remaining two-thirds of officers were of middle or lower class origin, most of them had received commissions during the War of Independence. Their careers had languished during the reign of Ferdinand V.II, but had resuscitated with the Carlist war and the advent of liberalism. Academy trained middle class officers increased in numbers after 1836, when proof of nobility for academy entrance was no longer required. A significant percentage of officers (perhaps 25 per cent) were from lower class backgrounds and had been promoted into the officer corps from the ranks. Guerrilla and colonial warfare had produced some outstanding generals of plebeian origin, like Espartero, but in general rankers could not expect to be promoted beyond major, and the growing emphasis on academy training meant fewer opportunities for similar advancement in the future.

Non-commissioned officers, who served as the crucial link between the military hierarchy and the troops, were kept socially and professionally isolated from their superiors. Nevertheless, during thirty years of nearly constant warfare, this group had prospered. Better pay (when pay was forthcoming) and the real possibility of promotion in to the officers' list made the army an attractive avenue of social mobility. As career opportunities for this group diminished, however, their political unreliability increased. From the 1830s to the1860s military discipline was constantly threatened by the discontent of sergeants and soldiers whose very real grievances were nurtured by radical politicians hoping to convert them into allies of popular revolution.

Upper and middle class officers were generally sympathetic to Moderado liberalism, while officers and NCOs from humble backgrounds leaned toward radicalism, but class origin was not an infallible predictor of political affiliation. The incorporation of Carlist officers in 1839 complicated an already .complex picture. To the extent that officers aligned themselves politically, it was more typically as clients of military and civilian politicians and in the expectation of career preferment. Frequent promotions and remunerative appointments were the lifeblood of such officers; denial of career opportunities eventually led middle class officers to collaborate with opposition politicians, irrespective of political leanings.

The army in war and revolution

Spanish officers viewed themselves as patriots, but they were not advocates of national expansion or wars of conquest. During the Liberal Union ministry of General Leopoldo O'Donnell (1858–63), however, the government curried favour with the army and the urban public with a series of foreign adventures in Cochin China, Santo Domingo, Mexico, and most successfully, Morocco. The war with Morocco, declared in 1859 after a series of perceived offences to the Spanish garrisons on the northern coast, resulted in a quick victory for the Spanish expeditionary force, which marched triumphantly into Tetuán six weeks after the war began. The 7000 Spanish casualties (attributable primarily to disease) purchased no new territory for Spain in North Africa, but did buy the government a brief respite from political conflict during the patriotic euphoria that followed, as well as a round of promotions for participating officers and troops.

The colonial and civil wars that broke out after the Revolution of 1868 provided greater tests of Spain's military preparedness. Taking advantage of the dynastic vacuum created by the abdication of Isabella II, the Carlists, led by a new Pretender, Carlos VII, resumed their offensive against liberalism. At the same time, Cubans demanding administrative autonomy and the abolition of slavery initiated a rebellion that caused the deaths of over 65000 Spanish soldiers over a 10-year period before the conclusion of a shaky truce in 1878. Both in the peninsula and overseas, the Spanish army was crippled by inadequate troop strength, lack of supplies, delays in pay, desertions, and low morale. Only the assertion of forceful military leadership after the Restoration of the monarchy in 1875 made it possible to bring these campaigns to a successful conclusion.

The antimilitarism unleashed by the Revolutionary Sexennium had a profound effect on the political and professional orientation of the officer corps. Antimilitarism was the obverse of Spanish militarism; it was a natural reaction against the army that made possible the exclusionary and repressive policies of the Moderados. More particularly, however, it was a response to the *quintas*, the unjust system of conscription that subjected the working classes to involuntary and inhumane servitude while permitting the middle and upper classes to purchase their way out of service. The advanced democratic platform of the revolutionaries of 1868 called for the replacement of the permanent army by the National Militias and the abolition of the *quintas*. Seeking to cement his popular base of support, the leader of the revolution, General Juan Prim, reduced the term of military service to one year and ordered the immediate promotion of all non-commissioned officers into the ranks of commissioned officers. But the need for troops to suppress the Carlist and Cuban uprisings led to new call-ups in 1872, provoking mass protests, defections, and a breakdown of military discipline. The first republican governments of 1873 responded to renewed demands for an armed people's militia by making all military service voluntary. Lacking a reliable army, they proved unable to suppress the cantonalist revolts aimed at dismantling the centralized state [see chapter 5]. Faced with wars on two fronts and fearful of a total disintegration of the state and its armed forces, the army intervened. Troops led by General Manuel Pavía entered the Cortes in December 1874 and dissolved the assembly, leaving power in the hands of a military cabinet.

General Pavía's coup was qualitatively different from the *pronunciamientos* that had regularly punctuated the political life of the Isabelline monarchy. Pavía acted on behalf of the army as an institution, in defence of its corporate interests, not as a surrogate for civilian politicians seeking access to power. During the year that followed, the military government headed by General Francisco Serrano satisfied the military's desire for order, respect, and national integrity, while pursuing victory against the Carlists and Cuban insurrectionaries. Its success convinced the Alfonsine faction in the officer corps that the moment had arrived to bring Isabella II's son back from exile. In December 1874 another military *pronunciamiento* led by General Arsenio Martínez Campos restored the Bourbon monarchy and ushered in a new era in Spanish civil–military relations.

After 1875, the agreement between the two dynastic parties to respect the legitimacy of the constitutional monarchy and to rotate peacefully in office eliminated the chief cause of the praetorianism characteristic of the first three-quarters of the century. With the Crown acting as the moderating power between the parties and with the perfection of the techniques of electoral manipulation, the army's functional role as the motor of a weak and unrepresentative party system disappeared. Leading generals with political aspirations were co-opted with noble titles and representation in the Cortes.

But the temporary elimination of praetorianism did not spell the end of Spanish militarism, for the underlying weakness of the state and the structural defects of the army remained intact. The officer corps, its numbers swollen still further by the wars and political turbulence of the 1860s and 1870s, continued to act as a largely autonomous pressure group. After 1875, officers were more conservative and nationalist and less socially prestigious. Recruited increasingly from non-noble military families and trained almost exclusively in the military academies, the officer corps was more conscious of itself as a group apart, although internal rivalries and individual ambition persisted. As political and social protest mounted after the 1890s, the army's police and judicial functions expanded. The army would use the enhanced leverage it acquired as the bulwark of the Restoration system to insist on protection from unwanted reforms and excessive political influence.

The army's insulation from civilian interference meant that military

budgets continued to be devoted to officers' salaries instead of modernization of equipment and training. Unable to meet the military challenges it
faced, first in Cuba and the Philippines, and later in Morocco, and under
attack from internal and external critics, the officer corps became increasingly divided and disruptive. But the dynastic politicians were too dependent
on the army to stay in power to insist on its reform, even though the
parliamentary monarchy was increasingly identified with military incompetence and arrogance. The military disaster at Annual in northern Morocco,
and the reformist campaign for 'responsibilities' that followed, finally
pushed them towards the timid assertion of civil supremacy over areas in
which the army had traditionally operated independently – especially, social
conflict and the Moroccan war. Thus challenged, the officer corps overcame
its internal differences and united behind the *pronunciamiento* of General
Miguel Primo de Rivera against the parliamentary regime. Like Pavía's coup
of 1874, the *pronunciamiento* of 1923 was undertaken by the officer corps in
defence of its corporate interests, rather than on behalf a civilian political
group. It owed its success, however, to conflicts over political legitimacy
similar to those that had made possible the military *pronunciamientos* of the
nineteenth century.

5

The left: from liberalism to democracy

DEMETRIO CASTRO

In the half century between the end of the War of Independence and the Revolution of 1868, the Spanish left underwent a complex course of change. We can discern two major phases in the historical evolution of the political forces that may be regarded as belonging to the left in this period. The first is the two decades between 1814 and 1833 in which liberals and absolutists were still locked in the battle for political control: the absolutists held the upper hand except for the brief period from 1820–23. During the next stage, from 1833 to 1868, civil war and military coups led to the definitive establishment of the liberal order.

At the beginning of this process the left comprised a broad array of personalities whose unifying element was their loyalty to the Constitution of 1812, with its recognition of national sovereignty and limitation of the monarch's powers. Contemporaries certainly did not speak of the left; the terminology of the day was composed of expressions such as the 'constitutional party', the 'patriotic party', as the advocates of new arrangements liked to call themselves, or the 'revolutionary party', which was normally used by its enemies. Only the need to resist the severe repression meted out by the governments of Ferdinand VII could maintain the unity of the constitutionalists, whose internal differences over the limits of change, the procedure for effecting it and role of popular intervention grew increasingly more pronounced. Disputes over the blame for the loss of power in 1823 and conflicts amongst liberal emigres served only to intensify these internecine struggles and gave rise to a radical faction whose partisans would come to be known *exaltados*.

The return of Ferdinand VII in 1814 and his decision to repeal the work of the Cortes of Cádiz were accompanied by the forceful repression of the liberals. Many were imprisoned, some killed, others exiled, and all reduced to silence by a pervasive censorship. A rudimentary but effective police system rendered all their attempts at political organization futile and the embryonic parties that had begun to take shape in the heat of the constitutional debates disappeared. The partisans of the liberal system found themselves forced to organize clandestinely and to conspire. Thus, from their very origin, Spanish liberals had a particular inclination for organizing themselves in secret societies.

Following the defeat of Carlism, this type of organization no longer made sense for the two liberal parties that emerged, the Moderados and the Progresistas. However, an extremist sector of the latter party that gave rise to the Partido Demócrata in 1849 did not completely abandon the formulas of clandestine organization, in the face of the intransigence with which the governments of both the Moderados and the centrist Union Liberal responded to their republican programme and proposed social reforms during the 1850s and 1860s.

There was, then, a relatively direct line between the clandestine conspiracies of the century's early decades and that pursued on the eve of the Revolution of 1868 by the democratic republicans, who, in turn, would inspire the organizational approach of some of the anarchist circles of the 1870s and 1880s. But secret organization was not the exclusive patrimony of the political circles that many considered as part of the left. In 1821, a sector of very moderate liberals formed their own semi-secret association, the 'Sociedad Constitucional' or the 'Sociedad del Anillo de Oro' (Ring of Gold Society). Two decades later, when the Progressives headed by General Espartero took power, their military backers organized an underground society, the Orden Militar Española, which they attempted to spread to all military outposts and garrisons in order to carry out a coup. In fact, the practice of military intervention in political affairs required a certain degree of conspiratorial activity, and such coups were a common recourse of moderates and progressives alike. Nevertheless, it would be the more radical sectors of liberalism, the progressives and democrats, who, unsatisfied with the degree of liberal consolidation attained and kept out of power, would display the greatest attachment to conspiracy and clandestine political manoeuvring.

Similar to the 'Ring of Gold' was the Society of the Comuneros, which was formed by *exaltados* in 1821 and which played a major role in the political agitation of the next two decades. They chose their name in honour of the members of the urban oligarchies who rose in revolt against Charles V in 1521 in defence of the tax and personal immunities then being encroached upon by the Crown. One of the communard leaders, Padilla, who was executed after the movement's defeat, became an eponymous hero of nineteenth century communards, and the most combative members of the society formed a special division called the 'sons of Padilla'. This was basically organized at the local level by parish or village, in *torres* (turrets), and at the provincial level in *merindades*, names evocative of the anachronistic universe of medieval Castile. It is impossible to know the number of members of each society, but the communard movement was able to establish a network of affiliates, especially in military units. Their orators participated in public debates, where they attacked the government for being less than energetic in implementing the liberal programme and for compromising with the absolutists, and they espoused similar views through newspapers such as the *Eco de Padilla*. They also agitated for popular mobilizations, which they achieved on various occasions, especially in Madrid. However, thwarted by provocateurs and spies, lacking clear concrete political objectives and convulsed by internal personal rivalries, the communards were politically ineffectual and succeeded only in doing the work of the absolutists by undermining the stability of the liberal government.

In their structure and internal life the communards reflected the masonic world which had inspired them, but during the Triennium they began to take up rites and structures of the *carbonari*, passed on by the refugee Italian revolutionaries living in Spain. The *carbonari* also traced their origins to freemasonry but they had developed a more clearly-defined political direction. The most important and active sectors were characterized by hostility toward the legitimist governments and by their advocacy of the republic as the most appropriate system for guaranteeing political liberties. Their radical politics and penchant for elaborate formulas of secret organization were very well received by the Spanish *exaltados*. The defeat of 1823 and the ensuing exile produced a further radicalization as some *exaltados* adopted republican principles, especially after the promulgation of the Constitution of 1837 with its revision of some of the tenets of the idealized Constitution of 1812. Most of the former *exaltados*, however, embraced the new constitution as members of the Progresista Party.

Republicans were a minority during the 1830s and 1840s, and their activities were confined to putting out a few short-lived newspapers and to popular agitation in some of the largest cities, especially Barcelona and, to a lesser extent, Madrid. In 1841 they managed to win office in the municipal governments of some cities, with important victories in Seville, Valencia and San Sebastian, and formed a small democratic caucus in parliament with left-leaning personalities from the Partido Progresista and other explicitly republican figures. The republicans' municipal successes did not necessarily mean they had attained wide social backing. In the larger cities control of the electorate through clientelistic politics was more difficult to achieve and there were larger concentrations of the middle classes and artisans who found the republican programme of slashing local taxes attractive, but there were incidents of fraud and violence as well.

These advances had their limits. When the Moderates headed by General Narváez took power in 1844, any further growth by the republicans proved impossible. Changes in municipal laws and a heavy-handed policy toward the press and freedom of association blocked republicanism's development as a party and made it even more difficult to criticize the form of government or the sovereign. Republicans were not the only victims: Progressives were systematically excluded from power by Queen Isabella's use of the royal prerogative and their electoral possibilities were undermined by a serious reduction in the number of eligible voters and the government's control of elections. As a result, Progressives and republicans alike dusted off the old conspiratorial strategies.

Well entrenched in the army, the Progressives engaged in conspiracies aimed at taking power through a *pronunciamiento* but all their repeated attempts at provoking a military uprising against Narváez failed. The severity with which he repressed the uprisings deepened the chasm between Moderates and Progressives, who returned to power only following the Revolution of 1854.

The republicans lacked the influence in the military that the Progressives enjoyed. They based their conspiratorial politics on the search for civilian support, even though this approach never had any real chance of success. Their most effective organization was established in 1842: the Confederación de Regeneradores Españoles, a secret society which drew on the experiences of the previous decades. Its structure mirrored the territorial organization of the Spanish state, with local circles, county and provincial units, and a central circle that operated at the seat of the executive power (usually Madrid), under the guidance of a Great Master. Into this eminently civil and territorial organizational structure they inserted a separate component corresponding to the country's military districts, each of which was assigned its own 'circle'. This was a telling indication of their conviction that taking power required the active involvement of the army. While the organization urged its members to participate in active support of the candidates favoured by the confederation and to occupy administrative and political positions, it likewise urged them to take arms and prepare for the use of force.

An even more remarkable feature of this organization was its ideology. In addition to the defence of national sovereignty and democratic principles, including universal suffrage, it displayed an incipient interest in social questions. Next to an express defence of individual property rights and a censure of 'communism', the Regenerators also included concrete formulas for providing material assistance to their more disadvantaged members and their families. This mutualism did not spring from any programmatic sense of socialism or social egalitarianism, but was modelled more on the confraternities of the Ancien Regime, albeit stripped of their religious elements. Such concern for social questions was unknown among the Progressives and reflects the attention that Republicans were beginning to pay to the working class movements that, by the early 1840s, had already emerged in Barcelona. Over the following decades this interest in what was then called the *clases jornaleras* (the labouring classes) and in their demands would grow without interruption within the republican movement. Republicans were agreed on the principle of 'emancipating' the labouring classes and of providing them with material improvements and 'moral' uplift, but they did not agree on how this was to be achieved nor how far this should go, and these disagreements created divisions which would only intensify over time.

Between 1844 and 1854, a younger generation of democrats, most of whom had not participated in the struggle against absolutism, drew closer to the workers and adopted some socialist ideas. The most notable was Fernando Garrido, a painter who had been exposed to the utopian socialist ideas of Charles Fourier. Garrido gathered around himself a group of co-religionists who shared his concern for the 'social question' and the problems of the *clases jornaleras*. He participated in a night school for workers and between mid-1846 and May 1847 edited two newspapers that published propaganda on the need to harmonize labour and capital to achieve a 'pacific democracy'.

Despite Garrido's Fourierist background, these young Republicans were not at all dogmatic. One group in Barcelona inclined towards the ideas of Etienne Cabet, which helped draw them closer to the artisans and workers whose numbers were growing. These utopian socialist doctrines were but an initial step in the evolution of the Spanish variant of 'Jacobin socialism', whose main pillars were defence of the 'right to work', that is the need for state intervention to assure dignified employment for all people willing and able to work, and the right of workers to organize in order to defend their interests against those of their employers. Such ideas were irreconcilable with the free enterprise dogma embraced by most radical liberals, progressives and democrats. These philo-socialist republicans were only a heterodox minority among the republicans but one whose activism earned them an influence that went far beyond their numbers. Within the republican movement they could gain acceptance only by exercising caution and discretion in expressing their socially oriented ideas and their public projection was stunted when, after the revolution of February 1848 in Paris, the government closed their newspaper. All in all, the republicans increasingly sought to broaden their social base amongst the lower-middle and urban lower classes and farmers, although only in Andalucia were they successful in sinking roots amongst the latter.

In the early months of 1849 the political organization that would bring together the leading factions and personalities of the previous years and serve as their vehicle for action in the mid-nineteenth century emerged: the Partido Demócrata . This new political force adopted that name not just to get around the veto imposed by the Moderate government on any party that questioned the form of government but also to broaden its potential appeal to allow inclusion of persons who, though still monarchists, desired serious reform of the basic political structures to achieve recognition of national sovereignty, wider or universal suffrage, and a curbing of the monarch's executive powers. In other words, not all members of the newborn party were republicans, but they were all democrats within the meaning of the term in the Europe of the time.

The party emerged, above all, as a result of a drive toward unification already at work within the republican movement, as well as from the schism of some sectors of the Partido Progresista's left wing, dissatisfied with what they viewed as excessive compromise with the policy of the Moderates. This realignment also received an indirect push from the European turmoil of 1848, and the accompanying exaltation of democracy as the amplification of liberalism in the sense of expanding and assuring equality and defending the rights of the majority. The new party did not manage to provide the left with full legal security. Political rights were exercised in a precarious climate under the wary vigilance of a government that regarded the republican programme as incompatible with the foundations of the regime. The republicans themselves, convinced that they would not be able to overthrow the monarchy, took advantage of the limited tolerance to disseminate their propaganda with short-lived newspapers and pamphlets, while stoking the embers of the old faith in clandestine activity and plotting.

It was in the 1850s and early 1860s that the old practice of subversive secret associations attained its maximum expression. The most far-reaching was the so-called Hijos del Pueblo (Sons of the People), which was to some extent a clandestine duplication of the party and which brought together a number of organizations, such as La Joven España, modelled on Mazzini's Young Italy. When the Progressives regained power following the Revolution of 1854 the unity of these organizations yielded to a series of autonomous and not always coordinated groups which returned to underground plotting once the Moderates had returned to power at the end of the decade. As a unitary organization it was ineffectual. Easily infiltrated by police spies, it does not appear ever to have posed a real threat to the stability of the regime.

Aside from Madrid, its strongest following was in Andalucia, where its base in the rural population of some counties was significant. Individuals left defenceless by economic and social changes found in the secret society a certain sense of shelter, solidarity and power on adoption of an identity as an *asociado* (member of the society). Hence the careful attention to initiation rites, secret oaths, the somewhat extravagant symbols, the internal segmentation according to levels of commitment, passwords and secret codes and, in short, the entire theatrical paraphernalia typical of such organizations. In some small villages in the provinces of Granada and Málaga practically all adult males were members and individuals who did not voluntarily join the local society were often forced in through ruses or outright coercion. Both were signs of the inability of the local authorities to control their activities.

These societies in all likelihood provided the foundation for the attempted insurrections in the province of Seville in 1857 and in Loja (Granada) in 1861. In both, hundreds of men, led or stimulated by democrats in the cities, took up arms, to be easily put down by the army in a few short days. The rebels' lack of clear ideas as to how to proceed suggests that they acted in the belief they were part of a broad national uprising, or that they could spark one, and reveals the impotence of the secret organization, its practical limitations and the capacity of this type of political militancy to distort its followers' grasp on reality. Such lack of realism was seen not just in isolated rural groups composed of politically inexperienced and uncultured individuals. On the contrary, young and already experienced republican leaders shared the same outlook. One of the most notable, Sixto Cámara, lost his life in 1859 in a failed attempt to trigger an uprising in Badajoz. On the whole, these experiences demonstrate the republicans' growing familiarity with political violence and the use of force, including threatening or punishing deserters and informers. If their insurrections were so infrequent and so ineffective it was due to the republicans' small numbers, deficient organization and lack of adequate weaponry and not to any distaste for the tactic.

At the same time that the groups in the orbit of the Partido Demócrata were pursuing their obsession with insurrection, their leaders in Madrid were engaged in heated doctrinal disputes. The party was a congeries of tendencies that were not easily harmonized. Any cooperation was more a response to government pressure than the product of a unity of interests. Resolution of their differences was secondary to the need to confront the forces that threatened their very existence. Some of their differences are explained by simple personal incompatibilities and rivalries among their leaders. Thus, when Nicolás M. Rivero used his control over the Democrats' first daily paper, *La Discusión* to turn himself into the effective leader of the party, García Ruiz and Emilio Castelar responded by starting their own papers. This was followed by an angry battle for control of the party's governing bodies in Madrid, characterized by an almost permanent exchange of invective and accusations between rival leaders and their followers, even though the political differences between them were minimal and somewhat artificial.

However, there were also far-reaching ideological or doctrinal differences in the party which began to emerge in the early 1860s. The origin of those disputes may be seen in the philo-socialistic conceptions of the young activists who joined the republican movement around 1848, although these views did not congeal into a unified outlook or win many supporters. In 1860 and again in 1862, Fernando Garrido maintained a running debate with the Democratic patriarch, José M. Orense, who advocated an individualistic interpretation, both politically and economically, of the republican programme, against the 'socialistic' position of his adversary, who was interested in the experiences of the cooperative movement and in State intervention to assure workers' rights. These differences did not have much repercussion at the time, but they were reproduced and amplified in mid-1864, when the party's unofficial organ, *La Discusión*, came under the control of Francesc Pi i Margall, a young writer and lawyer of Garrido's generation.

Pi was raised in Catalonia and had lived for a number of years in Madrid, where he had been an undistinguished member of the party. His ideas lacked consistency. When it came to the Catholic Church he was a radical. He was acceptably well versed in French socialist thought (and would for some time be influenced by Proudhon), but his position on the subject was always somewhat uncertain. When he took over at *La Discusión*, Pi ran a series of articles on 'socialism' in which he advocated the need for State intervention in the form of social welfare laws and measures to facilitate access to cheap credit as instruments for the emancipation of the labouring classes but not for collective ownership of property. In the final analysis, his proposals were not much removed from the democratic and republican ideal that took as its social model the individual, autonomous worker, peasant or artisan, who owned his labour and his own means of production and was thus able to lead a dignified life of austere comfort from the fruits of his toil. The proliferation of this type of worker–owner would eliminate the gaping inequalities of wealth and assure the well-being of every industrious man and his family. This was far removed from the world of the industrial proletariat, but to the extent that Pi envisioned any active social role for the state he clashed with the more classical liberalism then predominant among democrats. He drew a response from the standard-bearer of conservative republicanism, Emilio Castelar, and for weeks the two men carried on their argument via their respective newspapers while the members of the party found themselves compelled to line up behind one or the other. Castelar was the winner, and at the end of 1864 Pi had to leave the newspaper.

But such internecine squabbles were soon pushed aside by general political developments. Between 1866 and 1868 the Moderate regime, based on the Constitution of 1845, suffered its final crisis. This was due in part to the physical disappearance of the generals who had sustained it, Leopoldo O'Donnell and Ramon Narváez. Their deaths coincided with the deteriorating international economic situation of 1866, which had severe repercussions in Spain, and which was compounded by poor harvests and rising food prices. But the truly decisive factor was the political situation, marked by a profound delegitimization of the regime and of the person of the queen herself. For Progresistas and Democrats, the influence that the *camarilla*, a clique of palace personalities with close ties to the most intransigent sectors of the Church, held over the queen meant that the throne itself had been surrendered to the political heirs of the old-time absolutists determined to annul the achievements of the liberals. Indeed, the *camarilla* influenced appointments to high state office, imposed a policy of support for the Papacy by denying recognition to the new king of Italy, denounced university professors whose teachings did not adhere to the basic tenets of Catholic dogma, and, above all, vetoed any possibility of the Progressives forming a government. Inasmuch as Isabella II was identified with these policies, the Progressives lost all reason to abide by the constitutional order. They repeatedly refused to field candidates for elections and thus forsook any parliamentary presence, underscoring their alienation from a regime which they rightly felt excluded them.

In the mid-1860s, and not without misgivings from some of the party's civilian leaders, the future of the Progressives was placed in the hands of another general, Juan Prim. Prim threw himself into conspiratorial activity, trying to organize a *pronunciamiento*. The initial goal was to oblige the queen to call the Progressives to power, but this evolved into the idea of replacing the Bourbons on the throne. Not all Progressives shared this objective, but that did not deter Prim from repeatedly organizing military uprisings. None of these succeeded, but they did provoke severe reprisals, which only further eroded the legitimacy of the government.

Nor was the Partido Progresista very clear on its relations with the republicans. While they were broadly united on such issues as rejecting clerical influence in politics and education and recognizing the kingdom of Italy, the details proved more problematic. For example, not all Progressives were ready to accept freedom of worship, even if Catholicism remained the official religion of the state, whereas, with few exceptions, the Democrats defended this right and even the need for a secular state that was neutral on matters of religion and conscience. With respect to Italy, not all Progressives shared the Democrats' enthusiasm for Garibaldi. They also expressed misgivings about the somewhat demagogic populism to which the Democrats were prone and were deeply concerned about their nascent socialistic tendencies. Both groups defended the extension of individual rights, the elimination of all inherited social privileges, and granting the vote to all males of legal age. They advocated a more effective, streamlined and cheaper administration and the completion of the process of disentailment of the property of corporate institutions such as the Church and the municipalities. But on all these questions, there were differences of nuance and scope of sufficient import to prevent a genuine coming together. Democrats reproached Progressives for their timidity and lack of resolve for carrying through a vigorous consolidation of the liberal system; the Progressives rebuked republicans for their extremism and demagogry.

In the final analysis, Progressives and republicans sought their support from the same social base: the lower middle classes, the more economically stable artisans, and workers. This battle for clientele made full agreement between the two movements difficult, but faced with the common hostility represented by the Crown and its Moderate governments they managed to keep their rivalry under control. In any event, the Progressives refused to accept republicans in their conspiracies. Republican leaders were not allowed in the secret deliberations or juntas, although when it came to street battles with government forces, the presence of republican followers was more than welcome. In keeping with their long-standing approach to conspiracy, the Progressives entrusted the entire mission to the military *pronunciamiento*, so civilian participation was of secondary importance. In fact, they had cultivated their civilian support in a paramilitary organization, the National Militia.

In contrast, the republicans had no following in the military but were steadily attracting support in towns and in working class neighbourhoods of the major cities, especially Madrid. While they did not ignore propaganda, an arena in which they were devastatingly effective in undermining the monarchy's prestige by airing unwholesome aspects of the queen's marital life and her multiple amorous pursuits, they clung to their old penchant for conspiratorial insurrectionist activity. In 1866, a group near Barcelona that had accumulated a large cache of weapons was broken up, and in the months prior to the revolution of 1868, the Democratic Circle of Madrid, a political club that acted openly, instructed its members to organize into secret groups, stock arms and prepare to act.

Aware of their weakness, the Democrats sought to ally themselves with the Progressives in order to participate in the *coup d'état* they knew was being prepared. This alliance, as well as an even broader one with the more conservative Unión Liberal, was possible only because the Moderates had become more intransigent than ever. Thus, by 1868, political enemies of only a short time before marched together toward revolution and the overthrow of the regime born in 1833. If the goal then had been the installation of a liberal political system, now the objective was to strengthen it and revitalize political life by expanding individual and political rights. This required the participation of the majority of the population, especially the artisans and the working class of the incipient manufacturing centres, and such support could only be attained with the promise of social improvements. All these developments shaped the new democratic political landscape, the first glimpse of which could be caught in the 'Glorious Revolution' of September 1868. That revolution would also reveal the political ineptitude of both the Progressives, the 'historic' left of liberalism, and the newer left of Democrats and republicans, which was at least in part the product of their persistent fascination with the politics of conspiracy.

1868 and the 'Revolutionary Sexennium'

The military uprising that overthrew Isabella II in September 1868 enjoyed the support of a broad coalition of political forces. At its heart were the Progressives, and their military champion, General Juan Prim, for whom this revolutionary adventure was a last chance to come to power after decades of having been excluded by the royal prerogative. Their programme was not especially radical, but it did advocate the moralization of public life and greater respect for political rights and individual liberties, including the possibility of universal male suffrage, and this distinguished it clearly from the positions taken since 1856 by the Moderates and Liberal Unionists. Even some of the military leaders of the Liberal Union, angered by their exclusion from power since 1866 and the increasingly repressive tack taken by the Narváez and González Bravo governments, joined the conspiracy. Like the Progressives, they claimed to fear a possible dictatorship based on an alliance of Moderates, Carlists and ultramontane clergy.

The Unionist and Progressive conspirators had solid support in all areas of the country and among broad sectors of the elite: in the military, among large landowners, financiers and Barcelona industrialists. Even so, they felt unable to do without the involvement of the Democratic Party, all the while retaining their fear of the Democrats' radicalism and demagogy. For their part, the Democrats were divided, and some elements refused to back a movement whose goal was to change the occupant of the throne rather than abolish the monarchy altogether.

The military revolt began on 17 September and was followed in most of the cities and larger towns by popular uprisings that replaced the established authorities with revolutionary juntas composed, for the most part, of such eminently middle class types as journalists, lawyers and other professionals. The political make-up of the juntas reflected that of the forces involved in the conspiracy, with a clear predominance of Progressives and smaller numbers of Democrats and Unionists. Despite their minority position, the Democrats were able to leave their mark on the juntas' public pronouncements, which included demands such as the abolition of conscription and taxes on food-stuffs, freedom of religion and separation of Church and State, which left less radical coalition members either lukewarm or horrified. All this, plus the excesses committed in some places in response to Democratic demagogy, made fears of republican – and even social – revolution credible.

In fact, after a few weeks the left found itself almost totally excluded from control of the revolutionary process. When it became time to man the new political institutions even the most moderate Democrats found themselves relegated to such effectively powerless positions as president of the Cortes, mayor of Madrid or a few civil governorships. The Progressives, with Prim at their head until his assassination on 17 December 1870, dominated the government. They were also able to attract a segment of the Democrats, thereby breaking the party's fragile unity. In November 1868 some moderate Democrats, who came to be known as *cimbrios*, joined Unionists and Progressives in signing a manifesto defending popular sovereignty and uni-versal male suffrage but renouncing the Republic. With democratic rights, they argued, the form of government was immaterial.

The response of the Democratic majority was to become even more radical, transforming the party into the Federal Republican Democratic Party. 'Republican' was clear enough: they opposed the democratic mon-archy embodied in the Constitution of 1869 and in Amadeo I, son of Victor Emanuel of Italy, who was elected king in November 1870. Just what 'Federal' meant was much less apparent, even among party members them-selves. The word often provided the pretext for local groups to carry out their own political initiatives on the grounds of a supposed local or regional autonomy. Even Pi i Margall, who passed for the leader and theoretician of federalism, was never able to articulate a functional or coherent doctrine.

Between 1868 and 1872 the Federal Republicans participated in both municipal and national elections. In December 1868 they won the mayor-alties of twenty provincial capitals, including Barcelona, Zaragoza and Seville but rather than a solid base of support, these victories reflected a general lack of political mobilization, the errors of the Progressives and even the tactical votes of Moderates and Carlists who hoped to discredit the new regime by strengthening the radical left. Nationally, the Federal Republicans never won more than 10 to 15 per cent of the seats in the Cortes, too weak a minority to influence, let alone shape, government policy.

The decision of some Republican leaders to resort to armed revolt to achieve what eluded them through elections brought government repression and internal division, both of which weakened Federal Republicanism. Only the power vacuum created by the abdication of King Amadeo in February 1873 permitted them to come to power and install their desired regime. Their eleven months in power, from February to December 1873, were a catalogue of errors and chaos, including the revolts of the so-called Cantons in the south, and when General Pavía's coup chased them from power there was absolutely no serious attempt made anywhere in the country to defend the Republic. As events moved on, from General Serrano's conservative regime that lasted from January to December, 1874, to General Martínez Campos' coup that restored the Bourbons in the person of Isabella's son, Alfonso, the Republicans were engaged in the complex internal disputes that rendered them politically marginal. And there they would stay until the granting of universal male suffrage in 1890 and the emergence of a new generation of leaders, such as Alejandro Lerroux and Vicente Blasco Ibañez, made republicanism relevant once again.

II

THE RESTORATION, 1875–1914

The Bourbons returned to the throne in 1875 in the person of Isabella's son, Alfonso XII. The politicians who engineered this restoration also faced a daunting challenge: to construct a constitutional system that was more open than the one that had existed between 1843 and 1868; that was able to reconcile the Church; and that kept the military in the barracks. Under the leadership of Antonio Cánovas del Castillo and Práxedes Mateo Sagasta they managed to do just that, and the system they created, known as the Restoration, functioned smoothly for twenty-five years. On the face of it an advanced version of liberalism, including universal male suffrage as early as 1890, the Restoration worked only because of the systematic rigging of elections through networks of patronage and clientelism known as *caciquismo*. The construction and operation of this system, and the political culture it engendered, are analysed by Stephen Jacobson and Javier Moreno Luzón. Jacobson and Moreno Luzón also describe the increasing professionalization of Spanish society at this time and the corporatist approach to politics to which it gave rise.

The Restoration was a clever response to a difficult dilemma, but much like generals who prepare themselves to fight the previous war instead of the next, Spain's political leaders created a political system that spoke more to the circumstances of the past than it anticipated the challenges of the future. By the 1890s those challenges were real and pressing: rebellion in the colonies, especially Cuba; the emergence of regional nationalisms, especially in Catalonia; and the growth of a range of forms of mass politics with which the culture and mechanisms of the regime could not cope.

Spain had once controlled a global empire, but it lost the bulk of its imperial possessions in the first decades of the nineteenth century and by the time of the Restoration it was left with only Cuba, Puerto Rico and the Philippines, as well as some small enclaves in northern Africa. As its empire shrank, so had Spain's presence in the diplomacy of Europe. Spain remained outside the European alliance systems, and when it finally had to face the United States in 1898 it did so alone. The 'disaster' of 1898 and the loss of the colonies led many in Spain, including much of the army, to turn their attention to Morocco. These developments are the subject of Enrique Moradiellos' chapter.

In Spain, as elsewhere in Europe, colonial entanglements had significant domestic consequences. As Enric Ucelay da Cal explains in his chapter, one of these was to feed into the development of minority nationalisms that challenged the nationalism of the Spanish state. Moreover, the civil war atmosphere of the Cuban conflict gave these nationalisms and the reaction against them an intensity – what Ucelay calls 'hysteria' – that was new to Spain's political life. The Restoration also had to confront the increasing challenge of mass politics. As Pamela Beth Radcliff sets out, this took a variety of forms, and the diversity of the challengers meant that the political life of the period was much more vital than is usually believed. Radcliff works with a broad definition of politics which allows her to move beyond the formal organizations of Republicans and the labour left to include women and their neighbourhood-based, consumer-oriented actions. And as Edward Baker explains, the class and regional conflicts that shook Spain in this period, left their mark on the country's cultural life as well.

6

The political system of the Restoration, 1875–1914: political and social elites

STEPHEN JACOBSON AND JAVIER MORENO LUZÓN

On 29 December 1874, General Arsenio Martínez Campos issued a *pronunciamiento* in the Mediterranean town of Sagunto against the presidency of General Francisco Serrano, putting Spain's future in the hands of military and civilian monarchists who subsequently orchestrated the return of the Bourbons to the throne. In January 1875, the teenage prince Alfonso arrived in Madrid, while his mother Isabella II remained in Paris as a deposed monarch. The 'Restoration' (1876-1923) – as this new regime was christened – had a dual significance: on the one hand, it confirmed the triumph of the conservative order against the diverse leftist tendencies of the Democratic Sexennium (1868–74); on the other, it opened the door to an understanding between rivals historically faithful to the Progressive and Moderate political traditions. The ensuing period can be best understood as an ongoing process of dissent and compromise between those who aspired to recapture the democratic 'conquests' of the Glorious Revolution of 1868 and those who sought to maintain the status quo. Out of this equilibrium, an exceptional political system was born, the longest-lived in Spanish constitutional history and one that has remained the centre of historiographical debate to the present day.

Historical analysis has generally separated the Restoration into two phases. Using the Spanish–American War of 1898 as a convenient turn-of-the-century point of inflection, the most generally accepted line of argument has contended that this initially flexible political system, successfully organized by a select group of 'political friends', ultimately proved incapable of integrating new forces associated with the advent of mass politics in the twentieth century. Debates have revolved around whether this durable constitutional monarchy was beneficial to the development of liberal democracy or whether its oligarchical underpinnings retarded the emergence of mature participatory politics. Without dismissing the continued relevance of this discussion, our focus will be on the changing contours of political culture; the shift from clientelism to incipient corporatism and the professionalization and corporatization of society. This mixture of political and social history makes for an eclectic narrative, but one necessary to unearth the multiple layers and appreciate the many textures of this complex political topography.

The consolidation of constitutional monarchy

The new regime seemingly portended a return of the practices of the Isabeline period. Serrano and Martínez Campos – the two principal commanders during the Second Carlist War (1873–76) – appeared poised to occupy roles similar to those Espartero and Narváez had played following the first Carlist conflict (1833–39). However, times were not propitious for military governance in Southern Europe. In France, the mild-mannered Jules Grévy replaced Marshall MacMahon as President of the Third Republic in 1877. And in Italy, Garibaldi's military successes gave way to Cavour's conservative parliamentary pragmatism. Meanwhile, European armies assumed administrative roles in Africa, Asia, and the Caribbean, as the continent remained at peace, free of large-scale domestic and international armed conflict. Spain followed the trend of 'civilizing' domestic politics while augmenting military presence abroad. Following his triumph at Sagunto, Martínez Campos easily dispersed the last remaining Carlist troops in the Catalan and Basque Pyrenees. By early 1876, the victorious General departed for Cuba, and thereafter the military's chief theatres of operation remained overseas. On the Peninsula, the army acted solely in defence of 'public order' and did not seek to undermine the institutions of the state itself.

The Restoration Monarchy was marked by the imprint of the man responsible for the coronation of Alfonso XII, Antonio Cánovas de Castillo. Ex-member of the Liberal Union and head of the capital's small 'Alfonsist Party', Cánovas was a conservative statesman in a Europe of conservative statesmen, whose contemporaries included Bismarck, Disraeli, and Cavour. A scholar of sixteenth- and seventeenth-century imperial Spain, Cánovas was convinced of the necessity to overcome the turbulence of the nineteenth century using solutions borrowed from history. A steadfast Catholic, he believed nations received their mission from God, but that men had the capacity to interpret the signs of providence. In his judgement, Spain's greatness was dependent on the union of two components of the nation's 'internal constitution': the Crown and Cortes. History demanded the adoption of laws – the 'external constitution' – needed to ensure stability and solidify liberal gains. The figure of the King-Soldier, a symbol of and a check on the army, guaranteed the nation's welfare. Ever-conscious of the severity of the country's fiscal limitations and military vulnerability, Cánovas favoured prudence in international relations.

The Constitution of 1876 furnished the country with a workable political environment for almost half a century. It represented a compromise between those who sought to recoup the Moderate Constitution of 1845 and those who believed in the continued viability of the revolutionary Constitution of 1869. Faithful to the spirit of the former, the Canovist theory of 'joint sovereignty' between king and parliament replaced all references to 'popular sovereignty'. Inspired by the latter, the Constitution provided for basic rights of due process, assembly, and expression, although it allowed these to be expanded or contracted by legislative fiat. The king retained important powers, including the ability to appoint a government, to initiate legislation, and to convoke or dissolve legislative sessions, but in order to undertake any of these actions, he needed to act through at least one of his ministers. Following the British model, the Cortes consisted of two chambers, the Congress and the Senate. The former was elected by all citizens possessing the right to vote, while the latter consisted of a complicated composition of notables: some elected, some appointed by the monarch for life, and some who served due to their high personal status or in representation of the country's most prestigious religious, military, intellectual, or commercial institutions. Framers steered clear of both the Moderate principle of 'catholic unity' and the democratic right to 'freedom of religion' (*libertad de cultos*): Catholicism was declared the official religion, while confessional minorities and non-believers were afforded legal protection.

Cánovas' projects were aimed at ending the violence and chaos previously characteristic of Spanish liberal regimes. In order to achieve this goal, he designed a political system divorced from royal absolutism and military intervention. Again faithful to the British system, Cánovas sought to organize two political parties, one of them liberal–conservative and one liberal–progressive, which could together attract previously bellicose elements of the extreme left and right to civilian rule. The king was to be the arbiter in this system, colloquially referred to as the '*turno pacífico*' (the pacific turn). His role was to appoint governments alternatively representative of the two parties by favouring organizational cohesiveness and prejudicing internal dissension. Most recently educated at the British military academy of Sandhurst, Alfonso XII was familiar with the limited roles of army and monarchy within a parliamentary system. In theory, the game seemed relatively simple, but in practice it took almost a decade to definitively establish its rules.

Following years of *pronunciamientos*, cantonalist revolts, revolution, and civil war, this ideal two-party system was not to be created overnight. In fact, the Restoration's early years featured the return of governmental repression reminiscent of times past. During the second half of the 1870s, the various groups who would later form the Liberal Party had yet to achieve consensus. Meanwhile, Cánovas merged his Alfonsist followers into a broadly-based Conservative Party – formally called the 'Liberal–Conservative Party' – and quickly transformed it into a hegemonic power endowed with a mission to restore order. Aside from approving a Constitution, Conservatives limited suffrage and imposed rigid controls on speech, press, education, assembly, and oppositional parties. They centralized local administration and erected protectionist barriers, alleviating stress on industrial bourgeoisie wounded by the

Sexennium's free-trading measures. Not only did Conservatives temporarily quash the activities of the republican left, they obtained some of their greatest successes with respect to the right: they marginalized old Moderates who favoured the restoration of Isabella II; and, by the beginning of the 1880s, they attracted many distinguished members of the Catholic Union, who, following Pope Leo XIII's advice, recognized the legitimacy of the new constitution.

The country was not devoid of reactionary elements opposed to the liberal principles upon which Cánovas' system rested. Carlists continued to occupy the political far right. They represented those sectors of Catholic opinion faithful to the late Pope Pius IX's obscurantist dictates and unconvinced by Leo XIII's more pragmatic attempts to resituate the Church within a European liberal–conservative order. Although they continued to support the claims of the pretender Carlos VII, Carlists renounced an immediate return to the battlefield, choosing to contest elections and send deputies to the Cortes. At the outset of the Restoration, Cándido Nocedal led the party, although his death in 1885 was followed by the movement's splitting in two. His son, Ramón, led the splinter group, known as the Catholic 'Integrists', a faction who abandoned support of an alternative dynastic line but zealously occupied the reactionary vanguard in support of the traditional union of Throne and Altar. Integrists and Carlists were more influential on the grassroots level than in the world of high politics, collaborating within a number of influential newspapers and periodicals. Immune to papal persuasion but not populist rhetoric, they rallied around attractive slogans, such as the popular book title *Liberalism is a Sin* (1884). In this manner, old struggles were renewed in the realm of ideas as traditionalist attacks were generated from the periphery against the corrupt, liberal politicians of the central, laic state. Initially, such forces remained on the political fringe, but by the turn of the century Carlism and Catholic integrism came to be significant influences on the nascent movements of Basque and Catalan nationalism.

To the left of the Conservative party was a heterogeneous liberal organization headed by the politician destined to become the alter-ego of Cánovas, Práxedes Mateo Sagasta. Engineer, Freemason, and leader of the Progressive Party's right wing during the Sexennium, Sagasta was the Restoration's most remarkable coalition builder. In theory, his party – 'the Constitutionalists' – was faithful to the Constitution of 1869, but, like many of his colleagues, he participated in negotiations leading to the drafting of the Constitution of 1876. Martínez Campos led the right wing of what was to become the Liberal Party. After returning victorious from Cuba in the Ten Years War (1868–78), he briefly headed a Conservative government in 1879. Never compatible with the strong-willed Cánovas, who had stolen his thunder in 1875, the General abandoned Conservative ranks vainly in search of a larger role. To the other side of Sagasta was the 'Dynastic Left', composed of many notables associated with the Institution of Educational Freedom (*Institución Libre de Enseñanza*) and other distinguished democratic monarchists who had renounced republicanism following the fiasco of the First Republic.

Eventually, these former revolutionary groups came to accept the new constitution. In 1880, Sagasta's and Martínez Campos' factions came together to form the 'Liberal Fusion', and in 1885 Sagasta forged a union between the Liberal Fusion and the Left, to create the Liberal Party.

Liberals also abandoned their praetorian and populist past. The Sexennium's great orators, such as Cristino Martos, much like the generals Serrano and Martínez Campos, were eventually reduced to secondary although not unimportant roles. In their place stood notable statesmen and intellectuals of the period, like Segismundo Moret, member of the *Institución*, or the enigmatic Eugenio Montero Ríos, a professor of canon law at the University of Madrid who had authored the Sexennium's law of civil marriage.

Much as Conservatives were watchful over the manoeuvres of their absolutist rivals on the right, Liberals were wary of challenges generated from the various Republican groups on their left. The famous orator and university professor Emilio Castelar led the rather innocuous 'Possibilists', a collection of notables who envisioned using universal suffrage as a means of peacefully coming into power. They enjoyed substantial intellectual prestige but little social support. Francisco Pi i Margall's Federal-Republicans, most active in Catalonia, attempted to carry on the popular revolutionary tradition, although their strength among Barcelona's working classes was quickly losing ground to the anarchosyndicalist and communist doctrines of Bakunin and Marx. More threatening were Radicals linked to the military conspiracies of Manuel Ruiz Zorrilla, who from his exile in Paris vowed to end the illegal politics of electoral fraud by reverting to the equally illegal tradition of *pronunciamiento*. Radicals sponsored unsuccessful coup attempts in 1883 and 1886; thereafter this tactic began to disappear from the Republican repertoire.

Liberals governed the country throughout most of the 1880s. Between 1881 and 1884, Fusionists were followed in power by Leftists. In 1885, Alfonso XII died of tuberculosis, leaving his second wife María Cristina de Habsburgo pregnant with a male heir. Pursuant to a fictitious agreement later labelled the 'Pacto del Pardo' (The Pact of the Pardo Palace), the Liberal Party assumed power following the King's death and governed until 1890, a period known as Sagasta's 'long parliament'. Taking advantage of their extended tenure, Liberals not only undid some of the repressive measures of the late 1870s but also brought back reforms previously introduced during progressive and democratic eras. They instituted trial by jury and expanded freedoms of press and association, thereby facilitating labour-union organization and permitting a larger degree of political dissent. In the economic sphere, markets were partially opened to Europe. Moret attempted to end political isolation by secretly integrating Spain for a short period into the Triple Alliance. Their most remarkable achievement was the introduction of universal manhood suffrage in 1890.

The initial period of legislation by compromise also featured the promulgation of the Spanish Civil Code (1889), written by one of the century's most prolific legislators, Manuel Alonso Martínez. European civil codes often incorporated important land reforms, but Alonso Martínez was no Mendizábal, nor were the Liberals as enterprising as their Progressive predecessors had been. The Restoration was not to be accompanied by another round of ecclesiastical or civil disentailments. Instead, the Civil Code – one of the latest to appear in Europe – reconciled many differences plaguing Spain throughout the century. It gave legal validity to both civil and ecclesiastical marriage, although it prohibited divorce. Most notably, it preserved many customary or 'foral' laws governing family and property in the regions of Catalonia, Viczaya, Navarre, Aragon, Galicia, and the Balearic Islands. Forces opposed to the 'Bourbon' tradition of legislative centralization found their supporter in the Queen Regent María Cristina, symbolically representative of 'Habsburg' respect for the diverse customs of the 'foral' regions. The Civil Code of 1889 served as a counterbalance to the Constitution of 1876, preserving regional heterogeneity of private law within a political order of uniform public law and administration.

Clientelism and *'caciquismo'*

Restoration Spain was a solid liberal regime, one of the most juridically advanced in Europe, capable of integrating various groups who had previously wrought havoc on the country. However, political stability depended on a tacit accord between Liberals and Conservatives to alternate in power. The *turno pacífico* functioned properly only if the party appointed to form a government knew ahead of time that it would have a favourable parliamentary majority. Likewise, before a party abandoned power, it needed to be assured that such absence promised to be temporary. For these expectations to be met, politicians returned to the old habit of electoral manipulation. Previously a source of contention, this became a handy tool used to implement the various compromises inherent in the Restoration settlement. In practice, the political system functioned in reverse: rather than an electoral victory deciding which party would govern, a parliamentary majority was the handiwork of a cabinet appointed by the king, which crafted a favourable electoral result though control of the Ministry of the Interior (*Ministerio de la Gobernación*).

Results of parliamentary elections attest to the prevalence of such fraudulent practices. Figure 6.1 clearly shows the operation of the dynastic rotation, in which each governing party possessed an exaggerated majority. Universal manhood suffrage, introduced in 1890, made the system increasingly difficult to maintain but did not upset its basic workings.

Fraudulent elections were a consequence of the centralized state structure. Control over the polls depended on municipal government. Mayors of important towns and cities were appointed by the government and part of their job was to respond to orders dispatched by the civil governors. Provincial deputations, also under the governors' authority, functioned as

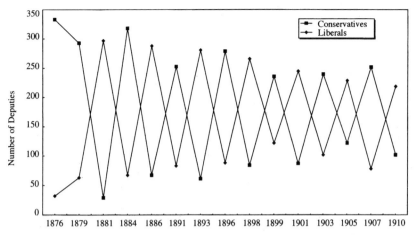

The "Turno Politico" of the Dynastic Parties Congress of Deputies

intermediary institutions with capacity to audit local governance and coordinate projects between towns. Civil governors, responsible to the Minister of the Interior, were roughly equivalent in their functions to French prefects, although the Spanish officials differed in the important respect that they were political appointees rather than civil servants. In order to obtain desired electoral results, civil governors replaced hostile town councillors with more compliant ones and dispatched agents to towns to prevent opposition victory. Judges played a more discreet role, mindfully fulfilling the wishes of the government upon which their careers depended.

Rigging an election was a complicated affair: the Minister of the Interior could not simply issue directives from the top down. If the map of Spain corresponded to a chess board in which each square (*casilla*) was an electoral district, then every *casilla* needed to be filled by a parliamentarian who more often than not had to be loyal to the government. The '*encasillado*' was the colloquial name given to this checkered design, the work of the Minister of the Interior. Negotiations took place at a number of levels between national, regional and local political elites, often originating with Cánovas and Sagasta and stretching to local party bosses, many of whom operated in remote areas. During such negotiations, municipal or regional interests were by no means discarded in favour of those of the capital. The search for electoral pacts was a necessity upon which the entire system depended and the *turno* needed to be maintained within all representative bodies: in the Cortes, deputations, and town councils. Moreover, the Spanish state was a weak administrative unit, centralized on paper but limited in its capacity to impose executive decisions from above. In order to accomplish even the most elementary of tasks – such as tax collection or conscription – ministers needed to act through local notables. Electoral organization was no exception. Such notables came to be denominated '*caciques*', borrowing a name

derived from Native American intermediaries who had fulfilled administrative functions in the Spanish empire.

The *cacique* was the true political protagonist of the Restoration. Without
much internal structure, local party organization often consisted of a handful
of public personages and their followers, many of whom aspired to
governmental posts. Party members littered the halls of elite sociability, such
as local men's clubs (*casinos*), theatres, religious and commercial organizations, and royal academies. Others wrote for the political press, the
proliferation of which greatly exceeded the public's capacity to read it. In
exchange for delivering the vote, local notables received various gifts from
those who wielded legislative power or exercised administrative prerogative.
Individual favours included the procurement of a government job, the resolution of a regulatory conflict, or the conferring of a military-service exemption.
Collective favours usually involved the concession of a public-works project
or other large-scale budgetary grants. Using the spoils system's well-known
incentives and rewards, political bosses were able to build clientelist networks
and gain influence in districts and provinces they represented. For example,
Alejandro Pidal – Conservative leader of the Catholic Union – controlled the
region of Asturias, where he succeeded in persuading the region's doctors to
exempt many of its youth from military service due to physical disability. The
Liberal Fernando León y Castillo constructed an electoral fiefdom in Las
Palmas on the Canary Islands, overseeing the development of the city's port
from his distant post as ambassador to France. The democrat Montero Ríos
controlled much of Galicia, while Juan Sol y Ortega served for years as
republicanism's perennial representative in Barcelona.

To be a *cacique* did not necessarily imply that one possessed specific social
or even geographical origins. Spain was a liberal society and its political
system, however corrupt, was flexible enough to incorporate persons from
various walks of life. None the less, *caciquismo* did exhibit some recognizable
social and geographical tendencies. It was strongest in rural areas and small
provincial cities, where lower classes depended on the mediation of local elite
to defend their interests, and in which middle classes searched, often in vain,
for jobs in the public sphere. Although many *caciques* were property owners,
most were recruited from the professions. Lawyers, merchants, doctors,
notaries, veterinarians, and municipal secretaries possessed a level of sophisti-
cation in administrative matters not shared by their fellow citizens. *Caciques*
were not unique to Spain but had their equivalents in other Southern
European liberal political systems. In Portugal, local notables, known as '*os
influentes*', were also called '*caciques*' and participated in a variety of the
turno, called '*rotativismo*'. In Italy, the '*grandi elettori*' formed the basis of
Giolitti's liberal regime. Likewise, liberal Greece, during the era of the
durable statesman Venizelos, was also buoyed by similar electoral devices.

Caciquismo was well adapted to the prevailing social conditions. Its elitist
configuration was the result of the stagnancy of a society lacking an associational tradition capable of addressing collective concerns in public forums.

Despite its apparent efficacy, *caciquismo* had a serious downside. A political culture in which interest overshadowed ideology dominated much of the country. Parties were no more than unstable alliances forged by local oligarchs, in which the distribution of spoils was more important than the development of political ideas or the elaboration of national platforms based on long-term goals and objectives. Electoral fraud and the misappropriation of resources undermined laws meant to guarantee equality of opportunity and neutralize government's discriminatory power. Justice, like the rest of Spanish administration, suffered from grave problems of corruption.

The '*fin de siècle*' crisis and 'regenerationist' responses

During the 1890s, Liberals and Conservatives continued to rotate in and out of office but electoral fraud, especially during the era of universal manhood suffrage, was becoming too obscene for many politicians to stomach. Until the last decade of the century, *caciquismo*'s critics had been chiefly republicans, but they were soon found among the dynastic parties. Conservatives exhibited two opposite tendencies: Francisco Romero Robledo, the one-time September Revolutionary, embodied the tradition of electoral management; while the 'gentleman' Francisco Silvela espoused a more ethical approach to politics. Conflicts between these two factions exploded in a series of corruption scandals in Madrid's municipal government, the residue of which split the party. Liberals were also divided. Their right wing was led by the jurist and *cacique* Germán Gamazo, a defender of agriculture's protectionist interests who also served in the prestigious position of dean of the Madrid Bar Association throughout most of the decade. On the left, the ex-Republican José Canalejas, son of a railroad magnate, was more representative of liberalism's urban constituencies.

During the closing years of the nineteenth century, colonial wars engulfed Spanish politics [see chapters 7 and 8]. The year 1898 involved much more than an embarrassing military defeat. Spain's humiliation triggered a collective 'crisis of conscience' which reverberated throughout political and cultural life. Writers and essayists carried events to an extreme, developing what became known as the 'literature of the Disaster'. The country's national – and even racial – ills would be cured by an aesthetic concoction of remedies past and future: anarchism, Catholicism, republicanism, Carlism, socialism, monarchism, and many avant-garde mixtures of the above. Alongside the intellectual movement, a more practical, though no less virulent, critique of the *caciquista* system also made its voice heard. Various commercial, professional, and agricultural groups – frustrated with governmental incompetence, resistant to paying taxes, and hamstrung by bureaucratic demands of clientelist networks – found their spokesman in Joaquín Costa, Aragonese notary, prolific critic of the Restoration, and literary demagogue.

In 1902, Costa published his most poignant condemnation of the regime, an essay entitled *Oligarquía y caciquismo*. The party he founded, the National Union, never became a significant electoral presence, but his arguments – used by democrats, economic liberals, and authoritarians alike – caused significant damage to the legitimacy of the political system.

'Regenerationism'– a nationalist call for change and progress – invaded society's most dynamic sectors. Neither dynastic party was able to avoid the reformist wave. In 1899, a coalescence of Conservative forces seeking to fill the void left by Cánovas, who had been assassinated in 1897, formed the Silvela–Polavieja government, a short-lived 'regenerationist' cabinet, first in line of what was to be many. Resentful of parliamentary pettiness, General Polavieja fashioned himself as a Spanish 'Boulanger', although his populist pretensions were unmasked by the fact that his chief backing came from Barcelona's industrial bourgeoisie, in search of political alternatives following the loss of Cuba, its chief 'protected' market.

In 1902, Alfonso XIII achieved majority, ending the Regency of María Cristina. Unlike his parents, the young King chose to intervene actively in politics, often becoming entangled in internecine party disputes. In 1903, Sagasta died, leaving both parties to confront the difficult task of renovating their leadership as well as their ideas. Conservatives and Liberals emerged from their predicaments in different manners but each designed a coherent reform project. However, to the detriment of the regime, the two projects were incompatible if not antithetical. Pathologically divided over sensitive issues involving Church and state, they sought to garner the support of the anticlerical left or the clerical right, hence radicalizing their respective positions. The *turno* continued to exist but compromise was no longer possible.

Francisco Silvela – who had taken over his party's leadership following Cánovas' death – first articulated the outlines of the Conservative response to the '*fin de siècle*' crisis. In 1903, Silvela ceded his post to Antonio Maura, a former Liberal who had abandoned Sagasta's party after emerging as the loser in its internal battles. As a Conservative, he was not without his adversaries, especially among the party's most oligarchical components. Both Silvela and Maura believed *caciquismo* to be the regime's principal enemy, as it isolated Spaniards from active participation in public life. In Maura's opinion, it was necessary to realize a 'revolution from above' as a means to create a citizenry dedicated to constitutional monarchy. This would, in turn, prevent a future 'revolution from below'. Their goal was the construction of a conservative democracy, not an unrealizable aspiration considering Spain remained primarily a rural and Catholic country.

Silvela and Maura attempted to institute a two-part programme meant to free the country from *caciquismo*'s shackles: first, electoral fraud needed to be eliminated, and second, government had to reflect society's 'vital forces'. Both goals were to be accomplished by decentralizing public administration in order to weaken the Ministry of the Interior, vitalize local government, and eliminate judicial and bureaucratic corruption. Maura also proposed to complement universal suffrage with a 'corporate vote' in municipal and provincial elections, a measure intended to promote and reward associational life. Conservative regenerationism possessed important support. The Church, for one, believed this 'corporativist' programme to be consistent with its interests. Moreover, Catalan regionalism placed its bets first with Silvela and then with Maura. By 1901, Catalanists had broken the back of the *caciques*' electoral dominance in Barcelona through the use of a modern propaganda organization directed by its political party, the Lliga Regionalista. Lliga adherents, many also practicing Catholics, generally believed in the strategic viability of a Catalanist–Conservative alliance.

The Liberal Party reacted more slowly to regenerationist influences. Montero Ríos and Moret, veterans of the Glorious Revolution, contested the party's leadership along with the younger Canalejas. Although many of their differences revolved around political networks, these politicians represented distinct strains of liberalism. Montero Ríos formed the right wing of the party – the individualistic, economically orthodox, and secular liberalism of the nineteenth century. Moret attempted to integrate Republicans through the formation of a 'Leftist Block', held together chiefly by an anticlerical platform. Canalejas promoted a new 'social liberalism', which shared certain characteristics with the French Radical Party or Lloyd George's project in England. All three considered Silvela and Maura's initiatives a grave danger to constitutionalism, equating regenerated Conservatism with a neo-Catholic resurgence.

Conservatives – in 1899–1901 and 1902–05 – and Liberals – in 1901–02 and 1905–07 – each had the opportunity to implement their respective programmes, although internal party divisions as well as fiscal limitations did not allow for great successes. To their credit, both parties succeeded in straightening out the disastrous situation of the treasury, in heavy debt following the colonial conflict. Both also collaborated in the construction of protectionist barriers which were among the highest in Europe. Conservative and Liberal projects finally came to a head during Maura's 'long government,' 1907–09. In the summer of 1909, the government went down in flames during the 'Tragic Week', a bloody anti-conscription uprising in Barcelona, triggered by a call-up of troops to fight in Spain's last important overseas holding, the Protectorate of Morocco. The revolt assumed anticlerical dimensions and Ancien Regime forms: mob violence resulted in the burning of Churches on a scale not seen in the city since 1835. In 1909, the supposed protagonists of the Tragic Week – including the then-innocent schoolmaster but former terrorist Francisco Ferrer – suffered summary executions by the Army, to the abhorrence of the European left.

Only after the horrors of the Tragic Week and Maura's fall were Liberals able to resolve their differences in favour of Canalejas, who governed between 1910 and 1912. In many respects, Canalejas' government represented the end of an epoch, during which time he was able to recapture the last conquests of the Democratic Sexennium. He abolished the hated '*consumos*' tax and institutionalized obligatory military service by abolishing the practice of purchasing exemptions. Canalejas' assassination in November 1912 and Maura's removal as Conservative Party chief in 1913 caused an ideological and leadership crisis within both parties, which, in many respects, was never resolved during the remainder of the Restoration (see chapter 12).

From clientelism to incipient corporatism

Political culture also experienced a slow but recognizable transformation due to the emergence of new professionalized middle classes, who came to fulfill technical roles in a modernizing society and who began to challenge the hegemony of traditional oligarchies through the exercise of more diffuse, corporate forms of power and influence.

In order to appreciate this phenomenon, it is perhaps necessary to temper the hyperbolic image of Spain generated in the years following the Spanish–American War, when regenerationist intellectuals succeeded in depicting the country as stagnant and traditional, isolated from the European mainstream. There was some truth to this image. While cities boasted the technological and cultural hallmarks of modernity much of the rural world was moribund, an embarrassment to cosmopolitan intellectuals, many of whom chronicled its ills and a few of whom proposed solutions. None the less, even this 'discourse of decadence', like the critique of political corruption, was by no means exceptional or even original. The reality was that Spain remained a liberal society undergoing similar stresses and strains to much of Europe. During the course of the Restoration, a skeletal political and administrative apparatus based on disorganized, clientelist, and local networks slowly evolved into a more complex entity. Elite society remained open to new-comers, as it had throughout the nineteenth century.

Education provided the most important avenue of opportunity for those who sought to better their station in life. Spain was well behind many of its neighbours in the fields of primary, secondary, and university education. The public system was under-funded, under-staffed, and open to a reduced number of students. None the less, Restoration politicians committed more resources than ever before to pedagogy. Silvela created the Ministry of Public Instruction in 1900, which inherited thousands of primary and secondary schools and a university system, previously organized within the Ministry of Public Works. Despite this administrative reshuffling, real accomplishments were more modest. Illiteracy rates remained abominably high, although they did exhibit an important downturn. According to official census information, adult (over the age of 10) male illiteracy declined from 52 to 42 per cent while its female equivalent dropped from 77 to 61 per cent from 1887 to 1910.

The Ministry of Public Instruction maintained the structure of Spanish education in existence since the Ley Moyano (1857), modelled after the French Loi Falloux (1850). Primary education remained essentially orga-nized by the municipalities. Public secondary schools ('*institutos*'), located in provincial capitals and other large cities, were generally staffed with a lay professorate. A candidate who successfully completed secondary-school exams received a Bachelor of Arts (equivalent of the French *baccalauréat*), a degree attesting to his knowledge of Latin, grammar, geography, history, religion, science, and mathematics. A student could then enter one of the universities, located in Madrid, Barcelona, Valencia, Zaragoza, Seville, Granada, Valladolid, Salamanca, Oviedo, and Santiago de Compostela, which awarded 'licentiates' (*licenciaturas*) in arts and letters, law, medicine, pharmacy, and natural sciences. Special public schools for industrial and civil engineers, machinists, architects, surveyors, primary-school teachers, veterinarians, nautical occupations, accountants, and other professions also existed in selected cities.

Public secondary schools possessed a monopoly on final examination and degree distribution, but parents were free to send their children to private schools for their coursework. In most of Spain, as in the rest of Southern Europe, private education was synonymous with Catholic education. The Church used seminaries to educate both aspirants for the priesthood and those destined for the university. The orders, most notably the Piarists and the Jesuits, also sponsored boarding and day schools. Less prominent were a number of elite private boys' schools, which featured a lay professorate but were by no means secular, as students normally attended mass and confession, undertook daily rosary prayers, and attended state-mandated religious education courses. It is important to note that private lay education's rise, quite noticeable in the larger cities in the 1870s and 1880s, did not continue throughout the Restoration. It was most prevalent in Barcelona, but even here religious orders began to expand their influence at the expense of lay schools by the turn of the century. Clerical influence was also omnipresent within the primary-education system. Church and State were never separate in Spain, and public and religious education overlapped, particularly in rural areas where parish and town worked in close collaboration.

In the mid-nineteenth century, universities could generally service public need. However, by the late nineteenth century, increasing demand forced reformers to allow students to study privately, requiring them only to attend up for exams at the university. Although this measure helped relieve numerical pressure on the public system, it also converted the university into as much a clearing-house for degrees as a place of learning. Moreover, the boom in higher education arguably had a limited social function. Despite high levels of illiteracy, Restoration Spain, like most of Europe, suffered from an excess of educated men: universities and secondary schools simply produced more graduates than the market could absorb. In France and England, colonial administration provided an easy outlet, but in countries lacking large overseas empires or internal bureaucracies, young, out-of-work, and underpaid professionals put increasing demands on the political system.

Scanty census information prevents an accurate determination of whether the number of professionals increased with respect to population during the

Restoration. Given demographic increases, it would be surprising if this were the case. None the less, Spanish schools were capable of producing the requisite personnel needed to carry out functions in a technologically modernizing society. During the Restoration, law remained a popular subject of study, yet medicine and science also became viable, though competitive, career tracks. Figure 6.2 demonstrates the increasing number of private doctors and pharmacists, and the decreasing number of private lawyers. This 'medicalization' of society – along with the expansion of the country's pedagogical edifice – was perhaps the most important social phenomenon transfiguring elite society.

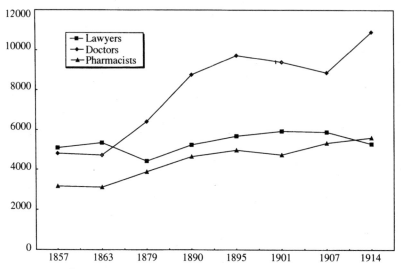

Private Legal and Medical Professionals in Spain (Excluding Basque Provinces and Navarre)

Restoration politicians also undertook an important reorganization of Spain's penal system. The comparatively low number of private lawyers does not mean that opportunities in the law were stagnant, only that business for barristers litigating civil disputes remained steady. Many persons touting law degrees found employment in state, provincial, or municipal judiciaries and administrations. Furthermore, the field of criminology took off during the Restoration, providing jobs in courts and prisons. A two-part reform of the judicial system, in 1882 and again in 1892, ultimately had the effect of creating new criminal tribunals located in all provincial capitals. This was accompanied by much needed advances in procedure, given that Spanish courts, throughout most of the nineteenth century, operated under many of the antiquated and barbaric practices of the Ancien Regime. The late coming of 'enlightened' legal reform was a double-edged sword in Spain as it had been in the rest of Europe: while these procedural advances theoretically provided the accused with increased rights, such innovations also streamlined justice, allowing authorities to punish delinquent behaviour and incarcerate at a quicker pace. By the turn of the century, criminal cases flooded the courts, tripling the number of civil cases. Parallel to increasing crime rates was the rise in penitentiary capacity. The years 1860–1905 marked the golden age of prison construction, as governments built 30 new institutions.

Urban professions formed the foundation of what was to become the corporate organization of the middle classes. Professional associations usually cropped up at the intersection of state and society, public and private: courts, schools, hospitals, and other places where independent practitioners sought to establish officially recognized bodies able to negotiate directly with regulatory authority. The liberal professions and their associational forms had been slowly coming into prominence since the late eighteenth century, but during the Restoration the presence of collegial organizations thickened and their influence grew. Juridical bodies formed the prototype. Bar associations – called 'colleges' (*colegios*) of lawyers – received their charters in 1838; notarial colleges received theirs in 1862; while those of solicitors (experts in court procedure) possessed the oldest organizations. Brokers involved in the exchange of goods, currencies, and financial instruments on various stock exchanges and other boards of trade also formed collegial associations. In 1904, an important reform in public health administration regulated and reformed medical and pharmaceutical colleges, which represented doctors, surgeons, and pharmacists in their relations with state medical inspectors and health authorities.

Despite the increasing importance of 'liberal' or 'free' professions, traditional methods of social ascension – the Church and the army – were still the most common. The coming of scientific, medicalized, and penitentiary society was not uniformly accompanied by an increase in lower-level professionalization. Nuns, monks, and friars doubled as nurses, teachers, social workers, and other employees of schools, poorhouses, hospitals, shelters, madhouses, and maternity wards, as they did in much of Southern Europe. Although the disentailing laws had removed the religious orders from ownership, many social welfare and charitable organizations were still staffed by regular clergy, who numbered more than 50 000 men and women at century's end. The secular clergy – tied to the fate of the state budget – saw their numbers decrease during the Restoration. The army was not as disadvantaged. By the early twentieth century, the Spanish Army had the highest officer-to-troops ratio in all of Western Europe, and its upper ranks, like the upper ranks of the clergy, were among the country's best paid officials. However, also similar to the two-tier structure of the clergy, the army's middle and lower strata – from lieutenant on down – received more modest salaries. By 1910, census data reveals some 96 000 officers and troops stationed on the Peninsula and in North Africa, a number much greater than the combined total of all civilian bureaucrats (excluding those employed in municipal government) during the same period.

Municipal government offered an important but not very lucrative alternative for the literate, although it was not uncommon for the same person to occupy multiple posts. Town and city judicial and administrative officials – many lacking university and some even secondary-school education – formed the bulwark of Spain's amateur bureaucracy. They were complemented by thousands of notoriously underpaid primary-school teachers, trained at public 'normal schools'. Although technically recognized as a national corps, teachers were for all intents and purposes municipal employees., This situation changed in 1901 when the Ministry of Public Instruction assumed responsibility for paying their salaries, a measure theoretically propitious to eliminating gross under-compensation in the poorest locales. Town government also employed a few thousand doctor-surgeons (*médicos titulares*), endowed with the difficult task of providing rudimentary care to the poor. In 1904, these general practitioners were upgraded in status and also became recognized as a national corps.

The remainder of the official state bureaucratic corps offered a limited number of opportunities to the educated. Telegraph and postal workers found themselves on the lower rungs. Civil, mining, and agronomical engineering corps, the clerical staffs of the Ministries and the bulk of the university and public secondary-school professorate occupied the middle levels. Senior professors were well compensated, as were medical personnel who directed and staffed hospitals and provincial health boards. At the top of the civil hierarchy were judicial functionaries – accused by Costa of forming the bulwark of *caciquismo* – who served as judges, prosecutors, state lawyers, court reporters, judicial secretaries, and property registrars. By the twentieth century, the state's considerable capacity to offer employment and distribute and redistribute resources was an irreversible trend. Although the country possessed only the rudiments of a modern civil service and although its treasury was continually in the red, its enterprising middle classes were not unaware that the larger and more bureaucratic states on the continent, such as Germany or France, marked the path over which Spain was destined to tread. Much as industrial entrepreneurs eyed steam power in England in the 1830s and brought it to Spain to reap profits, professionals – in search of status and stability – observed opportunities offered by more sophisticated continental administrations and sought to implant foreign models at home. As the Restoration progressed, the state offered more opportunities to the educated and the privileged, fuelling the *caciquista* system but also raising the stakes for its continued vitality.

Professionals and bureaucrats came to exert significant influence on the political process. In addition to officially chartered colleges and corps, the first decade of the twentieth century witnessed the formation of a fractured professional movement composed of underpaid, unsatisfied, and even out-of-work men and women. Teachers, engineers, higher- and lower-rung bureaucrats, judicial personnel, military officers, doctors, pharmacists, students, and other occupations formed local and national associations, leagues, and defence groups, using periodicals to help foster internal cohesion and voice demands in the public sphere. Industrial and agrarian protectionist groups, joint-stock companies, banks and railroads, along with the Church, were the most accomplished and experienced players. While these groups sought to defend or expand the influence of the privileged, others emulated their organizational styles to pressure government to limit the influence of oligarchy in state administration or the Church in education, health, and welfare. Increasingly, legislators and bureaucrats dealt directly with corporate entities when contemplating legislative or budgetary decisions, undermining 'back-room' methods of conducting political business. As voluntary associations and official institutions negotiated political or regulatory issues independent of traditional party networks, the basis of 'corporatist' or 'interest-group' politics began to emerge.

Conclusion

Spanish society changed greatly between 1875 and 1914. The Restoration had provided the country with stability which allowed for sustained, though uneven, industrial development and economic growth. The country still remained largely agricultural. Cities increased in population and generated phenomena previously unthinkable. New mass parties, like the Radical Republicanism of Alejandro Lerroux in Barcelona or Vicente Blasco Ibáñez in Valencia, or the middle-class Catalan nationalism of Francesc Cambó, displaced parties composed of old monarchist notables. Trade union federations, such as the socialist Unión General de Trabajadores (founded in 1888) or the anarchist Confederación Nacional de Trabajo (founded in 1910), augmented their influence. In 1910, Socialists elected their first deputy. Meanwhile, strikes multiplied and dynastic politicians began to think, albeit timidly, in terms of the social welfare of workers. Like much of Europe, Spain remained a 'divided society', exhibiting dramatic cleavages between privileged and dispossessed, landed and landless, capital and labour, centre and periphery, city and country.

In 1914, *caciquismo* continued to inform political life in much the same way as the critique of *caciquismo* still dominated political discourse. Two new party leaders, the Liberal Count of Romanones and the Conservative Eduardo Dato, represented the resurgence of oligarchical forces within the dynastic parties, highlighting the failure of more innovative politicians, such as Canalejas and Maura. Regenerationism continued to make its voice heard from within and without, from right and from left. Meanwhile, the middle classes were becoming professionalized, as universities and other schools continued to produce a technocratic elite which sought to occupy roles in pedagogical, penitentiary, and medicalized society, and who organized into associations to contest for political and economic power. The foundation had been laid for the transformation of the *caciquista* system, as corporatism would begin to replace clientelism as the characteristic threat to liberal politics in Spain as in the rest of Europe.

|7|

Spain in the world
from great empire to minor European power
ENRIQUE MORADIELLOS

'The dawning of the nineteenth century was a sad day for Spain.' These simple lines open Jerónimo Bécker's classic 1924 study of Spanish foreign policy throughout that century. The writer and occasional diplomat Salvador de Madariaga wrote in a similar vein some years later: 'In foreign, as in home affairs, Spain had to start in the nineteenth century from the bare ground. There was nothing.'[1]

It is certainly true, as both quotations express with pardonable hyperbole, that Spain experienced a radical change in its international standing, and hence in the character of its foreign policy, from the beginning of the nineteenth century. The country ceased to be the great world-wide empire it had been during the entire Early Modern period from the sixteenth to the eighteenth centuries and was reduced to the condition of a small European power. This transformation was the result of two simultaneous and connected processes: the irreversible loss, in two distinct periods, of its long-standing American and Asian empire; and the intense level of political instability, social conflict and economic backwardness which characterized the transition from the Ancien Regime to a liberal society and state.

The erratic foreign policy of Spanish governments during that period was the direct consequence of both processes. It should be remembered that from 1789 onwards the country consistently lacked what J.M. Jover called 'the indispensable primary instrument of any foreign policy: a solidly established state'.[2] Defying Leopold von Ranke's dictum, it might be said that nineteenth century Spain was a clear example of the primacy of domestic politics over foreign policy. The country's energies were so absorbed by the scale of internal problems that there was scarcely any strength left to attend adequately to external interests and problems.

Foreign policy at a time of crisis and transition

At the tail end of the eighteenth century the Spanish monarchy ruled over territorial possessions which were as far-flung as they were extensive. The Spanish empire was based on three very different and mutually distant geographical parts of the world: the vast possessions of the American continent from California and Florida in the north to the Antartic tips of Chile and Argentina in the south; the archipelagos of the Asian Pacific (the Philippines, Palau, Caroline and Marianas islands); and in Africa the garrison-towns of Ceuta and Melilla on the Moroccan coast and the colony of Fernando Póo, today's Equatorial Guinea.

Spanish foreign policy had as its main objective the defence of the motherland and the preservation of that huge colonial complex. In addition, there was the question of the recovery of Gibraltar, a key strategic position in the southernmost tip of the Spanish mainland overlooking the entry to the Mediterranean, which had been lost to Great Britain in 1704 in the course of the War of the Spanish Succession. Since the growing economic and naval power of Britain posed the greatest threat to Spanish interests, Spanish diplomacy had been directed since the beginning of the eighteenth century at the establishment of a close alliance with France with a view to strengthening Spain's military position in Europe and its naval strength in the Atlantic. As such, over the course of that century Spain's foreign policy held fast to a simple guiding principle: 'Spain plus France equals England'. Franco-Spanish support for the North American rebels in their war of independence against Great Britain was a clear example of this policy in action.

The eruption of the French Revolution in July 1789 and the parallel sparking of the crisis of the Ancien Regime in Spain irreversibly shattered the foundation of this long-standing foreign policy. After a brief period of confusion followed by a disastrous military conflict with the newly established French Republic, the Treaty of San Ildefonso of August 1796 saw the precarious re-establishment of the traditional Franco-Spanish marriage of convenience in the face of their joint British enemy. On this occasion, however, the fruits of this union were to be bitter for Spanish interests: in October 1805 virtually the entire Spanish navy was destroyed in an epic encounter with the British navy at Trafalgar (Cádiz). Henceforth, Spain ceased to be a significant naval power and lost the basic means of controlling its widespread overseas interests.

The irreparable loss of the fleet was followed three years later by the Napoleonic invasion of Spain and the initiation of a bloody and devastating War of Independence (1808–14). The consequence of these two events was the creation of a paradoxical and risk-laden situation which augured ill for the future: an imperial power without a navy and a series of distant colonies without a sovereign metropole. Out of the shadow of the Franco-Spanish conflict came Spain's own liberal revolution and the unleashing of a parallel process of colonial emancipation in its American possessions.

The immediate effect of the French invasion was to provoke a radical change in the foreign policy of the Spanish authorities who were resisting Napoleon. Their forced search for British diplomatic and military support concluded with the signing of a Treaty of Peace, Friendship and Alliance on 14 January 1809. Spain also signed a similar treaty with Russia, another of Napoleon's enemies, in July 1812. With the diplomatic backing of both alliances and the decisive military support of Britain the new authorities elected by the Cortes of Cádiz waged an exhausting war, dominated by guerrilla tactics, at the same time as they were undertaking a process of liberal social and institutional reform. By early 1814 their efforts had succeeded in expelling the French from Spain and restoring Ferdinand VII to the throne. However, on his return the king annulled all the Cortes' liberal reforms, initiating a prolonged period of political instability, economic weakness and a simmering discontent between absolutists and liberals that occasionally boiled over into full-scale civil war.

Despite the undoubted prestige Spain had gained from its proud resistance to Napoleon, the absolutist regime of Ferdinand VII was immediately made aware of its marginal status in Restoration Europe. Along with other small powers, Spain was excluded from the meetings of the Congress of Vienna (1814–15), in which only Great Britain, Austria, Prussia, Russia and France, the five great powers which would preside over what came to be called the Concert of Europe, took part. It was starkly apparent that Spain was no longer a great power, and the widespread rebellions in the American colonies had removed at source the basis of its former standing as a great imperial power.

To make things worse, both the diplomatic corps selected by Ferdinand VII and the policy he saddled it with were haphazard and unrealistic. An excellent example of this was the tautological directive sent to the Spanish delegates in Vienna: 'His Majesty decides in favour of what could be most conducive to the interests of the Monarchy.' This situation helps to explain the failure of Spain's attempts to gain the direct support of the European powers in its battle against the American insurgents. Besides Britain's self-interested opposition to any European involvement in the matter, these efforts were futile because Spain lacked the necessary material and political resources. Even so, in June 1817, Ferdinand VII formally joined the Holy Alliance of absolutist powers (Russia, Austria and Prussia). However, the fundamental objective of this diplomatic step was purely internal: to restrain the advance of liberalism on the continent and to achieve a guarantee of external support for his regime in the event of a new liberal revolution in Spain.

The greatest failure of Spanish diplomacy in the reign of Ferdinand VII was America. Between 1810 and 1825 all Spain's American colonies except Cuba and Puerto Rico achieved political independence after a lengthy struggle against the Spanish Crown which amounted, in several places, to open civil war. The emancipation process was led by the creole elite (the colonial-born Spaniards), fired by the previous example of their northern neighbours and at loggerheads with the Spanish administration as a result of long-standing socio-political grievances and economic ill-treatment. In fact, political and social power were denied to them by peninsular-born Spaniards, and the Spanish imperial system blocked their great prospects of profitable trade with foreign countries (by way of a high tariff barrier which ensured a captive market for Spanish goods). The French invasion of Spain revealed to the creoles the extent of Spanish decline and served as a catalyst in their prolonged struggle for political independence. Spain's military efforts to restore its authority proved fruitless and exacted a significant financial and human toll on the meagre resources of a mother-country already devastated by the War of Independence. The brief 'Constitutional Triennium' (1820–23) was unable to resolve the situation and this administration's own tragic demise also saw the disappearance of the Spanish empire in the American continent.

Significantly, the loss of the American empire coincided with another demonstration of the extreme internal weakness of the Spanish state. The French invasion of April 1823 – known as the '100000 sons of St Louis' – did not arouse the hostility of the Spanish populace on this occasion and easily dealt with the feeble liberal resistance. For the remaining 10 years of his reign, and until his death in 1833, Ferdinand VII restricted his diplomatic efforts, under the all too obvious political and military aegis of France, to guaranteeing the survival of his absolutist regime, preventing international recognition of the new American republics and saving Cuba and Puerto Rico from the imperial wreckage. The viability of these limited aspirations was determined less by Spain's ability to defend the two islands than by the mutual interest of Britain and the United States in keeping them out of other hands, namely those of Mexico and Colombia.

The foreign policy of liberal Spain

In the early 1830s, the Iberian Peninsula became the front line in the European struggle between liberalism and absolutism. Facing entrenched absolutist resistance and civil war, the unstable liberal regimes in Spain and Portugal were forced to turn to France and Great Britain for financial, military and diplomatic support. The two great liberal powers agreed to provide these by means of the Treaty of the Quadruple Alliance signed on 22 April 1834. By virtue of this agreement, the Iberian liberal regimes, which were not recognized by the absolutist powers nor by the Holy See, were placed under the diplomatic wing of France and Great Britain and sheltered from further hostile foreign interventions in their territory. In addition to the financial support given to the liberal forces in their war effort, British and French expeditionary forces comprising 7000 and 6000 men respectively fought against the Carlists. All told, these measures were a powerful contribution to the defeat of the Carlist and Miguelist threat and to the stabilization of the two liberal regimes on the Iberian Peninsula.

The involvement of Britain and France in Spain's domestic and foreign policy was gradually reduced as the liberal regime consolidated itself and as, from mid-century onwards, Spain underwent significant economic expansion and burgeoning industrial development. Nevertheless, the crucial importance of both countries in Spain's foreign policy continued throughout the nineteenth century and beyond. It was at this time that the new guiding principle of Spanish diplomacy took shape: 'When France and England march together, back them; when not, abstain.' Consequently, throughout the second half of the century Spain remained within the political and diplomatic sphere of influence of France and Britain. This was abetted by increasing French and British investment in the Spanish economy (especially in mining and railways) and by the renewed strategic importance of Spain to both countries (through neighbouring borders in the Pyrenees and Gibraltar, and due to Spain's proximity to Mediterranean and Atlantic areas of expansion and influence in Algeria and Portugal).

Breaking with the doomed pretensions of the absolutist period, liberal Spain formally recognized the new Spanish American republics: Mexico (1836), Ecuador (1840), Chile (1844), Venezuela (1845), Bolivia (1847), Costa Rica (1850), Nicaragua (1851), Argentina (1859), etc. Similarly, the governments of the decade of Moderate hegemony between 1843 and 1854 also achieved recognition from the Holy See with the signing of a Concordat on 18 March 1851. This wide-ranging diplomatic activity of the liberal state was made possible by an extensive rational reorganization of the bureaucratic apparatus at home and abroad from the late 1830s [see chapter 3]. Its only notable failure was its inability to achieve an international guarantee for the colonies of Cuba and Puerto Rico, in order to compensate for Spain's own military weakness making it difficult to defend them militarily should the need arise. In 1845, Great Britain confidentially proposed a three-way pact involving France, Britain and Spain aiming to guarantee these colonies from the threat of annexation by the United States. However, the Spanish authorities rejected the proposal for reasons of internal and external prestige and because they feared onerous conditions would be attached (basically the impossible acceptance of British colonial presence at Gibraltar). In any case, Spanish authorities were confident that Britain would in the event react promptly to protect her own interests by preserving the status quo in the Caribbean. Thus began Spanish isolation in the Age of Imperialism.

This blind faith that French and British interest in preserving the international status quo would suffice was a defining feature of Spanish foreign policy from the 1830s on. It undermined Spain's search for allies to guarantee its exposed overseas colonies and gave rise to a marked isolationist tendency in the face of great international conflicts. Spain's response to the Crimean War (1853–56) was exemplary, refusing to become involved in the confrontation between Russia and the Franco-British bloc, though her neutrality tended to favour the latter. The same caution was revealed in liberal Spain's foreign military undertakings in the 1850s and 1860s, namely the Franco-Spanish expedition to Cochin China (1857–63), the Moroccan War which resulted in the acquisition of Ifni (1859–60), the British, French and Spanish expeditionary force to Mexico (1861–62) and the War of the Pacific against Peru and Chile (1863–66). In all these cases Spain's military commitment was insubstantial and intended primarily for reasons of domestic prestige, with the backing or collaboration of the great Western powers and with no intention of undermining the cherished status quo. The slightness of Spain's relations with Portugal after 1833 is another example of the crucial Anglo-French influence on Spanish foreign policy. Given their opposition to a closer understanding between the two countries, the 'Iberista' movement rooted in the Portuguese and Spanish middle classes after mid-century came to nothing and was unable to break down the mutual ignorance and suspicion of the two Iberian states.

After the overthrow of Isabella II in September 1868 and during the six years of democratic rule that followed, Spanish foreign policy was marked by a combination of growing impotence and passive involvement in major international matters. The chronic political instability and social conflict of the period were exacerbated by the difficulties in finding a constitutional monarch for the vacant Spanish throne following the revolution of 1868. British and French vetoes of various candidates (including a Portuguese and a Prussian aspirant), along with the internal divisions among Spanish monarchists, undermined the threadbare credibility of the eventual winner, Amadeo of Savoy, a son of Victor Emanuel of Italy. In addition, the feverish search for a monarch through the courts of Europe, and particularly France's veto of a Prussian prince, provided the flimsy pretext for the Franco-Prussian war of 1870–71. In this conflict, Spain had no choice but to announce its neutrality and thus earned the resentment of both sides. This neutrality was enforced rather than borne of choice, given the internal situation of the country and the colonial war that had begun in 1868. The anxious and futile search for foreign recognition of the short-lived First Republic in 1873 was another proof of the acute internal instability of the new regime.

The Restoration: from isolation to disaster

The restoration of the Bourbon dynasty in 1874 under Alfonso XII calmed the social and political tensions inside Spain and this was faithfully reflected in the diplomatic sphere. The foreign policy framed by the architect of the new regime – conservative leader Antonio Cánovas del Castillo – was characterized by a desire for *recogimiento*, retrenchment and isolation, paired with the preservation of the status quo and the avoidance of any foreign conflict. This approach, with neutrality as its linchpin, was underlain by an acute awareness of the country's military and economic weakness.

Significantly, Spain took virtually no part in the scramble for Africa during the last third of the nineteenth century (with the forced exception of the conquest in 1884 of Río de Oro, later Spanish Sahara, right opposite the Canary islands), concentrating instead on retaining her colonies and holding onto Morocco. However, this policy of retrenchment meant that Spain risked finding itself isolated in the event of a threat to her overseas possessions. In 1887 Segismundo Moret, foreign minister in the Liberal government, attempted to avoid this danger by secret and indirect adherence to the Triple Alliance of Germany, Austria–Hungary and Italy, but the agreement was short-lived and did not constitute a commitment from any of those powers to intervene in the defence of Spain's overseas empire.

Without solid European allies and with insufficient defensive capabilities, Spain had to face a new and final colonial crisis after 1895. In February of that year a second and bloody war of independence began against the Spanish authorities in Cuba. By mid-1896 the independence movement had spread to much of the Philippines. Both wars were the latest result of the ongoing failure of Spanish colonial policy. In fact, since the loss of the bulk of its large American empire, Spain had proved incapable of modernizing its antiquated colonial system to integrate the colonial population by recognizing its political and economic aspirations. Continued rejection of calls for political autonomy and free trade joined with evidence of the military and economic weakness of the metropole to push the creole elites in Cuba and the Philippines towards the separatist option and armed insurrection. In 1894, the last year of peace, 43 per cent of Cuba's imports came from Spain while, high tariff barriers notwithstanding, 37 per cent came from the United States. The situation of Cuban exports was much worse: Spain took only 9 per cent compared to 88 per cent – mostly sugar, tobacco and coffee – that went to the United States. Therefore, it was already apparent that because of Spain's economic and industrial backwardness it could not supply the expanding Cuban market nor absorb more than a minimal part of Cuba's production. In both these areas the USA was an increasingly important client and exporter, and was able to guarantee Cuba's continued economic development both through the large volume of trade and through large-scale capital investment (concentrated in the mechanization of sugar mills and the setting-up of tobacco factories).

To make the situation worse, the Spanish colonial crisis of 1895 coincided with a period of colonial redistribution on a global scale. The 1890s saw the British ultimatum to Portugal regarding its South African expansion (1890), the Italian defeat at the hands of Abyssinia (1896), and the French retreat before Britain in Sudan during the Fashoda crisis (1898). This conjunction of forceful colonial redistribution proved fatal to Spanish interests: the failure of Spanish colonialism was obvious in both the Antilles and the Pacific, and these were both areas in which the United States had been developing as a nascent naval imperial power unchallenged by any other major power.

Between February 1895 and April 1898 Spanish authorities attempted to solve the colonial crisis by a combination of military force and political and economic concessions. On the one hand, they sent an army of 200 000 soldiers to Cuba to suppress a rebellion of around 40 000 insurrectionaries. On the other, they tardily accepted Home Rule and permitted free trade with foreign countries. But both were equally inadequate in dealing with insurrections that were generating a deep financial haemorrhage as well as causing serious social tensions back home – due to the unjust system of conscription that allowed the rich to buy their sons out and to the very high mortality rate among the conscripts, more of whom died from disease than in fighting.

At the same time, sucessive Spanish governments had to reject US offers to mediate in Cuba or to purchase the colony. These offers were unacceptable given the heightened nationalism both of contemporary public opinion and within the armed forces. Consequently, by April 1898, Spanish authorities found themselves thwarted. On the one hand they were economically and militarily too weak to crush the rebels or sustain a long drawn-out campaign. On the other, because of military feeling and the pressure exercised by the political opposition, they felt they could not give way to the United States and the rebels without putting the stability and very survival of the Restoration regime in jeopardy. In April 1898, General Correa, the Minister of War, publicly set out this unresolvable dilemma and its terrible consequences:

> I am not one of those who boasts about certain victory if war [with the USA] breaks out. But I am one of those who believes that this is the lesser of two evils. Worse would be the conflict which would break out in Spain if our honour and our rights were trampled.

Meanwhile the US government, galvanized by the chauvinistic sector of the press and public opinion, continued to demand a quick solution to the crisis in order to safeguard its economic and strategic interests in Cuba and the Pacific. For their part, all the major powers had signalled their resolute intention of not becoming involved in the growing dispute between the American colossus and what British Prime Minister Lord Salisbury called a 'dying nation'.

The conflict which resulted from the explosion aboard the battleship *Maine* at Havana Bay had, therefore, been anticipated for some time. (The explosion itself was either an accident or the work of Cubans who wanted to force the US to intervene.) On 23 April 1898 the United States declared war on Spain and immediately ordered its Atlantic and Pacific fleets to attack their Spanish counterparts located in the bay of Cavite in the Philippines and the port of Santiago in Cuba. The orders were carried out on 1 May and 3 July respectively. Both US fleets enjoyed overwhelming superiority in numbers and firepower, and destroyed the Spanish fleets almost without opposition in a matter of hours. The human cost of the battle at Santiago Harbour reveals the unevenness of the forces: 350 Spaniards died, 160 were wounded and 1600 were taken prisoner including the Spanish Admiral; in contrast one American was killed and four injured. Very appropriately, these spectacular naval defeats became known by Spanish contemporary public opinion and subsequent historiography as 'The Disaster of 1898'.

The loss of both fleets made it impossible for Spain to carry on a war so far from its own shores and so near the enemy's homeland. At the same time, the defeat had been so rapid and so complete that Spain had no choice but to sue for peace. In these circumstances there was almost no objection to the liberal government's request for an armistice on 18 July or to its renouncing sovereignty over all Spain's colonial possessions (Cuba, Puerto Rico, the Philippines and Guam) in the Treaty of Paris of 10 December 1989. Six months later, Spain sold the Palau, Caroline and Mariana Islands in the Pacific to Germany.

Aftermath of disaster: a new imperialism in Morocco

Although the Disaster of 1898 did not provoke the immediate collapse of the Restoration regime, it did occasion the abandonment of the policy of retrenchment established by Cánovas del Castillo. International isolation was widely perceived as being at the root of the war and subsequent defeat at the hands of the United States, and after 1898 Spanish governments sought to overcome it. Led directly by the new king, Alfonso XIII, they set out in search of an alliance that would guarantee the security of mainland Spain and its offshore archipelagos while supporting its old colonial pretensions in Morocco (the enlargement of Ceuta and Melilla and their hinterland). The hectic phase of imperialist rivalry in the first decade of the twentieth century, along with Spain's reduced standing as a minor southern European power, rendered such an alliance essential to guard against potential changes to the status quo in the Straits of Gibraltar and North Africa. Moreover, only such an alliance would make expansion in Morocco feasible, and this was considered by the king and the *africanista* ruling circles to be the last opportunity to gain a sizeable colony and to restore the military honour lost in 1898. Count Romanones, mayor of Madrid in 1898 and a future Prime Minister, would later recall that 'Morocco was for Spain her last chance to keep her position in the Concert of Europe.'

For obvious geographical and economic reasons, Alfonso XIII and his ministers concentrated their efforts on establishing such an alliance with the neighbouring Western Powers, Great Britain and France. The signing of the Entente Cordiale between these two countries in April 1904 was the vital precondition for the signing of the Franco-Spanish Agreements in October 1904. With previous British approval, both countries agreed to divide Morocco into two zones of influence and to coordinate their policies of colonial advance in the area. Anglo-French acceptance of an expanded Spanish presence in North Morocco derived from their common preference for having a neutral and small power on the African side of the Straits of Gibraltar. The energetic German protest against these agreements lay behind the international conference on Morocco held in Algeciras (Cádiz) in January 1906, which served only to emphasize German isolation and to reaffirm the new front formed by Britain, France and Spain. Spanish links to the allied bloc were ratified by the Cartagena Declarations of May 1907, by which the three countries exchanged mutual guarantees for the security of their Mediterranean and Atlantic territories and undertook to consult each other in the event of any change in this position.

After these preliminaries, the definitive Franco-Spanish Convention, establishing their respective Protectorates over Morocco, was signed in November 1912. Spain was left in control of a long northern strip of 20 000 square kilometres with under one million inhabitants. The strategically important port of Tangiers was detached and designated an international city. The lion's share of Morocco, 350 000 square kilometres and more than five million people, went to France, which saw its already large empire in North Africa further enlarged. The Spanish zone was an artificial entity, a totally unexplored mountain region, militarily indefensible and inhabited by fiercely independent tribes which had never been subjected by the Sultan's government. The only possible economic rationale for the costly conquest lay in the explotation of the Rif iron mines, actively encouraged by a powerful business colonial lobby well connected with high military and political sectors of *africanista* persuasion (a vague belief in Spain's historic destiny in North Africa).

Despite the limited size of this territory, its effective military occupation by a poorly trained and badly equipped conscript army posed major difficulties. As early as the summer of 1909 a rebellion of indigenous tribes had reached the walls of Melilla. The subsequent decision by the Conservative government of Antonio Maura to call up reservists sparked major social unrest in Barcelona, known as the Tragic Week. From that point on, the harsh war in Morocco, which ended only in 1926, represented a substantial human and economic burden which served to greatly polarize public opinion and further undermine the legitimacy of the Restoration regime. In the 1909 Melilla campaign alone the Army acknowledged more than 700 soldiers killed among casualties that totalled 2517. Independent sources put the figure as high as 4131. This growing 'blood quota' – paid exclusively by those too poor to buy their way out of military service – was the main reason for popular discontent with both the new imperialist adventure and the political system backing it.

On the eve of the First World War, then, Spain was embroiled in a very difficult colonial war which emphasized its inadequate military preparation, economic weakness and social and political instability. Thus, despite Spain's direct diplomatic links with the Anglo-French bloc, the government hurriedly declared its neutrality when hostilities started in the summer of 1914. Then as before, neutrality was not a position chosen freely after due consideration but the only conceivable policy for an internally divided country which was paralysed by its social tensions and all-too-obvious material limitations. Nevertheless, behind the official adoption of neutrality, Spaniards themselves were evenly split between Francophiles and Germanophiles, a division that responded quite closely to the political Left and Right, respectively. Against the backdrop of the Great War, Spaniards played out their own 'civil war of words'.

Although Spain did not enter the Great War and was spared the consequent human slaughter, the war did enter Spain by way of its huge political, social and economic impact. The massive economic dislocation and social distress brought on by the conflict – inflation, food shortages, industrial expansion, rural exodus, etc. – decisively eroded the fragile foundations of a political system based on the apathy and demobilization of the population. The result was the arrival of a new era of mass politics in which the ruling classes had to confront the threat of a radical change to the status quo. In such conditions, neutrality in the international arena was the unavoidable consequence of deep divisions at home. Once again, and not for the last time in the twentieth century, the primacy of domestic politics over foreign policy reasserted itself in Spanish history.

Notes

1 J. Becker, *Historia de las relaciones exteriores de España durante el siglo xix* (Madrid, 1924) vol. 1, p. 5; S. de Madariaga, *Spain: A Modern History* (London, 1961) p. 277.
2 J.M. Jover Zamora, *Política, diplomacia y humanismo popular en la España del siglo xix* (Madrid, 1976) p. 86.

8

The Restoration

Regeneration and the clash of nationalisms, 1875–1914

ENRIC UCELAY DA CAL

The revolution of 1868 codified Spanish democratic and nationalist discourse for the future: in the name of representative government, the naval ensign became a national flag, the imagining of a national matron, 'Hispania', appeared for the first time on coinage, and the national crest was designed. The so-called 'Revolución Gloriosa' of 1868 was a conscious echo of the founding myth of the British political system, the 'Glorious Revolution' of 1688. Triumphant Spanish liberalism claimed for itself a sort of 'Whig theory of history', with the sixteenth and seventeenth century opposition to absolutism (the 'Comuneros' and the 'Germanías' against Charles I, the legal protest of Aragon against Philip II's encroachments, the Catalan revolt against Philip IV's policy of coordination) as antecedents to the epic struggle for freedom begun against Napoleon and continued up to 1868.

The left liberal leader of 1868, General Juan Prim, was also an imperial champion, the hero of the successful Moroccan campaign of 1859–60, which had set off the important fireworks of rhetoric – novels, poems, painting, press – that reaffirmed national-liberal discourse as a font of renewed Spanish glory. Prim's reputation had been made amidst this outburst of national self-congratulation, in the glow of which it appeared that the Spanish people, united behind its leading institutions: Constitution, Crown and Army, would finally recover its rightful place among the European powers. Democracy would serve as the natural culmination of such a recovery. The ideological effectiveness of the fusion of these liberal arguments is shown by the immediate consensus they provoked. Despite bitter differences, the entire political spectrum, from the ultra-right Carlists to the extreme-left republicans accepted and adapted to the visual symbols of nationhood and Spanishness introduced by the new provisional government. Liberal reform finally had made institutional nationalism generally acceptable.

Yet democratization did not change a political tradition based on civil war into stable parliamentary competition wherein words and ballots replaced violence and bullets. Rather, democratization drew latent political warfare into the open. Civil war re-emerged, this time as a struggle between the defenders of the continuity of the liberal monarchy – that is, the survival of the joint symbols and the shared habits of the army and the Crown – against the opponents of such succession: Carlists from the extreme right and republicans from the extreme left. This opposition to the incipient democracy guaranteed the failure of its attempt to create a stable national state. There could be no clearer indication than the situation in the summer of 1873 when it had to confront a diverse group of enemies: Carlist rebels, Cantonalist rebels and Cuban rebels. There was even a small-scale conflict with the United States, the so-called 'Virginius' affair. All this discredited not only the Republican experiment; for many, the very word 'Republic' became synonymous with chaos. In January 1874 the army intervened and restored the Monarchy under Conservative auspices.

Against the Conservative tide, led by Cánovas, the liberal governments of the 1880s reintroduced and consolidated the programme of the 'Gloriosa': universal manhood suffrage in municipal elections (1882), the abolition of slavery in Cuba (1886) – as the Republic had freed the slaves in Puerto Rico –, a new commercial code (1886), right to association (1887), trial by jury (1888), a new civil code (1889), and finally universal manhood suffrage in national elections (1890).

The reforms that were still pending, above all of the armed forces and local government, would become the obsessive themes of all Spanish politics for the next century. Both subjects were at the core of any nationalist redefinition of Spain and were indissolubly linked. Although everyone agreed that the provincial system copied from France in 1833 was unsatisfactory, there was no consensus on how to best replace it. Also up in the air was the colonial question, which touched on both local and army reform. The implicit inclusion of Cuba in the already thorny field of local representation made it impossible to deal with by means of the usual juridical legerdemain, since it implied the uncomfortable adjustment of the military to civilian superiority, a circumstance officers were as loath to contemplate in practice as they were opposed to in theory.

The political shift after the culmination of liberalism

The late 1880s were a very important moment of change, in spite of apparent ideological continuity. Integrists (or ultra-Catholics) split off from Carlist dynastic legitimism, and there was a similar readjustment of republicanism as an electoral organization, a process that invited the definitive relegation of radicals and federalists. At the same time, the increased visibility of the labour movement coincided with the appearance of Catalan, Basque and Galician regionalism and/or nationalism. All of these redefinitions became visible between 1885 and 1892. Such changes meant that forces previously marginalized from the parliamentary system reincorporated themselves, even if they were inherently hostile to the existing constitutional order. In turn, such participation, under the appeal to full suffrage, meant that all manner of particularist reticence fuelled the appearance of regionalisms in the face of the rationalizing, democratic and unitary reform sponsored by Sagasta's liberalism. At the same time, the colonial mess in the Antilles introduced a civil war logic, born in the Cuban conflict of 1868–78, that made it impossible to achieve local administrative reform within metropolitan Spain.

Thus, the end of the 1880s and the early 1890s signified the end of old-style army revolutions and the assumption by the military of the role of absolute defenders of state continuity. As if in reply, literary regionalism produced a qualitative change in Galicia and especially Catalonia, where writing in local languages took on an ever more intense turn. Increasingly, there was pressure from sectors of the professional classes to turn the cultivation of literature from cultural politics into politics pure and simple.

As happened in contemporary societies as disparate as unified Germany, Great Britain (including Ireland) and the United States, the central (if not always the most explicit) political question in Spain was whether development would be directed by agrarian sectors best adapted ˙to rapidly internationalized market relationships or by industrial interests, who held out greater future promise of power and independence, but whose immediate health was more delicate and required stiff tariff protection. By the 1870s and 1880s, this debate began to go beyond abstract discussion as landowners who had purchased disentailed land began to exercise ownership at the expense of rural populations, leading to uprooting and economically driven migrations to the cities or to Cuba and Argentina.

Such social change generated considerable resentment in the popular sectors that were most subject to its effects. The expressions of such resentment were simple: either traditional protest, which was notoriously ineffectual; emigration; or some kind of organized corporative response, such as class unions or leagues. 'Workerism', the idea that labourers, both agrarian and industrial, should group themselves without the tutelage of middle class professionals, was increasingly called for from the poorest strata. From the 1880s on, there was a rapid expansion of working-class discourse, stressing the struggle between rich and poor, between those who toiled and the selfish exploiters, mixing traditional arguments with more radical ideological imports like Marxism and Bakuninism. The fashion of international revolutionary currents reinforced such notions, inculcating the sentiment that workers, by their very nature, were morally superior to the selfish and short-sighted bourgeoisie and thus capable of changing the nature of society and improving future humanity. Popular unrest, though held in check by the effective repression of the Civil Guard, led to growing networks of local agricultural and industrial unions which became increasingly active in the 1890s (see chapter 9).

Overall, the general trends of Spanish politics were not inherently different from those of most contemporary European or American states: nothing intrinsic to Spanish circumstance foreshadowed a particularly catastrophic passage from liberalism to democracy. Where Spain did differ significantly was in the stimulation of official nationalism, what has been called the 'nationalization of the masses', something which compared to the French Third Republic and Wilhelmine Germany, received little attention from the governments of the Restoration.

Decolonization and the rise of new nationalisms

The nationalist rhetoric in use in the last decades of the nineteenth century was loaded with clichés from the heady days of 1868 and their aftermath, but this language became increasingly outdated as society in both metropolitan and insular Spain adjusted to rapid transformation after a decade of abrupt ideological violence. New generations come of age after the Restoration transition.of 1875–76 clamoured for innovation and fresh ideas. Unexpectedly, these came largely out of the renewal of civil war in the Antilles. To a large extent, the appearance of new nationalisms of identity in Spanish politics was the result of what amounted to the first crisis of decolonization in European politics.

Spanish capitalism had developed within a distinctly imperial frame. Cuba was, after all, the most advanced regional economy within Spain: the first railroad in all Latin America (eleven years before the first line in the Peninsula), an independent bank of issue, direct access to the stock exchanges of New York and London. Could the more advanced regional economies of the peninsula not do as much and lead to a new, more powerful Spain, based on pluralism, development and democracy? But Cuba, marked by insistent fear of separatist conspiracy since at least the 1830s and by open secessionist revolt after 1850, revealed the 'true' nature of the Spanish imperial state: much pompous talk, but no effective action in a bureaucracy defined by military abuse and rampant corruption.

The rise of Cuban nationalist identity since the 1830s, with its permanent attraction to the United States, presented the first real alternative to Spanish institutional nationalism. Although initially pro-slavery, Cuban independentism edged towards manumission and race toleration in what remained an extremely racist society. The Spanish military had long enjoyed unchallenged protagonism in the 'overseas territories' in a notoriously corrupt environment. Peninsular immigration further complicated an already entangled social context, conditioned above all by the fact of slavery. The racial and sexual advantages enjoyed by even the poorest peninsular immigrant at the expense of free Afro-Cubans encouraged stubborn political attitudes rooted in the confusion between the privileges of class and colour. Accordingly, political alignments, especially with the 'Long War' of 1868–78, became increasingly 'national' in their polarization: 'separatist' (i.e. nationalist Cuban, presumably indulgent towards Blacks) versus 'Spaniard' (i.e. a partisan of continued military rule and its exclusivist advantages). In an independentist civil war, ideological definition became nationality, and, in turn, identity, overloaded with emotion, became hysterical: anyone who was not completely 'Spanish' without qualifiers or excuses was a closet traitor.

Such evaporation of ambiguity on what heretofore had been 'The Most Loyal Island' led quite naturally to a new ideological militarism, whereby the defenders of hardline decisions spoke their own language of identity as tough as that of any rebel, increasingly denying the respectability of any position other than undoubting fidelity to the metropolitan homeland. The result, in the colonies, was the appearance of a new and extremely emotional nationalism of identity, even in peaceful Puerto Rico. Such a discourse of 'unionism' was unknown in metropolitan Spanish politics until the impact of the second set of colonial wars in the 1890s. Then it was introduced primarily by the military press, which expressed opinions of middle-level officers discontented with the more political generals who controlled the army. Eventually, after 1898, this same opinion would blame the liberal government for a 'stab in the back', for wasting men and material in a struggle that somehow should have been won. In metropolitan Spain, 'españolismo' – literally "Spanishism' – became the expression of conservative resistance to demands for decentralization and to the rise of regionalism or competitor nationalisms.

The analogy between individual emotions and the acceptable limits of collective behaviour was thus turned into a ready-made ideology of national consciousness, redolent of threatened machismo and wounded pride, of which the military (and the ideological warriors who followed their lead) were to be the special guardians. Such sentiments were perfectly adaptable to models of *fin de siècle* European ultra-nationalism, given the interest shown by Spanish critics in the nationalist carryings-on of nearby countries. Throughout Europe this hysterical nationalism of identity was linked to imperialism and was made visible in imperialist crises of the 1890s in Portugal, Italy, France and to a lesser degree Britain, with the initially unsuccessful Boer War of 1899–1902, and Germany, with its ultimately futile race against British naval predominance.

While 'big' or 'imperial' nationalism showed a generalized crisis of nerves in the major powers, 'small' or 'anti-imperial' nationalisms spoke increasingly about their alleged right to self-determination, a doctrine of United States' ancestry given international recognition only with President Woodrow Wilson's 'Fourteen Points' in 1918. In the Spanish context, independentist ideas from the Antilles quickly followed an obvious connecting route and sprouted imitations in the Canary Islands, or at least among island emigrants in the Caribbean. Similarly, Catalan, Galician and Basque immigrant associations in Cuba and on the American mainland were inspired to copy the prevailing discourse of national self-determination common to almost all nationalisms in the Western Hemisphere and apply it to the nostalgic memories of the 'old country', in turn influencing metropolitan currents, until then more preoccupied with the defence of local rights and traditions. At the same time, however, racist themes also worked their way into anti-Spanish peninsular nationalisms, as they already had into dominant '*españolismo*'.

The experience of colonial civil war brought the new emotional mode of nationalism into peninsular politics. European influences were present, but played only a secondary role. The Cuban war in particular set off a dynamic of mutual antagonism, clearly visible by the 1890s, between the institutionally-minded official discourse of Spanish liberal-nationalism, built on institutional mechanics, and the emotional reply of nationalisms based on the search for identity. Colonial wars polarized what heretofore had been a debate between politicians, turning it into a potentially violent conflict between the officer corps, viscerally united after struggling incessantly against separatists, and the new alternative nationalist movements in the industrialized metropolitan regions. Hereafter, overwrought Spanish nationalism and its equally overwrought competitors fed off each other with a passion.

The Cuban war of 1868–78 had many long term implications. In metropolitan Spain, the conflicts led by left republicans in 1873–74, with the disastrous experience of the 'cantons', burned out the more abstract notions of self-determination that American influences incorporated into the Hispanic federalist tradition and marginalized its paladins, such as Pi i Margall. Nevertheless, since the underlying particularist impulses remained alive and well in Spanish society, the fate of federalism encouraged an ideological evolution toward more nationalist ideas of secession. A civil-war political culture, fed by both peninsular and colonial conflicts, encouraged the progressive redefinition of ideological attitudes surrounding identity: if citizenship was unavailable in any meaningful way for individuals, then the link between personal and collective selfhood served as a useful alternative, especially when the *fin de siècle* mix of heady racism from a more economically developed Europe legitimized such arguments with a scientific gloss and when Antillean race-feeling gave the whole business a hidden kick.

By the time the liberal government offered Autonomy Statutes to the Antilles in 1897, Cuba had been in revolt for two years. Delayed manumission of slaves only served to mix the implications of universal suffrage and full legal citizenship with an imperial and racist context that had thrived on postponing problems until violence broke out. Accordingly, the armed forces, especially the army, loomed behind the discussion on revision of state organization in the 1880s. External pressure on the often tenuously-held Spanish empire only worsened the deadlock between reformers and uncompromising defenders of unity at all costs.

No substantial reorganization of the administration could be carried out in the face of a Cuban nationalism that enjoyed implicit American support. This virtual veto of 'unconditional' interests in Cuba conditioned Spanish politics right up to autonomy for Cuba and Puerto Rico on the eve of the 'disaster'. Given the delays, Cuban independentism won over much of autonomist opinion with the expectation of United States' intervention.

Filipino nationalism, when it suddenly became a physical presence in the mid-1890s, was even more difficult for Spanish opinion to deal with than anything that had happened in Cuba. The novels of Dr Rizal, the founder and martyr of the Filipino cause, had asked for little more than access for Manila 'mestizos' to education in Spanish in the archipelago and some measure of promotion at the expense of priestly and military power. The garrison mentality of the Spanish army in the Philippines, little accustomed to any challenge beyond a disdained revolt of local troops in 1872 and semi-permanent troubles with the Moslems of Mindanao, dealt with such subversion by summary execution. The revolt led by Aguinaldo in 1896 produced even more vehement howls about masonic plots (and in fact the Katipunan, the Filipino party, was a semi-masonic organization). Faced with the need to deal with separatist revolts on two fronts a world apart, Spanish militarist propaganda could come up with no ideology better than the defence of Throne and Altar, a harkening back to Carlist truisms that boded ill for a traditionally liberal officer corps. Peninsular republicans, freemasons and anticlericals themselves, always hopeful of army intervention in their favour, were reduced to defending a patriotic perimeter of statehood, insisting on the Spanishness of the Antilles or the Philippines, while stressing the importance of civil liberties and a citizenship which had no meaning in the 'overseas territories', with the partial exception of Puerto Rico.

Thus, in the mid-1890s, the independentist explosions in Cuba and the Philippines gave free rein to hawkish and repressive solutions. In Cuba, the new commander, General Valeriano Weyler, was anxious to put into practice extreme anti-guerrilla measures: reconcentration of rural populations under military control, isolation of enemy groups, free-fire zones crisscrossed by patrols, all of which earned him the sobriquet of 'butcher' in the American sensationalist press and the respect of other professionals, like Britain's Lord Kitchener, who later would apply the same methods more effectively in South Africa. The entry of the United States into the Cuban struggle – the Americans' 'splendid little war' – produced a rapid military humiliation that annulled Spain as a power and brought the loss of her 'overseas territories' outside of Africa. The conflict began over the 'Cuban question', which had been a major reference point in American policy for over half a century, but President McKinley decided to include the Philippines among US war demands in reply to domestic opinion.

Perhaps the best illustration of the crushing nature of the defeat was the American conquest of Guam, in the Marianas. A light cruiser from Admiral Dewey's China squadron split off and headed for the island; upon arrival, the ship fired a salvo, and promptly was hailed by a representative of the governor, who profusely thanked the American captain for his salute to the Spanish flag but regretted that the small post lacked enough gunpowder for the reply protocol demanded.

Heretofore, the Cuban wars had been almost impossible to win, but Spanish arms had at least held their own. The diplomatic manoeuvrings of the Sagasta government while coping with American war fever did nothing to prepare Spanish opinion for the extent and depth of the defeat. On the contrary, militaristic nationalism dominated the internal comment; even the republican press in Barcelona ran doggerel that assured readers that a mature country like Spain, with centuries of warfare at her back, would quickly whip the inept 'sausage makers of Chicago'. The news of the naval rout off Santiago triggered panic in anticipation of American bombardment or invasion in some coastal areas like Mallorca.

The defeat of 1898, thus, was a psychological watershed, literally brought home with the traumatic disembarkment of the gaunt veterans of the conflict in the months that followed the hasty peace signed in Paris. The following years saw the military at their lowest prestige, with taunts and insults filling the opposition press, especially the publications of the new, rival nationalisms. Spanish officers, bitter at such treatment, tended toward a 'stab in the back' theory that argued that the true responsibility should be laid upon the Liberals, whose government led the war politically, and not upon those who had to do the fighting. An artillery officer like Francesc Macià, future leader of Catalan independentism, actually began his political career in indignation at the failure of the liberals to back the armed forces. Accordingly, the new nationalisms in Bilbao and Barcelona tended to see Teddy Roosevelt as the model most suitable for curing Spanish decadence and oppression – to them Spain exemplified the subjection of dynamic peoples at the hands of a ruined elite led by an inefficient military.

Spain's 'Disaster of 1898' thus fits into the chain of international imperialist rivalries and débâcles that dominated the 1890s. The consequences of such similar 'national crises' included public questioning of the existing political system, the increased visibility of working-class protest, and, last but not least, the rediscovery of the roots of national identity by new 'generations' of 'intellectuals' (this last a concept which arose in France at precisely that time). The so-called 'Generation of 1898' in Spain – like the 'Generation of 1890' in Portugal, the new nationalism of Maurice Barrès and Charles Maurras in France or the Italian 'Generation of 1905', among others – was really a loose-knit group of writers who represented a mood of revival, a call for the renewal of national energies and a patent disgust for the political 'truths' of late-nineteenth century thought. In social terms, the appearance of such critical 'intellectuals' throughout Europe was the result of the spread of the popular press, the formation of new cultural markets which permitted more authors to earn some kind of livelihood from freelance writing, and the progressive loss of control of the media by previously powerful newspaper editors and the lawyer–politicians who had run the press until then. Nationalist discourse, therefore, was in large measure an adjustment to changing opportunities for social advancement in an ever more urban and literate society. But 'intellectuals', although the most visible, were not by any means the only social sector to reflect an ambition for advancement by way of noisy ideological redefinition (see chapter 10).

The new Spanish nationalism or '*españolismo*' was linked to an equally new militarism, both products of the Cuban civil war and the ultrapatriotic, fiercely anti-separatist 'Voluntarios'. These notorious volunteer units composed of peninsular immigrants had backed army warmongers and formed the hardcore resistance to independentism and even autonomy from the 1860s to 1898. '*Españolismo*' stressed selfhood as the core of any programme to 'awaken' Spain from a lethargy increasingly blamed on the divisive tensions that liberal revolution had wrought. The practice of insubordination that had made the volunteers a decisive pressure group in colonial Havana was easily transferred to metropolitan life, even before 1898. The increasing attraction of burning or ransacking the offices of opposition newspapers was one such import, practiced in the mid-1890s, although the most famous instance would take place in Barcelona in 1905.

This kind of politicized semi-mutiny was qualitatively different from the earlier nineteenth-century militarism: then generals had sought power and had showered patronage on their supporters; now junior officers were challenging not merely civilian leaders, but also their own chain of command. The main thrust of the Cánovas transition and the settlement that had so favoured the liberals was to kick the generals out of the job of changing governments. This was achieved by the subtle technique of bringing the more outstanding army men into active politics, in part by judicious use of the king's prerogative to name senators. The younger veterans broke this comfortable arrangement, in the name of patriotism.

In 1905 the officers of the Barcelona garrison ransacked the offices of ¡*Cu-Cut!*, a Catalan periodical that had published a series of woundingly satirical anti-military cartoons. Their main goal was less to silence local anti-Spanish agitation than to break the will of the government and impose their own demands on the military hierarchy. They succeeded in both. Their action led to the Law of Jurisdictions (1906) which made press offences against the symbols of state subject to military rather than civilian courts. This foreshadowed a political future that was definitively troubled. With any slippage of liberal institutions, especially parliament, the defeated army, the self-proclaimed champion of extreme nationalism, could offer itself as an alternative to the jabbering politicians and the failure of 'partitocracy'. Military nationalists also appealed directly to the new king, Alfonso XIII, crowned in 1902, who did not seem averse to their affections.

The new competitor nationalisms formulated their alternatives to 'Spanishism' and its officer paladins in equally radical terms. The Cuban conflict had proven not only inextinguishable but contagious, and transformed constitutional, institutional discussion into an inexplicable redefinition of just what Spain was, as well as who should pick up the pieces. The 'problem of Spain', thus came full circle. Catalan and Basque nationalism now gathered on all sides of the historic conflict: if Spain was an empire, it was not a nation, but rather an oppressor of nations. If democracy was representation in the future, such citizenship should be realized in terms of historic parts, like Cuba, not of an outdated superstructure. Finally, such Catalan and Basque demands were formulated with the explicit idea that liberalism had merely been a last-minute try to give the dead husk of empire an appearance of life, typical of the outmoded proposals of liberals, full of fine talk of progress, which the end of the century was revealing to be hollow.

The success of the wars of national liberation in the colonies logically hardened nationalist responses. The antecedent to exalted Spanish nationalism had been the Moroccan War of 1859–60: the last victory of Spanish arms before the crushing humiliation of 1898. A small African triumph became the guiding light for the new militarist nationalism, locked into a dependency on French expansionism in the Mahgreb which would blossom as a full love–hate relation with all things Gallic, while the Spanish left – liberal, republican and working-class – all derived their inspiration from France and functioned within Jacobin parameters. With imperial collapse, Spanish leftists assumed the banner of unitary nationalism as the guide to democracy and, eventually, to progress and international recognition, in different ways.

If the militarists would not abandon the idea of empire and were partisans of a reborn 'Greater Spain', the patriotic left, as ever in French mould, took on the army as its major enemy in the years between the Dreyfus affair, which was at its height in 1898, and the separation of Church and State (1902–05). Accordingly, the left assumed a 'little Spain' outlook and dedicated itself to an exaltation of Spanish self-discovery. If the militarists wanted to regain a sense of outer projection of the state as a way of renewing nationhood, and thereby developing mass participation in public affairs, the left rejected anything but the exploration of inner space, the forgotten Spain that was the 'origin of the race'. This meant rejecting nineteenth-century stereotypes based on Andalucia (see Introduction), and emotionally exploring the dry Castilian countryside from whence everything worthwhile in Spanish history had once sprung. The great contribution of the writers of the so-called 'Generation of 1898' was really a 'little Castilian' perspective on an inward-looking, small-scale Spain, whose dreams corresponded to her resources. While some of the founding figures of this new left, such as Joaquín Costa, might have a soft spot for 'Africanism', the main drift of the reply to militarism rejected any appeal that was not to 'national policy' understood as exclusively internal development. Their point was that the best policy of identity and nation-building consisted in more and better schools, rather than a brighter place in the sun. The major difficulty was that there were other ways to turn inward.

The tension between inward- and outward-looking policies was also crucial for the nationalisms that arose in competition to Spanish identity. 'Catalanism' developed in a way that led to ever more explicit participation in elections: the 'apolitical' Unió Catalanista (founded in 1891) gave way to the Lliga Regionalista, which was born in 1901, and which, after barging into parliament in the 1901 elections, began to take a key role in local institutions such as Barcelona's municipal government or the provincial council and the limited 'home rule' Mancomunidad after 1914. With greater reluctance, Basque nationalists in Sabino Arana's Partido Nacionalista Vasco, formally constituted in 1895, also began to penetrate local office and, after 1911, to contest general elections.

In both cases, this step away from ideological purity towards political realism also meant dealing with a permanent series of ambiguities that exacted an important cost. Competing nationalisms were fundamentally anti-Spanish, yet they were acting in the Spanish political arena; thus they incorporated activists and sympathizers who were nationalists and others who were merely regionalists. By going for public office in town and provincial administrations on an anticorruption, pro-reform platform while defending an extreme doctrine of nationalist purity, both movements encouraged the formation of a practical wing, ever more willing to intervene in state politics (especially with the cherished theme of revamping local administration), and a hard line, permanently on guard against the taint of statist infection. Eventually, in the Basque case after 1921, and in 1919–23 among Catalanists, the movements split into separate, rival currents, much as Spanish nationalism was divided between the 'Greater Spain' militarist right and the 'Little Spain' left.

Nationalist contagion: urbanization, intellectuals and a service society

In the nineteenth century as before, Madrid was the focal point of social promotion, the mecca for all ambitious youth from the provinces. The rise of Barcelona as the capital of the industrial revolution in Spain made it a sort of alternative to such a central market of the vanities. The Catalan city had achieved Madrid's demographic size by mid-century and for over a hundred years the two cities would be locked in a bitter race for pre-eminence, the embodiment of the rivalry between political and economic power. The urban duel reinforced the centralism of political discourse arising in Madrid, which reflected the relative insecurity of an inefficient administration which pretended to overcome its deficiencies by a certain ferocity of tone and a fondness for harsh executive measures and police action. By way of reply, Barcelona became an anti-capital where any expression of radical dissent was sure to find some kind of haven. In essence, such discontents tended to coalesce around a zero-sum game for Spain, whereby Barcelona's claims would be recognized at the expense of Madrid's pretensions.

Fullblown Catalan nationalism, which had emerged by the late 1880s and early 1890s, became the clearest manifestation of such sentiments: rather than explicit independentism, 'Catalanism' leaned towards a formula on the Austro-Hungarian model or, for those who were more moderate, a monarchical federalism along the lines of Bavaria within the Kaiser's Germany. In contrast, other nationalisms remained mired in the contradictions between leading regional centres. Bilbao, itself really a conurbation rather than a single city, was never really recognized by other Basque cities as the local capital; in the same way none of the Galician towns was willing to yield to the pretensions of its rivals.

All anti-Spanish nationalisms were in fact a complex mixture of reactions between local, 'internal' migration and the arrival of outsiders. This led to a visceral racism at the root of Basque nationalism. In Galicia, with emigration from the region to Madrid, Cuba or Argentina as the dominant trend, the doctrinal pull was more diffuse. In Catalonia, however, with a major capital city rival to Madrid, nationalism reflected the tension between opposed migrations by a combination of linguistic affirmation (which permitted newcomers entry by simply speaking the local language instead of Spanish) and a preoccupation with demography (which led to the less fertile Catalans being urged to raise their birthrate). Regionalism became the equivalent recourse of those areas that could not affirm 'differential traits' such as race or language. In those cases, urban rivalry became a call for compensation in the face of alleged nationalist greed within a Spain willing to give similar treatment to all cities and communities. In all cases, however, the role of growing urban markets created rivalries between cities. As a result, regional cleavages took on more or less intensity depending on the demands being generated locally for greater social promotion, for more education, more access to bureaucracy and more recognition of the relevance of local networks.

The overall expansion of the Spanish urban system therefore had multiple cultural implications. Urban development, including the destruction of city walls and the construction of new districts (*ensanches*), confirmed cities as points of attraction for both skilled and unskilled labour. Similarly, urbanization gave increasing protagonism to new groups, who proclaimed the virtues of a new, modern life-style which would sweep away the backwardness of an allegedly unchanging agrarian society. An urban way of life, however, looked beyond mere industrialization to the service society, with the idea that the state should be an active model for such change (see chapter 6). Any expansion of public welfare automatically meant more public servants. Therefore, any serious reform of the state, especially in the direction of offering more and better services, meant a debate over the nature of bureaucracy and, ultimately, about what kind of nation was being built: a republican People or a Catholic faithful? Administered by whom: Spanish or Catalan functionaries? What special opportunities were there for youth? Or finally, to pose a question that was formulated seriously only after the First World War: just men or also women?

After the traumatic turn of the century, nation-building in Spain was universally called 'regeneration', by which most commentators meant a genuine national revival to realize what the liberal revolution had left undone. The hurried changeover in 1902 from the regency of the queen-mother to her sixteen-year-old son, King Alfonso XIII, seemed to echo such sentiments. With its overtly biological meaning, 'regeneration' was to bring Spain into the modern world, refuting all those who claimed that it was a hopeless, decadent and regressive society or that the Spanish 'race' was beyond all recovery. There was equally general agreement that the impulse for rebirth would come from the cities, although there was some dispute as to whether vitality lay in an outstanding industrial metropolis like Barcelona or in smaller provincial capitals, purportedly full of untapped human resources.

The diverse 'modernisms' that shook Spanish cultural life from the turn of the century onward were a direct expression of the fusion of urban demands for representation and meritocratic jobs and the interconnected requirements of an incipient consumerism. Especially when seen from Madrid, democratic rights were not merely a question of eliminating *caciquismo* but also one of cultural politics. Spaniards, the left argued with growing aggressiveness, would have to be taught civics in schools that were still unbuilt. This was the greatest sin, the prime failure of liberal reformism. In leaning towards the Church, conservatives were incapable of even understanding the nature of the problem. From Barcelona, the growing expansion of literary Catalanism was inseparable from its mutation into a political movement: any push towards linguistic Catalanization (together with the lexical and grammatical standardization of the language, successfully realized by Pompeu Fabra in 1913–18) meant the provision of public services, especially education, in Catalan, a direct rebuttal of the liberal tradition of unified standards.

The 'Restoration' had represented the triumph, more apparent than real, of lawyers over soldiers, but when the military failure in 1898 landed on the lawmongers' lap, the officer corps claimed to be yet another party injured by scheming politicos. Everyone accepted that Spain was governed by an 'oligarchy' which used electoral fraud to stay in power. This was true, in one way or another, of most of the existing parliamentary systems, but the idea, especially as expressed in Costa's 1901 *Oligarquía y caciquismo*, provoked lamentations over Spain's exceptional backwardness and provided a conceptual meeting-point for protest politics of the left and right, even of Spanish nationalists with their Catalan or Basque competitors.

The attack on the elite of the liberal professions came from the hoards of less successful law graduates, of minor journalists and of unknown writers who envied even these. The demand to open up the political system hinged on turning the bureaucracy into a civil service: democratized meritocracy against the exclusivism of the few who had 'made it'. Military men could agree with such an idea and even purport to lead it, but it was the journalists and educators who became the standardbearers of the new message, leading a mass of schoolteachers dedicated to the proselytism of radical democratic or '*obrerista*' values.

The dynastic parties found themselves increasingly unable to keep up with the organizational changes their position as constitutional instruments required. The rotation between liberals and conservatives took for granted that other forces could be 'transformed' slowly, with individual leaders drawn away from anti-system protest by the lure of 'real' politics. The shock of imperial defeat destroyed the calm required for this process and, after the turn of the century, antisystem criticism harped insistently on electoral fraud and called for a drastic, almost apocalyptic, renewal. In the face of even such extreme calls for change, the dynastic parties were unable to change themselves, from congeries of 'notables' and their clients to modern electoral machines, with large memberships and a network of street-wise, local entities. Republicans, and even Carlists, had painfully achieved this transformation in the 1890s; accordingly, both were anxious to disassociate themselves from insurrection. Ultimately, the two constitutional parties would fall apart under this pressure, parliament would cease to be an effective legislative tool, and King Alfonso XIII would become ever more involved in cabinet combinations, with the army looming as the possible reply to parliamentary failure (see chapter 12).

In many ways, the greatest success story in this process was the Catalan Lliga Regionalista. Operating out of Barcelona, the Lliga managed to establish a working monopoly of 'Catalan' discourse, but it had a hard time breaking the hold liberals and conservatives had on much of rural Catalonia. Nevertheless, the Lliga's greatest success came from presenting itself as a serious alternative, not so much to liberalism or to the parties as to the political system itself, all the while working within it. Its leading figure, Enric Prat de la Riba, achieved control of the administration of Barcelona province in 1908 and turned it into a power base from which flowed all manner of cultural initiatives. The attack on the Lliga's papers by officers of the Barcelona garrison in 1905 was countenanced by two successive liberal governments. This led the regionalist party to put together 'Solidaritat Catalana' or 'Catalan Solidarity', a surprising coalition of opposition parties from the Carlists to a part of the republicans, joined in a fear of the Law of Jurisdictions. 'Solidaritat' proved victorious in the 1907 elections, sending to parliament a 'Catalan delegation' whose spokesman, Francesc Cambó, became a leading figure in Madrid for almost thirty years.

Lliga leaders like Prat de la Riba or Cambó may have been lawyers, but they were also essentially outsiders of rural origins (Cambó was the son of rich peasants) who triumphed by imposing themselves on the Barcelona bourgeoisie. Similarly, their fiercest local enemies, the left republicans and 'españolistas' of Lerroux's Radical Party, which emerged in 1906–08 in opposition to 'Solidaritat', were also penniless, immigrant lawyers for whom Barcelona was a city of opportunities. Others, like Lerroux himself, were journalists who took to the bar as soon as he was able. All the new organizations that definitively transformed Spanish politics between 1906 and 1907 made proposals for increasing social mobility: they all appealed to new urban clienteles by promising them the key to the future in abstract or ideological terms and with very practical appeals for collective promotion.

Accordingly, Lerroux pretended to supersede the old formula of a 'republican union' with a new French-style 'radicalism' which signalled the appearance of new immigrant, liberal professionals willing to lead school teachers and workers in the transformation of Barcelona into a 'democratic' and 'wholly Spanish' city of open opportunity. In a similar vein, novelist Vicente Blasco Ibáñez's Valencia republicans advocated the triumph of the 'progressive' city, capable of turning peasants into businessmen, against the unreformed Catholic rural hinterland. The same was true of their rivals: the Lliga represented the renovation of Barcelona's bourgeoisie under the direction of migrants from other parts of Catalonia anxious to redefine the parameters of social ascendancy in Spain's economic capital by applying the techniques of private practice to public service. Finally, the anarchosyndicalist reply to 'Catalan Solidarity', 'Solidaridad Obrera' (or 'Workers' Solidarity'), which also appeared in Barcelona in 1907, promised the control of the future directly to the most literate, ambitious and upwardly mobile among unskilled labourers. Radiating out from Madrid, the Socialists made even more explicit the capacity of well-established trades like railway men or printers to lead the disciplined working class to a meeting of minds with the new service industries. Although it later matured as a social movement, Basque nationalism would also present itself as a mechanism for controlling social promotion. Very much a reaction against rapid and savage industrialization and the immigration it prompted, Basque nationalism called for the segregation and expulsion of non-Basque racial elements, while protecting local migrants in the name of preserving religious tradition.

Conclusion

The post-liberal, or even antiliberal, nationalisms claimed to go beyond liberalism in the name of an 'authenticity' based on 'difference'. Even the new Spanish nationalism that arose at the end of the century wanted to assume Spain's 'different' nature. All so-called 'regenerationist projects', Catalan and Basque as well as Spanish, rejected liberalism in the name of something less artificial. Only Santiago Alba, in some sense Costa's heir, tried to renew Spanish nationalism by working within the liberal paradigm; only Andalucian nationalism, a movement born in the 1910s calling itself 'liberalist', considered itself to be in some sense an heir to liberalism. By the end of the First World War, 'regenerationism' itself was dead, regionalisms were increasingly replaced by competing nationalisms and republicans everywhere were trailing behind the lofty aspirations of the 'workerists'.

In the face of so much literature lamenting the grevious exceptionalism of Spanish politics, it should be noted that moving from a liberal system to rough hewn democracy was a Europe-wide problem. It can even be argued that this very problem was an important reason for the frivolity with which many political leaders made the decision to go to war in August 1914. Even in Britain, for all the reforming zeal of David Lloyd George, the Liberal government failed to meet the challenge of labourism, women's suffrage and Irish (including Unionist) pressure. In fact, the Liberal Party itself did not survive the long term challenge of adaptation after the passage though the Great War.

In spite of its neutrality, the First World War had an enormous impact on Spanish society (see chapter 12). Proximity to the European conflict, plus a small war of her own in the recently-acquired Moroccan protectorate, imposed the reordering of Spain's capitalist structure, while at the same time overloading the mechanisms of politics, altering labour sociology, and changing the style of ideological confrontation in the major cities. A struggle to determine the direction of economic growth and which social sectors should pay the price of change emerged and would continue for 25 years, up to the end of the Civil War of 1936–39.

|9|

The emerging challenge of mass politics

PAMELA BETH RADCLIFF

One of the major themes of late nineteenth and early twentieth century western European history is the emerging political role of the 'masses' and the challenge that this mobilization posed to the oligarchic liberalism of the nineteenth century. While in theory liberalism espoused universal citizenship, in practice, property, race and gender qualifications limited citizenship and political access to an elite few. Over the course of the nineteenth century, groups excluded from this elite ruling class, from poor men to women, mobilized against this exclusion. The challenge for the liberal state was to achieve a delicate balance of integration, accommodation and repression that would neutralize or channel this mobilization while protecting and democratizing basic liberal institutions. Those that failed to achieve this balance would become vulnerable to attacks from mass mobilizing forces on both the left and the right, i.e., primarily communism and fascism.

Despite the prevailing image of Restoration apathy and stagnation, significant oppositional movements emerged outside the formal institutions of the regime, where they laid the groundwork for the eventual collapse of the Restoration and the democratic experiment of the 1930s.

The Restoration regime and mass politics

Spanish liberalism has been traditionally portrayed as uniquely unresponsive to the challenge of mass politics. In particular, the early Restoration regime (1875–1914) has been viewed as a highly oligarchic, 'managed' political system, in which true pluralism continued to be sacrificed in exchange for stability and order. After the disastrous experiment in democratic mass mobilization under the First Republic (1873–74), the Restoration followed as a reaction to, and a defence against, further outbursts of uncontrolled popular political fervour.

From this perspective, historians accepted that 'politics' under the early

Restoration was controlled by a cadre of elites. In turn, the exclusivism of the Restoration regime appeared to provide powerful evidence for the weakness of Spanish liberalism and thus its marginalization from the rest of western European civilization. Compared to the increasingly expansive and contested liberalism of Britain after the Second Reform Bill (1867) and France after the establishment of the Third Republic (1871), Spain's early Restoration regime seemed both uniquely unyielding and politically enervated.

While many of the details of the Restoration's oligarchic liberalism cannot be disputed, this overall portrait of political apathy and stagnation has been overstated. Thus, while it is true that official Restoration politics was designed to minimize unchannelled mass participation, it was not an entirely closed or repressive system. Although the regime did attempt (with mixed success) to suppress certain forms of mass politics, it also created a framework of basic liberal freedoms, including guarantees of freedom of the press and association and the crowning glory of universal male suffrage (1890), that opened up a broader space of political contestation. Protected and encouraged by these rights, segments of the excluded 'masses' used this space to organize and exercise their collective voices in what would become a multi-faceted challenge to the Restoration.

Thus, the Restoration's role in the emergence of mass politics was a paradoxical one. On the one hand, many of the institutions and mechanisms of the regime acted to control or suppress mass political participation; on the other hand, the liberal identity (epitomized by the press and suffrage laws) embraced by the regime provided a space in which mobilization could occur on the margins of the narrow realm of official politics. The end result was mixed. Through the regime's repressive and manipulative techniques, the elites maintained their nearly exclusive access to formal power. However, the mobilization that sprouted in the cracks of the system opened up a larger political arena where forms of mass politics could develop. Whether or not these movements aimed to reform or overthrow the Restoration regime, the proliferation of 'unmanaged' mobilization undermined the long-term stability of a regime whose survival depended on widespread apathy and passivity. In other words, whatever the specific content of the protests, the fact of mobilization itself constituted a political challenge.

Social and economic context for mass mobilization

While the Restoration system provided the ambivalent political space .for mass mobilization, Spain's changing economic and social landscape helped shape the forms it took. The relationship between social and economic change and political mobilization is not a direct one, but significant social and economic transformations that threaten to uproot people from their old ways of life, push them into contact with new ideas and environments, and present them with novel survival challenges often do generate political mobilization.

Spain's social and economic transformation paralleled that of other western European countries, but it was slower and more regionally uneven than in the most industrialized nations. Thus, by the early twentieth century, while a majority of the population still worked in agriculture and lived in rural settings, a significant minority of the population were employed in industrial and service jobs and resided in expanding urban areas. Much of the urban industrial population was concentrated in three regions of the country: Asturias, Vizcaya (the Basque Country) and Catalonia. As in other countries, these urban, industrial areas were often the locus of new forms of mass mobilization such as trade unions and populist political parties, as well as older forms of collective action like consumer riots. By the early twentieth century, this mobilization was beginning to break the hold of *caciquismo* in urban centres, as local bosses lost control of increasingly pluralistic environments.

However, mass mobilization was not confined exclusively to these urban industrial settings. Although the Spanish countryside had been historically quiescent, especially compared to its French counterpart, from the late nineteenth century agrarian revolts became an increasingly common feature of the political landscape. The root of this new activism lay in the dramatic social and economic transformation of the countryside that occurred over the middle decades of the nineteenth century. The long process of disentailment was intended to consolidate the liberal principle of private property and motivate the new owners to invest in and improve their land. While the transfer of land resulted in some increased productivity, it also had the effect of worsening the condition of the poorest sector of the farming population, the landless labourers, or *braceros*.

Concentrated heavily in the south and west, which were dominated by huge estates called *latifundia*, the *braceros* had always eked out a marginal existence. What made their situation more tenuous, however, was the loss of municipal common lands that had acted as a buffer against seasonal unemployment and perennially low wages. In addition, historians have argued that the new liberal property relationships erased the vestiges of an older paternalistic model of employer/employee relations that had blunted the edge of worker discontent. Thus, the economic and social changes in the agrarian sector created a fertile context for the intensification of mass mobilization at the end of the nineteenth century.

Interpreting mass mobilization

Within this political and economic framework, various forms of mass mobilization evolved, but they all shared several characteristics. First, they were united by their appeal to the lower classes, and often specifically to the working class. In traditional Marxist terms, this political fault line between rich and poor was explained as the fruit of class struggle, an inevitable conflict grounded in the contradictions of capitalism. Instead, I argue that the emergence of mass politics can be understood as a more general post-Enlightenment conflict between the political and economic elites who controlled access to power (while claiming universal access) and those who felt actively excluded from such power. Within this conflict, I would identify class as an important axis around which mass mobilization and politicization in the industrializing world occurred, but not as its exclusive source. In addition to class, other axes of solidarity revolved around neighbourhoods, gendered sociability patterns, and the 'networks of debt' established between shopkeepers and their poor clients. These axes were linked by social and economic ties, but not necessarily by strict class identity. The result is a more complex arena of politicization that yields a richer portrait of the diverse forms of mass mobilization.

In addition to the general appeal to the lower classes, the diverse forms of mobilization shared another important characteristic that helps explain their marginalization in traditional political histories of the period. That is, all of these oppositional movements were most successful in mobilizing the 'masses' outside the framework of national political institutions. Given the context of the Restoration, in which access to formal power was limited, it follows that mobilization was likely to occur outside the channels of the formal political system, either in 'direct action' appeals or in the less restricted arena of the liberal public sphere. This mobilization has often been neglected by a conventional political model that emphasizes electoral impact and the ability to shape governmental policy. Thus, a full understanding of the dimensions of mass mobilization requires a more inclusive definition of politics that encompasses a broader arena of struggle.

Moreover, such mobilization was most likely to emerge out of local rather than national political dynamics. Thus, most forms of mass politics under the Restoration were essentially local in scope, and even into the 1930s, the political centre of gravity for mass politics remained at the local level. The result was a clear gap between local political cultures, especially in the emerging urban centres, and their national counterpart. While the national political culture remained elitist, cities around the country developed well-articulated oppositional cultures that injected pluralism and mass participation into their local political arenas. Not surprisingly, it was in these cities that the *caciquista* system first began to break down and where the foundations for the Second Republic were being laid.

Although this more vibrant political culture was limited largely to the minority urban centres, and thus could be contained within the rural-dominated Restoration regime, the accelerating growth of cities in the early twentieth century resulted in a subtle shift in power relations by the 1930s. After decades of local-level transformation, the national consequences of this shift would become suddenly apparent in the dramatic April 1931 election, when the urban vote against the monarchy convinced Alfonso XIII that he should abdicate the throne. While to many this vote seemed like a sudden shift of opinion, in fact oppositional groups had been preparing the ground at the local level for decades before finally breaking the surface of national politics.

Within this common framework of mobilization, we can identify several oppositional traditions that challenged the elite nature of nineteenth century liberalism. The first tradition was embodied in the republican movement, which sought to democratize liberalism by integrating the masses through a more inclusive notion of citizenship. Thus, Spanish republicans, like their French counterparts, sought to mobilize the masses within a cross-class alliance that could undermine the lingering hegemony of a monarchist/ clerical elite and provide the foundation for a strong, liberal democratic state. As such, the republicans operated in a liminal area between the official political realm and the arena of popular politics. The second tradition was embodied in the competing anarchist and socialist labour movements, which sought to mobilize workers through appeals to class solidarity and visions of a radically egalitarian alternative to liberalism. And finally, in contrast to the other two, the third tradition was dominated by women, an informal consumer politics that challenged the 'hands off' economic policies of the liberal state with its radical direct action.

Republicanism and mass politics, 1875–1914

At first glance, late nineteenth century Spanish republicanism appears to be far removed from the world of mass politics. In fact, republicans were such a marginal force in the official political life of the Restoration that they have been virtually ignored in the historiography of the period until recently. General texts on the period focus on the sterile infighting between the major republican groups and their leaders and point to their dismal electoral showing in national elections. The problem with these accounts is that they equate the failure to carve out an important space within the official political realm with a lack of influence on political life, more broadly conceived. By extension, the republicans' ambition to foment a new kind of mass politics was not taken seriously by historians who had written them off as non-players. Following this logic, it was easy to assume that liberalism in Spain put down few roots among the masses, thus paving the road for inevitable polarization.

This traditional view of republicanism relied on two basic assumptions: that it .was a marginal political force, and that, as a 'bourgeois' liberal movement, it had already lost the working classes to anarchism and socialism. Neither assumption, however, has stood up to the combined assault of recent research and, equally important, new ways of thinking about politics.

As a result, I would argue that Spanish republicanism played a fundamental role in the formation of a mass political culture in the late nineteenth and early twentieth centuries.

Within a traditional definition of politics, there is no question as to its marginal status. Republican parties never managed to upset the managed alternation of power between the Conservatives and the Liberals that defined the entire Restoration. Moreover, republicans never posed even a vague electoral threat to this system. Between 1875 and 1890, they won a measly 3.34 per cent of all parliamentary seats. Significantly, even after the passage of universal male suffrage in 1890, the republicans captured an average of about only 30 seats, or 6 per cent of the Cortes. Thus, at the level of national political power, the Restoration mechanisms of exclusion effectively neutralized republicanism as a democratizing force.

This marginalization was exacerbated by the organizational weakness and internal divisions of the republican movement. After the collapse of the First Republic, republicans split into a number of competing parties, each orbiting around its own national leader. The factions did divide over substantive issues, such as centralism vs. federalism, and political vs. social democracy, but such debates tended to get lost in the virulence of personal attacks. As a result, the parties rarely achieved an electoral alliance, let alone a coherent oppositional platform. After the turn of the century, a new generation of republican leaders like Alejandro Lerroux and Melquíades Alvarez sought to renovate the movement, but their 'new' republican parties still failed to crack the ceiling of national political power.

To get a fuller picture of republican influence on mass political culture it is necessary to go beyond a conventional 'top down' approach to political history. To begin with, the focus on national politics underestimates republican presence at the local level, which was the real source of its strength. In fact, given the divisions and disorganization at the national level, it could be argued that republicanism was virtually a local phenomenon, and more specifically, a local urban phenomenon. Evidence of republican strength can be found in the results of municipal elections after 1890, where the first cracks in the *cacique* system surfaced. Thus, republicans won 16 per cent of the seats on city councils in 1903, and the majority in a growing number of cities over the next two decades. In many cities, republicans virtually took over the local political establishments, as with Lerroux's Radicals in Barcelona, Alvarez' Reformists in Oviedo, and the Blasquistas in Valencia.

Nevertheless, local electoral victories had limited impact, given the centralized nature of Restoration politics. Between the appointed mayors and provincial governors, the civil guards and the military units stationed in urban areas around the country, even republican-dominated city councils had little room in which to stake out an independent course. If we look, however, to the broader arena of hegemonic struggle, the picture is quite different. It was in this broader contest over competing systems of power and legitimacy that the republicans carved out a powerful space, articulating an oppositional paradigm of the social order that was crucial to undermining the 'total social authority' of the Ancien Regime.[1]

They articulated this oppositional paradigm in the public sphere, the space between society and the state in which voluntary 'publics' struggled to assert their competing visions of the world. It is this powerful presence in the public sphere that most clearly exposes the internal contradictions of the Restoration system. While the regime manipulated elections to control access to formal power, it defended the basic liberal reforms of freedom of press and association that opened up access to the public sphere. Thus, the Restoration implicitly encouraged the formation of a thriving public sphere that provided an alternative space for mass mobilization.

The rise of the public sphere is associated with the growth of urban culture, which includes not only the press but all the institutions of urban sociability like concert halls, theatres, cafes, voluntary associations and bullrings. It is this local process, which takes off in scattered urban centres in the late nineteenth century, in which the republican movement was deeply involved. Through its press, its voluntary associations and their activities, republicanism played a central role in constructing an independent political life that flourished outside the restrictions of formal political institutions. In the process, it introduced its oppositional paradigm into the public discourse, where it muddied the clarity of the dominant hegemonic framework.

Republicanism could have this impact because it was much more than an electoral movement dedicated to installing a new regime. In the words of José Alvarez Junco, 'more than a simple current of opinion or a political party, republicanism was an entire conception of the universe, a collection of beliefs about the future and the destiny of humanity, guided by reason'.[2] At the centre of this world view was the broad mission to 'modernize' Spanish society following a European model of progress, as it was imagined from Spain.

From this perspective, the monarchist and clerical establishment was an Ancien Regime anachronism that Spain had been trying to shed since the early nineteenth century. In common with other regenerationists of the period, the republicans portrayed the country as crushed beneath the weight of a stagnant aristocratic/ecclesiastical elite. To regenerate itself, the country needed to slough off its old leaders, cut the manacles of *caciquismo* and clericalism, and integrate both the progressive middle classes and the alienated and marginalized masses into a society in which they were true citizens. Because of the close association between Church, monarchy and 'backwardness', the republican vision was as anticlerical as it was antimonarchical. Republicans sought to construct a truly 'modern' Spain that was secular, republican and vaguely democratic.

This project was as much cultural as it was strictly political. Thus, republicans sought, not only to alter the political structure but to construct the intellectual and symbolic foundations for a new society. If the

republicans could create a nation of people who thought like citizens, not
subjects, who were capable of informed participation in the future democratic society, they could undermine the hegemony of the traditional elites,
erode the stability of the Restoration and usher the country into the twentieth
century.

The essence of this transformation was education, to which, like liberal
democrats elsewhere, they ascribed almost mystical powers. Education, in
the broadest sense of the word, performed the double function of preparing
people for their role in the new society and of helping to construct its
foundations. Their ideas on pedagogical content were simple. If you gave
individuals an education that stressed independent thinking, freedom from
religious indoctrination and intellectual exploration, they would naturally
reject the hierarchy and blind faith that tied them to the Ancien Regime and
embrace the liberal democratic values of republican culture.

Achieving this transformation was an especially daunting task in the
Spanish context. In the first place, they had to create a new educational
agenda, but more importantly they had to reach the millions of Spaniards
who were simply left out of the existing, and inadequate, state educational
system. In contrast to the French republicans who made universal education
a priority of the Third Republic, the Restoration state had no interest in
stirring up a demobilized and apathetic population. Thus, Spanish republicans had to pursue this goal from outside the system, and in their urban
strongholds they created an alternative network of voluntary institutions and
means of communication that served tens of thousands of mostly working-
class men around the country. For example, in Barcelona, which spawned
the most impressive array of these institutions, in 1910 there were between
50 and 65 primary and adult schools, 42 neighbourhood centres with 9000
members, and a dozen worker *ateneos*.[3]

It was through this public sphere network that republicanism made its
crucial contribution to mass political culture in the late nineteenth and early
twentieth centuries. In simple terms, this network undertook the basic
process of politicizing workers, of providing them with a space where they
could learn, discuss and begin to articulate a political identity. And, because
the existing regime relied on popular apathy and social disarticulation to
maintain itself, this process was inherently oppositional and deeply political,
whether or not specific ideological beliefs were transmitted.

The significant participation of urban working-class men in the republican movement and the impact of the latter on working-class politicization
has only recently been recognized, as old assumptions about class and
political orientation have broken down. The standard line, in Spain as in
France, was that 'bourgeois' republicanism passed the torch of working-class
politicization to the 'authentic' working-class organizations during the revolutionary period that began in 1868 and ended with the First Republic in
1874. At this point, the torch passed to the emerging anarchist movement,
which dominated the Spanish branch of the First International. (The Socialist

party did not become a major contender in the labour movement until the First World War.)

However, the relationship between republicans, anarchists and workers, as well as socialists, has proven to be more complicated. What local historians have discovered in republican strongholds in the late nineteenth and early twentieth centuries is a largely undifferentiated milieu of popular politics, in which republicans and anarchists, and in some cases socialists, participated. The ideological affinity between republicanism, especially federalism, and anarchism has often been acknowledged, but their cohabitation of social and political space is only now being recognized. Especially before the First World War, the line between republican and 'workerist' political culture was not clearly drawn.

The fuzzy distinction between the groups was reinforced by their common marginalization from the official political realm. As outsiders and victims, they had plenty of opportunities for commiseration and cooperation. Straightforward cooperation existed in joint campaigns against persecution and for the benefit of political prisoners. But at times there was a more subtle symbiosis, particularly between republicanism and anarchism, in which republicanism acted as the unofficial political wing of the anarchist movement and the latter as the trade union wing of the republican party. This level of implicit collaboration was never openly declared, since anarchism officially rejected electoral politics, but it worked precisely because the two movements claimed leadership over different operational spaces. Thus, anarchists could quietly vote for republican candidates, while, in contrast, socialists and republicans fought for the same ballots. As a result, anarchism tended to take root in republican strongholds, while socialism had to find new political spaces. Thus, the Socialist party did well in newly created industrial towns, especially mining communities, and developed a strong rural base among unorganized poor peasants. This porous boundary between republicans and anarchists was not completely sealed off until the Second Republic, when republicans migrated from the margin to the political establishment.

More subtle but perhaps more significant than their institutional collaboration was the overlapping cultural milieu in which (mostly) republicans and anarchists sought to mould workers' minds and bodies. This milieu produced a whole range of institutions, from laic schools to choirs, masonic lodges, neighbourhood improvement associations, cultural centres, 'freethinking' societies, and worker *ateneos*, which were like sociable debating clubs. The central principles circulating in this milieu were secularism, anticlericalism, rationalism, and the pursuit of human perfection through self-improvement. There were doctrinal divisions between anarchists and republicans, notably on the issue of class conflict vs. class harmony, but as Pere Solà has noted, there was a permanent oscillation between these two visions rather than a definitive break between them, especially in the early years.[4] The result was a broad oppositional culture that quickly permeated the urban working-class milieu with its inherently subversive general principles and associational practices.

Although its contours were broad and loosely defined, this oppositional culture owed more to republican liberalism than to anarchism. In both theory and practice, it followed a democratic/civic ethos more than a proletarian one. In fact, anarchist and later socialist cultural theory relied heavily on 'bourgeois' 'free thinking' models, and it was not until the Second Republic that working-class parties consciously began to articulate a proletarian culture. In practice, republicans, anarchists and socialists sponsored their own cultural organizations, but neither anarchists nor socialists ever established the 'cradle to grave' subculture of the German Social Democratic party.

Until the consciously working class parties defined an alternative proletarian public sphere in the 1930s, the plethora of voluntary cultural organizations that encouraged workers to sing, learn to read, attend lectures, collaborate on neighbourhood projects, and socialize together, all contributed to building a broadly democratic public sphere. And whether their participants called themselves anarchists, republicans, socialists, or carried no political affiliation, they moved within a cultural framework that, in essence, had been imagined and designed by republican liberalism.

As a result, the republican movement played a crucial role in the creation of an independent sphere of associational life that reached into the lower classes. This sphere then provided a framework in which 'unmanaged' public opinion and the broader process of politicization could flourish; in other words, it helped construct the civic building blocks of a democratic mass political culture. Paradoxically, however, the republican movement could not channel this mass mobilization into their own specific political project. Thus, many workers who began their political life as republicans later migrated to anarchism or socialism. The failure to republicanize the masses in formal political terms can be attributed to the weaknesses, both external and internal, that were outlined earlier. The failure also helps account for the ease with which republicanism has been dismissed as a force in mass politics in the late nineteenth and early twentieth centuries. But the reality is more complex. Republican activity in the public sphere helped set in motion a destabilizing process that made it difficult for a regime that relied on apathy and demobilization to sustain itself indefinitely. But at the same time that republicanism succeeded in undermining hegemony in its urban centres, it could not assert its own hegemonic leadership as a replacement. The upshot was a hegemonic crisis which was eventually settled through direct armed confrontation: the Civil War.

The labour movement

The major alternative to the republican movement in the mobilization of working class men was, of course, the labour movement. Like the rest of the industrializing world, Spain experienced a wave of class-based association-ism in the later nineteenth century that came to be one of the dominant modes of mass politics after the First World War. In this formative period, the success of trade union mobilizing was limited by a variety of constraints that kept it from posing a powerful challenge to either the existing Restora-tion system or the republican democratic organizations. These weaknesses at the national level led to the same kind of historiographical neglect of the labour movement during this period, especially from 1888 to 1910, as characterized the scholarship on republicanism. Nevertheless, as with the republican movement, the labour organizations were able to carve out their new political space in a number of local settings, thus establishing the infrastructure for their explosion after the First World War.

While Spain's labour movement did fit into the larger European pattern of mobilization, its specific parameters were unique to its own political, social and economic context. Its two most striking characteristics were its regional and local diversity and the long term ideological/institutional division between socialists and anarchists/anarchosyndicalists. Outside of Spain, by the end of the nineteenth century, anarchism had either been defeated by Marxism or reformist trade unionism, or had withdrawn from the labour movement to pursue individual acts of terror. This combination of compet-ing worker organizations and local diversity insured that no coherent national labour movement, embodied in an organization like the German Social Democratic party, could emerge. As with republicanism, the story of the labour movement has to be told from the bottom up, rather than inferred from its national profile.

The local diversity of the labour movement evolved largely from the unevenness of Spain's economic development. Thus, in the late nineteenth and early twentieth centuries, the labour movement took root in two different kinds of localities: urban, industrial settings and latifundia regions. As noted earlier, in the urban settings the labour movement formed part of a broad populist political culture. As a result, the urban worker was more likely to have had some experience with associationism, in addition to being more literate and better paid. In the latifundia regions, especially western Andalu-cia, organized oppositional culture was difficult to sustain, given the power of rural *caciquismo* in setting up relations of political and economic depend-ence, and the workers' extreme poverty and lack of individual or collective resources. In these poorest areas, the labour movement found plenty of discontent but no sustained associational tradition on which to build.

As a result of these different contexts, two distinct labour movement cultures emerged, one urban and one rural. The rural labour movement was more erratic in organization, tended towards greater violence, favoured spontaneous direct action tactics and embraced more radical ideals. In contrast, the urban labour movement developed more permanent organiza-tions and paid more attention to 'reformist' issues like work conditions and cultural infrastructure. While there were exceptions to this rural/urban dichotomy, this general division in priorities and tactics survived into the 1930s and provided an ongoing obstacle to united action.

Another important obstacle to unity was the clash between socialism and anarchism/anarchosyndicalism. The split within the European labour movement surfaced during the early years of the First International in the 1860s, when Bakunin and Marx faced off with their conflicting visions of mass mobilization. At first, the Spanish International was dominated by the anarchist or 'anti-authoritarian' tendency, but in subsequent decades the Socialists established a foot-hold in the labour movement. Both anarchists and socialists shared the eventual goal of a radically egalitarian society, but differed on the best way to achieve it. Following Marx, socialists stressed the value of a strong and efficient organization which would pursue the eventual seizure of power in the name of the proletariat. In the meantime, the Socialists pursued a short-term strategy of electoral conquest and shop floor negotiations for better working conditions.

In contrast, anarchists eschewed what they saw as the authoritarian hierarchy of socialist organizations and relied on loose, decentralized federations and both spontaneous mass uprisings and individual acts of violence to generate revolutionary energy. However, after the turn of the century, a new version of the 'anti-authoritarian' tradition emerged, in the form of anarchosyndicalism. Anarchosyndicalism, embodied in the Confederación Nacional de Trabajo (CNT), formed in 1910, sought to combine the revolutionary spontaneity of anarchism with the organizational structure of syndicalism. In so doing, anarchosyndicalism took on more of the institutional trappings of a trade union movement, including permanent economic organizations, strike funds, short term goals and so on. As a result, in shop floor praxis, anarchosyndicalists and socialists often fought for similar improvements in wages and working conditions.

Where they differed dramatically, however, was in their relationship to electoral politics. While the anarchosyndicalists rejected all ties to the state, the Socialists sought to use its institutions to further the revolution. Thus, the Socialists participated in electoral politics, while the anarchosyndicalists supported what they called direct action, which meant 'that the workers deal directly, without intermediaries, whether they are workers or politicians, or bourgeois or authorities, with those with whom they have a conflict'.[5] Their ultimate 'direct action' weapon was the general strike, which was supposed to cripple the bourgeois capitalist system through the withdrawal of its labour force. Even such apparently clear ideological differences should not be exaggerated, since anarchosyndicalists still participated in the electoral process, at least indirectly in their alliances with republicans. Beyond these structural differences was a more ineffable difference in tone: moderation for the Socialists and intransigence for the anarchosyndicalists.

This difference in tone suggests that the urban/rural split should overlap with the socialist/anarchist one. While it is true that the socialists established early strongholds in the mining and metalworking industries in the north, and that anarchism found immediate resonance among the poor *braceros* of the south, the full picture is much more complicated. Thus, the anarchists also developed urban industrial strongholds like Barcelona and Gijón, and the socialists developed their own rural base, especially in the western border regions, New Castile and eastern Andalucia.[6] As a result, it is impossible to maintain the argument that anarchism or socialism appealed to a certain type of worker in a particular economic environment.

These conclusions contradict most of the traditional assumptions about the shape of the labour movement in Spain. While a number of paradigms have emerged, most of the explanatory models rely on some linkage between 'backwardness' and anarchism, which is simply not sustained by the evidence. Anarchism and socialism were each found in both the 'modern' urban industrial settings and in the 'traditional' rural agricultural ones. Furthermore, these models fail to take into account the heterogeneity of the anarchist movement, which makes it difficult to treat as a coherent phenomenon. Anarchism operated according to fiercely federalist principles that allowed each local federation to adapt to its own environment without having to follow a fixed platform imposed from above. Once again, it is important to emphasize the local centre of gravity in Spanish political culture.

The most convincing paradigm regarding the 'causes of anarchism' is a political model that focuses on the unresponsiveness of the Restoration state. Thus, in broad terms, anarchism/anarchosyndicalism thrived on the widespread suspicion of the possibility of change through governmental channels. In other words, it reflected the crisis of political legitimacy that plagued first the Restoration Monarchy and later the Second Republic. Thus, the anarchist movement symbolized the political scepticism that the republicans had to overcome in order to consolidate popular support for a liberal democratic state and that the socialists had to overcome to convince the masses that they could vote their way to the revolution.

But even this explanation does not account for local variation. Why, in some cities and towns, did Socialists predominate over republicans and anarchists, while in others the Socialists barely existed? While the inflexible and weakly reformist state provided a common political denominator, its differentiated impact spawned a variety of local political responses or dynamics. Within this spectrum, certain dynamics favoured the insertion of the anarchosyndicalist, and others of the socialist movement.

The political geography of the province of Asturias provides a good example of such local dynamics. The largest labour movement in the province was the Socialist party and its trade union affiliate, the UGT. The backbone of the UGT in Asturias were the miners who worked in the cluster of mining towns in the central basin. Within this socialist bastion, however, there were two strongholds of anarchosyndicalism: the major industrial city of the province, Gijón, and the town of La Felguera, where nearly all workers were employed by a single metallurgical factory.

Structural economic explanations for this division are difficult to sustain.

Thus, some historians have suggested that Gijón's anarchist tendencies (like Barcelona's) were rooted in the decentralized structure of industry in the city, which provided a better fit for loose anarchist federations, or in the rural southern origins of workers, who presumably brought their anarchist affinities with them. The first hypothesis is contradicted by the neighbouring town of La Felguera, a one-company town in which all 5000 metal workers belonged to the CNT. The second would require a differentiated immigration pattern between socialist and anarchist strongholds, which was not the case. Significantly, both hypotheses implicitly rely on the teleology that equates backwardness with anarchism and advanced consciousness with socialism.

More convincing than either of these economic-based arguments is one that focuses on the distinct shape of local political cultures and the configuration of political space. In Gijón, for example, a powerful conservative establishment and a venerable republican tradition left little room for a socialist labour movement that depended on electoral conquest and moderate shop floor tactics. Thus, the conservative stranglehold on the city helped legitimate the political cynicism of the anarchosyndicalists. In contrast to a mining town like Mieres, where a workers' party had a real chance of taking over the municipal government, in Gijón this possibility was unlikely even if every worker in the city voted for the Socialist party.

Further, Socialists had to compete against an entrenched republican movement, particularly in its federalist incarnation, that touted a similar platform of municipal reform. The anarchosyndicalists, on the other hand, did not directly challenge the republican movement with an alternative political party, but maintained enough flexibility to manoeuver within the existing system without being tainted by its failures. Thus, in places like Barcelona and Gijón, anarchism and republicanism could often co-exist in a complex political environment with no clear distinctions between political and anti-political, or reformist and revolutionary. Furthermore, as has been pointed out, federalism and anarchism shared a certain outlook. Thus, anarchism must have seemed more familiar to a working class weaned on federalist ideology.

Once the anarchosyndicalist movement established itself, its survival probably depended as much on the self-propelled tradition it created as on a fervent commitment to anarchist ideology. In simple terms, the labour movement in Gijón (as elsewhere) became identified with anarchosyndicalism. Although the socialist movement struggled along, joining the UGT meant living on the margin of the community to which most of one's co-workers belonged. As new generations were born into the city, this tradition would also be passed on from father to son. By this point, the CNT stood as much for a way of life as it did for a specific ideology.

In contrast to Gijón, the mining towns proved to be more open to socialist appeals. In these towns, which exploded from sleepy villages to small cities over the course of a couple of decades, the Socialists faced no competing existing political traditions. Furthermore, their electoral tactics could show more positive results than in a complex city like Gijón; in most of the mining towns, Socialists took over the municipal governments soon after the passage of universal suffrage. In this context, the Socialists had no trouble defining their political space. And just as with the CNT elsewhere, once the Socialists established their local dominance, it was much easier to maintain this political niche than it was to challenge it. Nevertheless, despite the local successes of the Socialists in regions like Asturias and Vizcaya, their overall growth in Spain was slow until the 1930s, when the optimism of the new Republic and a broader recruiting strategy turned the movement into the largest political party in the country.

What, then, was the general impact of the labour movement on the emerging culture of mass politics in late nineteenth and early twentieth century Spain? In terms of national politics or economic policy, its impact, like that of the republicans, was minimal during this period. Through the use of spectacular if inconsistent acts of repression, like the massacre in Jerez de la Frontera in 1892, the Montjuic trial in 1896, or the trial of Francisco Ferrer in 1909, the regime managed to keep the labour movement destabilized and on the defensive. The strategic and organizational difficulties of bridging the gap between the Andalucian *bracero* and the Barcelonan textile worker were equally debilitating, as was the competition among republicans, socialists and anarchists.

And yet, in conjunction with the republican movement, the labour movement played a key role in building pluralistic local political cultures, in politicizing workers, and in expanding the limits of political discourse in dozens of urban public spheres around the country. Even during the decade of the 1890s, when repression crippled trade union organizations, anarchists were able to continue their cultural and educational activities. In later decades the impact of the labour movement would be more differentiated from that of the republicans, but in this formative period, the labour movement was part of a broader populist political culture in which republicanism was still the major current. What the labour movement offered at this point was a potential radical alternative to the democratization of liberalism envisioned by the republicans. If Spanish liberalism could not be adapted to the new world of mass politics, then the labour movement, especially in its anarchist incarnation, stood ready to absorb the disillusioned masses.

Women and consumer politics

While the republican and labour movements constituted the major mass political movements of the period, they offer a distinctly masculine version of politics. Both of these movements comprised mainly working-class men, so they tell us little about the political role of women of the lower classes. In fact, it is common to assume that since most women did not join the ranks of unions or political parties they were largely apolitical. Likewise, since women were identified with the private sphere of home and family, their absence from the nineteenth century public sphere has often been taken for granted. Thus, women, especially from the working classes, are often written out of the narrative of modern politics.

Through questioning narrow definitions of modern politics and the public sphere, however, we can locate working-class women's sphere of political activity. This activity emerged out of the daily networks of female sociability, which were the marketplace and the neighbourhood instead of the trade union, the *ateneo* or the *tertulia*. For women involved in the daily provisioning of their families, one of their main common concerns was guaranteeing the consumption of goods and services necessary for basic survival and comfort. As a result, their political action often took the form of the consumer protest, well-known to historians of early modern Europe, but often overlooked as a 'modern' form of politics. In fact, this form of protest survived in the twentieth century as a predominantly female form of politics. When women took to the streets to protest high prices or shortages, they crossed the line from private consumer to political actor: they mobilized collective resources, they occupied public spaces, they tried to influence government policy and they often succeeded in doing so. Moreover, through the consumer protest, working-class women provided an alternative blueprint for political opposition, a blueprint that lacked formal structure but which retained significant power to mobilize community action, once again at the local level.

Because of the social division of labour in industrial societies, women remained the most sensitive to marketplace issues and continued to mobilize around them. And because of their continued marginalization in formal political systems, they still embraced forms of direct confrontation that bypassed legal mechanisms of redress. While the incidence of the traditional food riot declined along with subsistence crises, it was replaced by battles over prices, rents, services and shortages of other essential goods. Women did not always dominate these struggles, but they often did. Moreover, when women organized protests, it was more often than not around these kinds of broadly-defined consumption issues. As a result, these protests constituted the most coherent expression of working-class women's political identity.

The coherence emerged, not from the links of formal organizations or ideological manifestos, but from the strikingly similar way that these public protests unfolded, in both content and form. The participant was the irate consumer, angry at the government or a businessman for not providing the expected goods or services that popular notions of justice demanded. Organization was spontaneous, often unfolding at the immediate location of the problem and always remaining local in scope. Targets and goals were usually specific, and the participants were often prepared to hold the line until these goals were met. Moreover, within the limited scope of the attack, they were willing to employ coercion and violence to achieve their aims. The drama of members of the 'weaker sex' engaged in violent public confrontation was often enough to bring the authorities to their knees.

While consumer protests were a more or less constant feature of urban life during the nineteenth and early twentieth centuries, there were periods of greater intensity, arising from a significant disruption in the distribution and access of acceptably-priced basic consumer goods, such as bread, meat, and coal for cooking and heating. One such period was the turn-of-the-century, when a series of bad harvests sent agricultural prices spiralling and sparked a series of riots across the country. Significantly, the inability of the government to remedy the situation became an important contributing factor to the larger political crisis unfolding after 1898. Furthermore, the riots offered a specifically gendered reading of the crisis, employing the powerful metaphor of the (male) government as failed breadwinner. Through this discourse, they exposed the shame of a government incapable of providing for its 'weaker' members and thereby questioned its masculine legitimacy to rule on its own paternalistic terms.

So how, then, did this tradition of collective action figure into the emerging mass political culture of the early Restoration? On the most basic level, the consumer protest remained part of the basic repertoire of collective action up to the Civil War. Thus, it joined the strike, the election and the cultural event as one available mass political weapon. And while the consumer protest was not linked to a formal institutional base, it did help to solidify the new working-class neighbourhoods, which would become important informal units of association in the emerging urban political cultures. More subtly, it articulated a set of issues that could appeal to a broad spectrum of lower-class people, especially women, and provide a basis for community mobilization that extended beyond the workplace or the city hall.

Finally, the consumer protest contributed to the larger oppositional task of undermining the legitimacy of a regime that depended for its survival on apathy and apoliticization. While the consumer protests never directly attacked the regime or the political system, they did demonstrate the sterility of the regime, even on its own terms. In this way, the waves of consumer protests opened the door for the republican and labour movements to propose alternatives to the existing system that were better equipped to serve its population's basic needs. Within this gendered framework, female consumer rioters can take their rightful place as modern political actors in a complex drama in which the future of the Restoration was at stake.

Conclusion

Thus, female consumer rioters joined republicans, anarchists and socialists in an emerging arena of mass politics nurtured by the ambivalent liberal identity of the Restoration regime. Significantly, most of this political activity has been invisible in traditional histories of the Restoration, which have taken its exclusivity and stability at face value. As this chapter argues, however, despite the lack of popular access to formal 'high politics', opposition thrived in a broader oppositional arena that existed outside the narrow confines of a conventional model of politics. Located largely at the local level, different groups mobilized for either inclusion, reform or destruction of the Restoration system, but through alternative political forms. Given the restrictions of Restoration liberalism, these groups were most successful when they pursued their political goals outside the national electoral arena. Thus, the republican and labour movements pursued politicization through the relatively open public sphere, while anarchists and consumer rioters adopted direct action tactics that bypassed formal mechanisms of redress. Only by re-defining mass politics to include the broader arena of hegemonic struggle can we view the full spectrum of political conflict brewing beneath the surface of the apparently stable regime.

Why is such a re-definition important to our understanding of Spanish history? If none of these forms of mass politics succeeded in forcing the Restoration elites to accept greater pluralism, why do they need to be resurrected from historical obscurity? Aside from the desire to produce a more nuanced view of Restoration politics, this exploration of the origin of modern mass politics throws light on the crisis of the 1930s. It demonstrates that, in fact, there was a core of politicized masses who provided a real constituency for the democratic regime inaugurated in 1931. However, it also illustrates the tremendous challenge that the Second Republic faced in attempting to integrate a plethora of distinct local political cultures into a pluralistic but coherent national political culture. Clearly, the Republic was never able to rise above this political fragmentation and unify the nation. In fact, one could argue that there was never one Republic, but a number of local, or in some cases, regional Republics, that struggled unsuccessfully to define a common destiny for the Spanish nation. Their failure to do so opened the door for the conservative counter-revolution, which solved the problem (temporarily) by re-creating a culture of demobilization and apathy.

Notes

1 John Clarke and Stuart Hall's definition of hegemony, in 'Subcultures, Cultures and Class', in *Resistance Through Ritual: Youth Subcultures in Post-War Britain*, edited by Stuart Hall and Tony Jefferson, (London: Hutchinson Press, 1976), p. 38.
2 José Alvarez Junco, *El emperador del paralelo: Lerroux y la demagogia populista*. (Madrid: Alianza Editorial, 1990), pp. 185–6.
3 Joan Culla y Clara, *El republicanisme lerrouxista a Catalunya (1901–1923)*. (Barcelona: Curial, 1986), p. 103.
4 Pere Sola, *Els ateneus obrers i la cultura popular a Catalunya, 1900–1939*. (Barcelona: Ediciones la Magrana, 1978), p. 187.
5 Anarchosyndicalist leader Angel Pestaña quoted in Manuel Pérez Ledesma, *El obrero consciente*, (Madrid, 1987), p. 261.
6 Tim Rees alerted me to the creation of local Socialist unions decades before the formation of The National Farmworkers' Association in the 1930s.

|10|

Fin de siècle *culture*

EDWARD BAKER

Spanish intellectual and cultural life has often been seen as the result of the disastrous defeat in the Spanish–American War of 1898. Such a perspective obscures the fact that what happened in Spain was part of ·a broader European *fin de siècle* that saw, among other things, an increasing public role for intellectuals and a questioning of nineteenth-century verities of rationality and progress. The loss of empire coincided with the spread of the ideas of thinkers such as Bergson and Nietzsche, and the result was, as José Alvarez Junco has argued, that Spanish intellectuals responded with an irrationality that can be seen in six features of their work. They were essentialists, seeing Spain not as a product of history but as an eternal, metaphysical entity. They were idealists because the country they imagined was not based on social, economic or political realities but on a national spirit. Like so many European intellectuals of the time, they were racialists, believing that biology determined being and action. They were populists, hoping for national redemption at the hands of the lower classes. They were paranoid, constantly positing an opposition between Spain and some 'other', usually 'Europe' that sought to destroy Spain's position in the world. (At the same time, some saw 'Europe', i.e. science, as Spain's salvation.) Finally, they were *machistas*, seeing Spanish defeat as a loss of national virility. What they wanted was regeneration, of the nation and of the race, but this was a goal that could be both understood and achieved in various ways, and that would lead Spain's intellectuals along different political paths.

The 1898–1936 period was the Silver Age of Spanish literature, a worthy modern-day successor to the sixteenth- and seventeenth-century Golden Age. The extraordinarily rich and varied literature of this period did not seek merely to replicate or reproduce historical developments. In a society as complex as that of early twentieth-century Spain, in which a modern, secular intelligentsia began to perceive itself as an agent not only of intellectual and artistic creativity, but of political and social change as well, literature possessed a very broad thematic and formal range of expression and a significant measure of autonomy, as well as the ambition, if not the capacity, to engage the conscience of an entire people. Viewed in historical perspective, that new intelligentsia was engaged in the same dialectic of class conflict, regionalist demands, and the clash of archaicism and modernity that moved all of Spanish society toward the war of 1936–39, and it understood literary creation as an important aspect of its individual, collective, and nearly always public activism.

Modernism and the *fin-de-siècle* crisis: the Generation of 1898

In the aftermath of the defeat of 1898, a scholar and intellectual of great distinction, Joaquín Costa (1846–1911) sounded an alarm. In this he was far from alone, but his voice was both vastly learned and thunderously eloquent in an age that still prized eloquence. (*Oligarchy and Rural Bossism as the Present-Day Form of Government in Spain*) *Oligarquía y caciquismo como la forma actual de gobierno en España* (1901) was a lengthy essay in which Costa contrasted written law with unwritten political reality. It was also an opinion survey conducted under Costa's direction by one of Madrid's most notable liberal intellectual institutions, the Ateneo or Atheneum. Costa argued that the Spain of the Restoration was not a sovereign nation, that its written Constitution was nothing more than paper, and that the people's sovereign will had, in effect, been sequestered and replaced by a gerry-rigged but effective tripartite governing mechanism: 1) the oligarchs, what today would be called the 'political class'; 2) the *caciques* or rural bosses who effectively controlled elections and, in general, political life at the local level; and 3) the governors of each of the 50 provinces, political appointees beholden to the central government who acted as a link connecting Madrid and the local bosses. In sum, the Spanish state, far from being the instrument of popular sovereignty, represented nothing and no one beyond itself and its political agents, and the social contract, the philosophical and juridical foundation of liberal governance, had in reality been nullified.

In this era of high nationalism nothing could be more damning than the chapter heading which began his essay: 'Spain is not a sovereign nation'. To the young writers, artists and intellectuals who came to be known as the Generation of 1898, it provided an explanatory device and an ideological focus for their disaffection with the Restoration polity. The young writers' uncompromising rejection of Restoration politics, culture, language and *ethos*, their intensely ethical sense of what Spain was not and should become, drew them together in the late 1890s and the first few years of the twentieth century.

They were the *intellectuals*. This word, which has an infinitely familiar ring to twentieth-century ears, is actually of fairly recent coinage. It was first so used in France in the context of the Dreyfus Affair late in the nineteenth century, in Spain its currency dates from the beginning of the twentieth century. It began as a term of opprobrium used to distinguish dissident writers and thinkers who were not, or were not yet, attached to the dominant cultural and political institutions of their various countries. They deemed it their moral duty to intervene in the widest range of public affairs and were 'anti-national', that is, they stood in opposition to conservative conceptions and conventional notions of national culture and traditions. In the Spain of 1900 the intellectuals distinguished themselves by being *against*: the torture of the prisoners in Barcelona's Montjuic fortress in 1896; the policies and politicians who led their country into an imperial war with the United States; the political monopoly of the two dynastic parties of the Restoration, Cánovas's Conservatives and Sagasta's Liberals; the language, gestures, culture, ideologies – including, of course, that of the Church – and, in general, the conventional, unreflective *modus vivendi* of Restoration society. At the turn of the century, the relative unity of the intellectuals as a definable group within the sphere of culture and its intersection with politics was based upon their opposition to all the things, people, practices, symbols of what, quite correctly, they regarded as official Spain.

One of the characteristic expressions of this momentary unity of the younger generation of intellectuals was a typical product of both European and American literary and cultural modernity, the so-called little review. One of the distinguishing features of literary and artistic modernism was a sharp separation between 'high' and 'low' culture, and the little review was one of the salient expressions of a modernist literary and intellectual elite. In turn-of-the-century Spain little reviews' titles almost invariably conveyed a sense of symbolic generational break with the immediate past: *Germinal*, after Emile Zola's naturalist depiction of French proletarian life, *Joventut*, 'Youth' in the language of Catalonia, *Vida Nueva* or 'New Life', *Gente Nueva*, 'New People', *Electra*, *Helios*, etc. The little reviews were almost inevitably short-lived and provided a space of aesthetic, ideological and political dissidence for writers who had not yet been, and in some cases would not be, absorbed into the dominant cultural and political institutions of the Restoration, including the institutions and forms of political behaviour that linked the press to the state.

Electra (1901) was one of the most representative of the little reviews. It brought together in its pages very nearly all of the most important writers of the group later called the Generation of 1898. The review's name was taken from a play, *Electra*, by the older novelist, Benito Pérez Galdós (1843–1920). Its debut in a Madrid theatre in January, 1901, was rendered memorable when one of the writer-journalists of the younger generation, the then radical Ramiro de Maeztu (1874–1936), stood up in the middle of the anticlerical play, cried out 'Death to the Jesuits!' and singlehandedly started a riot.

The review *Electra* was short lived – it did not survive to 1902 – but it was symbolically important because it was a simultaneous expression of aesthetic and ideological dissidence. It gathered in its pages what in retrospect would be the key writers of the so-called Generation of 1898: Miguel de Unamuno (1864–1936), Ramón María del Valle-Inclán (1866–1936), Manuel (1874–1947) and Antonio Machado (1875–1939), Pío Baroja (1872–1956) and José Martínez Ruiz (1873–1967), who in the future would be known pseudonymously as 'Azorín'. *Electra* and other little reviews of those years united two ultimately conflicting tendencies. One was the *fin de siècle* aestheticism with roots in Baudelaire and French symbolist poetry which was known in the Spanish-speaking world as *modernismo* and which had its first flowering in the 1880s and 1890s in Latin America. The other was the desire for political, economic and moral reform lead by Costa and known as *regeneracionismo*. Momentarily united, the modernist and regenerationist impulses define the aspirations of an entire generation of young writers and thinkers who would come to be known as the Generation of 1898.

Spain's turn-of-the-century modernist literature manifested itself in every genre, but its greatest achievements are those of poets such as Antonio and Manuel Machado, and Juan Ramón Jiménez (1881–1958). They were profoundly influenced both by French symbolists such as Charles Baudelaire and Paul Verlaine, as well as the early Latin American modernists, most notably the Nicaraguan poet Rubén Darío (1867–1916). Their poetry brought about a revolution in poetic language and form by breaking radically with the literature of the Restoration. Much of Restoration literature, particularly its prose fiction and drama, was based on two aesthetic effects. The first is pure denotation, an aesthetic that commonly we associate with the doctrine of realism, a verbal art that seeks to represent on the printed page the appearances of the external world. The second effect is rather different. The sentimental corollary of pure denotation in the fiction of the time is a psychological one that we could call empathetic proximity, the sense that we as readers are close to the characters of the realist novels, that we are able to enter their social world and individual psychology, that we can share their thoughts and feelings. In the English-speaking world we are all familiar with these aesthetic effects through the work of Charles Dickens. In the Spain of the 1880s and 1890s, the novels of Benito Pérez Galdós played a similar artistic role. Just as we can with the characters of Dickens's London, we can follow Galdós's characters step by step through Restoration Madrid and empathize with their struggles and triumphs, their lives and deaths by reading ourselves into the weave of the narration.

If realism is an aesthetic of familiarization and proximity, modernism, whether in prose or verse, relies on defamiliarization and distantiation. By way of contrast with Galdós, Pío Baroja created distance through systematic and pervasive misanthropy. Where realism employed denotation to achieve aesthetic effects in which external reality – or its appearance – was referred to or represented, modernism relied on distance and the self-referential use of language and form. In Unamuno's novel *Niebla* (*Mist*, 1914), the protagonist, August Pérez discusses with his friend Víctor Goti what would happen if there were an author hiding behind the furniture taking notes on his conversations. Leaving aside that this observation is Unamuno's way of ridiculing the convention of the omniscient narrator, the putative author's readers would think that nothing was happening, due to the banality of the conversation. Here Unamuno enunciates one of the core truths of modernist literature: the reality of literature takes place on the printed page; that flat surface is its privileged space. Fictional characters are not people and unlike people do not have insides because the printed page does not either.

Authors, however, can also problematize their subjectivity and can create poetic subjects to be intensely and minutely explored. The modernism of 1900, as exemplified by Antonio Machado's *Soledades* (Solitudes, 1903) and *Soledades, galerìas, otros poemas* (solitudes, galleries, other poems, 1907), plumbed the inner workings of a fragmented and decentred subjectivity and the difficult and enigmatic language of the fragmented subject's projection upon the external world. This sort of poetry seems withdrawn from the world, its lyric delicacy, enigmatic beauty and complex subjectivity seem infinitely distant from the concerns of daily existence, not to mention the exigencies of a deeply conflicted society. In a post-imperial Spain that obsessively questioned its place in Europe and the world, this poetry, along with the symbolist lyric of Antonio's brother Manuel, and Juan Ramón Jiménez, and the exquisite decadentist prose of early Valle-Inclán, seems out of touch. However, in addition to modernist lyric's enduring lessons in poetic language and form, there is in that body of work an attitude of dissidence and a gesture of protest against the debased language of Official Spain.

At the same time, there were other more visible signs of dissent in the work of those young writers. The 'Disaster' of 1898 called into question Spain's status as a sovereign nation; it also brought to the forefront the country's standing in the concert of Europe. If in 1900 the very word 'Europe' represented a synthesis of power, wealth, knowledge, culture, in a word, *civilization*, was Spain a European country at all? Unamuno had already posed the question of Spain's relation to Europe in an influential series of essays on nationality and culture, *En torno al casticismo* (*Regarding Span-ishness*, 1895). The word *casticismo* resists translation. It comes from *casta*, that is, caste, and has both biological and cultural overtones. It connotes everything that distinguishes one species of animal or one nation from another, and in these essays Unamuno attempted to delineate the character-istics that distinguish Spain – its culture, its people, its history – from other nations. In the early decades of the twentieth century, Spanish writers and intellectuals would almost inevitably take sides in the polemics between Europeanizers and *casticistas* on the Europeanization of Spain. Although later in life Unamuno was to become one of the most vociferous of Spain's *casticistas*, in the waning years of the nineteenth century he was very much a Europeanizer, but with a twist. Rather than accepting the protectionist essentialism of the *casticistas*, he declares that Spain is an undiscovered country and that the process of discovery can only be undertaken by Europeanized Spaniards. We know nothing, he writes, of our landscape and of its inhabitants, of the life of the Spanish people. He argues, then, for a dialectic of Europeanization and *casticismo* in which modern cosmopolitan intellectuals will be the true discoverers of Spain and the Spaniards.

For most of the twentieth century, Spanish intellectuals have been obsessed with themselves and their country and its culture, and have regarded Spain from the standpoint of its exceptionalism. None the less, the sense of an abyss separating the country from Europe was, in fact, shared by many other Europeans. In Czarist Russia, the debates between Europeanists and Russophiles covered the same territory as the polemics between Spanish Europeanizers and *casticistas*, and the feeling of being at best on Europe's periphery was experienced by virtually all of the stateless nationalities of the Austro-Hungarian empire. All of them experienced the same distance from the seats of wealth, power and knowledge that they synthesized in the word 'Europe'.

If Europe was the utopia of modern Spanish intellectuals and writers, we could then argue that Spain for them was the polar opposite – a dystopia. Valle-Inclán stated the case for dystopian Spain most forcefully and effectively in his play *Luces de bohemia (Bohemian Lights*, 1924). Valle-Inclán combined an ideological question that reverberated throughout Spain with a complex and rigorous aesthetic, the *esperpento*. Here again we have a word that defies translation. An *esperpento* is a grotesque or deformed person or thing. A truly hideous painting, for example, can simultaneously provoke laughter and horror, and in the throes of that violently contradictory sentiment we can call the painting an *esperpento*. In *Luces de bohemia* Spain is an *esperpento* and the aesthetic of deformity that Valle-Inclán creates to reflect it is the art of the *esperpento*. The bohemian poet Max Estrella argues that Spain is a grotesque deformation of European civilization and that if artists aspire to reflect that reality, they should trade in ordinary mirrors for the concave ones on the storefront of a well-known pharmacy on the Callejón del Gato in the old part of Madrid.

If Europe was utopia and Spain dystopia, Castile was Spain's dystopian heart and soul, because for many Castilian-speaking intellectuals, Spain was reduced to Castile. As historians and writers, scholars and ideologues elaborated the virtually metaphysical construct that was Spanish nationalism, they found the essence of Spain in Castile. If there was such a thing as a stable and more or less unchanging national character, and for nearly all of them there was such a thing, that character was unmistakably Castilian. Many of these intellectuals were from the periphery and came together in the national capital. Madrid was the meeting place for writers, artists and intellectuals of every stripe, and it was the starting point for the ones who would attempt to come to grips with the crush of reality and myth that Castile was becoming for all Spaniards in the age of high nationalism.

The intellectuals and their project

The modern, critical and to varying degrees disaffected intelligentsia that arose in *fin de siècle* Spain reached an initial maturity in the second decade of the century. One of the most notable expressions of that maturity was, once again, a periodical. But in this instance it was not a little review, for the centripetal force of the little reviews had been dissipated by 1905. It was, rather, an ambitious journal of culture and politics the title of which, *España* (*Spain*), is suggestive both of a collective fixation and a project. The progressive intelligentsia increasingly refused to see Spain as a nation with a more or less fixed and stable past, a history, a set of traditions to be cultivated and maintained, or, for that matter, questioned and rejected. Rather, they conceived of it as a project, the ongoing task of an entire polity whose collective mind they aspired to be. This aspiration was most clearly delineated by a young German-trained philosopher, José Ortega y Gasset (1883–1955), who held the Chair of Metaphysics at the University of Madrid. Ortega's father, José Ortega y Munilla, was both a novelist of some note and the director of the most important independent Madrid daily newspaper, *El Imparcial*.

Before he had reached his 20s, Ortega cut his teeth on the paper's pages, and his presence was felt in its distinguished Monday literary supplement; in fact his philosophical vocation was inseparable from his presence in Madrid's periodical press – dailies, weeklies, monthlies – from 1902 until the outbreak of the Civil War in July of 1936. In this, as in many other questions, his reasoning was clear and simple: in Spain, unlike the Germany where he received his philosophical training, there were no specialized journals of any note and virtually no reading public for them. In Spain, a philosopher had the obligation to think in public, as the ancient Greeks had done in the agora, the public square or marketplace, and in the early twentieth century he believed that the best and most available agora was the press. At the age of 25, he brought out his first journal of opinion, *Faro* (*Lighthouse*). He then went on to create *España* in 1915, left it a year later, and in 1917 inspired the creation of the best daily paper of pre-War Spain, *El Sol* (*The Sun*). Finally, he founded Spain's most influential journal of the arts, letters, and thought, the *Revista de Occidente* (*Occidental Review*, 1923–36). The latter are the years of his best known and most frequently translated essays, *The Dehumanization of Art* (1925) and *The Rebellion of the Masses* (1929). These were the culminating works of a thinker whose vast learning and remarkable analytical and phenomenological precision were, however, repeatedly marred in the 1920s by the empty elitist gestures of a provincial Nietzschean.

It is impossible to exaggerate Ortega's influence on the thought and letters of the more than two decades preceding the outbreak of the War. From the very outset he desired to be a public thinker and to a very great extent he achieved what he had proposed. That achievement began with a public speech, *Vieja y nueva política* (*Old and New Politics*, 1914) intended as the founding document of the Liga de Educación Política (League for Political Education). In this speech the young philosopher argued very convincingly that there were, in effect, two Spains, one purely official, the other a vital, living organism, and that official life, in an advanced state of petrification, was utterly oblivious to the real life of the nation. Ortega described official Spain as the immense skeleton of an organism that had evaporated, vanished, and that was left standing through sheer inertia.

As a political project the Liga de Educación Política was stillborn, but the ideas behind it inspired the creation of *España*, published weekly from January 1915, to February 1924. *España* was incomparably the best Spanish journal of ideas and opinion during the nine years of its existence. It brought together the now somewhat older writers who had begun fighting the literary and cultural wars at the end of the nineteenth century with younger ones who, like Ortega, were very often university-trained intellectuals and academics rather than creative writers. The review combined arts and letters with progressive politics and ideas in a perfectly unselfconscious way that, as we will soon see, would be called into question during the 1920s, with the advent of the phenomenon of 'pure' poetry and the 'dehumanized' novel. In the years of the First World War, the review was staunchly on the side of the Allies and against Germany, in a controversy that split Spanish writers, artists and thinkers into opposing camps. It stood for centre-left thought and quality in the arts and letters, and worked under the assumption that there was no significant, underlying conflict between one and the other. *España*, in sum, was the venue of a progressive intelligentsia of a nation in the throes of modernization, perhaps the last publication that brought together nearly all progressive writers and thinkers. It was the gathering point of a principled opposition, that of the intelligentsia, to a visibly disintegrating Restoration monarchy.

Regional renaissance: Catalonia and Galicia

The second half of the nineteenth century and the early years of the twentieth witnessed a rebirth of national literature in Catalonia and Galicia. Both Catalan and Gallego had been the vehicles of an important vernacular literature in the Middle Ages, and both were revived in the mid-nineteenth century as a consequence of the stirrings of regional nationalism and Romanticism's fascination with the local and the particular. However, in the broader historical context of twentieth-century Spanish culture, these movements can also be seen as part of a modern, post-Romantic regionalization of Spanish literature after four centuries of political and cultural centralization.

In Catalonia, and especially in its capital Barcelona, the defeat of 1898 was seen in a very different light than from Madrid. Catalan criticism of the Spanish state proceeded from two directions. The first was a nationalism that mobilized the bourgeoisie and engendered a *Renaixença*, a cultural rebirth that recuperated and vindicated Catalan language and culture. The second was the labour movement, which was mainly anarchist in inspiration. Within this polarity of bourgeois nationalism and proletarian revolutionary internationalism, an exceptionally dynamic culture would emerge.

The most visible face of Catalan cultural life was in architecture. Unlike Paris, Barcelona was never transformed by a Haussmann, nor could it boast a grandiose plan of modernization like Vienna's Ringstrasse. The change it underwent, however, was typical of European cities in which a new, nineteenth and early-twentieth century addition, in Catalan the *eixample*, built on a grid, stood against the old, in this case, medieval and early modern city. Barcelona's was designed by Ildefons Cerdá, one of the most notable theorists of the new urbanism in the nineteenth century, who none the less is not nearly as well known as the other important Spanish urbanist, Arturo Soria, the designer of Madrid's Lineal City. With few exceptions modernist architecture flourished in the *eixample*, the newly built city of the Barcelona bourgeoisie.

Barcelona's and, indeed, Spain's greatest architect was Antoni Gaudí, the fervent Catholic whose Sagrada Familia, the Church of the Holy Family, is a stupendously excessive hymn to both soaring faith and untrammelled modernity. Although somewhat less exuberant, his houses such as the Casa Batlló and the Casa Milà are surely no less modern, as is the most accessible of his works, the Parc Güell. Named after one of Gaudí's patrons, Eusebi Güell, this popular Barcelona park was paradoxically the result of a failure. Originally conceived a century ago as a bourgeois housing project, it never got off the ground, but remains today as a park built around an open plaza with benches winding around it that are decorated in exquisite multi-coloured ceramics. In addition, both the Casa Batlló and the Casa Milà, known as La Pedrera or the Quarry because it resembles a vast and wondrous heap of stone, are among the finest examples of domestic architecture in early twentieth-century Europe. Gaudí's work is both varied and abundant, but he was not the only talented architect working in Barcelona. Built on the same block as his Casa Milà are two minor masterpieces by excellent architects, Josep Puig i Cadafalch's Casa Amattler, and Lluis Domènech i Montaner's Casa Lleó Morera. Although built in vastly different modernist styles, Gaudí's houses share an attention to interior design with those of Puig i Cadafalch and Domènech, so that the actual dwellings are animated by the same spirit as the exteriors.

Barcelona, not Madrid, was also where modern art flourished in Spain. A semi-adolescent Pablo Picasso got his start illustrating the menu for the famous cabaret 'Els Quatre Gats' which opened in 1897. The cabaret exhibited the works of Catalan modernist painters and promoted such small art forms as puppetry, of which there was a long tradition in Catalonia. It was also the home away from home of the excellent post-impressionist painters working in Barcelona at the turn of the century: Santiago Rusinyol,

Isidre Nonell, and especially Ramón Casas. Of the three, Casas was probably the most talented, both as a painter and as an illustrator. Both his painterly ability and his illustrator's topicality were on display in Els Quatre Gats, where he executed a mural-size dual portrait of himself and the owner of the place, Pere Rumeu, an interesting character in his own right, on a tandem bicycle. Rusinyol was both a painter and a writer, as well as a collector with a good eye, as the Cau Ferrat, his house in Sitges, now a museum, attests. Nonell, in all probability, exerted the most direct influence on the young Picasso. Unlike Casas he was a good colourist whose subject matter was almost invariably the unadorned wretchedness and the deformities of Barcelona's sub-proletariat, especially women. There is something more than a faint echo of both qualities in Picasso's early work, particularly his Blue Period, and even, perhaps, in the subject matter, although not at all in the handling of a somewhat later one. 'Les Demoiselles d'Avignon', (1906–07) a key painting in the emergence of cubism, evokes not the discreet charm of the southern French town but the bordellos of Barcelona's Carrer d'Avinyó. By the time of 'Les Demoiselles d'Avignon', of course, Picasso was firmly and permanently entrenched in the capital city of modernist culture, Paris.

Paradoxical as it may seem, Catalan literary modernity was built on the ruins of *modernisme*, the *fin de siècle* movement that was a rich mixture of art nouveau and symbolism. The movement that replaced *modernisme* was called *noucentisme*, a neologism invented by the essayist Eugeni d'Ors (1882–1954). The word means 'nineteen hundredism', but it plays with the Catalan word for 'new' and it signalled a generational break with the modernists and the doyen of Catalan letters, the poet Joan Maragall (1860–1911). The break took place on political as well as literary grounds, as the *noucentistes* abandoned the apoliticism of their predecessors and aspired to become both a modern intelligentsia and the intellectual wing of the regionalist political party, the Lliga.

Galicia too experienced a literary rebirth, the *Rexurdimento*, a literary and cultural resurgence which recuperated a rich medieval tradition and set the stage for a revival of poetry in Gallego. Catalonia was Spain's richest industrial region, but Galicia was very different, a poor, heavily populated region with a high rate of migration, both to other parts of Spain and abroad, especially Cuba and Argentina. Even so, Galicia could boast three exceptional poets: Rosalia de Castro, Eduardo Pondal and Manuel Curros Enríquez. Castro, who wrote in both Spanish and Gallego, ranks as one of the three best lyric poets of the nineteenth century.

Galicia barely experienced the modernizing influences that shaped Catalan literature. Instead of a *fin de siècle* modernism or *noucentisme*, its twentieth-century literature was a continuation of the *Rexurdimento*'s romantic localism with strong Celtic overtones. This continuity is found in the work of the most important poet of the period, Ramón Cabanillas (1876–1959), who can be seen as a transitional figure between the late nineteenth-century romantics and the avant-garde writers of the 1920s and 1930s.

Modern Galician literature began with the 'Nos' group and their journal, *Nos* (*Ourselves*). The review was founded in 1920 by Vicente Risco (1884–1963) and was published until the outbreak of the Civil War. With far fewer material resources and on a much smaller scale, *Nos* met the same needs of a modern intelligentsia as did Ortega's *Revista de Occidente* during those same years. Until the advent of the Nos group, Galician literature was more localist than nationalist, and was less a literature than a miniscule group of poets who doubled as both writers and readers. What we can call the 'Nos period' was characterized by a degree of modernity and cultural maturation as well as the advent of modern prose writing.

High modernism: from Juan Ramón Jiménez to the Generation of 1927

Spain remained neutral during the First World War, but the sea change in literature that took place in much of Europe during the War and its immediate aftermath also occurred in Spain. In Spain the transformation was first and most visibly registered in the field of poetry and is associated with the name of Juan Ramón Jiménez, who was awarded the Nobel Prize for Literature in 1956, and with one of the finest books of poetry in modern Spanish literature, the *Diario de un poeta recién casado* (*Diary of a Newly Wed Poet*, 1917).

In 1916 Jiménez crossed the Atlantic and landed in New York. The purpose of his voyage was marriage to Zenobia Camprubí, a young Puerto Rican educated in the United States. The literary consequence was a diary in verse and prose that permanently altered the landscape not only of his own work but of Spanish poetry in general. Not just the landscape but the seascape and, most particularly, the cityscape was changed as well, for in the New York pages of the *Diario* we have some of the finest urban poetry of modern Spain, and a remarkable foretaste of Federico García Lorca's more familiar *Poeta en Nueva York* (*Poet in New York*, 1941). The *Diario* was both an opportunity for a still young poet who was an aesthete with somewhat solipsistic overtones to open up to the world, and to solidify and, in effect, modernize his solipsistic tendencies. But in this instance we have not so much a solipsism of the poet, the writing subject, as the self-referentiality of the text, the poetic object in itself. The *Diario* is the first great book of Spanish poetry that systematically proposed and fully achieved one of modernism's fundamental propositions: the self-contained and self-referential book. The *Diario* is a collection in which each poem *may* be read individually but *must* be read in relation to all the others, for it is in that relation where meanings are fully revealed.

The work of the five or six years immediately following the *Diario* is distinguished both for its enormous quantity and its astonishing quality, and for its distantiation from a turn-of-the-century modernism that by the second decade of the century had lapsed into a purely gestural aestheticism and an overblown musicality. The *Diario* is, thus, a momentous break from earlier forms of modernity and a giant step toward the high modernism of the inter-war period, the modernism of the earliest manifestations of the Spanish avant-garde and the early maturity of the so-called Generation of 1927. In the poetry, and in general, the literature, of high Spanish modernism we should make certain distinctions between the avant-garde of 1919–25, and the subsequent work of the Generation of 1927. The avant-garde produced more heat than light, more movement than purpose, more sound than substance, as it engaged in the unceasing creation of movements and produced a remarkably small amount of enduring literature. The most important of them in Spain, *Ultra*, was not much more than a series of gestures, most of which were borrowed from Italian futurism and its debrained fascist cult of the machine, speed and violence, and from the aimless French avant-garde of the immediate post-war that had not quite yet evolved toward surrealism. *Ultra* left us next to no good poetry, and yet in one regard it was quite fruitful, for it placed on poetry's centre stage a single rhetorical figure, what José Ortega y Gasset would call 'the advanced geometry of metaphor', which provides one of the keys to the poetry of the 1920s and beyond. It also contributed an appetite for cinema, which would be a key element in the aesthetics of the new writers.

The vacuity of much of Spain's avant-garde poetry stands in stark contrast to the achievements of the Generation of 1927, so-called because of its celebration in that year of the third centennial of the death of the seventeenth-century baroque poet, Luis de Góngora. It is not simply that there were a few remarkable poets, like Federico García Lorca (1898–1936), whose poetry and drama are familiar to anglophone readers, or Vicente Aleixandre (1898–1984), who was awarded the Nobel Prize for Literature in 1977. It is rather that there were a number of poets, such as Jorge Guillén (1893–1984) and Luis Cernuda (1902–63), whose accomplishments are equal to theirs, and numerous others whose legacy is a poetic *oeuvre* of surpassing beauty and complexity. Among them are Pedro Salinas (1891–1951), Gerardo Diego (1896–1987), Emilio Prados (1899–1962), Manuel Altolaguirre (1905–59), José Bergamín (1897–1983), and finally, because at 95 years of age he is the only poet of his generation who is still living, Rafael Alberti (1902–). It would also be unjust not to mention a great scholar and critic, Dámaso Alonso (1898–1990), whose editions of Góngora's poetry served to focus attention on the affinities between the baroque and the poetry of high modernism, although his most important volume of poetry, *Hijos de la ira* (*Children of Anger*, 1944), dates from the post-war period.

There is a vast distance separating the symbolists of 1900 from the poets of the 1920s and 1930s. That distance can be measured in aesthetics, in the way of conceiving of and writing poetry, but it is also one of generational style. The turn-of-the-century poets and writers often adopted bohemian forms of behaviour; they were more likely to be found in cafés than in libraries. With the exceptions of Unamuno, who held the chair of Greek language and literature at the University of Salamanca, and Pío Baroja, who was trained as a physician but immediately abandoned the practice of medicine, the writers of 1900 were fundamentally self-taught. By way of contrast, the younger writers of the twenties, particularly the poets, were in many cases not only university-trained, but were among the finest scholars and critics to be found in the Spain of those years. Dámaso Alonso, Jorge Guillén and Pedro Salinas held university chairs Salinas taught first at the Sorbonne and later at Cambridge, and Guillén was his successor at the Sorbonne. In 1929, Ernesto Giménez Caballero published an inquiry in his review, *La Gaceta Literaria* (*The Literary Gazette*), in which he asked older writers what they thought of the younger poets, and Antonio Machado, one of their most uncompromising critics, admitted that they were far less provincial and much better educated, or at least more educable, than their predecessors. By way of example, we need only compare Manuel Machado's often shoddy and improvised translations of Verlaine with Guillén's impeccable translations of Valéry.

One of the few characteristics that the younger poets did share with the writers of the Generation of 1898 was the institution of the little review. Unlike the turn-of-the-century reviews, those of the twenties and early thirties were often associated with a single poet or editor: Jiménez's *Indice*, Gerardo Diego's *Carmen* and Manuel Altolaguirre and Emilio Prados' *Litoral*. The reviews functioned, as they had earlier in the century, as a form of internal communication among poets who cultivated a poetics and a vocation that marked them off both from earlier poets and from Spanish society. In this regard, *Revista de Occidente* (*Occidental Review*) deserves special mention. A monthly founded in 1923 by José Ortega y Gasset, it was not a poetry review, nor was it little. At the time, Ortega was at the height of his power and influence both as a philosopher and as a creator of publications that almost immediately became major cultural institutions in Spain. In this new and immensely influential review, the word 'occidente' has the same resonance as *abendsland*, literally 'twilightland', in Oswald Spengler's *The Decline of the West*, and it conveys the sense of the defence of European high culture, civilization's sole guarantee against decadence, barbarianism and chaos, the rule of the masses.

Nowhere was the influence of Ortega and *Revista de Occidente* clearer than in the emergence of the 'dehumanized novel', so-called because it followed the aesthetic postulates that Ortega had expounded in his essay *The Dehumanization of Art* (1925). With the term 'dehumanization' Ortega synthesized high modernism's rejection of romanticism's postulate of an emotional bond between the literary text and the reader, and realism's belief in denotation as the supreme value in art. 'Dehumanized' art requires distance rather than proximity, the absolute autonomy and, in consequence, self-referentiality of the work of art, which will be free both of nineteenth-century sentimentality and the often facile musicality of symbolist lyric. In one of *Revista de Occidente*'s all-important publishing ventures, Ortega launched a 'dehumanized novel' series, the *Nova novorum*, that feature works such as *El profesor inútil* (*The Useless Professor*, 1926) by the leader of the school, Benjamín Jarnés (1888–1949), as well as works by the poet Pedro Salinas, Antonio Espina (1894–1972), and other young writers.

The great literature of the younger generation, however, is to be found in poetry. It is impossible in this space to do justice to the artistic achievements of the poets of the Generation of 1927, which were profound, numerous and enduring, but there are a few, Guillén, García Lorca, Aleixandre, Cernuda and Alberti, whose work merits special mention. Guillén was the eldest of the five. He published his first book, *Cántico* (*Canticle*, 1928), when he was in his mid-thirties and at the height of his first poetic maturity. *Cántico* stands along with Juan Ramón Jiménez's *Diario* as a work that embodies the modernist ideal in which a book must be read, at least at one level, as a single self-referential text, and there is no work of modern or contemporary Spanish poetry of greater formal perfection. As its title suggests, it is an ode to the joy of human existence, an exaltation of a *natural* world that is well made. I emphasize natural to distinguish it from the *social* world, which for Guillén is not necessarily well constituted, as he demonstrated in his subsequent work, the appropriately titled *Clamor* (1957–63). For even in the mid-1920s, when he defended pure poetry, he did so in a habitually nuanced way; as he wrote in a letter to Fernando Vela, the managing director of *Revista de Occidente*, in 1927, we must advocate a poetry that is 'rather pure but not too much'.

The only Spanish poet – and playwright – who has won a permanent audience in the English-speaking world is Federico García Lorca. Until 1929, Lorca's finest lyric poems synthesized a modernist sensibility with traditional Spanish song forms, but in 1929 he journeyed to New York and produced a series of poems that reflected the greatest and most brutal of modern cities. He spent his months in New York at Columbia University, just a few blocks south of Harlem, New York's vast black ghetto, and many of his poems captured the social, racial and psychological violence of that place. Like Lorca, Rafael Alberti had cultivated traditional song forms, particularly in his youthful volume, *Marinero en tierra* (*Landlocked Sailor*, 1924), which won him the National Literary Prize in 1925. However, just before his friend Lorca departed for New York, Alberti had completed one of his finest works, *Sobre los ángeles* (*Regarding Angels*, 1928), and was beginning what may today stand as his finest book, *Sermones y moradas* (*Sermons and Dwellings*, 1929–30).

The mention of these two works, along with *Poeta in Nueva York* and Vicente Aleixandre's *Espadas como labios* (*Swords Like Lips*, 1932), inevitably brings up the presence of surrealism in the Spain of the 1920s and

1930s. With the publication of the French poet André Breton's first surrealist manifesto in 1924, the most important movement of the twentieth-century modernist culture – literature, painting, cinema – had its start. Surrealism began in France with poetic readings of Freud and the search for a mode of poetic composition that was, or that the surrealists wanted to be, not only an exploration of the unconscious, but one that employed the very methods of the unconscious. The surrealists aspired to reproduce the movement, the shape, the feel of the unconscious immediately, that is, without the mediation of the logic and reason of conscious thought. Thus, they conducted experiments in what they called automatic writing, the attempted transcription of the grammar and syntax and substance of dreams as they occurred.

In Spain the greatest modernist artists were engendered in Barcelona, but Paris was the heart of modernist art and Picasso was neither the first nor the last of Spanish artists to take up residence there. There is a very real sense in which by the 1920s Paris was the centre of Spanish painting. José Victoriano González, the great cubist painter known by his pseudonym Juan Gris, was born in Madrid in 1887 and emigrated to Paris at the age of 19. There he met Picasso and made a living, as he had in Madrid, as a magazine and book illustrator. He did not exhibit for several years but early in the second decade of the century his work turns up in the major cubist shows. That work, both in its analytical and synthetic phases, is characterized by an extraordinarily lyrical line, an elegance of composition and a sense of colour's role in composition, that gives him a place of honour among the earliest and greatest of cubist painters – Picasso, Braque, Léger, and Juan Gris.

In the Paris of the 1920s, several Spanish artists made significant and, in some cases, key contributions to surrealism. Chief among them were the Mallorcan painter Joan Miró and the Aragonese film maker Luis Buñuel. If only for his notoriety, the Catalan Salvador Dalí, the most overrated painter of the twentieth century, also deserves mention. In addition, he collaborated on the script of the 1929 surrealist film classic, Luis Buñuel's *Un chien andalou*. The film was based on two dreams that Buñuel recounted to Dalí. The first, and one of the most arresting images in film history, is the opening scene of *Un chien andalou*, in which a cloud cuts the moon in two and a razor does likewise to an eye. The second dream was that of a hand filled with ants. The next year Buñuel made *L'âge d'or* and shortly thereafter returned to Madrid.

During these years, Spanish film, with the exception of a handful of avant-garde improvisations, was the bailiwick of producers who cranked out genre movies filled with bullfighters, flamenco dancers and non-stop melodrama. The first great film made in Spain, and one of the most distinguished documentaries in all of film history was Buñuel's *Tierra sin pan*. This work is the result of an encounter between the modernity of a young cinematic genius and the millennial wretchedness of a remote region of Extremadura, Las Hurdes, the poorest place of a very poor country. But that encounter takes place at the level of determinate absence. In 1932 Buñuel documented the unrelieved misery of a place where, just as in Carlo Levi's superb memoire of political exile in a southern hamlet of Mussolini's Italy, *Cristo si è fermato a Eboli*, Christ, that is, civilization itself, never ventured. What does go forth with Buñuel to las Hurdes is a deity of modern culture and, like God, it is the one thing we never see, but it is also the thing by virtue of which we see what had until then been rendered invisible, the misery of an entire people. That thing is the movie camera, virtually the only object involved in Buñuel's film that could not have been in that ghastly place in the year 1000. The most stunning aspect of this film is its very condition of possibility, the unregistered encounter between the wealth, power and knowledge objectified in the technology of that machine, and the millennial wretchedness which it had been brought from Madrid to record. There is, then, a very real sense in which *Tierra sin pan* is as much about asphalt, that is, about Madrid and its culture, as it is about land and bread. With *Tierra sin pan* a pre-war cinema of high quality begins and simultaneously comes to an end.

For all the Spanish contribution to surrealism in France, in Spain itself there was never an organized surrealist movement and the acceptance of surrealism among the major Spanish poets of the twenties has often been called into question. This does not diminish surrealism's great importance in the Spain of the 1920s and 1930s. Surrealism was an infinitely liberating experience for Spanish poets. It opened them and their poetic language to primal, violent dream states, frequently tragic but often traversed by the kind of nihilistic humour that the painter Salvador Dalí raised to an art form and in the last, meretricious half of his life, turned into a ready source of income. Surrealism, with its revolutionary overtones, was also for some poets a step toward a poetry that was less concerned with purity of diction and form and more engaged with the world, in particular the world of politics.

From purity and dehumanization to a literature of social commitment

The series of political crises that occasioned the fall of the monarchy and the proclamation of the second Republic on 14 April 1931, did not of themselves effect a sea change in the course of literary creation in Spain. In fact, the rejection of 'dehumanization' was already taking place at the close of the decade of the twenties. It is no accident that the prime examples of a 'rehumanized' novel, José Díaz Fernández's *El blocao* (*The Blockhouse*, 1928) and Ramón Sender's *Imán* (*Magnet*, 1930) thematized Spain's colonial war in Morocco. Poetry would soon break with the ideal of purity, whether relative or absolute, that had been so important in the 1920s. By 1930 there was an emerging sense that the ideal of purity that had arisen in the previous decade had either been fulfilled or, alternatively, should be rejected for a more socially engaged literature. We have seen that for García Lorca New York had the same revulsive effect as the Moroccan War had for

Sender and Díaz Fernández, and that the revolutionary dimension of surrealism had for other poets and writers. At the same time, in 1930, Díaz Fernández expressed the need for a renewed social engagement in literature in a series of essays published in a volume called *El nuevo romanticismo* (*The New Romanticism*), in which he argued for a synthesis of humanism and modern machine culture. Díaz Fernández had already brought those ideas to bear in his novel *La venus mecánica* (*The Mechanical Venus*, 1929). *El nuevo romanticismo* expressed the author's and many other writers' and readers' rejection of Ortega's ideas on 'dehumanized' art, and postulated a politically engaged and progressive modernism that would be one of the salient characteristics of the literature of the 1930s.

The Second Republic was in many ways a culminating moment for Spanish letters. Several of the older writers, those of the so-called Generation of 1898, created some of their most enduring works during those years. Among them are Unamuno's novella of religious crisis, *San Manuel Bueno, mártir* (*Saint Emmanuel the Good, Martyr*, 1934). It is a work with strong Dostoyevskian echoes about a village priest who has lost his faith and goes to his death with his secret intact in order to preserve the faith of his parishioners. In *Juan de Mairena* (1936) Antonio Machado invented the last and most engaging of his apocryphal poets and philosophers. Finally, in the late 1920s and early 1930s Valle-Inclán wrote his 'Ruedo Ibérico' series, which by any standard are the finest cycle of historical novels in Spanish literature.

Just as important was the emergence of new voices and the renewal of relatively young ones. With support from the Republic's Ministry of Education, García Lorca founded an alternative theatre, La Barraca (The Shack). La Barraca, a student enterprise, took remarkably modern productions of Spanish classical theatre – works by Lope de Vega, Pedro Calderón de la Barca and other seventeenth-century dramatic poets – to rural Spanish audiences which often had not seen anything of the kind since the time, in the seventeenth century, of wandering actors who put on shows in towns and villages. These experiences, in turn, strongly influenced Lorca's rural dramas of unrequited passion and violence, *Bodas de sangre* (*Blood Wedding*, 1932), *Yerma* (*Barren*, 1934) and *La casa de Bernarda Alba* (*The House of Bernarda Alba*, 1936).

The new literary voices of the 1930s were both numerous and talented. Among the younger poets, the most memorable is surely Miguel Hernández (1910–42). Hernández was not only endowed with an immensely original and powerful poetic voice, he was a social oddity. Nearly all of the great Spanish poets of the period were recruited from a higher or lower stratum of the bourgeoisie. Some, like Juan Ramón Jiménez and Federico García Lorca, belonged to families that were quite prosperous, and others, such as Antonio and Manuel Machado, who came from a family of intellectuals, lived in much more precarious circumstances, but in nearly every case there was access either to money or to high culture or to both. Hernández was the exception to the rule, for he was a shepherd, not like the idealized courtiers that were the stock-in-trade of Renaissance bucolic literature, but simply a shepherd. His first book, *Perito en lunas* (*Expert on Moons*, 1933) reveals a young poet who has both fully assimilated the technical lessons of the 1920s, particularly the use of baroque metaphor, and a rigorous sense of form. Just as his first book deployed a classic Renaissance form, the octave, his next book, *El rayo que no cesa* (*Ceaseless Lightning*, 1936) is, if possible, even more classical on a purely formal plane, for the single most dominant form in that book is the sonnet. Its tone, however, is social and earthy in the manner of Pablo Neruda's *Residencia en la tierra*, and metaphorical in the manner of the Generation of 1927.

Along with the new poetry there is a new narrative that merits more attention than it has received. Max Aub (1903–72) began his literary career in the twenties under the influence of Ortega y Gasset's ideas on the novel and 'dehumanized' art. Although his greatest works were written after the Civil War in exile in Mexico, during the Republic he wrote one of the finest novels of the period, *Luis Alvarez Petreña*. The protagonist of the novel, a failed artist and an equally failed human being, is Aub's way of squaring accounts with the 1920s and his own artistic past.

The Republic witnessed a flowering of social and political narrative. Following *Imán*, Ramón Sender wrote one of the best and least known political novels of twentieth-century Spain, *Siete domingos rojos* (*Seven Red Sundays*, 1933), and an excellent historical novel which won him the National Literary Prize in 1935, *Mr Witt en el cantón* (*Mr Witt in the Canton*), about the revolutionary uprising of 1873 in Cartagena. In addition to Sender's, there are important political and social novels by César M. Arconada (1898–1964), including *La Turbina* (*The Turbine*, 1930) and *Reparto de tierras* (*Redistribution of Land*, 1934), and by the prolix and unclassifiable Joaquín Arderíus (1890–1969).

Postscript

On 18 July 1936 the Civil War broke out. Salamanca, Unamuno's home city, was the seat of the provisional military government, the nucleus of what for the next 39 years would be the dictatorship of General Francisco Franco. In that place and in those circumstances the commemoration of 12 October, the Día de la Raza or Day of the Race in the language of Spanish nationalism, took on very great importance. In that commemoration, an aged and ailing Miguel de Unamuno shared the speakers' rostrum with the commander of the Foreign Legion, General Millán Astray, who gave a delirious harangue, a veritable model of the fascist cult of violence, in which he cried '¡Muera la inteligencia!' These words can be interpreted in two ways, first 'Death to intelligence,' or, alternatively, 'Death to the intelligentsia.' Unamuno replied courageously, 'Vencerán, pero no convencerán.' In effect, he stated, you may prevail by force of arms, you may very well be victorious but you will not persuade the Spanish people. Unamuno died two and a half months later and did not live to see how right he was. As right as José Ortega y Gasset who, from exile, wrote Unamuno's obituary, and with it the obituary of the entire pre-war intelligentsia. In it he observed that with the death of his always vociferous rival, and in the midst of the war's cacophony, a fearful silence had descended upon Spain.

SPAIN IN THE INTERWAR CRISIS OF LIBERALISM, 1914–1939

The First World War opened a long period of crisis that affected all of Europe. Neutrality was no escape: Spain did not intervene in the war, but the war intervened in Spain and brought the Restoration under pressures to which it would eventually succumb. But while the interwar crisis was shared, the specific form it took and the ways in which it played itself out varied from country to country. In Spain, liberal constitutionalism was succeeded by a military dictatorship, Spain's first, in 1923. However, General Primo de Rivera failed in his attempt to institutionalize his rule by creating a single-party regime on the fascist model, and was removed from power in January 1930. The attempt to return to the Restoration system failed and led instead to a democratic republic. Facing a host of domestic problems and an unfavourable international political and economic environment, the Second Republic's attempts at progressive reform generated increasing opposition which, in turn, produced further polarization. But when the right tried to deliver the coup de grace, by means of a military coup, the result was a civil war that lasted three years and thrust Spain into the centre of European power politics.

This section opens with an overview of Spain's economic development between 1780 and 1930 by Leandro Prados de la Escosura. Prados questions the predominant view that Spain was an economic failure; he argues, instead, that Spain experienced sustained and significant economic development, especially in the two decades before the Civil War, while at the same time falling further behind countries such as Britain and France. Some aspects of the pessimistic view remain valid, but Spain enjoyed enough of the attributes of modern economic growth for its experience to be much closer to the European vanguard than to the contemporary 'Third World'. This economic growth, and the social and cultural changes that flowed from it, set the stage for the political crisis that followed.

Luis Arranz, Mercedes Cabrera and Fernando del Rey take up the fate of the Restoration during and after the First World War. The *turno*, on which the system was based, was already under severe pressure. It survived attempts by a range of opposition forces – Catalan nationalists, Republicans, Socialists and anarchosyndicalists – to use the renewed political activism of the military to overthrow it in 1917, but the end was not far off. Attempts to incorporate some opposition forces were inadequate and in September 1923 the king sanctioned a twentieth-century *pronunciamiento*. The authors see this outcome as far from inevitable, but made possible by a series of weaknesses in Spanish political life: the fragmentation of the dynastic parties; the divisions and lack of a committed parliamentary approach of the Socialists and Republicans, and the spread of a climate of opinion, Regenerationism, which favoured efficiency over democracy and viewed the death of liberalism with indifference and even satisfaction.

Javier Tusell and Genoveva Queipo de Llano see the dictatorship of Primo de Rivera, which lasted from 1923 to 1930, as a step away from democratization that furthered polarization and radicalization. Primo sought to embody the Regenerationist dream of the 'Iron Surgeon', who would excise the cancerous elements from political life. He also adopted a heightened nationalism, which was reflected in his policies towards Catalonia, Morocco and the economy. Perhaps the most striking feature of his rule, however, was his toleration of the Socialists and his desire to involve them in the institutionalization of the regime. They refused, joining a diverse group of political and social forces in opposition. When the economic prosperity that had buoyed the regime disappeared with the Depression that began in 1929, Primo was dumped, but the attempts to return to the *status quo ante* failed and brought a second republic rather than a return to the Restoration.

Nigel Townson's point of departure for analysing the Second Republic is to see it 'in its own right' and not just as the prelude to the Civil War. He emphasizes the complexities of national politics and the 'labyrinthine reality' of the years 1931 to 1936 against older interpretations that have focused on a bipolar left–right division. The Republic ran aground on a series of socioeconomic and cultural conflicts that split classes as well as bringing them into conflict. The class struggle in the cities and the countryside was important, but so were the struggles between Catholics and anticlericals, regional nationalists and centralists, republican and non-republican middle classes and anarchosyndicalists and socialists. Only a 'greater commitment from all the forces of the Republic to compromise and the rules of parliamentary democracy' could have overcome such deep and multiple conflicts. These divisions, as much as those between workers and bourgeoisie, were responsible for the collapse of the broad coalition that had brought the Republic into existence as well as for providing issues around which a renewed right could coalesce in a new party. The failure of its legalist tactics and the victory of the Popular Front in the elections of February 1936 led the right to a more traditional approach: the military coup.

This time, however, the *pronunciamiento* produced civil war. The Spanish Civil War was the product of domestic conflicts, but foreign intervention quickly enmeshed it in the broader power politics of Europe. In turn, this internationalization led to a complex struggle whose roots were defined in manicheistic terms of good versus evil, a definition whose life was prolonged by the Cold War. In his chapter, George Esenwein goes beyond this morality play perspective to view the Civil War in its full complexity. Esenwein discusses such classic issues as foreign intervention and the conflicts among the forces in the Republican zone, but he also examines more neglected matters, such as cultural life and gender relations. He also provides a narrative of the events that led to the victory of the Nationalists and the creation of the dictatorship that would dominate Spain for the next 36 years.

11

Economic growth and backwardness, 1780–1930

LEANDRO PRADOS DE LA ESCOSURA

During the nineteenth century Spain underwent a complex transition from a colonial empire under the Ancien Regime to a modern nation with a liberal system of property rights. The nature of this transition has led to a negative view of post-imperial Spain. This is particularly true of its economic performance, which has frequently been described using words such as stagnation, backwardness and failure. In the Spanish context, these concepts can be traced back to Jaume Vivens Vives, who first described the pre-First World War Spanish economy as underdeveloped.

Gabriel Tortella was the first to undertake a study of long-term economic trends during the nineteenth century, and he concluded that 'the Spanish economy offered a picture of stagnation when contrasted with most of its Western European neighbours'. Nicolás Sánchez Albornoz has painted a more complex picture, highlighting the paradox of the level of growth Spain achieved during the nineteenth century alongside the continuously widening gap that separated Spain from other western European economies. He also stressed the dualistic nature of the Spanish economy, and described the nineteenth century as a transition from a traditional European economy to a modern condition of underdevelopment.

The concept of failure, which O'Brien and Keyder define as 'opportunities missed, leads lost and output foregone because of a neglect of best economic practice', was first applied to the Spanish case by Tortella, who saw the key to Spain's nineteenth century as 'an effort to industrialize that failed'. Later, Jordi Nadal developed a definition of failure as the inability to reproduce the English model and described Spain's economic performance between 1830 and 1913 as 'the failure of the Industrial Revolution'. But rather than equating Spain with the developing countries of the late twentieth century, Nadal saw it as a 'late joiner, as an attempt, largely thwarted, to join the ranks of the first comers'.

The inability of Spain to develop economically according to the 'European' model can only be understood through a study of the endogenous and exogenous elements[1] common to most historical interpretations. Among the endogenous factors, agriculture has been given a central importance. For Tortella, natural resources and property rights are major obstacles for Mediterranean economies such as Spain's: low productivity and the retention of a large percentage of the labour force produces low levels of per capita income and narrow domestic markets for manufactured consumer goods. In addition, agricultural backwardness is seen as contributing to high mortality rates and slow demographic expansion.

Not all historians put the blame so squarely on agriculture. Sánchez Albornoz cites the lack of dynamism of the Catalan textile industry, and recent studies have stressed the importance of the mediocrity of the industrial sector. Pedro Fraile asserts that in the century after 1830 the growth elasticities[2] of the cotton and iron and steel industries were lower in Spain than in other nations, and Tortella emphasizes the attitudes of Spanish entrepreneurs who sought tariff protection rather than facing competition in international markets.

The role of government is another endogenous element. Historians have pointed to a number of ways in which government policy hindered economic development: the diversion of capital into agriculture through the disentailment process and the application of budgetary policies leading to rising interest rates and the crowding out of private investment.

But historians of nineteenth century Spain have tended to give greater weight to the exogenous forces, especially the loss of the Latin American colonies and the subsequent gradual integration of the economy into the broader European economy over the course of the century. For Vicens Vives, the loss of the empire was the major obstacle to Spain's economic modernization, as the regions most deeply involved in colonial commerce failed to achieve modern economic growth. This line of reasoning has been dominant for more than two decades, although historians have not provided much empirical evidence to support it. Tortella has been one of the few dissenters: 'the cost of losing the colonies', he writes, 'cannot be considered as a vital factor in Spain's backwardness'.

The various analyses of Spain's 'failure' or 'backwardness' or 'retardation' have rarely been accompanied with solid quantitative evidence, let alone systematically tested with the statistical and econometric models now available. Comparisons, both explicit and implicit, of Spain's economic performance with that of other European nations are based on limited or shaky empirical evidence; in most cases, 'guesstimates' or proxies of structural change are designed to test the extent to which the Spanish experience fits the British paradigm of modern economic growth. Moreover, the various hypotheses that have been proposed as explanations of Spain's relatively poor performance have not been subjected to the empirical tests now common in British, French and German economic history. This delay has been due to the inadequacy of the official statistics and the fact that the task of data reconstruction had hardly begun until the 1970s.

The rest of this chapter summarizes my research on the process of change in the Spanish economy during the transition from a colonial economy to a peripheral nation. The chapter is structured as follows. Section 1 proposes a definition of backwardness. Section 2 confronts the crucial question of the loss of empire. The negative effects of the loss of empire varied by both region and economic sector, but the overall effect appears to have been milder than is generally believed and in the short run probably fell below 6 per cent of GDP. The loss of the Latin American colonies cannot be held responsible for more than a small part of the pervasive and long-term retardation of Spanish agriculture, industry and finance from 1820 to 1914. Section 3 analyses the role of the agricultural sector, which accounted for about half of GDP and employed about two-thirds of the labour force throughout the century. The picture is more optimistic than is usually presented: output appears to have increased steadily over the century, and more rapidly than population, and this was due, at least in part, to improvements in the productivity of land and labour, especially a shift from subsistence to commercialized agriculture and the response to foreign demand for agricultural products.

The degree to which agricultural backwardness was responsible for the weakness of industrial development is examined in Section 4. Spanish industrial production showed far from unimpressive growth, but compared to both the pioneering industrial nations and the later comers, the rate of growth was quite slow. This difference was due less to the size of the domestic market than to the levels of exports, itself a result of a basic lack of competitiveness. Finally, Section 5 questions the view that foreign trade had negative effects on Spanish economic development; rather than the product of dependency, backwardness in nineteenth-century Spain seems to have been 'its own doing'.

1   Backwardness, growth and structural change

Structural change in the Spanish economy can be compared to a 'typical' western European standard which establishes the degree of convergence and pinpoints the possible sources of divergence. In general, Spanish development did not follow western European patterns of structural change, but on the other hand there are no similarities to patterns in the contemporary Third World. The emerging picture is one of a retarded economy with low investment rates, a weak industrial sector, a large subsistence agriculture, a low degree of openness, a delayed demographic transition and limited rates of human capital formation. At the same time, from the 1830s on, it experienced a sustained increase in real per capita income and by 1930 had reached levels of per capita income similar to those of Italy in 1914.

Spain experienced consistent economic progress but along its own, idiosyncratic path, but at the very moment that it began to enjoy sustained growth it also began to experience relative backwardness: the Spanish economic structure began to diverge from that of other European countries and the difference in per capita income grew. The reality of structural change and per capita income growth preclude considering Spain as an under-developed semi-colonial economy. They also preclude describing the Spanish economy as stagnant. The concept of 'backwardness', which is compatible with growth and change, is perhaps the most applicable to the Spanish economy before the First World War.

2   The loss of empire

For many scholars, the loss of the bulk of the American empire by 1820 and the subsequent reorientation of the economy towards Europe have been seen as inimical for Spanish economic development before 1914. My own approach has suggested that the effect of the loss of empire was smaller than that posited by other historians. On the basis of a reconstruction of commodity trading between Spain and the colonies from 1784 to 1820, together with data on central government revenues, I calculated upper-bound estimates of the repercussions of colonial independence on trade in commodities and services, on investment and on revenues. Trade flows and government revenue did decline, and domestic investment also fell despite the fact that colonial emancipation also produced a repatriation of capital. The manufacturing industry may have been the most affected because the colonies had provided it with a protected market. Financial, commercial and transport services in cities like Seville and Cádiz, which had been closely linked to colonial trade, also suffered.

It is also important to analyse the gains obtained from patterns of trade and specialization produced by the colonial market. The composition of colonial imports suggests that the possibility of increasing production by reallocating resources would have been small and that most gains possibly resulted from an improvement in the patterns of consumption. Nevertheless, colonial products could have been obtained on the international market so that colonial trade would only have been beneficial if Spain had been able to acquire those commodities at prices below those of the market. The assumption here is that Spain's entry into the international market as a purchaser of primary products would not have significantly altered prices, as Spain was a small country and consequently a price taker.[3] Moreover, Spain did not depend on the colonies for masses of raw materials. For example, the Catalan cotton textile industry depended less on raw cotton from the colonies than on cotton yarn imported from Europe. This situation only emphasizes the weakness of the Catalan spinning industry at this time.

Industrial exports such as textiles, iron and steel, paper, milling and spirits certainly stimulated the development of manufacturing in the peninsula. What has to be asked, however, is whether the ratio between foreign trade and national income represents the externalities[4] for the economy derived from the growth of industrial exports. The highly protectionist nature of colonial legislation made Spanish manufactures artificially competitive in Latin America, but even so, the lack of competitiveness of these industries at the end of the eighteenth century was such that Spanish merchants imported and then re-exported to the Indies large quantities of foreign manufactures, even though these were subject to high taxes both on entering Spain and leaving it again. The loss of the colonies was most acutely felt by industry and by specific regions, especially Andalucia and Catalonia.

The evolution of particular industries after 1820 demonstrates that the medium and long-term consequences of Latin American independence depended on the flexibility and dynamism of the industry concerned. For example, the Basque iron and steel industry became uncompetitive from the 1770s on. Colonial markets accounted for at least a third of Basque production at the end of the eighteenth century, but demand from Spanish America, together with domestic demand, seems to have offset the decline in European demand. The Valencian silk industry presents a similar picture: between the 1790s and the 1820s, net exports of raw silk rose while net imports of silk textiles also increased.

Colonial markets were central to the Catalan textile industry, but even so, as much as 80 per cent of the demand for its products came from within Catalonia. Indeed, the maturing of the textile industry coincided with the loss of the colonies and their overseas markets. Instead of relying exclusively on import substitution[5] to stimulate growth, Catalan textile production grew at the same time as an increase in the smuggling of British cotton textiles into Spain through Spain and Gibraltar. This complementary expansion of both domestic production and contraband can be explained through rising demand, derived to some extent from the substitution of cotton for more traditional fibres such as wool and linen, and the lack of an integrated domestic market.

The loss of the colonies definitely had a negative effect on the Spanish economy, especially in the short term. Trade in goods and services fell sharply and investment levels declined. Domestic industry lost a protected market and the government's fiscal difficulties worsened as it lost an important source of revenue. That said, the true sources of Spain's post-imperial shortcomings are to be found elsewhere.

The quantitative evidence available suggests that the loss of the colonies had a less profound and widespread impact on the Spanish economy than has generally been thought. The most competitive and flexible sectors of the economy eventually adapted to the new circumstances. This was particularly true of commercial agriculture, which found growing markets in north-west Europe.

3 The performance of Spanish agriculture: a reassessment

The role of agriculture in retarding Spain's economic development has been a favourite topic of historians. Tortella has noted that agricultural stagnation, and the inability of agriculture to grow more quickly than the population, explains, at least in part, the delay in Spain's modernization. More recently, James Simpson has described the nineteenth century as Spanish agriculture's 'long siesta', during which it grew only slightly more than did population. My own estimates question these negative assessments. Moreover, I find the sources of agricultural growth to have been different from those suggested by Tortella and Sánchez Albornoz: where Tortella attributes growth to 'technology', I find it in the reallocation of cultivated land in favour of more valuable crops. Thus, the relative decline of low-value cereals and legumes and the relative growth of higher value and more labour intensive crops increased the demand for otherwise underemployed labour. The result was an increase in output per worker employed in the agricultural sector.

The picture for the first half of the nineteenth century broadly agrees with the historical literature that suggests an expansion of production in line with population and a tendency for output per worker to fall. What is not clear, however, is whether the increase in supply of cultivable land until mid-century, itself a product of disentailment, led to a decline in yields, as some scholars have claimed. Land productivity did not change much between 1800 and 1869, and the danger of periodic harvest failure remained.

When we come to the second half of the century the picture changes. The data reconstruction exercises show an increase in the growth of output compared to the first half of the century. This led to a greater per capita output, while the efficiency in the use of land and labour, measured in output per worker and per hectare, also increased. It does not seem likely then, that the productivity of either land or labour declined due to the lack of technological change. The data do show that at the turn of the century the performance of the sector was marked by increased output per hectare, due to the relative decline of cereals, and an increase in labour productivity.

The measured increase in labour productivity raises the question of the extent to which the retention of a large share of the active population in agriculture was the result of general agricultural stagnation, or whether it reflects the inability of the 'urban sectors' of the economy to absorb labour at a rate that might have stimulated agricultural modernization. Since agriculture appears to have been more dynamic than is commonly assumed by historians, the implication is that other activities must bear a larger share of the responsibility for Spain's economic backwardness. Moreover, part of the cause for the inefficiency of agriculture can be found in inappropriate economic policies. Less tariff protection for cereals would have led through the price mechanism to a more intense reallocation of labour to commercial agriculture, industry and services.

Consideration of sectoral productivity and the gap between agriculture and the rest of the economy makes an enlightening test. Historians have long pointed to the weak demand for industrial goods in the agrarian sector as a major cause of backwardness. A comparison of agricultural output and productivity between Spain and other European countries might cast some light on the contribution of agriculture to the creation of a demand for industrial goods. Agricultural output grew faster in Spain than in France or Britain during the nineteenth century, although output per male worker grew more slowly in Spain, widening the gap which was already apparent in 1800.

Did natural endowments such as altitude, soil and precipitation determine the crop mix in Spain, especially the reduced weight of livestock and the importance of cereals? Or was this mix the product of the system of landholding, the endowment of human capital and protectionist policies? In other words, did Spain face natural limits to agrarian development or was agriculture hindered by inefficient resource allocation? Natural conditions certainly played a role: geographical studies show that soil quality, precipitation, temperature and topography meant that Spanish land could not reach the yields available in France or Britain. Given this lower quality of land, Spain would have needed a higher land–labour ratio and a greater emphasis on livestock to reach French or British levels of output per worker. Why this did not happen; why a greater and more widespread release of labour did not take place and why a traditional labour-intensive agriculture emphasizing cereal production and using marginal lands persisted for so long, remain the key questions. My own research has produced quantitative evidence that indicates that responsibility for the slow, but not unimpressive, growth of Spanish agriculture rests with factors that retarded the release of labour from the sector, encouraged cereal production and retained marginal land in production. This retardation can be attributed to protectionist policies and the inability of non-agrarian sectors to draw labour away from agriculture. Within these constraints, agriculture was responsive to markets and to incentives to specialize, and ready to adjust its use of the scarce factors of production.

4   Industrial growth and the market

The standard historical explanation of the weak performance of Spanish industry emphasizes the small size of the domestic market and the constraints imposed by the low per capita income of the rural population. This hypothesis can now be tested with newly available data by comparing levels of industrialization in Spain with levels in other European economies with similar per capita incomes. The results of my research refute the argument that the lack of domestic demand was the main obstacle to industrial growth in Spain; it also underscores the lack of connection between Spanish industry and the international market. Industrial exports accounted for a very low proportion of national income. The gap that separates Spanish industry from that elsewhere in Europe narrows when only domestic consumption is considered, that is, when exports are excluded from the comparison. In contrast, at similar levels of income, Spain exported many fewer industrial products. All this makes it difficult to conclude that the lack of domestic demand was the main factor holding back industry in nineteenth century Spain.

Industrial productivity and competitiveness differences are but the consequence of the growth gap between Spain and the more advanced European economies. If we compare industrial output per worker at similar levels of per capita income, we find that for the per capita income attained by Spain in 1910, its industrial output per worker was 124 per cent of that in Britain (which reached the same level of per capita income in 1830); 101 per cent of France (which reached that level in 1860) and 87 per cent of Germany (1880). This simple exercise points out that productivity differences diminish when comparing countries with equal per capita incomes and suggests that more backward European countries must specialize if they are to develop a manufacturing sector with an active presence in international markets.

The quantitative exercises I have developed cast serious doubt on the traditional explanation for Spain's industrial backwardness. The low per capita income associated with a backward agricultural sector is not a sufficient explanation for lagging industrial growth. Rather than the constraints of the domestic market, the inability of industry to export and the low level of industrial productivity go a long way to explaining the phenomenon. In this context, the attitudes and strategies of Spanish industrialists becomes very relevant. Their response to competing internationally was to redirect their efforts to the home market and seek tariff protection.

5 International trade and economic backwardness

Spanish trade grew impressively between 1815 and 1914, especially during the period of liberal government policy. Although exports were always dominated by primary products, trade patterns do show that Spain responded with a remarkable degree of flexibility to changes in international demand. The expansion of imported raw materials and capital goods at the expense of foodstuffs and consumer goods again affirms the responsiveness of trade to the demands of a growing economy.

The role of foreign trade in Spain's economic modernization was certainly positive: it opened larger foreign markets for goods such as minerals and metals as well as labour-intensive products. Trade also broadened the market for productive factors: it induced and stimulated the shift of workers from the subsistence sector into more valuable and labour intensive cash crops, and it led to land and mineral deposits being put to more intensive use. Consequently, national purchasing power increased and Spain was able to import capital goods and raw materials, thus avoiding potentially serious bottlenecks for growth. Trade stimulated the creation and integration of financial and land markets and foreign demand promoted expansion of the railway and shipping.

Trade grew much more rapidly than GNP, but for all its dynamism it was too small to have a substantial impact on the national economy. The counterfactual argument that there was a more efficient growth path independent of the international economy does not seem plausible. There is no quantitative evidence to support a theory that productivity in the export sector was inferior to that in sectors serving the domestic market. In addition, the domestic market does not appear to have offered any equally efficient alternative allocation for those factors of production used for exports. On the contrary, one could argue that a larger export sector would have increased levels of both employment and productivity, resulting in higher income. Thus, trade emerges not as the hegemonic element in Spain's economic modernization but, rather, as a small but indispensable stimulus of development.

Historians have frequently premised their interpretations of the secular retardation in southern and eastern Europe on the Prebisch–Singer doctrine[6] of relative price deterioration. My research demonstrates that from 1784 to 1913, the opposite happened: at least with regard to Britain Spain's net barter terms of trade[7] improved by a substantial margin. Single factorial trade estimates (corrected for unemployment) also show favourable trends in Spain, due mainly to increased opportunities for employment from enlarging the foreign trade sector. When levels of welfare or trends in the double factorial terms of trade[8] are measured, the results show that relative income evolved favourably in Spain against Britain due to the creation of new jobs.

During the nineteenth century, Spain's foreign trade followed a sustained growth path with higher rates than the economy as a whole. Changes in world demand influenced exports more significantly than did gains in competitiveness. It was in primary products that Spain enjoyed its comparative advantage. While Spain's exports were less diversified than those of more advanced European economies, changes in the products it did export show that Spain's export composition was much more flexible than in today's less developed countries. Moreover, structural changes in imports were closely related to the transformation experienced by the domestic economy.

Spain's foreign trade did exhibit a merchandise trade deficit,[9] but this was much smaller than has usually been contended. It was also less permanent, becoming a surplus after 1870. Even so, it is likely that, other than in the early years of the century, the current account balance[10] was negative. This deficit was financed through direct foreign investment, but from the 1880s onwards the decrease in foreign debt, the slowdown in foreign investment and the rapid increase in immigrant remittances combined to produce a surplus during the first decade of the twentieth century.

Gains from trade seem to have been proportionally related to the intensity of export activity. Spain did not develop a large export sector, but exports did grow faster than domestic product and their contribution to growth was especially important between 1860 and 1890. Linkages between trade and the domestic sector appear to have been limited, but international trade did help extend the market, make use of idle resources, improve the transportation system, create processing industries in mining regions, increase the propensity to save and create a modern financial system. Foreign demand also helped increase productivity in both mining and agriculture, facilitate the shift of labour from subsistence to commercial activities and create new jobs for unemployed workers. Thus, the limited size of linkage effects did not mean that trade had a negative effect on growth. Indeed, during the three decades when Spanish policy was most 'free trade' (1860–90) growth rates were similar to those in Europe's advanced economies while the years of protectionism (1890–1913) saw Spain's rate of growth fall behind. The Spanish case is one in which trade played a complementary rather than a leading role in the process of growth.

On the other hand, for most of the nineteenth century Spain did not experience the deterioration of prices for primary exports predicted by Prebisch and Singer. Between 1880 and 1913 the drop in relative export price was more than compensated for by the effect of new jobs and, to a lesser extent, by improvements in productivity. The result was an increase in the absolute welfare levels of the owners of the factors of production in the export sector and in relative levels compared to more advanced countries. Thus, any ground Spain lost to its European neighbours cannot be attributed to its specialization along the lines of comparative advantage[11] and the explanation for the growing divergence between living standards in Spain and elsewhere in Europe must lie outside the export sector.

Conclusions

Historians of nineteenth and early twentieth century Spain have interpreted its transformation from colonial empire into nation in terms of failure, backwardness and stagnation. My research questions these views; the main findings and questions raised can be summarized as follows:

1 Real per capita income experienced a sustained and, in historical terms, far from negligible growth over the long nineteenth century, and this accelerated in the two decades before the Spanish Civil War. Despite this, Spain's relative levels of income worsened over the same period; per capita income fell from two-thirds of British levels at the time of the Napoleonic wars to half in 1930.

2 Spain's pattern of development between 1850 and 1910 did not follow the western European 'norm'; there was a long delay between the start of modernization in 1830, as measured by rising real income per head, and the beginnings of structural transformation, which came only at the end of the century.

3 There is no conclusive evidence to support the view that the loss of empire was responsible for Spain's economic retardation. Despite the undoubted negative effects in the short run, the overall impact on GDP was less than 6 per cent, far less than estimated by historians, and concentrated in particular regions.

4 Agricultural production grew in both absolute and per capita terms during the nineteenth century, due to increases in productivity and larger amounts of resources used. Foreign demand actively promoted improvements in organization and resource allocation. While this evidence casts serious doubt on the argument that agriculture was at the root of Spain's industrial failure, it cannot dispute the fact that Spanish agriculture was less buoyant than its British or French counterparts: productivity grew more slowly and differences increased.

5 The key to the mediocre performance of Spanish industry was the failure to gain access to foreign markets, not the limited size of the domestic market. Between 1800 and 1910 manufacturing output and productivity increased, albeit more slowly than elsewhere in western Europe. There was a slight improvement in the level of industrialization per capita between 1910 and 1930, but this did not even begin to cut into other countries' lead in productivity. There can be no doubt that industry shares the responsibility for Spain's slow and insufficient modernization in the early twentieth century.

6 Exports represented only a small part of Spain's GDP, but they acted as a significant – and perhaps indispensable – stimulus to economic modernization. Foreign demand induced more efficient allocation of resources and the exploitation of natural advantage, especially in minerals and cash crops. Exports and imports displayed a degree of flexibility and the long-run balance of payments evolved in such a way as to render comparisons between nineteenth century Spain and contemporary Third World underdevelopment totally inappropriate. Theories of dependency formulated for Latin America have but limited relevance to nineteenth century Spain. Specialization along the lines of comparative advantage provided Spain with both absolute and relative improvements in welfare as measured by real terms of trade.

7 The most appropriate term to describe Spain's economic performance during the long nineteenth century is backwardness. A number of the essential elements of the traditional, pessimistic view resist modern quantitative reconstructions: low levels of human and physical capital formation; a large traditional agricultural sector; an inefficient, overprotected manufacturing sector run by entrepreneurs who shrank from

competition; and reduced openness to foreign markets. Even so, the old pessimism must be at least partially abandoned. Nineteenth and early twentieth century Spain enjoyed sustained growth in real GDP per capita and per worker, populations growth and moderate changes in economic structure, and these are all components of the classic definition of economic growth in modern nations. Spain did fall behind the advanced countries of western Europe, but its route to modernization was much closer to that of the western elite than that of today's developing nations of the Third World.

Notes

1 Economic variables whose values are determined by others in an economic model (endogenous) or those not so determined (exogenous).
2 The responsiveness of the value of an economic variable to changes in the value of another, related one.
3 A country which has such a small proportion of the total output or sales that it can exert no influence and must take market prices as its own.
4 The benefits or costs derived from the actions of another party.
5 Replacing imported goods with those produced domestically.
6 As the terms of trade move against them, developing countries should use protection and import substitution to promote industrialization and thus reduce income inequalities among nations.
7 The most common measure of the terms of trade (values of goods traded between nations), calculated as the ratio of the index of export prices to that of import prices.
8 A measure showing the welfare effects of the terms of trade, calculated by multiplying the net barter terms of trade by the ratio of the productivity change index for the two countries' export industries.
9 Trade deficit in goods, with services not included.
10 A section of a nation's balance of payments accounts composed of visible and invisible trade plus private and official transfers of capital.
11 Specialization in economic activities that an individual or nation performs relatively better than others.

|12|

The assault on liberalism, 1914–1923

LUIS ARRANZ, MERCEDES CABRERA and FERNANDO DEL REY

Between the Tragic Week of July–August 1909 and the beginning of 1913 the long-established collaboration between the two principal political parties, the Conservatives and Liberals, broke down. The outbreak of the First World War in August 1914 thus found Spanish political life in the midst of a grave crisis. Even so, the rotation in power between the anti-Maura faction of the Conservatives and the Liberals was sustained until the summer of 1917. Then Catalan regionalists, republicans, Socialists and anarchosyndic-alists, the political forces opposed to the *turno* system, took advantage of renewed military intervention in political life to attempt to overthrow the regime. They failed, but from 1917 until 1923 Spain was governed by a series of coalition governments which attempted to fuse the dispersed dynastic parties in order to keep the Restoration alive through very difficult circum-stances, including ongoing pressure from the army, class conflict in Barcelona and military defeats in the country's Moroccan Protectorate. These coalitions also sought, with some success, to bring some of the opposition groups into the government. The Catalan Lliga came on board in October 1917, and the moderate republicans of the Reformist Party did so in December 1922, in time to join the last cabinet of the Restoration, which lasted until the military coup led by General Miguel Primo de Rivera in September 1923.

The crisis of the dynastic parties, 1909–13

The main reason for the end of collaboration between Conservatives and Liberals between 1909 and 1913 was the absence of any agreement over the future direction of the constitutional monarchy. During the early years of the twentieth century the Restoration did not face any significant organized opposition, on the right or the left, nor did it face any intense pressure for democratization. This absence of any incentive from without, combined with the characteristics of the two dynastic parties, led to the emergence of a profound disagreement over where to take the regime. On the Conservative side, first Francisco Silvela and then Antonio Maura held that the future of the Monarchy lay in administrative decentralization and making universal suffrage more effective, as well as a rigorous defence of public order that clearly eliminated political violence as a tool of opposition. This conception required that both the *turno* and the role of the Crown be redefined, and Maura knew that it would require the collaboration of the Crown and the Liberals. However, both his overall political position, which many saw as excessively clerical, and the corporative aspects of his programme for reforming local administration meant that Maura did not enjoy the same room for manoeuvre as had Cánovas during the 1870s and this collaboration escaped him.

For their part, the Liberals oscillated undecidedly between a number of alternatives: the continuation of a cautiously pragmatic liberalism; a French-style anticlericalism as the basis of political mobilization and to draw the Republicans into the orbit of the Monarchy, or the adoption of a new, more socially-oriented liberalism of the sort personified by the British Liberal leader, David Lloyd George. Fearing that Maura would be able to mobilize the largely dormant Catholic vote for the Conservatives, which would keep them out of power permanently, they preferred to let the Crown keep its determining role in the *turno* which meant that they were, for all practical purposes, uninterested in making the system more genuinely democratic. Thus the Liberals were in tune with Alfonso XIII, who came to the throne at the age of 16 following an almost exclusively military and technical education. Young Alfonso had not fully assimilated the lesson that the survival of the monarchy demanded constitutional reform, and he preferred to entertain the anticonstitutional pressures of the military rather than try and lead a more mobilized and conflictive public opinion into constitutional channels.

Following the Tragic Week, the Liberal leader Segismundo Moret chose to ally himself with the republicans against Maura's government, and went so far as to demand that the king dismiss his Conservative prime minister. Maura's response was to declare the political collaboration between the two dynastic parties at an end. Three years of Liberal cabinets followed, but the Liberal party was becoming increasingly splintered. Moret and his policy of drawing closer to the republicans were challenged by two other key figures, Manuel García Prieto and the Count of Romanones. They supported José Canalejas for the leadership of the party, and in 1910 Alfonso called on him to form a government. Canalejas came from a Republican background, but he had reached the conclusion that using the Crown was a more effective way to achieve reform than was attempting to mobilize the voters. Canalejas gave the Liberals a new programme: a combination of mild anticlericalism and social liberalism; he broke the relationship with the Radical Republicans and sought to reestablish a working relationship with the Conservatives. And, despite the long, firmly centralist tradition of his party, he also displayed some sympathy for the demands of the Catalan regionalists.

Maura distrusted Canalejas' anticlericalism, while his more socially-oriented liberalism brought him into collision with republicans and Socialists, who did not forgive his having abandoned Moret's left bloc. The antimonarchical left criticized Canalejas unmercifully and tried to force him from power through an unsuccessful general strike. When Canalejas was assassinated at the end of 1912, none of his efforts to patch up relations with the Conservatives had yet to bear any fruit. His death also removed the firm hand that had kept internal dissension under control, and the party reverted to a factionalism in which personal and political motives were closely connected.

For his part, Maura made the grave mistake of presenting the king with an ultimatum: that the Conservatives would remain in power until the Liberals renounced any idea of working with the republicans and Socialists, or if they refused, the Liberals could remain in power but the Conservatives would refuse to succeed them. This ultimatum was in flagrant contradiction with Maura's own advocacy of democratization, as it made the Crown the sole arbiter of political life. He also failed to recognize that republicans and Socialists had achieved neither revolution nor reform while Canalejas had been in power. All this cost Maura the leadership of the Conservatives, who were not ready to join him in defying the king nor in running the risk of pushing the Liberals back into the arms of the antimonarchist opposition. Moreover, many Conservatives did not share Maura's view of the necessity of replacing a system based on the influence of local notables and the trading of favours with a more professional style of politics based on mass mobilization behind a defined set of policies. Thus Maura was replaced as leader by Eduardo Dato, whom Alfonso called to power in October 1913.

The passionate war

Catalan regionalist leader Francesc Cambó wrote that the First World War created a 'profound spiritual disturbance' throughout Europe which threatened the continent with a 'crisis of anarchy'; it was a 'revolutionary hurricane' after which nothing would remain as it had been.

Spain's neutrality did not shield it from the effects of the cataclysm, and the War had a major influence in shaping the social political processes of those years, and especially from 1914 to 1921. The war shook the bases of the Spanish economy; it increased social mobilization and social conflict; it strengthened nationalism, especially of the Catalan and Basque varieties, which were confronting the centralist state; it opened the door to corporatist ideas and anti-individualist policies that became alternatives to the parliamentary system of the constitutional monarchy, and all this reinforced the political culture of regenerationism. As a result, the regime was subjected to increasing criticism from both the antimonarchist left and the antiliberal right, which were quite effective in undermining its intellectual legitimacy and increasing its political isolation.

To a certain point, this political radicalization fed on the economic repercussions of the Great War. In general terms, the war had permitted significant capital accumulation: business profits in shipbuilding, metallurgy, textiles and coal skyrocketed; for cereal and livestock producers they were more modest. The rate of social change speeded up, accelerating a process that had been underway since the beginning of the century. Immigration from the countryside to the cities and industrial zones increased, especially in Cataluña and the Basque country. The percentage of the labour force engaged in agriculture declined by 15 per cent between 1910 and 1920, while the industrial labour force grew by 40 per cent and the service sector by 16 per cent. The economic growth of these years permitted the reduction of Spain's external debt and a formidable increase in the Bank of Spain's gold reserves.

Not all the by-products of Spain's neutrality were positive. For a large part of the population, the war years were anything but a good business opportunity, because foreign markets were not interested in importing or exporting certain products and raw materials. Citrus fruits, one of the country's leading exports, suffered, while wood imports dried up, leading to increased construction costs. The railroad system was frequently unable to meet the growing demands put on it because of the scarcity and high cost of coal.

To understand the political mobilization that the war produced, it is essential to keep in mind the spread of the idea that the profits were being enjoyed by only a minority. The myth of the 'gutless' *nouveau riche* capitalist was widely believed. Stereotypes such as these were important in bringing people into the street to protest, but the inflation produced by the war was also a significant factor. Inflation derived from the export of basic necessities, but it also derived from artificially-generated shortages created when producers or middle men engaged in hoarding in order to push up their profits. Spain suffered lower levels of inflation than other neutral countries, but the effects were particularly harsh in the final year of the war, after prices had risen 61.8 per cent and wages only 25.6 per cent.

The lower classes were the most sensitive to the effects of inflation and they were the first to mount public protests and demand that basic subsistence products be reduced in price. Between 1916 and 1919 such protests often led to violent outbursts that resembled the food riots of earlier times. The labour unions were quick to capitalize on this popular mobilization; never had they had such a large membership. The Socialist Unión General de Trabajadores (UGT) went from 114 000 members in 1914 to 211 000 in 1920, while the anarchosyndicalist Confederación Nacional del Trabajo (CNT) mushroomed from some 15 000 members at the beginning of the war to 700 000 in 1919. Inflation also hit the pocketbooks of the middle classes: civil servants, white collar workers, professionals, small manufacturers, and even the middle ranks of the army, and they responded by taking up corporatist responses which often looked much like the actions of unions. Even the businessmen who did best out of the economic boom launched an offensive against the proposal by the Liberal finance minister, Santiago Alba, to impose a tax on war-related windfall profits.

This corporativism called into question the liberal tradition of the nineteenth century. Although such theories had been around for a long time, it was only after the War that they enjoyed conditions which favoured their spread. The consequences were quick in coming, as classic parliamentary government lost its legitimacy across wide sectors of the population. Other sites challenged parliament as the centre for political activity; not just the streets but also *ad hoc* institutions designed to speak for special interests. Moreover, from the unions, from employers and from intellectuals came demands for the state to take a direct role in regulating social and economic relations, as had been done in such a spectacular fashion in the combatant nations. Established politicians went part way in this and tried to control prices, supplies and trade; they created or revived organisms to represent the different interest groups involved; they tried to strengthen social policy and encouraged collective bargaining with the state as ultimate arbiter.

Neutrality and the attempts at revolution, 1914–1917

It was the Conservative prime minister, Eduardo Dato, who had to confront the outbreak of hostilities in August 1914 and who defined the policy of strict neutrality which would remain essentially unchanged throughout the war. All the politicians of the monarchy upheld neutrality, although some, such as the Count of Romanones, openly displayed their inclination to intervene on the side of the Entente. None of them denied that Spain's interests were connected to France and Britain, but nothing could convince a majority of Spaniards to give up neutrality. The brutal submarine campaign that the Germans unleashed at the beginning of 1917, which sank a number of Spanish merchant vessels, made neutrality more difficult to sustain, but Conservatives and Liberals alike never lost sight of the fact that to intervene in the war would in all likelihood have been a political and economic disaster for the country, and might even have led to civil war.

The bitter polemic between *aliadófilos* (partisans of France and Britain) and *germanófilos* (partisans of Germany) made fears of possible civil conflict credible. Both groups idealized their respective heroes and subordinated a realistic analysis of Spanish interests to their political passions. Both sides, and especially Germany, gave large sums of money to the Spanish press, and the never-ending nature of the war combined to sustain the debate and raise its temperature. The pro-German camp saw in Germany an authoritarian and nationalist monarchy, a model for rebuilding Spanish grandeur and for undermining the support for liberalism among the more conservative sectors of society. They never suggested that Spain intervene in support of Germany; their goal was to ensure that Spanish neutrality did not benefit the Entente.

The political consequences of the war, and especially of events such as the entry of the United States and the fall of the Czar in Russia in 1917, were most immediate among the *aliadófolos*. Around 1913 the more moderate republicans had toyed with the possibility that Alfonso XIII might let them join the Liberals in government, but the war brought more radical elements to the forefront of republican politics. The Radical Republican party of Alejandro Lerroux, along with the Socialists, identified the cause of the Entente with political revolution and the creation of a republic in Spain, a position adopted by the moderate republicans of the Reformist party when it became clear that the king was not going to challenge the policy of neutrality. Although their position was not entirely clear, the *aliadófilos* did not generally advocate Spain becoming a combatant; rather, they proposed a form of neutrality that would benefit the Entente and give Spain a full role in the idealized democratic order they believed would follow from an Entente victory.

This radicalization of the left became visible after 1916 but it did not produce any nightmares for those in power. Things changed when the Lliga Catalana adopted a position of confrontation to the *turno* system. The Lliga was a conservative party and although its ability to mobilize people politically was modest, it had been able to push the dynastic parties to the margins of political life in Cataluña.

Difficulties in getting approval for its budget forced the Dato government to resign in December 1915, and the Count of Romanones took advantage of this situation to return to power and try to definitively establish his leadership of the Liberal party. Romanones put another Liberal chieftan, Santiago Alba, in the ministry of Finance. Alba attempted to introduce a programme of economic and fiscal reform, whose centrepiece was a tax on wartime windfall profits. This bill faced vocal opposition from the Lliga and its leader, Cambó, and was defeated in parliament. This defeat on a money bill did not topple the Romanones government; rather, it fell because of the openly pro-Entente turn of its foreign policy once the Germans began to attack Spanish merchant vessels. In April 1917 Romanones was succeeded by his rival, García Prieto, who returned to the policy of strict neutrality, a policy which the left saw as favouring Germany.

The Liberals' stretch in office provided the opportunity for an understanding between the Conservatives and the Lliga. The core of the Lliga's programme was decentralization, beginning with broad autonomy for Cataluña, something which many saw as sneaking separatism. In 1913, the Dato government had allowed the deputations of the four Catalan provinces to create a single administrative organism: the Mancomunidad. For his part, Cambó sought support against Alba's tax bill and movement towards the political as well as administrative autonomy of Cataluña. Above all, he wanted to break the two-party system. However, negotiations between Cambó and Dato broke down once the Conservative leader became convinced that the king would not invite Maura to form a government and once the Catalan leader realized that the Conservatives wanted only to convert the Lliga into the Catalan branch of their party.

In the Spanish revolutionary tradition, whenever civilian politicians had had recourse to the use of violence they had called on the military. The appearance of the so-called Juntas Militares de Defensa made this possible again in 1917. The overwhelming majority of opinion held that the Spanish armed forces were not prepared to intervene in the European war. The unprecedented deployment of resources by the combatant nations led to the realization that the technical level of the military had to be increased, as did the degree of selectivity of officers, especially in the infantry. The problem was not new: it had been around at least since the defeat in 1898 and had been brought to the fore with the war in Morocco. The Romanones government had initiated these reforms, and the Juntas were the embodiment of the resistance, especially from the infantry. Bringing together officers between the ranks of lieutenant and colonel, and led by the Barcelona garrison, the Juntas hid their bureaucratic inertia behind other slogans: opposition to battlefield merit promotions, favouritism within the king's military entourage and economic hardship caused by inflation, all of which they clothed in a confused rhetoric of national regeneration.

It was García Prieto who had to deal with the Juntas, and rather than accept their demands, which would have meant the collapse of the chain of command, he chose to resign. The Liberals retained the majority in parliament, but the king called on the Conservatives to form a government. Surprisingly, the Dato cabinet did not receive the support of all political forces in the face of the humiliation of civil authority posed by the Juntas and their demands. Dato realized that the emergence of the Juntas was the stimulus the Lliga and the antimonarchist left needed to undertake the attack on the regime they had been promising, and this led him to accept the Juntas' demands and rescind the disciplinary measures which had been taken earlier.

Since the beginning of the war, parliamentary activity had been limited by the fear on the part of weak governments that the chamber would become the principal site of the conflict between *aliadófilos* and *germanófilos*. The appearance of the Juntas gave the opposition the occasion to attack the government for its refusal to call parliament into session by calling an 'Assembly of Parliamentarians' in Barcelona in July 1917. Because this gathering had the appearance of becoming a constituent assembly, and thus revolutionary, all Liberal or Conservative deputies and senators, who together constituted some 80 per cent of the total, stayed away. The Assembly's objectives were confused: on the one hand it demanded that the government open parliament, while on the other it demanded that a provisional government convoke a constituent assembly. Dato allowed the Assembly to meet but then dissolved it before its deliberations had advanced very far.

Because it had failed to attract any monarchist politicians, even dissidents such as Maura or Romanones, the Assembly's representativeness was very much in question. So was its independence from the Juntas Militares. Indeed, both Cambó and the leader of the Radicals, Alejandro Lerroux, had had contacts with the Juntas. Thus, an Assembly of Parliamentarians who were overwhelmingly republicans and *aliadófilos* was attempting to take advantage of the actions of seditious military officers who, as well as professionally mediocre, were by and large *germanófilos*.

The final challenge the Dato government faced in the summer of 1917 came one month after the meeting of the Assembly of Parliamentarians: a general strike called by the two union organizations, the UGT and CNT. Given the close relationship of the Socialist Party (PSOE) to the UGT and its participation in a committee of Reformists and Radicals whose goal was to overthrow the regime, these parties must also be considered responsible for the strike. Such a strike had been in the offing since March, but it was not called to coincide with the Assembly of Parliamentarians and when it finally did happen, it was not connected to any other political initiative. In fact, the strike was triggered by a small local dispute which led to a protest strike by the railway workers' union. The UGT leadership was unable to control the situation and was forced to declare the general strike before it was ready to do so.

But this was only one of the many problems which undermined the strike. The unions lacked any political support: the Lliga denounced it as 'stupidity'; Lerroux disappeared to France; and after a vain attempt to convince the leaders of the UGT to call it off, Reformist leader Melquíades Alvarez went to ground in his political stronghold of Asturias. Not even Pablo Iglesias, the venerable leader of both the PSOE and UGT, was in agreement: he urged that the strike be limited to a one-day action in solidarity with the railway workers. The strike also lacked effective leadership because the clandestine committee in charge was arrested on the second day of the conflict. Moreover, there was no coordination between the CNT and the UGT. The strike was supposedly revolutionary, but the manifesto which announced its goal of replacing the regime also declared that it aimed to do so pacifically.

The strike failed almost immediately in Madrid and Barcelona; only in the coalfields of Asturias and – to a lesser extent – the iron mines of Vizcaya did it amount to a serious problem of public order. In many places, nothing happened at all. The unions' failure put in evidence the incapacity and lack of unity of the political opposition to the monarchy. Nowhere was this clearer than in their analysis of the behaviour of the Juntas Militares, without whom there would have been no Assembly and no general strike. All the 'regenerationist' hopes placed in the Juntas were dashed when the army repressed the strike with startling severity.

Yielding to the Juntas in order to defeat possible revolution had paid off for the Dato government, but it was unable to escape responsibility for what had happened. The Juntas denounced the government as the enemy of 'regeneration' and blamed it for the harshness of the repression. For their part, both Maura and the Liberals stood by as the Lliga, the republicans and the Socialists denounced the government furiously. In November 1917 the king finally pulled the plug on Dato. The Liberals still held a majority in parliament but they were so divided that they were unable to put together a new cabinet. In the end, García Prieto came to power at the head of the monarchy's first coalition government, composed of representatives of almost all parliamentary parties including the Lliga.

The post-war social crisis

When the First World War finally came to an end, Spanish public opinion was dominated by the question of autonomy for Cataluña and – to a lesser extent – the Basque provinces, but this issue was soon eclipsed by social conflicts which, between 1918 and 1921, reached an unprecedented level of intensity. Never had Spain seen so many strikes nor so much violence and terrorism. The focal points were Andalucia, the scene of the 'Bolshevik triennium' of 1918–20, and greater Barcelona, where the conflict continued until 1923.

The mobilization of the southern agricultural labourers is striking because it took place after decades of relative calm and in a region where the union presence had been unstable. During the 'Triennium' the number of unions and strikes in rural Andalucia skyrocketed. The most active area was the Guadalquivir valley and the provinces of Cádiz, Córdoba, Sevilla and Jaén. The goals were clearly economic: wage increases, a shorter working day, the abolition of piece work, but they also carried an openly political intent. The unions' language was impregnated with the myth of the recent Bolshevik revolution and this encouraged the use of violence against both people and property. In the middle of 1919 the government sent 20 000 soldiers to the south; by closing union offices and newspapers and arresting hundreds of union leaders they eventually, and bloodlessly, brought the strike wave to an end.

In Cataluña social conflict took much more violent, and degrading, forms. In addition to a strike wave which dwarfed those anywhere else in the country, Cataluña became notorious as the home of a terrorism which appeared to be endemic. The numbers speak for themselves: between 1916 and 1923 more than 300 people were killed in the province of Barcelona alone. The victims included workers of varying political affiliations, businessmen, police officers and innocent bystanders.

The principal instigators of this social conflict were the anarchosyndicalists of the CNT. The 'Canadiense' strike, against Barcelona's electricity and street railway company, in February 1919, literally kept the city in the dark for weeks. It also marked the point of no return, after which the CNT began a spiral of radicalization which, together with the subsequent repression in 1921–22, was the main cause of its decline. Under the influence of the Bolshevik revolution, the Socialists also became more radical and abandoned their alliance with the republicans and its goal of the bourgeois republic for the dictatorship of the proletariat. Even so, a great majority within the UGT refused to join the Communist International, and many fewer Spanish Socialists joined the new Communist party than was the case in other European countries. As small as it was, the Communist schism added its share to the violence that had long characterized the relationship between Socialists on the one hand and anarchists and syndicalists on the other.

The radicalization of the Socialists was provoked, above all, by their rivalry with the CNT, whose membership had vastly increased. Even so, they continued to have recourse to state agencies such as the Social Reform Institute and the newly-established Ministry of Labour, although this did not imply any support for the constitutional monarchy itself. The Socialists monopolized the workers' share of representation in these bodies, vetoing the presence of Catholic unions and taking advantage of the anarchists' rejection of any involvement with political institutions. This dogmatism, combined with the radicalization of some employers' groups, prevented the consolidation of a system of labour relations based on mutual recognition and peaceful collective bargaining with the State as arbiter. And nowhere was this clearer than in Barcelona.

It was these circumstances that inspired the radicalization of those groups: businessmen, middle classes, non-revolutionary workers, military officers and clergy, who saw in the unions' offensive the beginning of revolution, anarchy and chaos. Their position was characterized by a fear of Bolshevism and a counter-revolutionary drive based on militarism and an authoritarian corporativism. Thus, they denounced the liberal system as useless and corrupt and encouraged the military to intervene in order to replace 'old-style' liberal politicians with a government of technocrats and representatives of economic interest groups.

The constitutional monarchy struggles to survive, 1918–1923

Between 1918 and 1923 there were four general elections and eleven very diverse governments. The system could no longer deliver a parliamentary majority, which meant that coalition governments became the norm.

The first coalition government, headed by García Prieto, held 'renovation' elections in February 1918. The Ministry of the Interior did not intervene on behalf of government candidates, in large part because with a coalition government it was hard to know just how to intervene. Moreover, the internal divisions within the dynastic parties meant that the old two-party system was, in fact, evolving into a multi-party one. Even adding all their factions together, neither Liberals nor Conservatives could sustain a stable majority.

The situation was further complicated by the presence in the cabinet of the Lliga Catalana. The Lliga had participated in the Assembly of Parliamentarians, and reaped the benefits by doubling its number of seats. On the other hand, the republicans suffered a major defeat, although some of the seats they lost went to their Socialist allies, whose number of deputies increased from one to six. These results confirmed that the republicans had not yet become a significant force for democratization and that Spanish socialism remained more a union movement than a political one. Indeed, only a half of the members of the UGT voted for PSOE candidates. The antimonarchist left continued to have only a meagre presence in parliament.

Unable to maintain a parliamentary majority in the face of such serious

Table 12.1 Spanish governments, 1917–1923

Dates	Prime Minister	Composition
1–11–1917/21–3–1918	García Prieto	Coalition of main monarchist parties, including the Lliga
21–3–1918/9–11–1918	Maura	'National government' composed of the leaders of the monarchist parties
9–11–1918/5–11–1918	García Prieto	Alliance of Liberals and democrats
5–12–1918/15–4–1919	Romanones	Predominantly Liberal
15–4–1919/19–7–1919	Maura	Maura's Conservatives, with some support from Dato
19–7–1919/12–12–1919	Sánchez Toca	Dato's Conservatives
12–12–1919/5–5–1920	Allendesalazar	Dato Conservatives, Liberals and democrats
5–5–1920/8–3–1921	Dato	Dato Conservatives
8–3–1921/13–8–1921	Allendesalazar	Conservatives, Liberals and democrats
13–8–1921/8–3–1922	Maura	Conservatives, Lliga, Liberals and democrats
8–3–1922/9–12–1922	Sánchez Guerra	Conservatives, Lliga, Liberals and democrats
9–12–1922/1–9–1923	García Prieto	Coalition of all Liberal groups
1–9–1923/13–9–1923	García Prieto	Coalition of all Liberal groups

issues as Catalan autonomy, the Juntas Militares, social conflict and the need to pass the first budget since 1915, García Prieto resigned at the end of March 1918. This produced a political vacuum, and only the King's threat to abdicate convinced the leaders of all groups loyal to the monarchy to collaborate in a coalition cabinet which, because of its breadth, was christened the 'national government'. At its head was Antonio Maura, whose stature, absence from government since 1909 and long-standing criticism of the *turno* made him the ideal person to direct such a coalition. Maura was convinced that a coalition government was essential if the constitutional monarchy were to be reinvigorated, but he also realized that his government was not really a coalition with a shared programme, but a conglomerate in which each party retained its own.

The new government was greeted with relief, and even enthusiasm, by parliament and much of public opinion. It did achieve some goals, such as reforming procedures so that parliament conducted its business more efficiently, but the end of the war led some of the groups in the government to reassert their independence. The most impatient was Santiago Alba, leader of the so-called Liberal Left, who sought to get republicans and Socialists to collaborate with him in renewing the regime. A confrontation with Cambó over the budget gave him the opportunity to resign. But Dato also bolted, leaving Maura with no choice but to bring his government to an end at the beginning of November 1918.

In line with the international climate, the next two governments were Liberal ones, headed by the leaders of the party's most important factions, García Prieto and Romanones. The parliament returned in the 1918 election gave the Liberals only a plurality, and then only if they stuck together. The fragility of García Prieto's position was increased by the repeated refusal of the moderate republicans and Socialists to support him, and when the peace negotiations opened in Paris he was pushed aside by Romanones, who had been the strongest supporter of the Entente during the war. In addition, he was also much more open to negotiating an autonomy statute with Catalonia. But in the early months of 1919 the ongoing social conflict in Barcelona led Romanones into a direct clash with the military authorities there and his government fell.

This was followed by an abrupt, but ephemeral, turn to the right, as Maura returned to power at the head of a cabinet composed solely of his followers and with the reluctant support of the more numerous Dato wing of the party. Maura held elections, but did so without restoring the constitutional guarantees that Romanones had suspended. For the only time in the history of the Restoration, a government lost an election. Maura faced a highly fragmented parliament and a dangerous conglomeration of protesters: the republicans and Socialists were joined by the Romanones Liberals, for whom the circumstances in which the election had been held rendered the government illegitimate. After four months Maura was forced to resign.

From July 1919 to December 1922 there were six governments, based primarily on Dato's Conservatives, who emerged from the elections of 1919 and 1920 as the largest parliamentary bloc. These Conservative governments had to get a budget through parliament, which Allendesalazar achieved in 1920, and deal with the Juntas Militares, which were finally dissolved in 1922. By far the greatest problem they faced, however, was the social conflict in Barcelona, and they confronted it in different ways. During their first months in office, Sánchez de Toca and Dato took a conciliatory approach; later Dato and then Allendesalazar supported a 'dirty war' and harsh repression. These oscillations reflected the fierce struggle within the CNT between those who believed that it would not survive without negotiations and some sort of political intervention and those who countenanced anything, including the terrorist tactics of the so-called 'action groups', to prevent the CNT from taking a reformist approach. The result was *pistolerismo*, with gangs of gunmen littering the streets of Barcelona with corpses. In March 1921, Dato was himself assassinated by anarchists.

The attitude of the Liberals to these Conservative governments moved between neutrality and support; when the situation was particularly serious they even joined the government. Among Liberals, Romanones was the most reticent. For its part, the Lliga never hid its preference for participating in cabinets only when Maura was in charge. The republicans and Socialists remained permanently in opposition, faithful to their traditional revolutionary strategy of isolating the monarchy from its Liberal support, although after mid-1920 the radicalization of some socialists and pressure from Communists and anarchosyndicalists made this impossible. They vigorously defended civil authority in order to criticize the weakness of successive governments in dealing with the Juntas Militares, even though in 1917 they had tried to use the Juntas to stage a revolution. At no point did they consider collaborating with the government in order to better defend civil authority against military pretensions. Socialists, along with republicans, never got beyond constantly repeating that there could be no solution to such political problems so long as the monarchy remained in existence.

By 1921, the worst of the social conflict appeared to be over, but it was followed by an even graver problem. In the summer, Spanish troops attempting to put down a revolt in the Rif area of the Moroccan Protectorate suffered a serious defeat at Annual. The responsibility for the tragic outcome of this risky operation reached the governing Conservatives, but also the military command in Morocco and the king himself, an enthusiastic supporter of Spain's colonial presence in North Africa. Just when it looked as though the Restoration had miraculously survived its worst moments and when the enemies of the regime appeared exhausted, Annual gave them a new and very powerful weapon.

Maura returned to power on 14 August 1921 at the head of another coalition, but one which was very different from the earlier 'national government'. Then he had had to accept the leaders of all parliamentary groups; this time he chose his own ministers, and while he included lesser figures from those groups which most supported the *turno*, the cabinet was dominated by people who opposed it: Maura himself, Juan de la Cierva and Cambó. Maura sought to carry through an ambitious set of policies, and he put Cambó in the key Finance ministry. Yet the very nature of the government meant that its support was limited, especially as there were many Conservatives who were determined to prevent Maura from becoming party leader following the death of Dato.

Maura was able to restore the military situation in Morocco with few problems, but in March 1922 his government fell over the level of ongoing military commitment it should make there. He was succeeded by the leader of the largest Conservative faction, José Sánchez Guerra, who not only undertook a policy of constitutional normalization, especially in Barcelona, but also ordered a thorough investigation of what had happened at Annual. The report was brought to parliament in December 1922, but because a number of leading Conservatives had been deeply involved in the Annual affair, the government resigned in the midst of a tumultuous debate.

This left the way open for the Liberals to return to power, but they did not return united. Instead, they formed a 'Bloc' of all the factions within the party plus the republicans of the Reformist party, whom Romanones had been courting for 10 years. The new cabinet had an ambitious programme that included electoral reform (proportional representation), establishing a Civil Protectorate in Morocco and freedom of religion. This last goal did not include revoking Catholicism's status as the official religion of the state but, as in the past, religion would be the Achilles heel of a Liberal administration.

The most dangerous issue was the question of the 'responsibilities' for Annual, and the government decided to deal with it, come what may, creating a special commission that included representatives of all the parliamentary parties, republicans and Socialists included. There is no reason to believe that the dynastic parties would not have been able to deal with this issue and save the Crown, although the Conservative party would likely have sustained heavy damage. Nevertheless, the Crown lost its nerve. Spurred by the revival of social conflict in Barcelona and the reappearance of a radicalized Catalan nationalism, the Captain General of Cataluña, Miguel Primo de Rivera, staged a *pronunciamento*, something the Restoration had succeeded in eliminating from Spanish political life for nearly half a century. The entire political process halted on 13 September when the king abandoned his constitutional government and, on the eve of the return of parliament from its summer recess, gave his support to Primo de Rivera's coup. Constitutional and parliamentary politics were suspended by the beginning of a dictatorship which would last seven years.

Conclusions

The establishment of a dictatorship was far from inevitable, and Alfonso XIII's decision to renounce constitutional government, something Spain had enjoyed since 1834, was undoubtedly more responsible for this outcome than anything else. The magnitude of this error would be revealed in all its brutality in the bitter isolation he suffered in April 1931.

But the Restoration had a number of shortcomings beyond Alfonso's personal weakness. Of these, the excessive fragmentation and personal rivalries within the Liberal and Conservative parties stood out. This was the product of the absence of a shared vision for renewing the regime and of leaders capable of uniting people behind it. There was no sense of 'constitutional engineering', of the need to change the electoral and party system, that had been so important in the early days of the Restoration. It was not clear whether there would be a return to the old two-party system or whether the new pattern of coalition governments would be consolidated. What is clear, is that reforms, and especially the most important ones, were undermined by the ambitions of the principal party leaders who were afraid to yield any advantage to their rivals.

This situation shows that, despite what its critics said, the regime was neither immobile nor paralysed: the incorporation of the Lliga Catalana and the Partido Reformista into the government is proof of that. Moreover, despite the very difficult circumstances, some 'silent' reforms were enacted in a range of areas: social and labour legislation, parliamentary and administrative modernization and fiscal and banking reforms, many of which lasted for decades.

For their part, republicans, Socialists and anarchosyndicalists were much more heterogeneous and deeply divided than the dynastic parties. If their respective political and doctrinal traditions had encouraged them to develop a strong electoral and parliamentary approach, this might well have pushed the monarchy's political leadership into democratic competition, as happened elsewhere in Europe. Such political activity might also have led the anti-regime left to value the existing constitutional guarantees and to try to extend them. However, many on the left were within a revolutionary tradition for which the state was less important than smaller units: the municipality for republicans, the union for Socialists and anarchosyndicalists. Yet, as the events of the summer of 1917 revealed, they were no more skilled as revolutionaries than they were as reformers. Indeed, they were little more than subversive forces which continually speculated with the monarchy's problems, hoping against hope that some *deus ex machina* – the victory of the Entente, the Juntas Militares or the defeat in Morocco – would do their job and liquidate the regime.

For the republicans this was a period of profound decadence brought about by a lack of a programme, leadership and unity. Their reformist wing delayed 10 years before deciding to join a Liberal government. For their part, after 1920 the Socialists used rhetorical radicalism to hide their political inhibition, whether it was towards the monarchy, towards a future republic or, above all, towards revolutionary unionism. In this camp, the revolutionaries and terrorists within the CNT always defeated the more moderate elements who advocated a compromise that would permit CNT unions to continue to exist and, together with the UGT, control labour relations.

A final significant element of weakness was the strengthening of a climate of opinion which, since 1898, had attacked the legitimacy of the Restoration. The ideas of Regenerationism had changed the liberal concept of the purpose of the state. Instead of dividing and controlling political power and creating a legal framework in which individuals and groups with differing ideas and interests competed peacefully, Regenerationism called for a strong political authority which would encourage or create those social, economic and educational realities that society did not produce. (That such demands contradicted their complaints about the excess of bureaucrats went unnoticed.) The tremendous capacity to coordinate all aspects of national life that had been shown by combatant states during the First World War only furthered such demands, although they could still be considered compatible with constitutional government and liberal politics. The triumph of Bolshevism and then of fascism shattered this view: antiliberalism moved from being the politics of nostalgia for an idealized past or the justification for the conservatism of an elite to becoming the shared banner of the radical right and the revolutionary left. The result of this doctrinal ferment was the indifference, and even outright satisfaction, produced by Primo de Rivera's coup. The liberal system, which had been painfully constructed during almost a century and consolidated during the nearly 50 years of the Restoration, was cast aside as a superfluous adornment and the principal obstacle to the rapid transformation of the country. Time would show, however, that the countries which conserved the constitutional legacy of the nineteenth century would best resist the totalitarian challenge of the 1930s. Spain would not be among them.

|13|

The dictatorship of Primo de Rivera, 1923–1931

JAVIER TUSELL and GENOVEVA QUEIPO DE LLANO

At the beginning of 1923, the political situation had become very difficult, and from various sectors of the political spectrum, including the intellectual world, calls for an authoritarian solution increased. It is not surprising that the strongest support for this idea came from the right, but to understand the initial support enjoyed by the dictatorship it is important to keep in mind the broad extent of the clamour. The crisis of liberal parliamentarianism in Spain did not arise out of the birth of mass democratization or the spiral of social tensions into violence, as in Italy, nor did it spring from an external defeat for which the military were held responsible, as was the case in Turkey. Similar factors were at work in Spain, but there the worst moments of violence had already passed, and there was no trial of those deemed to be politically responsible for the disastrous conduct of the Moroccan War which would end in executions. The most peculiar thing about Spain, in fact, was that virtually no change was made in a political system whose popular support was constantly eroding, but for which no alternative was offered. This explains the initial success of the regime, as well as Primo de Rivera's declared intention that there would be a return to reformed liberalism.

The *coup d'etat* and the composition of the regime

Even before General Primo de Rivera's revolt in Barcelona, a group of generals in Madrid were involved in a conspiracy which was far from discreet. Prior to this an attempt had been launched by General Aguilera in collaboration with certain intellectuals. The rebellion which was to prove successful was led by a soldier with political aspirations, who had some links with the vague ideology of *regeneracionismo* and at the same time a member of the most famous military families of the Restoration.

Miguel Primo de Rivera, Captain General of Catalonia, engineered a *coup d'etat* in Barcelona on 13 September 1923. He immediately published a

manifesto in which he outlined in superficial form a programme in keeping
with the *regeneracionista* spirit so prominent since 1898. This manifesto
declared that the moment – 'more feared than hoped for' – had arrived to
dispense with 'the misfortunes and wickedness which began in '98'; the
political elite had 'hijacked the popular will' and now the military, which had
until then provided 'the only feeble restraint' on the corruption, were
assuming full power in order to impose a new regime. Primo de Rivera was
confident that he would have the support of all those who 'were perfectly
distinguished by their virility'.

King Alfonso XIII did not intervene except to 'acknowledge the victor'
and public opinion received the coup well, so that Primo faced hardly any
opposition. The new dictator affirmed that his aims were not political; on the
contrary, he only came to purify the political world through the establishment of a temporary authoritarian regime and thus, by playing the role of
Joaquin Costa's 'Iron Surgeon', he would relieve the nation's ills. One of the
dictator's first declarations warned that he 'had no experience of government
and his methods were as simple as they were guileless'. To his simplified way
of thinking, sincerity, kindness, industriousness and life experience would
suffice to confront the country's problems.

Primo de Rivera had stated in the manifesto that the government would be
run either by military personnel or by civilians under his patronage. At first,
until December of 1925, he opted for the former arrangement: the responsibilities of governance were shared between him and a military directorate,
composed of several army generals and a single admiral. By appointing
Primo de Rivera as *Ministro Universal* without convening the legislature, the
king had violated the Constitution.

The cleansing of the corrupt *caciquista* practices was one of Primo's
declared objectives and in the first months of the regime, until April 1924, he
attempted to implement what Costa had called a kind of 'political surgery'.
The reform of the local administrative apparatus consisted of a series of
measures whose aim appeared to be the destruction of the oligarchy and of
caciques. All local governments and municipal bodies were dissolved and
replaced in each district by military government delegates who applied at the
local level what Primo was carrying out on a national scale. But the
government's efforts in this area were a failure in the end. Ramón Pérez de
Ayala wrote that at most a few particular *caciques* left the scene, only to be
succeeded by new ones. When the parliamentary system disappeared, *caciquismo* not only endured, but increased its power, unconstrained by public
opinion.

According to *regeneracionista* thought, an Iron Surgeon must not only
eliminate political corruption but promote a new political system. In light of
this, Primo de Rivera created the Patriotic Union as the official party in April
1924. At first, the dictator indicated that the party would include anyone
who supported the Constitution of 1876, which in fact he had already
violated. Despite this declaration, the party was later endowed with a

programme which argued for a new constitution with a single legislative chamber subject to approval by plebiscite. Primo de Rivera's definition of the Patriotic Union was confusing: 'a political party, but apolitical, which exercises a politico-administrative function'. The government showed an apparent preference for party members when it came to distribution of official jobs, although it was not an official state party on the fascist model. Rather, it was an archetypal personalistic group, which only acted on orders from above and had no life of its own. Other parties, including the Socialists, were allowed to exist, although subject to limitations.

The dictatorship's most valuable partnerships came from the extreme right, such as some of the followers of the former Conservative leader Antonio Maura, who were moving towards an authoritarian position. Nevertheless, Maura himself condemned the new regime, labelling it a 'figurehead of the military junta,' and indicating that any hopes for the regeneration of the country resided in 'a revival of public spirit'. There were also intellectuals like Ramiro de Maeztu and Eugenio D'Ors who were enthralled by the 'magical spell of order'.

Initially, Primo de Rivera considered his dictatorship as temporary. Although he professed admiration for Mussolini, his regime always had more in common with Eastern European dictatorships like that of Pilsudski in Poland, which also featured a military man atop an authoritarian regime. The Polish dictator also counted on the support of a political group whose composition was confusing (it called itself 'The Non-Partisan Block in Support of the Government') and above all on a mentality which was characteristic of the moment. The *sanacija* which Pilsudski wielded was the equivalent of the Spanish autocrat's *regeneracionismo*. Primo was a soldier well integrated into traditional circles of power and a product of an officer corps which had long considered a certain liberalism to be part of the norm. Mussolini was something very different: a journalist with intellectual pretensions and a former revolutionary socialist desperately seeking a political role for himself through the mass mobilization of war veterans.

In Primo de Rivera's case, just as in Italy and Poland, nationalism played a very important role in defining the regime. At first the Spanish dictatorship stirred the enthusiasm of one sector of Catalanism, which was concerned with the government's passivity in the face of social conflict in Barcelona. Like many other political forces in Spain, Catalan nationalists were prepared to welcome an 'Iron Surgeon' in the hope that he might transform the government's view of autonomy. It did indeed appear at first that the dictator was disposed to support the work of the Mancomunidad of Catalonia. But Primo de Rivera's sympathy for Catalanism was short-lived and his years of government soon became a march toward the centralization of the Spanish state. The definitive break came with the publication of the Law of the Provinces (March 1925), drafted by José Calvo Sotelo, one of the young technocrats who would play such a crucial role in the development of the regime. In practice the law obstructed the organization of further supra-provincial entities. As a result the relationship between Catalan political forces and state institutions became conflictive. Some of the Lliga Catalanista offices were closed, its daily newspaper was shut down, and some of its members were detained. Beginning in 1926, Primo de Rivera in fact prohibited any attempt by the Catalanists to resume their political propaganda. Francesc Cambó, principal leader of the Lliga, never trusted the dictatorship. He engaged in public argument with Primo on occasion and, near the end of the regime, published a highly critical book. In other regions where autonomist movements existed, the impact of the dictatorship was much the same. Basque nationalism took refuge in cultural demonstrations. In one case after another there was a movement towards radicalization on the part of the youngest sectors, the consequences of which were made evident in the 1930s.

Morocco

As he had with the Catalan question, Primo de Rivera quickly backtracked on his previous statements about Morocco. He had originally declared himself in favour of abandoning Morocco, but when he became dictator and head of the government, he did just the opposite: not only did he refuse to leave, he undertook the occupation of the whole northern part of Morocco which had been designated as a Spanish 'protectorate'.

His change of heart was determined by fierce opposition by officers in the colonial army, of whom Francisco Franco was one of the leading figures. After an initial disastrous attempt near the end of 1924 to exchange Ceuta for Gibraltar with the English, he gave the order to withdraw from the zone of Yebala and Xauen. The retreat was very difficult, since Spanish troops had to endure both abominable weather conditions and the attacks of Abd-el-Krim, whose troops, while not numerous, knew the terrain very well. This operation took a catastrophic toll on the Spanish troops, with casualties which exceeded those of the Battle of Annual in 1921. The retreat, as much as the apparently decisive victory of Abd-el-Krim, provoked profound disillusionment in the Spanish army in Africa, which it demonstrated by protesting against the dictator and his Moroccan policy. This convinced him that the protectorate should not be abandoned.

Initially, all Primo could do was lament the grave military setback, but mistakes by the rebel leader Abd-el-Krim provided the opportunity to resume the offensive. Believing that he had rid himself of the Spanish, and having under his command over 100 000 troops and more than 200 cannon, in April 1925 Abd-el-Krim opted to attack the French part of Morocco. This led to talks between France and Spain. In June, an agreement was reached in Madrid through which a certain degree of autonomy was promised to the tribes of Yebala and the Rif, and the decision to act forcefully was announced. Spanish forces soon grew to 200 000 men, and French troops to 300 000. As Salvador de Madariaga later wrote, 'the success of the Moroccans produced what years of Spanish diplomacy had not managed to obtain from France: a united policy in the face of a common enemy.' This was much more than the adversary could withstand.

The outcome of the Spanish and French collaboration was not long in coming. The landing at Alhucemas Bay, in September 1925, was a complete success and marked the beginning of the end for the Moroccan revolt. Faced with enemy troops which were far superior in number and, for the first time, engaged in a coordinated effort, Abd-el-Krim had virtually no hope of resisting. The final important battles took place in May of 1926, and at the end of that month the rebel leader surrendered to the French, and was banished to Reunion Island. The Spanish government protested bitterly that he had not been handed over to them to be tried. Towards the end of the year Spanish troops were drastically reduced, and by June 1927, the fight was considered to be definitively terminated and no further casualties were sustained.

The success in Morocco brought Primo de Rivera great popularity at home and in turn encouraged his foreign policy to become more assertive. For instance, in 1927 he demanded that the privileges granted to Spain by the 1924 agreement on Tangiers be increased. Likewise, Spain repeatedly demanded a permanent place on the Council of the League of Nations, even though it had withdrawn itself from the League for a number of years. This type of foreign policy embodied Primo de Rivera's deeply felt and pretentious nationalism, although he was never prepared to challenge the traditional Anglo-French mediation of Spanish foreign policy.

The civil directorate: political, economic and social aspects

The successful solution of the Moroccan problem, which had been a nightmare for Spanish rulers since the 1890s, encouraged Primo to find formulas to formalize his regime and stay in power. In December 1925, he named a government composed largely of civilians, although the Home Office was headed by the notoriously brutal General Martínez Anido. He also announced that, for the time being, elections would not be called and censorship would be maintained.

The formation of a civilian government did not, in and of itself, resolve the regime's future. Within a year, the dictator had announced his intention to convene an Advisory Congress, whose purpose would be to put the regime on firm legal footing, a plan which was endorsed by six and a half million people in a plebiscite. Nevertheless, without the cooperation of certain members of the old elite and of the king himself, the effort to convene the Advisory Congress remained paralysed.

In the meantime, the dictatorship's civilian government undertook active economic and social policies. It was here, and especially in its enthusiasm for economic nationalism and state intervention, that the regime best embodied the regenerationist programme. In this field, Primo de Rivera favoured interventionism and nationalism, rejecting free market competition as 'useless' and harmful for national power, and encouraging production by means of monopolies (such as the state oil and telephone companies, CAMPSA and Telefónica) and a complicated bureaucracy of a series of regulatory councils. Chief among these was the National Economic Council, which oversaw the regulatory Committee of Industrial Production, which was in turn charged with issuing permits for the establishment of any new industry.

The dictatorship significantly increased state revenues, through the emission of debt rather than a more effective collection of existing taxes. These were used to undertake a sweeping programme of public works, such as a massive expansion of the highway network, and the beginnings of a tourist infrastructure through *Paradores Nacionales*. He also initiated a policy of interventionism in the railroads, which would eventually result in nationalization. He also set up the *Confederaciones Hidrográficas*, agencies to promote irrigation and other water related projects. As was the case in Morocco, Primo jumped off from projects which had originated in the previous era but had never been concluded because of the instability of the parliamentary regime.

On balance, the economic policy of the dictatorship was largely successful, but one must bear in mind that General Primo de Rivera was favoured by coming to power in an era of clear economic boom, which was a global phenomenon in the decade of the twenties. Public works substantially stimulated the production of cement and steel, and the rate of industrial production increased by 40 per cent. The regime did not take on the issue of the redistribution of wealth, nor did it address either tax or agrarian reform, so that its actions in the end benefited the well-to-do above all. In any case, to present the dictatorship's economic interventionism as any sort of Keynesianism *avant la lettre*, would be mistaken. Primo de Rivera had much more to do with the traditional paternalism of the Spanish right, or the straightforward nationalism of the Iberian military. In its final years, the dictatorship was faced with an economic crisis produced by the devaluation of the peseta, a predictable result of its policy of massive emission of debt, and it did not make even minimal progress in formulating either a diagnosis or a solution.

The regime did not ignore social issues. On these matters, as with so many others, the dictator was well-intentioned, but his was an approach steeped in paternalism and based on a concept of interventionism which extended the bureaucracy and, as a result, the inefficiency of the state. The regime's social policy was overseen by the Minister of Labour, Eduardo Aunós, an old Catalan nationalist who had evolved toward the authoritarian right. A National Council on Labour, Commerce and Industry was created in April

1924, as a high-level advisory body. Two years later, the government issued a Labour Code, which included previous stipulations regarding labour contracts, accidents, and industrial tribunals, and was deeply influenced by Mussolini's Labour Charter.

The dictatorship's most brilliant work in this area – and its most debatable and enduring – was the creation of a corporatist system. Its primary building blocks were the *comités paritarios*, or arbitration committees, with a second tier of provincial committees, capped by national *Consejos de la corporación*. At each level employers and workers had an equal number of democratically elected representatives. The system's critics attacked it as a mere imitation of fascism's syndicalist system, and Aunós had in fact travelled to Italy a few months before the appearance of the project in the 'Madrid *Gazette*'. This corporativist organization, however, derived from social Catholicism, and it was clearly distinguished from the Italian fascist case by the democratic election of its representatives and by the participation of the socialist union federation UGT.

There is no doubt that, under the dictatorship, the working class benefited from the stability of employment rates and from the extension of social security. On the other hand, salaries remained essentially static, with a tendency to go down: according to official statistics, for 52 occupations, 18 saw their wages increased, 6 remained the same, and 28 saw them lowered. Between the strong functioning of the economy, government repression – particularly of the anarchists – and the weariness of the workers' movement, there were very few open social conflicts in this period, a remarkable change from the class warfare of 1919–23.

The labour movement

The most spectacular feature of the dictatorship's relationships with workers' movements was without doubt its collaboration with the Socialist party. It was in fact not an alliance as much as a continuously changing process, vague in its content, and steeped in doubt on both sides. Primo de Rivera's propaganda periodically asserted that the only honest party from the previous era was now collaborating with the regime, and indicated furthermore that socialism would combine with the Patriotic Union to create a new social and political system. Francisco Largo Caballero, the executive director of the UGT, joined the Council of State as a representative of labour, upon his election by the members of his party who sat on the Labour Council. The situation began to change, however, in 1927 when the Socialists refused to send any representatives to the Advisory Congress, in which six places had been reserved for them by Primo de Rivera. From that point on the change was complete, as the anticollaborationist line triumphed, represented by those, such as Indalecio Prieto and Fernando de los Ríos, who supported a liberal and humanistic socialism, close to republicanism.

The tiny Communist party, on the other hand, had been declared illegal near the end of 1923, and continued to be irrelevant for the whole period. As for the CNT, it was in bad shape before Primo came to power and the regime relegated it to such a semi-clandestine status as to create the impression that it had disappeared altogether. Repression was often severe but also selective. Some local offices were closed under various legal pretexts and the main anarchist newspaper, *Solidaridad Obrera*, was banned. The CNT was also suffering from increasing internal conflict between Angel Pestaña and the syndicalist sector on the one hand, and the more ideologically driven and violent Iberian Anarchist Federation (FAI), founded in 1927, on the other. The former was tolerated at times, but the latter was destined to have much more relevance in the decade of the 1930s, due to the romantic aura which was produced by the persecutions it endured. Catholic syndicalism, for its part, failed to prosper, continually complaining about the regime's preference for the socialists. By contrast the *sindicatos libres*, yellow unions created by employers during the crisis of 1919–23, enjoyed the protection of General Martínez Anido and did experience some temporary growth.

The failed consolidation of the regime

One of the series of changes of direction which occurred throughout the six-year tenure of the dictatorial regime involved the convocation of an Advisory Congress in September 1927. Primo de Rivera had already announced some time before that he would convene such an assembly, but he had declined to do so until now in the face of strong opposition from the old political elite, including, it seems, the king himself. Now he announced that the Congress would be called 'to prepare and present in a step-by-step process to the Government, over a three-year period, a first draft of a constitution'. All the Congress members were selected either directly or indirectly by the government – despite the fact that many held views which hardly coincided with those of Primo. In addition, the operation of the Advisory Congress provided clear evidence of Primo de Rivera's bias against parliamentarianism: all the work was done by committee, only subjects proposed by the government were addressed, and there was a time limit on discussion.

The Congress was a disaster from the start, since it failed to include most of the opposition to the regime, as Liberals, Socialists, an important sector of Conservatives, and the majority of intellectuals who were selected, refused their nominations. The draft prepared by a Congressional committee failed to satisfy even Primo de Rivera himself, who would have preferred a more authoritarian document. The person most harmed by the Congress was Alfonso XIII, because it accentuated the sense that he had been disloyal to the Constitution without signalling either an alternative path or a return to normality.

The opposition

The deliberations of the Congress proved the catalyst for the emergence of some opposition to the regime, practically non-existent until then. It was to be expected that opposition would come from the old political elite, but this was not at first the case, as the latter chose a wait-and-see approach born of the sense that the *coup d'etat* had been inevitable. As time passed the attitude of the old elite began to change, due primarily to two factors. In the first place, the dictatorship's activism against the oligarchy and *caciquismo* was beginning to disrupt the clientelistic models on which the old political system was based. Second, the continuous accusations of administrative immorality which Primo de Rivera levelled at all those politicians who had preceded him, turned them into mortal enemies.

The opposition of these old politicians was totally ineffective, and never went beyond veiled accusations at banquets or malicious gossip. Occasionally, they also appealed to the king himself against the dictator. This achieved little more than making the king's position even more uncomfortable, as he found himself faced by the whole of the old political elite. Alfonso XIII attempted to modify Primo de Rivera's antagonistic views toward them, but found that the autocrat was very difficult to control in any respect.

The exception to the rule was the leader of the Conservative party, José Sánchez Guerra, whose opposition went beyond mere words. When the Advisory Congress was convened he opted for exile abroad, where he devoted himself to plotting with disaffected army officers. Opposition from the army was prompted by Primo de Rivera's attempts at military reform, such as a system of advancement based on war merits rather than seniority. This favoured officers who had been involved in the North African campaign, such as Francisco Franco, whose earlier opposition was evolving towards support. By 1925–26, the military began to coordinate with the politicians and in June 1926, they staged the 'Night of San Juan' (*la Sanjuanada*), a failed but important attempt to overthrow the dictator.

The most serious conflict with the military came when Primo attempted to apply his promotion system to the Artillery Corps. In the face of staunch opposition, he was obliged to dissolve the entire body. From that point on, an important portion of the young artillery officers adopted a markedly pro-republican stance. They were joined by several generals who opposed Primo de Rivera for personal and ideological reasons. This opposition did not mean that Primo's military policies were unjustified. The dictator did accurately perceive the defects in the armed forces, and sought to resolve them. He did succeed in reducing the officer corps by 10 per cent, the troops by around a third, and the number of cadets even more drastically (from 1200 in 1922 to 200 in 1929.) He also created, in February 1927, the General Military Academy and named General Franco its first director.

Another sector of Spanish society which faced off against the dictatorial regime were the intellectuals, whose numbers might be scant but whose influence on society was undeniable. The first significant clash between Primo de Rivera and the intelligentsia took place in February 1924, when Miguel de Unamuno was removed as chancellor of the University of Salamanca and exiled to the island of Fuerteventura. Later he chose self-exile in France. There the Basque author, in conjunction with Eduardo Ortega y Gasset, published a number of *Hojas Libres*, pamphlets which were very critical of both the regime and the monarchy. As time went on, tensions between the dictatorship and the intellectuals increased. Like Unamuno, another prominent figure in Spanish literature, Ramón del Valle-Inclán, experienced a radicalization in opposition to the monarchy, and his grotesque tale, 'The Captain's Daughter', was withdrawn from publication.

Initially, Primo de Rivera had had some support in the world of culture, so unanimously critical of the corrupt parliamentary system; most strikingly, the country's leading public intellectual, José Ortega y Gasset, also thought that the general could clean up the system and then lead the evolution towards liberal reforms. Over time, Primo also benefited from the support of those who were evolving towards authoritarianism or open fascism (Ramiro de Maeztu, Eugenio D'Ors, Ernesto Giménez Caballero). But the support of Ortega y Gasset and other liberal intellectuals was short-lived and had vanished by 1925, when it became clear that Primo intended to stay in power. Even the poets of the generation of 1927, who were largely uninterested in politics, ended up opposing Primo de Rivera.

The intelligentsia's protests were not very effective until March 1929, when university students began to demonstrate in the streets. This provoked the closure of the Universities of Madrid and Barcelona and the substitution of their chancellors. Primo de Rivera showed himself particularly inept in dealing with the students' increasingly combative attitude, provoking the indignation of the academic establishment, and leading to a group of prestigious scholars abandoning their teaching positions. The political belligerence of the intellectuals would survive Primo's own downfall and would turn against the monarchy itself.

The collapse of the dictatorship

By the end of the 1920s, Primo was facing an increasingly active opposition. In January 1929, Sánchez Guerra led a military uprising in Valencia, which was followed by another in Ciudad Real. In some garrisons, principally in the south, conspiracies continued to be hatched by members of the old political elite and high-ranking military officers. These events exacerbated the dictator's indecision. He was very conscious of the need to 'get ready for the Judgement Day', especially because his own ministers were insisting that elections were necessary. The problem was just how to do it, however, and Primo found himself at a dead end.

As his perplexity increased, so did the deterioration of the economic situation. The Finance Minister, Calvo Sotelo, could not work out how to deal with the devaluation of the peseta, something which greatly damaged Primo de Rivera's sense of national pride. As a result of both the deterioration of the economic situation and the attitude of the Socialist Party, social conflicts became more numerous, resulting in a considerably greater number of work-days lost, harming the economy even further.

The seriousness and uncertainty of the situation induced Primo de Rivera to survey opinion among the upper echelons of the military. Their response was not enthusiastic, and on 30 January 1930 he offered his resignation to the king. It is no surprise that the king reacted with unfeigned indignation and severity, since this procedure had never been discussed and left him to take all the blame. Upon abandoning power, the dictator fled to Paris, where he would die suddenly a short time later. It was one of those very rare instances in history in which a dictator voluntarily relinquished power.

Overall assessments of the dictatorship often note that it was positive in economic terms and negative in political ones. Such judgements are basically correct, although some nuances are required. In the area of economics and the Moroccan war, Primo succeeded in carrying out what others had already thought about, although he enjoyed an exceptionally propitious set of circumstances – the general economic expansion of the twenties and the collaboration with France. The dictator's failure in the political realm stemmed from his inability to carry out the *regeneracionista* programme which he claimed to be his own. With this, he also wreaked considerable damage on the monarchy as an institution, since Spanish public opinion correctly blamed the king for the dictatorship. In some circles, and especially among the authoritarian right, the general would be elevated to a semi-mythical status, with Alfonso XIII playing the villain's role.

The *Dictablanda* and the road to the Republic

The man selected to succeed Miguel Primo de Rivera was also a general, Dámaso Berenguer. He was a cultivated, intelligent and equitable person, who had distinguished himself over the previous six years by his moderate opposition to the dictatorial regime. He was the most liberal of the three figures suggested by Primo de Rivera as potential successors. When he immediately announced his intention to return to constitutional norms, public opinion was conspicuously favourable, and his relatively liberal measures, like restoring the professorships of those who had resigned or been dismissed under the previous regime, were well-received. The military conspiracies which had proliferated in the last stages of the dictatorship all but disappeared. The new regime was baptized by public opinion with the name *dictablánda* (a pun on the Spanish word for Dictatorship) which means a softer regime.

Nevertheless, the Berenguer government suffered from a number of major deficiencies from the start. First, in spite of their declared intentions to liberalize the regime, the new cabinet retained many of the authoritarian prerogatives of the dictatorship. Second, Berenguer tried to return economic policy to the former liberal orthodoxy, precisely at a moment when the world was suffering the impact of the Depression. Most seriously, however, Berenguer's long-run project was only to turn the clock back to September 1923, as if nothing had happened. He only thought of restoring the 1876 Constitution, and even of reconstructing the *cacique* system. To a large degree, this anachronism was inevitable, given that the majority of monarchist politicians on whom he was depending continued to be anchored in the *cacique* past. Perhaps a more skilful politician, such as Francesc Cambó or Santiago Alba, could have offered a more innovative solution. The king had appealed to both men, but the former was ill and Alba was too alienated from the monarch, whom he considered indirectly culpable for the persecution to which he had been subjected under the previous regime.

Public opinion, which had been all but dormant for the previous seven years, now began to play an active part in political life. The difficult economic situation contributed to this, since Spaniards were beginning to feel the effects of the global crisis, and in a few Andalucian provinces drought conditions provoked work stoppages and labour conflicts. Even more important than this was the blossoming of impassioned political mobilization during this period, which was a result of the general modernization of Spanish society, the ramifications of which could not be perceived during the dictatorship. This situation was aggravated by the fact that the monarchy had now to suffer the consequences of having abandoned the Constitution. The king and General Berenguer were confronted with violent offensives from across the political spectrum. The most effective opposition to the Berenguer government came in fact from a coalition of republicans and socialists known as the Pact of San Sebastian, reached in August 1930. The pact brought together republicans of every hue, from long-time radical demagogues such as Alejandro Lerroux through intellectuals like Manuel Azaña to former monarchist politicians such as Niceto Alcalá Zamora and Miguel Maura. The alliance also included the Socialists and the Catalan republican left, led by Francesc Maciá, a former army officer who had led a failed conspiracy against Primo de Rivera. This alliance would later function as both a provisional republican government and an electoral alternative.

Most ominous for the monarchy was the disaffection of many of its former supporters, both among the middle classes in general and among the political leaders. The collaboration of an important sector of the intelligentsia and a portion of the army further increased the strength of republicanism. The former responded to the call for a '*Agrupación al Servicio de la República*', which emerged from a manifesto drafted by Ortega y Gasset, Ramón Pérez de Ayala and Gregorio Marañón. As for the army, the republicans benefited from the mood of generalized protest evident in some garrisons, like the artillery unit, and also from the conspiratorial tradition within the officer corps, especially among the youngest. It was they who led the uprising of December 1930, in Jaca and Madrid, which the government put down, but only at the cost of considerable damage in the court of public opinion.

Most counterproductive of all for the monarchy was the slowness with which Berenguer proceeded. When he attempted to hold general elections without convening municipal elections first, a broad segment of political forces refused to participate. Faced with the gravity of the situation, King Alfonso turned to some monarchist politicians who had distinguished themselves by opposition to Primo de Rivera. None of them, however, had much interest in stepping into power at a juncture when saving the monarchy looked to be an impossible task.

The king finally dismissed Berenguer and replaced him with Admiral Aznar, who formed a broad monarchist coalition which included the Catalan regionalists. His programme included elections, beginning at a municipal level, a revision of the 1876 constitution and regional autonomy for Catalonia. However, it was too little, too late: public opinion continued to turn against the monarchy and even the monarchist politicians were divided. Even so, Aznar kept his word, and municipal elections were held on 12 April 1931. After such a long period of electoral abstinence, the populace was awakened in a most impassioned way: Spain had never known elections in which all citizens, across all classes, were so interested. The republicans took election day as an opportunity to hold a plebiscite on the monarchy, while the monarchists reverted to offering the same kinds of candidates they had always had for municipal posts – local notables without any real national significance. The monarchy was damaged as a result. The ardour with which the public viewed the electoral contest was most evident in the big cities, where public opinion was both highly articulated and beyond the control of the government.

In the cities and larger towns, the republican–socialist coalition's triumph was crushing; they won all major cities and every provincial capital but one. In the smaller locales, where *caciquismo* continued to predominate, the monarchists prevailed. The way in which the latter identified with the monarchy struck a Spain which was in ferment as decrepit and anachronistic. Spanish society gave the impression that it was dispensing with monarchist institutions because these were an impediment to its modernization. Once the results were known, the development of events convinced the republicans of the possibility of taking power immediately. For his part the king, after thinking for a time that he would not abandon the throne until after national elections had been held, ended up giving up royal authority and abandoning Spain. The Republic was proclaimed on 14 April 1931.

The change produced in Spain by this chain of events was much more important than the mere transition from one regime to another. What changed was political life itself. In 1923 Spain had a political system of oligarchic liberalism; in 1931 it had a mass democracy. The republican experience represented a much more significant change than did, for example, that of the Portuguese Republic of 1910. It was the first experience with democracy in Spain's history and, like Weimar Germany, it was a regime of strong reformist character.

Historians have interpreted Primo de Rivera's regime in quite diverse ways. Many have cast it as the forerunner to the Franco regime, but the latter's immense degree of repression and will to endure are beyond any comparison with the former. Shlomo Ben Ami has argued that the Dictatorship was an attempt at 'fascism from above', but this is also debatable: Primo de Rivera did not exhibit a totalitarian will, or revolutionary demagogy, or any commitment to creating a single-party state. Primo de Rivera's regime should not be interpreted in light of what followed it, but rather of what preceded it. It was a step backwards on the road towards democratization. By delaying and repressing the political mobilization, it led to polarization and radicalization. Not only did it bring down the monarchy; by the abruptness of the transition and the almost complete renewal of the political elite, it also gravely damaged the democratic experiment which was already facing a very difficult future.

|14|

The Second Republic, 1931–1936

Sectarianism, schisms, and strife

NIGEL TOWNSON

Studies of the Second Republic have finally emerged over the last decade or so from the lengthy shadow of the Civil War. The Manichean image of a Spain divided into two during the conflict of 1936 to 1939 has long been projected back onto the 1931 to 1936 period, above all by the Franco dictatorship of 1939–75 but also by many of its detractors, thereby obscuring the labyrinthine reality of the regime's democratic years. The establishment of parliamentary democracy in Spain in the 1970s, and the corresponding decline of the Civil War as the quintessential point of political reference, gradually altered the historiography of the Second Republic. Local and regional studies, together with a greater appreciation of the complexities of national politics, have revealed a more rounded picture. If the Republic of 1931 to 1936 is to be understood in its own right, and not as a mere prelude to the fratricidal slaughter of the regime's last three years, then the Civil War itself should not be seen as the inevitable outcome of the vicissitudes of the first six.

The provisional government

The Republican–Socialist coalition that came to power with the advent of the Republic in April 1931 faced a series of redoubtable obstacles if the new regime was to be consolidated, let alone fulfill the widespread expectations of reform placed in it. The very nature of the transition, whereby Alfonso XIII peacefully vacated the throne following the adverse result of the municipal elections of 12 April, was a constraint on reform. Given that the pillars of the monarchy, such as the Church, the army, and the landowning oligarchy, had abandoned the king out of expediency, as opposed to an identification with the republican cause, the desire for change of the Republic's supporters was circumscribed by the extant social and institutional might of the Ancien

Regime. By comparison, the republican movement was fragmented and weak. Its greatest bastion, the socialist trade unions, the General Union of Workers (Unión General de Trabajadores), was far from truly nationwide in scope, while the myriad republican parties, though well supported in a significant number of towns, were highly localized and lacked a national structure.

The abortive coup of December 1930, when the Republican–Socialist coalition had attempted to topple the monarchy through a general strike in conjunction with a rising by military sympathizers, had revealed the coercive limits to the antimonarchist movement. Once in power, the republicans were in a far better position, with the forces of the right demoralized and in disarray, to carry out a thoroughgoing revolution by means of force, but they lacked the unity of purpose, the necessary strategy, and, above all, the will, for such an enterprise. On the contrary, the peaceful nature of the transition and the surge in support for the antimonarchist cause since the fall of the dictatorship of General Primo de Rivera in January 1930 had convinced the republicans that a democratic parliamentary regime could meet the varied hopes deposited in it.

The dilemma of the antimonarchist *pueblo* of 1930–31, which ranged from unskilled workers to shopkeepers, landowners, artisans, industrialists, landless labourers, and the professional classes, and included a great many former monarchists together with the uncommitted middle classes, the '*clase neutra*', is that it was a populist movement created out of a common opposition, but bereft of a common programme. In reality, the crowds that thronged the squares and streets of Spain on 14 April in celebration of the Republic's proclamation harboured a multitude of fissiparous, often contradictory, interests. The provisional government itself, divided as it was between recent Catholic converts to the republican cause, socialists, conservative republicans, and left-wing republicans as well as Catalan and Galician nationalists, possessed neither a common programme nor a shared vision of the Republican state. Given the range of expectations, from traditional republicans to republican converts, monarchists, and the working classes, the government faced a daunting task if the Republic was to be consolidated as a parliamentary democracy.

The reformist aspirations of the provisional government were also hindered by the republicans' very conception of change. Reliance on a limited, unreformed, and weakly integrated state as the instrument of reform and the neglect of other means of enforcement was to prove a devastating mistake given the intractability of structural problems such as the *cacique* system and the acute socio-economic inequalities of Spanish society. The poverty of economic thought, reflected in an unquestioning adherence to the orthodoxies of a balanced budget and low taxation, was, given the worldwide recession, the huge deficit inherited from the dictatorship, and the tenuous fiscal resources of the Spanish state, a further critical constraint on the republicans' room for manoeuvre. The provisional government thus embarked on major reform at a time of global depression and political uncertainty, confronted not just by its own divisions and the diverse expectations of its popular base but also by the strictly circumscribed resources of the Spanish state.

The political instability of the Republic was to lie not in a straightforward dialectical clash between the 'proletariat' and the 'bourgeoisie', but in a number of socio-economic and cultural conflicts not only between, but also within, and beyond, the classes. Thus the history of the Second Republic was not shaped by the struggle between the workers and the employers or that between the landowners and the landless labourers alone – central as these confrontations were to the regime's trajectory – but also, for example, by those between Catholics and anticlericals, radical and conservative republicans, regional nationalists and centralists, the republican and non-republican middle classes, as well as between anarchosyndicalists and socialists. Significantly, the first major schism suffered by the antimonarchist cause occurred within the working class. There was not one, but several, working class organizations in Spain, with the socialist and anarchosyndicalist movements the most important. Initially, the anarchosyndicalist National Confederation of Labour (Confederación Nacional del Trabajo, or CNT) had welcomed the Republic as an opportunity to liberate many of its militants from jail and to organize itself relatively unhindered, having been severely repressed under the Primo de Rivera dictatorship. However, the introduction of the Socialist-inspired labour legislation of April–May 1931, designed not only to improve the lot of the workers but also to entrench the Socialists within the state – and, in the process, win the CNT rank and file over to the socialist cause – together with heavy-handed repression of the anarchosyndicalists by the Republican authorities, combined to distance the CNT rapidly from the new regime. This was virtually a rerun of events under Primo de Rivera when the socialist UGT had collaborated with the dictatorship in order to further their own interests at the expense of the CNT.

The prompt reassertion of this traditional cleavage within the organized working class played into the hands of the Iberian Anarchist Federation (Federación Anarquista Ibérica, or FAI), a product of the repression of the dictatorship which militated from within the CNT to advance the anarchist tradition as opposed to the more moderate syndicalist one. The syndicalists may have held the upper hand at the National Congress of June 1931, but thereafter the FAI and other CNT radicals came to dominate the movement, the July 1931 stoppage in Seville, which claimed 20 lives, being a foretaste of the FAI-inspired twin-track strategy of strikes and insurrections. The alienation of the CNT deprived the regime of the support of a substantial section of the organized working class and had immense repercussions. Not only did the CNT's actions heighten social and political tension, but its soaring growth over the next two years was to undermine the Socialists' own commitment to the Republic.

Republicans and Socialists in power, 1931–1933

Despite mounting internal disputes over the extent and nature of reform, the Republican–Socialist coalition won a landslide victory in the general election of June 1931, the Spanish Socialist Workers Party (Partido Socialista Obrero Español, or PSOE) emerging as the single largest party with 117 seats, followed by the Radical Republican Party (89), the left republican Radical Socialist Party (55) and Acción Republicana (26), and the Catholic Conservative Liberal Republican Party (Derecha Liberal Republicana, or DLR) (27). The only sizable non-republican rightwing group was the Agrarian group with 24 deputies. However, the composition of the Constituent Cortes provides a misleading snapshot of the balance of forces within the Republic. First, the right, still disorientated and disorganized, was underrepresented. Second, many monarchists, convinced that the monarchy itself was a lost cause, had joined the republican parties, some even standing in the general election as republican candidates. The failure of the progressive administrations of 1931–33 to take such recent converts realistically into account would frustrate and even prevent the application of reform, especially the labour laws, and thereby undermine relations between the left republicans and their socialist allies.

The disharmony within the ruling coalition was highlighted by the ructions and recriminations that characterized the constitutional debate of July to December 1931. Discussion of the religious clauses caused the Cabinet's first split when the Catholic Prime Minister, Niceto Alcalá Zamora, and his party colleague, Minister of the Interior Miguel Maura, resigned in October 1931; the Cabinet therefore lost its only Catholics, and with them the goodwill of many fellow believers. The political damage was partially rectified by the election of Alcalá Zamora as President in December 1931, only to create a new set of problems as the vain and volatile ex-monarchist minister (acting much like the king he had served), exacerbated the instability of the regime by his excessive interference in governmental affairs.

Once the Constituent Cortes had fulfilled its principal task by passing the Constitution, it was hardly surprising that the tensions within the Republican–Socialist coalition came to the surface. The Radicals, voicing the opposition of the propertied urban and rural middle classes to the labour legislation as well as their anxiety at the burgeoning economic crisis, wanted the Socialists out of the government, not least so that they could dominate an all-republican administration. By contrast, the left republicans, led by premier Manuel Azaña, believed that the Socialists' continued governmental participation was essential, both to pass the laws supplementary to the Constitution and to keep the socialist trade unions under control. Underlying these strategic concerns were two contrasting visions of the Republic. For the left republicans, as for the Socialists, the Republic was consubstantial with the 'modernization' of Spain; this implied not just the classical liberal reform of the country's political institutions but also, and more radically, its economic and social reform. For the inappositely named Radicals, the Republic was largely an end in itself, a change of political regime that would open up the channels of influence to the middle classes and extend secularism, but alter little else.

The Radical exit from the government in December 1931 represented a fundamental split in the republican movement which deprived the Azaña administration of the support of the largest of the republican parties. More than any other republican party, the Radical Party articulated the concerns of the industrial and commercial classes, the *patronal*, and the middle-class professional associations. In hindsight, an all-republican administration, complemented by the benevolent opposition of the Socialists, might have done more for the stability of the regime by consolidating urban support and the republican alliance; the industrial and commercial middle classes, unlike many landowners, were prepared to work within the legal framework of the Republic. As it was, the left Republican–Socialist government, which would rule for the next two years, was left to advance its programme of reform on the sole basis of an interclass alliance between the socialist working class and the progressive middle classes.

The opposition of the Radical Party to the left Republican–Socialist coalition was initially ambivalent as the Radicals endeavoured to keep the alliance with the left republicans open, in the conviction that the government would soon fall and give way to an all-republican administration, while also consolidating their appeal amongst the conservative middle classes. The longer the Azaña administration continued in power, the more the Radicals' equivocal posture gave way to a critical and even threatening one, climaxing in July 1932 with the Saragossa speech of the Radical leader, Alejandro Lerroux, in which he effectively called on the Socialists to leave the government before the army intervened. The following month, on 10 August, a motley group of monarchists led by General Sanjurjo attempted to overthrow the Republic in a *coup d'etat*. The fact that Lerroux was involved in the abortive coup – though never proven at the time – demonstrated the degree to which he was the focus for disgruntled monarchists. The failure of the so-called '*Sanjurjada*' did not alter the fact that for the Radical Party and its middle class supporters, especially the industrial and commercial groups, the prime objective remained the removal of the Socialists from office and the modification, if not overturning, of the labour legislation in the belief that this would quash the burgeoning workers' protest.

Social conflict

Labour conflict was greatest in the countryside, the most important sector of the Spanish economy, partly because of the wretched inequalities of rural life and partly due to the previous absence of a legal framework for labour relations. The most strife-ridden area was the south with its vast landed estates, the *latifundios*. Traditionally, landowners had enjoyed almost absolute power over the labourers, based on their hegemonic control of local institutions (the town council or *ayuntamiento*, the judiciary, the Civil Guard, and provincial officials), the zealous backing of the Church, and the constant surplus of hired hands. With the advent of the Republic, the rural status quo was transformed. The 1931 labour reforms, comprising the introduction of arbitration committees (*jurados mixtos*), the prohibition on outside labour being contracted as long as local labourers remained unemployed, and the obligation of proprietors to cultivate their land (thereby eschewing lock-outs), permitted the workers finally to organize and defend themselves against the landowners, a process reinforced by a shift in the balance of power as many *ayuntamientos* fell under the sway of republicans and socialists.

This radical realignment of the rural order was challenged by the landowners through the rejuvenation of old agrarian associations, the creation of new ones, and obstruction of the reforms at the local level. At the same time, they vigorously promoted the political cause of the non-republican right. The proprietors' goal was simple: to overthrow the Socialists and their legislation and return the countryside to the monarchist status quo. Rural labour relations were therefore radicalized not just because exports declined and unemployment rose but also because the workers became increasingly dismayed at the uneven application of the labour legislation and the slow pace of agrarian reform. Like the landowners, the *patronal* objected vociferously to the Socialists' ministerial presence and reforms, blaming them, together with the more general failure of the government to uphold 'law and order', for the depression and extensive worker unrest. However, the *patronal's* protest, unlike that of most landowners, was directed not against the Republic as such but against the Socialists. The less extreme approach of the urban employers, in large measure due to an established tradition of industrial relations, was reflected in the nature of its revisionist campaign, which consisted of courting public opinion and lobbying political parties while struggling to bring the congeries of highly localized and sectorial employers' bodies into a more effective national framework.

The impact of the worldwide depression on relations between the workers and the employers under the Republic has often been underestimated. While it is undoubtedly true that, largely because of the limited export–import market and strong protectionism, the 1929 Crash had a limited overall effect on Spain, it should be stressed that several leading industries, such as construction, metallurgy, and mining in Asturias, as well as a number of agricultural export sectors, were badly hit by the global economic crisis. The challenge posed by escalating unemployment was compounded by chronic structural underemployment, altogether affecting up to nearly two-thirds of the workers in some southern provinces. By the winter of 1932–33, the exiguous public works funds had been exhausted, and, to make matters worse, there was no social security benefit for the workers to fall back on.

Relations between workers and employers were therefore to deteriorate in urban and rural areas alike because of the unremitting rise in unemployment from 1931 onwards.

If the consolidation of working-class support for the Republic was complicated by the sectarian division of the workers between the CNT and the UGT, the middle classes presented an even more perplexing panorama. The damage wrought to the Republic by the split between Radicals and left republicans in December 1931 and by the internal schism of the Radical Socialist Party in September 1933 was limited insofar as these splits took place within the republican movement. While the multifarious fissures of republican politics, ranging from the innumerable local and provincial autonomous groupings that made up the weakly integrated national parties to the many regional entities, represented only a part of the middle classes, a far greater source of instability lay completely outside the Republican camp: the Catholic middle classes. Given the paramount importance of anticlericalism to the cultural identity of the republicans, this middle-class religious divide represented a fundamental challenge to the consolidation of the regime.

The resurgence of the right

While the failed coup of 10 August 1932 had demonstrated that the new regime had little to fear from the monarchist opposition, the emergence of the non-republican or so-called 'accidentalist' right, according to which a regime was to be judged by its content and not its form, was a different proposition altogether. The anticlerical reforms of 1931, particularly article 26 of the Constitution, provided the non-republican right with a revisionist banner around which to rally the majority of Catholics. Acción Popular, originally a lobby group centred on the Catholic daily *El Debate* that soon transformed itself into an umbrella organization of regional parties, was therefore able to draw on the formidable resources of the Catholic Church. Also crucial was the economic and organizational backing of the agrarian associations, especially the National Catholic Agrarian Confederation (Confederación Nacional Católico-Agraria). Thus the defence of religion and that of property, as embodied in the party slogan of 'Religion, Fatherland, Order, Family and Property', were inextricably linked. Acción Popular subsequently formed the cornerstone of an even broader coalition, the Spanish Confederation of Autonomous Right-Wing Groups (Confederación Española de Derechas Autónomas, or CEDA), which on its foundation in February 1933 boasted more members, over 700 000, than any other party. The singular achievement of the 'accidentalist' right was to forge, out of an alliance between small and medium landowners and the landowning oligarchy, the first mass Catholic party in Spanish history. The refusal of the CEDA to commit itself to the Republic, as embodied in its 'accidentalist' stance, along with its explicit determination to supplant the Republic by an authoritarian regime based on corporatist Catholic principles, represented a deep-seated cleavage not just within the middle classes but in the Republic itself.

The end of the Republican–Socialist coalition

The crushing of the '*Sanjurjada*' gave the Azaña administration a renewed sense of purpose and unity as the Radicals rallied behind it in defence of the Republic and the right was temporarily disarmed. The government took advantage of this honeymoon to pass two critical pieces of legislation, the Agrarian Reform bill and the Catalan Statute. However, the government's new lease on life came to an abrupt end in January 1933 with the repression of a CNT insurrection that had stretched from Catalonia to Cádiz. In the southern village of Casas Viejas, the Republic's own security force, the recently created Assault Guards, killed 22 peasants, most of them in cold blood. Although the Azaña administration was not directly implicated in the massacre, its image was badly tarnished. The Casas Viejas incident was also symbolic of the reformist government's inability to tackle the structural problems of rural society such as the inequitable distribution of land, unemployment, and *caciquismo*. Much the same could be deduced from the defeat of the ruling coalition in the municipal elections held in predominantly rural areas three months later.

During the summer of 1933 the government's standing deteriorated still further as both the economy and urban labour relations reached their nadir. The *patronal*'s antisocialist campaign, boosted since February 1933 by the Radical Party's declaration of outright opposition to the government, reached its zenith in July 1933 with a national congress in Madrid of over 1000 representative bodies. There is little doubt that the campaign of the *patronal* played its part in the two major republican splits of the first *bienio*: the separation of the Radicals from the Azaña administration in December 1931, and now, in the summer of 1933, the breakup of the Radical Socialist Party over the same question of socialist participation in the government. The tension was heightened by the fact that the peak of the *patronal*'s protest coincided with an intensive period of CNT mobilization. Consequently while the left republicans' commitment to the Azaña administration was being undermined by the opposition of the industrial and commercial middle classes, the Socialists' own commitment was flagging as a result of the halting progress of reform and the ascendancy of their revolutionary rival.

The government, besieged by the CNT, the *patronal*, and by its own internal divisions, was further weakened by the uproar which greeted the passing in June 1933 of the Law of Congregations. This anticlerical measure, which prohibited the Church from pursuing its extensive educational activities, outraged the Catholic opposition and prompted the personal protest of the Pope. As a Catholic, a constitutional revisionist, and an opponent of the

Azaña administration – to the extent that he had been plotting its downfall in collaboration with the opposition – President Alcalá Zamora readily withdrew his support from the Cabinet. However, Azaña returned as prime minister as there was no alternative, but, three months later, the President again withdrew his support following the government's poor performance in the elections for the Tribunal de Garantías Constitucionales (Supreme Court). Once the Radicals proved unable to secure a parliamentary majority, the President brought the Constituent Cortes to an unceremonious close.

The governments of 1931–33 had carried out the most sweeping series of reforms in modern Spanish history, touching on virtually all aspects of national life. These included a major expansion of public education, the separation of Church and State and other restrictions on organized Catholicism, the partial modernization of the armed forces, a far-reaching new electoral law, the wide-ranging labour reforms, the much-anticipated Agrarian Reform Law, and a statute of regional autonomy for Catalonia. The chief failure was in agrarian reform. Instead of mobilizing rural opinion behind the Republic through a meaningful redistribution of land, the tardy and overly complex Agrarian Reform Law, limited both in scope and resources, engendered widespread frustration. The reforms also failed to consolidate the ruling coalition, as reflected in the growing disillusionment of the Socialists during the summer of 1933 and their refusal to ally with the left republicans in the general election later that year. Part of the problem lay in the left republicans' greater interest in cultural and institutional rather than social and economic issues. In any case, the left republicans and the Socialists both overestimated the capacity of the state and the Cortes to implement change, a situation accentuated by the sometimes disastrous lack of experience and expertise of the ministers, and underestimated or ignored the extent to which interventionist economic and fiscal measures could have boosted their reforms. The upshot was that by the time of the 1933 general election the left republicans had lost the crucial support of the Socialists whilst alienating Catholic opinion and the conservative middle classes of a secular outlook.

The centre-right in power, 1933–1935

The general election of November 1933 resulted in a hung parliament. The fact that the Socialists won only 62 seats while Acción Republicana and the Radical Socialists plummeted to less than a dozen was partly due to the introduction of female suffrage and to anarchist abstention, but the principal reason for defeat was that the new electoral system, ironically passed earlier in the year by the left Republican–Socialist majority, heavily favoured broad coalitions. As a result, the decision of the Socialists to stand alone in the election, despite the entreaties of their former left republican allies, was fatal to the cause of the left. This strategic blunder did not prevent both the

Socialists and the left republicans, following their defeat, from vigorously contesting the validity of the elections. The largest single force in the Cortes was now the accidentalist right, the CEDA having amassed 115 deputies, though it had fallen short of an overall majority. The leading republican party was again the centrist Radical Party with 104 deputies, an improvement on its 1931 performance but a disappointing result after two years in opposition. Although the distribution of votes among the left, centre, and right was roughly comparable, the pendulum effect of the electoral law, which castigated the disunity of the left, meant that the only majority possible was a coalition between the centre and the right. Given the CEDA's equivocal stance towards the Republic, the President called upon the Radical Party to form the first government of the ordinary Cortes.

The Radical-dominated Cabinet formed in December 1933 was a minority administration that depended for its parliamentary survival on the CEDA. Although the Radical Party and the CEDA held a number of conservative goals in common, such as the modification of the labour and agrarian reforms and an amnesty for the monarchist rebels of 10 August 1932, and while their symbiotic relationship was consistent with Lerroux's claim that the Republic would be consolidated only through the incorporation of the non-republican right, the arrangement remained a marriage of convenience between two forces that were at once allies and rivals. Separated by strategic and ideological differences (many Radicals, for example, were masons, in contrast to the Catholicism of their CEDA counterparts), the most crucial of which was the extent to which the reforms of the first *bienio* should be rectified, the collaboration between the Radical Party and the CEDA ushered in a period of political instability.

The immediate challenge to the new-found political hegemony of the centre-right was the CNT rising, its greatest under the Republic, launched on 8 December 1933. The rebellion's complete failure and the severe repression that followed may have blunted the CNT's insurrectionary fervour, but a different revolutionary spirit was astir elsewhere within the organized working classes. By the summer of 1933 the Socialists had become openly disenchanted with the Republic, a process accelerated by their departure from the government in September 1933 and consolidated by their humiliation in the general election two months later. They now rejected not just political alliance with the republicans but – on the grounds that 'bourgeois' parliamentary democracy had little more to offer than the monarchy – the Republic itself. The Socialists therefore proclaimed that should the CEDA, which although not a fascist party itself admired the Nazis and their legalistic tactic for the conquest of power, enter the government they would declare a revolution.

The sharp rise in labour strife in 1933–34 is partly explained by the Socialists' more radical stance, but the main reason was material: the deepening economic crisis and the undermining of the labour legislation. However, the Radicals' reform of the labour laws cannot be equated with their wholesale destruction. In the ten months before the October 1934 uprising, local studies show that conditions of employment in the urban areas did not deteriorate much, if at all. Although the Minister of the Interior, Rafael Salazar Alonso, took a hardline approach to all trade union mobilization, he clashed continually with the more conciliatory Minister of Labour, José Estadella, whose relative even-handedness – including the arrest of recalcitrant employers – eventually alienated the *patronal* from the Radicals, a crucial loss of social support in the party's escalating struggle with the CEDA. By contrast, in the rural areas the Radical administration obliged its accidentalist ally, which regarded the countryside as its personal domain, either by overturning the extant legislation or by turning a blind eye to violations. The landowners' counteroffensive was summed up in their vindictive exhortation to unemployed labourers to '¡Comed Republica!' ('Let the Republic feed you!').

The uneasy relationship between the CEDA and the Radical Party, reflected in the government's uncertain agenda and the lack of solid public support, was partly due to their conflicting interests and partly to the opposition of a sizable minority within the Radical Party to the alliance with the accidentalists. This led the CEDA to engineer the expulsion of two Radical critics of collaboration, one of which was the party's deputy leader Diego Martínez Barrio, from the Cabinet in March 1934. Unable to reach a compromise with Lerroux, in May 1934 Martínez Barrio headed a major Radical split, taking with him 20 deputies, up to one-fourth of the rank and file, and the most liberal section of the party's social base. The schism underlined Lerroux's determination to maintain the alliance at all costs, not least because it made the party even more dependent on the CEDA.

Despite the departure of the Radical dissidents, relations between the Radical Party and the CEDA remained discordant. In April 1934, Lerroux, as a direct result of the amnesty granted to the monarchist insurgents of 10 August 1932, was dismissed as prime minister by Alcalá Zamora and replaced by Ricardo Samper of the PURA (Partido Unión Republicana Autonomista, the Valencian affiliate of the Radical Party). Clearly the President aimed to further his own centrist designs, given that Samper was neither the choice of Lerroux, nor, unlike the Radical leader, a zealous advocate of the CEDA alliance (the PURA and the Derecha Regional Valenciana, the CEDA's affiliate in Valencia, were bitter enemies). Over the next few months, an isolated and beleaguered Samper would struggle to contain an ever-widening opposition front, ranging from the landless labourers in the south to the Basque and Catalan nationalists in the north, while contending with the disagreements of hardline Cabinet colleagues, the waxing impatience of Lerroux and the party, and the increasingly vociferous criticism of the CEDA.

The first major mobilization against the Samper administration was the June 1934 strike of the landless labourers trade union, the FNTT. Undoubtedly motivated in large part by the deterioration in working conditions under the government of the centre-right, the labourers also harboured vague expectations of a social revolution which, however, was doomed from the outset by the lack of a simultaneous strike by urban workers. The failure of the strike, the greatest in Spanish agrarian history, greatly strengthened the landowners, further shifted the balance of local power to the right as numerous left-wing *ayuntamientos* were overthrown, and dealt a devastating blow to the socialist movement. In the light of the revolutionary strike launched by the Socialists later in the year, the stoppage of the FNTT, the largest union in the UGT, was a profound strategic mistake.

CEDA criticism of Samper was not so much concerned with the FNTT strike as his handling of the challenges posed during the summer of 1934 by the Catalan regional government, the Generalitat, in a dispute over its legislative rights, and by the Basque nationalists, who, with the opportunistic backing of the Socialists and left republicans, orchestrated a drawn-out campaign of public protest at the blocking of the Basque autonomy statute. Ostensibly exasperated by the prime minister's conciliatory approach to the two disputes, in reality the CEDA gladly exploited its differences with Samper to bring the government down, engineer its own entry into the Cabinet, and trigger off the socialist revolution.

October 1934

The entry of the CEDA into the government on 4 October 1934 was the signal for a socialist general strike and an armed uprising that amounted to a fullblown insurrection in Asturias but little more than skirmishes elsewhere. As in December 1930, the Socialists harboured the vague belief that the 'revolutionary *pueblo*' would be joined by the army, but the nineteenth century *pronunciamiento* model was again found wanting: clearly the largely defensive rising owed more to an over-optimistic preconception than a realistic grasp of the dynamics of an armed insurrection. A second, but logistically unrelated, rebellion took place in Catalonia where the Generalitat government half-heartedly declared a Catalan state within 'the Spanish Federal Republic'. The Catalan rebellion and socialist stoppage were soon brought under control by the authorities, but in Asturias the workers forcibly took over much of the region, declared the establishment of libertarian communism, and defied the army for two weeks before admitting defeat.

'October 1934' was at once a demonstration of the unity and division of the opposition. United by a shared antagonism to the centre-right government, the progressive middle classes, organized working classes, and Basque and Catalan nationalists were none the less divided by the lack of a common strategy or vision. As far as possible, the Socialists aimed to keep the revolution to themselves, spurning the advances of the left republicans, the Catalan nationalists, and of other working class forces. The rising was further weakened by the immobilization of the FNTT as a result of the June

1934 strike, while the involvement of the CNT in neither the Socialist enterprise (with the notable exception of Asturias) nor the Catalan rebellion gravely undermined both. The October insurrection also demonstrated that for the Socialists parliamentary democracy was not an end in itself but a means for the achievement of meaningful reform. Once the Republic no longer served that purpose, the Socialists were prepared to break with it.

The October 1934 uprising and the resulting repression polarized politics to an unprecedented extent and would remain the fundamental point of political reference until the outbreak of civil war in July 1936. The corresponding loss of legitimacy of the Radical Party's centrist strategy permitted the CEDA to shift the balance of power steadily to the right, manifested in its ever greater Cabinet presence and substantial inroads into the Radicals' extensive control of local government. The rearguard action fought by the Radicals over the extent to which the reforms of the first *bienio* should be overturned and over the scope of the post-October reprisals only partially constrained the right's pursuit of revenge. The counteroffensive in the Cortes, crystallized by the quashing of the Agrarian Reform Law, was more than matched in the countryside. No longer inhibited by the socialist trade unions, now underground, or by left wing *ayuntamientos*, few if any of which were able to function after October 1934, the landowners were at liberty to reassert the pre-Republican status quo. Wages plummeted and working hours soared, while many militants, if not in jail, were sacked. Untrammelled by the trade unions or ministerial strictures, the *patronal* also took eager advantage of the rarefied political climate by sweeping aside earlier collective agreements and foisting new, retrogressive terms of employment on those workers not incarcerated or blacklisted.

The popular front and the election of 1936

The indiscriminate nature of the right's politics of persecution, symbolized in national political terms by the arrest of Manuel Azaña, proved counterproductive insofar as it reunited the fragmented forces of the opposition out of a fear that the Republic itself was under threat. Reconstruction of the coalition of 1931–33 proceeded uncertainly. First the various republican parties reached an understanding in April 1935 before the moderate socialists agreed to join on principle. However, the socialist left, essentially the UGT and the Socialist Youth under Largo Caballero, blocked any further progress. The left's resistance was eventually overcome by a combination of circumstances: the multitudinous rallies held between April and October 1935 by Manuel Azaña, who did more than anyone to revive the republican ideal, the crumbling of the government coalition in late 1935, and the lack of an alternative strategy with the election imminent. The last-minute adherence of the Communist Party gave the alliance its name – the 'Popular Front'.

The Radical-CEDA coalition finally collapsed in December 1935 following the exposure of Radical corruption. In reality, the 'Straperlo' and 'Tayá' affairs were minor cases of venality that were initially exploited by the opposition but transformed into national scandals by a vengeful Alcalá Zamora, embittered by the personal feud with the Radical leader over the President's cessation of several Lerroux Cabinets. Although the perfidious logic of the CEDA's ascendancy, predicated upon the decline of its ally, together with the Radicals' loss of political credibility since October 1934, had reduced the Radical Party at both national and provincial levels to a shadow of its former self, the scandals were none the less crucial to the sinking of the CEDA's strategy. Once the Radical Party had imploded, Alcalá Zamora, fearful of the pronounced authoritarian proclivities of the CEDA leader, Gil Robles, chose to call a general election rather than confer the premiership on the CEDA leader.

The general election campaign of February 1936, divided by the exigencies of the electoral system between two broad coalitions of left and right and dominated by the rhetorical imperatives of the October 1934 uprising, has magnified the image of a bipolar battle between the 'two Spains'. In fact, both alliances were deeply flawed and inherently unstable. On the one hand, the Popular Front was a circumstantial coalition of a strictly electoral nature. On the other hand, the forces of the rightwing conglomeration, ranging from conservative republicans and the CEDA to monarchists and the extreme right-wing Bloque Nacional, were at such odds ideologically that they failed to forge a common programme, ultimately agreeing only on their 'anti-revolutionary' status.

The Popular Front's narrow electoral victory resulted in the formation of a purely left republican government, the socialist left having vetoed PSOE participation. Thus a broadly-based electoral conjunction of the working classes and progressive middle classes was reduced overnight to a narrowly-based government of middle class professionals. Efforts to incorporate the Socialists, most notably in May 1936 when the moderate socialist leader Indalecio Prieto was offered the premiership after Azaña replaced Alcalá Zamora as President, repeatedly foundered on the intransigence of the UGT. The Popular Front, in other words, had ceased to exist as the trade unions and political parties had split apart.

During the spring and early summer of 1936 the government and parties were steadily eclipsed by the trade unions as power passed from the Cortes into the streets. Worker mobilization not only secured an amnesty for the October 1934 rebels but also forced the *patronal* to accept the readmission of blacklisted activists and the restoration of the former terms of employment, thereby recovering many of the losses of 1933–36. Similarly frustrated by the delays and disappointments of parliamentary reformism, the landless labourers in the south and west also took the law into their own hands, seizing and settling more land in a matter of months than in the previous five years. Symptomatic of the schism between the trade unions and the parties was the fact that legislation passed later that summer by the Cortes merely rubberstamped the workers' *fait accompli*.

Amongst the working classes an overwhelming presentiment of revolution reigned, but neither the CNT, scarred by the failures of the past, nor the UGT, confronted by a left republican government, possessed the will to seize the initiative. By contrast, the forces of the right were busily preparing the ground for a coup d'etat. Following the defeat of the 'antirevolutionary' coalition in the general election, the CEDA's legalist tactic, considered by much of the right to be redundant, gave way to the 'catastrophist' solution of the extreme right. While the strategic military support for the rising was orchestrated from behind the scenes by the monarchists, the necessary insurrectionary climate was fomented by the violence of the Falange, the miniscule but highly militant fascist movement, on the streets, and in the Cortes by those deputies who beseeched the army to intervene. The calculation of the catastrophists was that spiralling public disorder and the corresponding loss of state authority would become a self-fulfilling prophesy and force the hand of the army. In the event, the failed coup of 17–18 July was converted into civil war by the vacillations of the republican government, the divisions of the army and Civil Guard, and the mass resistance of the organized working classes. Thus the crisis of state which had given birth to the democratic parliamentary pretensions of the Republic was ultimately to be determined by the more traditional political expedient of force, albeit with the novel embellishment of large scale foreign intervention. Certainly a less feckless administration than that of Casares Quiroga could have eschewed civil war by snuffing out the military uprising at its inception. Surmounting the deeper sources of the conflict would have required a greater commitment from all the forces of the Republic to compromise and the rules of parliamentary democracy, as opposed to the sectarian politics of patrimony that characterized the regime.

|15|

The Spanish Civil War

GEORGE ESENWEIN

Shortly after it broke out, the Spanish Civil War acquired an international significance that continued to resonate long after the conflict had ended. At the time, the underlying complexities were not immediately apparent, and most people reduced its meaning to a black and white struggle between binary opposites, such as 'good' and 'evil', socialism and capitalism or Bolshevism and fascism. This manicheistic perspective was well suited to the ideologically-charged post-First World War intellectual climate. Both the Cold War and the Franco regime blocked the emergence of a more nuanced view. Only many decades after its conclusion did the Spanish Civil War cease to be portrayed as a morality play and only then did aspects of the conflict, such as gender issues and cultural life, begin to receive the attention they deserved.

Summarizing something as complex and controversial as the Spanish Civil War inevitably leaves the historian with the risk of oversimplification and with many difficult decisions about what should, or should not, be included. For this chapter, the decision has been to reveal something of the underlying complexities of the conflict without sacrificing the coherency of the story itself. In addition to a general outline of the events themselves, there is a discussion of the major social and political issues they raised and, as an indication of the directions in which the historiography is evolving, a consideration of some of the gender and cultural aspects of the war.

From military rising to civil war

Though the generals who rose against the Republic on 17 July 1936 were confident of an early victory, their attempt to seize power and establish a military directory met with only partial success. Only about one third of Spain was theirs, most of it in the conservative northern and central countryside. In major urban and industrial areas the military rebellion was crushed by trade unions, improvised popular militias, and the military and police forces who remained loyal to the Republic, although in some cities with leftist traditions, such as Zaragoza and Seville, the insurgents quickly gained the upper hand by moving to control military garrisons and other strategic facilities, thereby preventing leftist organizations from mounting an effective response.

Because their plans for achieving complete military control of Spain had failed, the insurgent generals, joined by an assortment of right-wing civilian groups, were forced to conduct a civil war against the Republican government. The country was now split into mutually hostile zones.

The early weeks of Spain's civil war were characterized by a wave of terror that swept through both the Republican and Nationalist camps. Though stemming in part from the pent-up passions of a politically and socially divided country, this terror also sprung from longstanding ideological differences. On the republican side, the initial confusion caused by the breakdown of government authority led to terrorism and violence on an unprecedented scale. In some instances, the triumphant left-wing unions and their *checas* (secret police units) wasted no time in rounding up suspected rebels or rebel sympathizers. Known Falangists and other anti-leftists were primary targets, though mere middle-class Catholics also fell victim to the 'street justice' meted out in the heat of the moment. Those condemned to death were forced to undergo the harrowing ritual known as a *paseo* ('taking someone for a ride') which, in most cases, meant being carted off to the outskirts of town to be summarily shot alongside other suspected 'enemies of the people'.

Perhaps the most shocking form of violence committed during the so-called 'Red terror' was the ferocious assault against the Catholic Church. Apart from sacking and burning Churches and convents, and attacking religious monuments, a certain number of revolutionaries set about killing some 7000 clergymen and women in what turned out to be the greatest clerical bloodletting in modern times.

The reign of violence on the Republican side was matched by the terrorism that occurred in Nationalist Spain. At least in the opening phases of the war, personal vendettas, mob violence as well as the ghastly '*paseos*' mentioned above were also commonplace in Nationalist-occupied towns and villages. Militants of leftist parties or trade-unions, or simple non-Catholics fell prey to these bloody purges. Yet there were differences between the Red and White terrors. For example, more so than in the Republican zone, the lines separating terrorism against civilians from 'military action' became blurred under the Nationalists. This was true above all because the Nationalist rebels relied on repression both as a means of securing recently conquered territory and for establishing their control over the daily life of the local population in the rearguard.

Contrary to what Franco and his followers claimed during and after the war, 'Red terror' also differed from the repression in the Nationalist zone in that it was not sanctioned by the Popular Front government. This is illustrated by the fact that violence of the kind described above was drastically curtailed in most regions following the reestablishment of central and local government authority. As early as 23 August, the government established Popular Tribunals, which attempted to regularize the trials of those suspected of being pro-'Fascist'. Repression in the Nationalist zone, on the other hand, persisted throughout, and even beyond, the war. Thus while it true that the sheer number of those killed by military authorities declined as the war progressed, executions became regularized under a military court system established behind-the-lines and continued for several years after the war ended in 1939.

The Republican zone

The July military rising not only triggered a civil war but also unleashed a popular revolution of massive proportions. Because the rebellion had caused the partial – or, in some cases, complete – breakdown of formal government institutions, Spain's revolutionary forces – as represented by the anarcho-syndicalists (CNT–FAI), left socialists (PSOE–UGT) and Marxist revolutionaries (POUM) – were offered the opportunity to radically transform society. The result was one of the most profound and far-reaching social revolutions in the world since the Russian revolution of 1917. The degree and intensity of these revolutionary experiments varied from place to place. But in regions where the anarchosyndicalists were preponderant, the revolution embraced nearly all aspects of society. Apart from collectivizing agricultural and industrial enterprises, the anarchists set about building the basis of a so-called free-communist world (*comunismo libertario*). In some areas, money was completely abolished, Church buildings were put to secular use, and everything – from cigarettes to luxury hotels – was considered public property.

Throughout the summer of 1936 power in the towns and countryside remained scattered among hundreds of revolutionary or popular front committees, and regional authority resided in various types of provisional bodies – such as the Central AntiFascist Militias Committee in Barcelona and the Council of Aragón. Even in the Basque country, which was otherwise untouched by the revolution, the defence committees or juntas which were used to put down the military rising temporarily displaced central government authority and thereby prepared the ground for the emergence of an autonomous Basque state. During the brief time the Madrid government ceased functioning the independence of the Catalan government evolved to the point that it behaved as though it were a separate country. In many respects, then, Republican Spain during the first 10 months of the war existed as a mosaic of satellite states, each possessing varying degrees of independence.

Not all republicans welcomed these revolutionary transformations. In the

Basque country, for example, no revolution occurred. Instead the conservative and mostly Catholic Basque nationalist organizations quickly assumed political and economic control of the region. Their opposition to the Francoists, like that of the Catalan regionalists, was based on their desire to give full expression to their own cultural and political identities. A coalition consisting of the moderate socialists of the PSOE, the middle-class republican parties, and the communists of the PCE and PSUC were also strongly opposed to revolutionary developments in the Republican zone. In the immediate aftermath of the uprising, republican representatives remained in charge of the Popular Front government despite the fact that real power had devolved to the working-class organizations and civilian groups who had helped to put down the rebellion. Though some, like the 67 year old prime minister Francisco Largo Caballero, were sympathetic to the revolution, the main objective of the new regime formed in September 1936 was to restore state authority throughout the Republican zone to prosecute the war more effectively. Of all the republican parties, it was the PCE and PSUC – led by the strategic anti-fascist shift of the III International in 1934 –-which took the lead in defining the political agenda for the Republic. Both inside Spain and abroad, they promoted the idea that the war was being fought to defend a democratic Republic against the menace of fascism. Their moderate message appealed to a wide audience, but particularly to the middle-class republicans who, lacking enough popular support, had stepped aside and allowed the Socialists and their political allies to take over the reins of government, but now felt threatened by the revolution.

For the first few months of the war no single political force was powerful enough to impose its own agenda, and therefore various strategies were tried simultaneously. But for several reasons the centralized programme of the Popular Front parties prevailed. Thanks partly to the binding sense of solidarity that arose in the initial stages of the war and partly to the gathering momentum of centripetal forces inside the government, the process of reconstituting state authority in Madrid was well advanced by the autumn of 1936. But given the dynamics of the anti-centralizing forces, it was evident that recovering state control would be uneven, and that it would be especially difficult to achieve the full integration of the various political entities that existed in the Republican zone.

From a military point of view, the major obstacle the republicans had to overcome was how to cobble together an effective fighting force. Though most senior officers had remained loyal to the Republic, the Army itself was in a state of dissolution. Not only had the rebellion shattered its internal chain of command but the emergence of independent civilian militias had further eroded the integrity of the Army. This was not least because the militias' themselves were operating independently of one another, rarely paying any regard to the actions or needs of other units. The blatant shortcomings of these improvised military apparatuses, which were graphically exposed in the early weeks of fighting, only served to reinforce the arguments of those in the Republican camp who insisted that the war had to be conducted along conventional lines.

Partly for military reasons and partly because they sought to use the army as a vehicle for advancing their own political agenda, the communists of the PCE and PSUC were among the first to call for the militarization of the militias as well as the creation of a unified military command (*mando único*). In fact, they were instrumental in creating the basis for a government-controlled Popular Army, which came into being towards the end of 1936. Their efforts to dominate this new structure were reinforced in October 1936 by the arrival of the first shipments of Soviet supplies and equipment as well as the first units of the Communist International's (Comintern) volunteer army, known as the International Brigades.

Originating from countries around the globe, the estimated 40 000–50 000 men and women who served in the International Brigades embodied the anti-fascist political passions that were aroused by Spain's conflict. Though organized and directed by the Communist International, not all the volunteers were communists. Some were liberal school teachers and middle-class professionals, while others were working-class youths who simply wanted to act on their deeply-held political convictions. But whatever their class origin or ideological background, all had come to Spain in the belief that they could help stop the spread of fascism by supporting the republican cause.

The communists' plan to bring the Popular Army under their control benefited from the support of the International Brigades in several ways. Both the Brigades themselves and the internal command structure of the Army were welded together by a network of political commissars, whose theoretical role was to ensure the loyalty of the regular officers and to maintain the morale and education of the troops, although in practice they were used by the communists both to indoctrinate the army and to influence the course of military affairs. The International Brigades also contributed to the communists' efforts to present the Spanish Civil War as a major flash-point in the global struggle against fascism. Stalin in particular wanted to dramatize the danger fascism posed to all democratic societies that failed to oppose it, and the example being set by the self-sacrificing International Brigades was frequently invoked in the communists' diplomatic and political propaganda to underscore this urgent message.

Nationalist Spain

The various insurgent forces who were fighting against the republicans came to be known as the *Nacionales*, Nationalists, a label that was used above all to imply the legitimacy of their movement. In contrast to the regional or separatist movements on the republican side, nationalism on the right referred to a concept of Spain defined wholly by national institutions like the

Catholic Church and social practices, like the Castilian language, which had for centuries been associated with things Spanish. Equally important in this connection was the fact that there was a consensus among the various Nationalist civilian parties about the need for placing a military victory over their opponents above all other considerations. Thus, while not everyone shared the same vision of Spain's political future, they all accepted the military's leadership. This did not mean that the military could dispense entirely with civilian assistance. Groups such as the Carlist Requetés and the Falangist militias had proved to be indispensable allies in the early stages of the conflict. Furthermore, the army relied on the activities of civilian organizations both to help them maintain public order and to oversee essential operations in the rearguard. The Falangist Feminist Section (Sección Femenina), for instance, was one of several women's organizations that provided vitally important social welfare programmes, such as orphanages and soup-kitchens (*Auxilio Social*).

Over the course of the war the military greatly expanded its role. The first attempt to consolidate military rule came with the creation of the National Defence Committee, which had been set up in late July to coordinate the Nationalist war effort. And even though the committee gave greater coherence to the rebel command, the body still lacked an executive head. General Sanjurjo, the nominal head of the uprising, had died *en route* to the rebellion. Other possible candidates included General Mola, the main figure behind the July conspiracy; General Cabanellas, the most senior member of the committee; and General Francisco Franco. Of the three, Franco was by far the most capable military leader. More important, he was the only person who commanded the respect and allegiance not only of the majority of the ruling junta and civilian parties but also of the foreign powers aiding the Nationalists. On 1 October 1936, the National Defence Committee decided to invest both military and political authority in General Franco. In the following months he took further steps to consolidate his power, culminating in April 1937, with the amalgamation of all the Nationalist factions into a single party under his control, the Falange Española Tradicionalista y de las JONS (FET).

Given that the forces supporting the rebellion comprised a wide spectrum of right-wing opinion, the task of defining a political agenda would not be an easy one. This is reflected in the fact that Franco's blueprint for rule was constructed around very different and often contradictory ideas. On one level, the institutional basis of his regime was not formally defined as 'fascist', though the main structures of the *Estado nuevo* incorporated many fascist ideas and organizational principles. For example, the 'Fuero del Trabajo', or Trade Union Unity Act, passed in 1938, was closely patterned after the Labour Charter earlier adopted in Mussolini's Italy. As a result, all unions in the Nationalist camp were merged into a state-controlled vertical structure, the Spanish Syndical Organization (Organización Sindical Española).

Yet not all aspects of the Francoist state conformed to the fascist model. A major pillar of the regime both during and following the war was the Catholic Church. More than any other institution, the Catholic Church embodied the beliefs and values of the Nationalists, most of whom followed Bishop Pla y Deniel and other Church officials in picturing the civil war as a crusade against the godless enemies of the 'spiritual' Spain they were defending. The Church also played a major role in defining the social and intellectual life of the Francoist state (see chapters 16 and 18).

Franco's efforts to unify the Nationalist movement greatly benefited from the relative economic stability which his side enjoyed throughout the war. Though they could not rely on Spain's traditional financial institutions to fund their cause, the Nationalists managed to secure support through private funding and foreign loans. Much of Franco's war was underwritten by economic arrangements with Italy and Germany as well as capitalist concerns such as Texas Oil and Firestone, who provided supplies on credit.

Foreign intervention

To understand the international response to the Spanish Civil War, it is necessary to bear in mind the fear of another general European war that informed much diplomatic behaviour, especially in France and Britain. The post-First World War settlement had excluded Germany, blamed for having caused the war, and Russia, viewed as a threat to the capitalist and liberal order of the Western countries, from the great power system. Policy towards Spain would be marked by this fear of communism, which in part blinded Britain, France and the United States to the real menace posed by the rise of fascism.

For Great Britain and France, the fear that Spain's war might possibly exacerbate social tensions at home and, worse, spill over into the general European arena carried the most weight in their joint decision to pursue a policy of non-intervention. In France, the question of whether or not to become involved in the Spanish situation was complicated by the pro-Republican sentiments of Leon Blum's Popular Front government, although these yielded in the face of domestic political concerns and the absence of British support. Fearful that France might find herself isolated at a time when her major rivals, Germany and Italy, were gaining strength, Blum decided to embrace non-intervention as a necessary evil.

In Britain, the Conservative-dominated National government was above all interested in protecting British strategic and economic interests in an increasingly volatile situation. In the first instance, the government were concerned that the Spanish coasts of the Straits of Gibraltar remained in friendly hands. There was also the question of the naval balance of power in the Mediterranean, and Britain quite naturally did not want to see strategic areas like the Balearic Islands fall under the political influence of hostile powers. From a purely economic standpoint, the British government did not want to lose control over her considerable economic interests, particularly her mineral resources, in Spain.

There was only one multilateral effort aimed at blocking foreign involvement in Spain. Fearful that the civil war could trigger a larger European conflict, British and French diplomats urged all nations to adopt a hands-off policy. Under their initiative, 27 countries signed a Non-Intervention Agreement in August, 1936 and one month later a Non-Intervention Committee was set up in London. This was meant to give some teeth to the Agreement but because the Committee could neither prosecute violators under international law nor enforce any of its decisions, the non-intervention policy was condemned to futility.

Prior to the July rebellion, Germany had not paid much attention to Spanish affairs, but this soon changed. Only five days after civil war had erupted, General Franco dispatched a delegation to request troop-transport planes from Hitler. Upon reading Franco's pleas for support, Hitler decided to intervene. Within days 20 Junkers-52 were making their way to Morocco. This decision was more than just a knee-jerk response to the threat of communism. From a diplomatic standpoint, Germany had much to gain from intervening. Above all it offered Hitler the opportunity to undermine France's role as a major power and he reasoned that the defeat of a left-wing government in Spain would further this goal. A war in Spain also provided a much welcomed distraction that would give Germany the breathing space she needed to pursue her expansionist plans in Austria and eastern Europe.

In exchange for aiding the Nationalists, Germany also hoped to reap more concrete advantages. German economic relations with the rebels were secured early by the creation of import–export companies which served as a conduit not only for funnelling supplies to the Nationalists but also for extracting mining concessions from Franco. In this way, Germany managed to gain access to Spain's rich mineral resources. Besides the transport planes and fighters they had delivered to Franco at the beginning of the war, the Germans also sent the fighter pilots and specialists needed to operate and maintain this equipment. By late October, Berlin decided to formalize their air combat role in Spain by officially forming the Condor Legion, which included seven thousand military pilots. As the war progressed, the Condor Legion became ever more vital to the Nationalist war effort.

The Italians were even more generous with their aid. Mussolini extended credit to Franco so that he could pay for weapons, military equipment and supplies which Italy shipped to the Nationalists throughout the civil war. Towards the end of December 1936, the first group of Italian volunteers (Corpo di Truppe Volontarie) landed, a fighting force that would grow to around 72 000 by war's end. Mussolini decided to intervene on the side of the Nationalists for a variety of political and pragmatic reasons. By helping a pro-fascist movement he hoped to limit French influence in Spain while at the same time strengthening the Italians' presence in a vital part of the Mediterranean. Mussolini was also convinced that the future of Italian interests was bound up with her image as an aggressive power. Demonstrating Italy's growing military prowess could only enhance the 'forceful' image that Mussolini was seeking to cultivate. Finally, Mussolini believed that Italy's military accomplishments in Spain would impress others, particularly Germany, of her value as a potential ally. In fact, it was largely thanks to the common ground they established while assisting the Nationalists that both Germany and Italy began to draw closer together, forging a bond that first took shape with the Rome–Berlin Axis, formed in November 1936.

Spain's unexpected civil war was not at first viewed as being of great importance to the Soviet Union, not least because Moscow, like many other foreign governments, believed that the conflict would be a short one. But when it became apparent that both Germany and Italy were helping to extend the conflict, the Soviets could no longer afford to ignore the Spanish situation. Stalin's decision to intervene on the republican side was conditioned by his belief that, in order to check the spread of fascism, it was in the Soviet Union's best interests to secure stronger ties with the Western democracies. He had already taken steps to improve diplomatic relations with the French – their pact of Mutual Assistance was signed in May 1935 – and Stalin was convinced that by helping the republicans in Spain it would be possible for the Soviets to draw closer not only to France but also to Great Britain.

The cementing of Soviet–Republican relations came about when republican leaders agreed to have Spain's considerable gold reserves transported to Russia for safe-keeping. This important transfer, estimated at the time to be around $518 million, secured the Soviet government's assistance, making them the major supplier and distributor of arms and military equipment to Republican Spain. To ensure that Soviet interests were being served, the Russians exercised their power of monopoly over these vitally important resources. The leverage that Soviet supplies and prestige bestowed upon the communists enabled them to dominate all the major military campaigns conducted by the republicans. As the war progressed, communist commanders increasingly determined military priorities and their preponderance throughout the infrastructure of the Popular Army made them indispensable for every major military operation carried out between 1937 and the end of the war.

Both the United States and most Latin American countries refused to be drawn into a foreign adventure. In the latter case cultural and historical ties that bound Spain's former colonies were not enough to counteract the profound divisions that the conflict roused in every country; only Mexico sided clearly in favour of the Republic and decided to send modest amounts of aid. As to the United States, the Roosevelt administration tended to be sympathetic to the republican side but adopted a policy of neutrality. Overcoming the entrenched isolationist mood of the country was one reason, and Spain was certainly not viewed as being of great economic or political importance to the United States. It was also true that, in an election year,

Roosevelt could not ignore the fact that significant numbers of the voting public, including the greater part of the large and influential Catholic community, were pro-Nationalist. In the end the US decided to enforce an arms embargo on Spain, a policy which dovetailed with both Great Britain's and France's efforts to seal off the Spanish conflict.

Military engagements: 1936–1937

For the first six months of fighting, the Nationalists completely dominated the war. The northern city of Irún fell to the rebels on 5 September and further inroads into republican-held areas of the Basque country were made that same month. The Nationalists were also advancing rapidly along the Guadarrama front (north of Madrid), on the Castilian plains towards Toledo and in the south and southwest.

More than anything else, the Nationalists were determined to take Madrid, convinced as they were that once it was captured the war would be effectively over. By early September they were at the point of mounting such an offensive when Franco decided to send relief forces to Toledo. Although this decision inevitably dissipated the momentum of the Nationalists' march towards the capital, they were poised to take Madrid by the first week of November. However, Franco's troops were unexpectedly halted on the outskirts of the city and the stalemate would last until the final days of the war in 1939.

Undaunted by this setback, the Nationalists launched a series of new offensives. At the end of January, the commander of the Army of the North, General Mola began an ambitious campaign aimed at securing the northern regions still under republican rule, Santander, Vizcaya and Asturias. In this same period, Queipo de Llano's Army of the South was scoring a string of Nationalist victories, securing the strategically important port of Málaga on 8 February.

At this critical juncture the republican forces were desperate for a military victory. Their opportunity came on the north-eastern Madrid front: with the Italians leading, the Nationalists attacked the town of Guadalajara on 8 March in the hope of opening a back door to the capital. Their assault was quickly thwarted by some of the Republican army's best units, including the communist 11th Division led by Enrique Líster and the anarchosyndicalist 14th Division under Cipriano Mera. Though in strictly military terms this was a minor victory, it was widely perceived as a major triumph for the republicans.

During the first year of fighting there were also singular episodes which came to symbolize the epic struggle gripping Spain, and for some, the world beyond. The two most famous were the seige of Alcázar in Toledo and the bombing of the small Basque town of Guernica. The Alcázar was the historic military fortress of Toledo, where some 1100 persons (mostly members of the civil guard and a few cadets), sought refuge after their failure to take the city in July 1936. They demonstrated remarkable perseverance in the face of repeated republican attempts to flush them out, until September 1936, when Franco's forces liberated the fortress. The case of the ancient town of Guernica, symbol of the Basque liberties, was totally different. On the afternoon of 26 April 1937, a market day, a fleet of German airplanes swept over the town for more than three hours and dropped an estimated 1000 high explosive bombs, and perhaps as many as 3000 two-pound aluminium incendiary bombs. The bombing raid was then followed up by aerial machine-gun attacks directed at fleeing civilians. In the aftermath, over 1600 men, women and children lay dead or dying in the smouldering rubble. Although the Nationalists at first firmly denied any knowledge of the air raid, there were numerous survivors and physical evidence to attest the atrocity, and the case generated a considerable amount of negative publicity for the Nationalist cause, among other reasons because Pablo Picasso took it as the motif for his celebrated masterpiece 'Guernica'.

The Basque country, as well as Santander and Asturias, were particularly vulnerable to the Nationalists because they had been almost immediately physically cut off from the rest of Republican Spain. From July 1936 until it fell to the Nationalists in June 1937, the political and economic environment of the Basque country bore little resemblance to that elsewhere in Republican Spain. At the beginning of the war, an alliance of the conservative Basque National Party (PNV) – the preponderant party in the region – socialists, communists, and other republicans had prevented any serious outbreak of anticlerical violence and had also acted as a brake on any attempts at collectivization. The anti-revolutionary trajectory of Basque politics was reinforced when the left-dominated ruling bodies that had emerged in the wake of the rebellion were replaced by a moderate Basque government. With the passage of the Basque autonomy statute in October and the ascent of the ardent nationalist José Aguirre as President, the PNV quickly asserted a commanding influence over the course of events. However, surrounded on all sides by rebel forces, the Basques could do little to defend their homeland. This was particularly true after the Nationalists launched their northern offensive in the spring of 1937. Following the destruction of Guernica in April, the Nationalists penetrated deeper into Vizcaya. By June only Bilbao was still holding out, but on 19 June the Basque Government negotiated a surrender, which saved the industrial belt of Bilbao from serious damage.

Cultures in conflict

The civil war also pitted opposing cultures against one another. In many ways, including their profoundly differing views on gender, religion and interpersonal relations, Republican cultural life stood in stark contrast to that being promoted in the Nationalist camp. Yet within each zone cultural differences also existed among the different political and social groupings; in addition to the larger competition to lay claim to Spain's cultural identity there was also a struggle for cultural dominance inside each of the two warring camps.

The social code that informed Nationalist daily life was a mix of traditional and newly adopted customs and values. While it was relatively easy to assert the old ways of doing things – most were accustomed to a society dominated by the military and Church – imported social habits were not so easily accommodated. Many pro-Nationalists were disgusted by the introduction of fascistic trappings and symbolic rituals borrowed from Italy and Germany.

Daily life under the Nationalist umbrella also had to conform to the dictates of Franco's emerging military regime. In many instances this involved physically erasing vestiges of lay progressive Republican culture. Throughout recently conquered areas, for instance, religion was reintroduced into schools and other walks of life that had been secularized under the Republic. Crucifixes again adorned the walls of schools and prayers were *de rigueur* in the classroom.

Men were expected to participate fully in the martial order: those who were not fighting were expected to play a public role that demonstrated their masculine or 'virile' traits. Needless to say, alternative lifestyles were not tolerated and those identified with these 'subcultures' faced certain and severe punishment. An example of the latter can be found in the execution of the internationally renowned playwright and poet and Federico García Lorca, whose homosexuality posed a threat to the traditional social code of behaviour that was being imposed by the right.

Women engaged in activities that were largely defined by the male-dominated military and Church hierarchies. Most accepted that their role in the war was to stay at home and uphold the Catholic and conservative traditions associated with motherhood and the nuclear family. But even if they deferred to male authority, not all women remained secluded in the confines of their homes, especially those who belonged to female-led political organizations like the Falangist Sección Femenina and the Carlist Margaritas. They, along with other activist women, supported the war effort by taking on public duties. In an effort to integrate women into the new social order the Franco government required all women between the ages of 17 and 35 to perform war-related social services.

The Nationalists employed a variety of media to disseminate their political and cultural messages. One important means of mass communication was posters and public notices. Poster art, especially the work of Carlos Sáenz de Tejada, extolled the values of 'traditional' Spain by linking Catholic spirituality with the sombre images of war. Posters were also effective vehicles for stirring up anti-communist sentiment. In many of these, republicans of all stripes are caricatured as the harbingers of the Bolshevik menace.

Franco himself became the focus of Nationalist iconography, frequently portrayed as a modern-day 'El Cid', the national hero who was leading the Nationalists' crusade to reunite and strengthen a decadent and divided Spain.

As different as Republican political groups were from one another, the outbreak of war provided the catalyst needed to unite their different 'cultural communities' temporarily under the banner of anti-fascism or Popular Frontism. With the exception of the culturally conservative Basque national-ists, republicans supported a cultural agenda that contrasted sharply with that in the Nationalist camp. The vast majority of republicans defended a secularized state and society, most also accepted a pluralistic society which could accommodate a wide range of social beliefs and practices. Cultural cooperation on the left was manifested in a variety of ways, the most obvious being the emergence of numerous multi-partisan organizations throughout the Republican zone.

Underneath the veil of the unity, however, the Popular Front 'cultural community' was deeply divided. This was evident in many spheres and can be briefly illustrated by examining the Republican parties' differing respon-ses to gender relations as well as to varieties and production of their poster art.

Though republican groups of all political shades promoted women's issues, what precisely this entailed differed from party to party. For the female activists belonging to the middle-class Esquerra or other Catalan parties, promoting civil and social rights for women was intimately bound up with their national identity, whereas women affiliated to the Madrid-based Izquierda Republicana adhered to the classical liberal model of feminism which articulated female emancipation in terms of rights such as the vote and divorce.

Like almost all other republican women's groups, the communist-inspired women's organizations, Agrupación de Mujeres Antifascistas and Unió de Dones de Catalunya, were more interested in mobilizing women for the anti-fascist cause than in radically redefining gender relations. Despite their declared intent of recognizing women as full members of 'public' Spain, communist groups appealed to women to help the war effort by performing traditionally-defined women's tasks. As one communist slogan put it: 'Women defend your bread, your liberty, and the future of your children, by fighting against the oppression of Fascism through the women's brigades in the army of production.'

For the far left feminism meant something altogether different. In contrast to their communist and middle-class republican counterparts, members of the Marxist Female Secretariat of the POUM were not concerned with protecting women's legal rights as defined by liberal democratic institutions, because they believed that the liberation of women was only possible within the context of a communist society. The most radical women's agenda was adopted by the Mujeres Libres, an anarchosyndicalist female organization affiliated to the CNT–FAI. Like the POUM, members of Mujeres Libres rejected the label 'feminist', which they saw as bourgeois. Instead, they saw themselves as an integral part of the working-class revolutionary movement which sought to overturn capitalism and replace it with a system based on libertarian principles. Even more radical were Mujeres Libres' attempts to transcend age-old female stereotypes and abolish sexist social practices which had effectively excluded women from being treated as men's equals in society. Those who enlisted to fight in the militias, for example, forcefully challenged the commonly-held view that a woman's place is in the home.

Despite their commonly shared concerns for women and women's issues, these various Republican organizations never managed to create what Mary Nash has termed a transpolitical women's movement. Nor were they able to alter significantly the traditional boundaries of gender relations. This was not least because, with the possible exception of the Mujeres Libres, female-led groups never challenged male hegemony in cultural and political affairs by establishing autonomous bodies that set their own agendas. Instead most deferred to the male-dominated unions and party structures that were already locked in intense political rivalries. In practice, the subordination of female organizations to the male hierarchy meant that the strategies of women's groups were more concerned with politics than with gender issues per se.

Along with the press and radio, posters were employed as the principal medium for promoting the sectarian views of the various parties. Poster artists like Josep Renau were particularly adept at combining avant-garde techniques and styles (like photo-montage and cubism) with political and social messages. Like the advertising posters they supplanted, their role was not just to grab the attention of passers-by but to influence them to respond to their pointed messages. Posters mirrored the distinctive cultural codes of the different republican parties. The refrains found in anarchist culture were easily identifiable: most emphasized the need to end illiteracy, and equated revolutionary transformations with the struggle against fascism. The posters issued by Catalan and Basque nationalist parties, on the other hand, laid stress on their overriding concern for obtaining home rule in Republican Spain. The communists, for their part, presented a unified and coherent image of the war, promoting the idea of the Popular Front and even including the identifying insignia and colours of all the republican parties, but subordinating revolutionary messages or images to their professed goal of winning the war against fascism.

The profusion of political and social messages found in poster art produced at the beginning of the war reflected the political diversity and spontaneity that characterized early Republican Spain. In this period, poster art reached its greatest point of artistic development. As the war dragged on, however, Republican propaganda became less colourful and kaleidoscopic in its themes. Harrowing pictures of children mutilated by bullets and bombs and stern messages that dwelled on the dangers of rearguard traitors increasingly displaced the mostly positive and affirming images associated with the initial stages of the revolution and war. Following the violent political clashes of May 1937, poster art increasingly echoed the homogenized political thinking of the triumphant anti-revolutionary forces of the Popular Front government.

The struggle for power in the Republican zone

The Spanish Civil War was defined as much by events behind the front lines as by military campaigns. The dynamics of Republican politics revolved around three major axes: 1) the revolution triggered by the military uprising; 2) the regionalist movements in Catalonia and the Basque Provinces and 3) the efforts by anti-revolutionary forces to impose their own agenda on the Republican zone.

In its early stages, the revolution in Republican Spain moved with such velocity that it often blurred political borders that had formerly divided the Spanish left. In parts of the south and the Levante both socialist (UGT) and anarchosyndicalist unions (CNT-FAI) cooperated in setting up agricultural and industrial collectives even while they disagreed on the nature of the new society.

Both the urgency and fervour with which the anarchosyndicalists embraced the revolution testified to their abiding belief that the historical moment to destroy what they regarded as the irredeemably corrupt and oppressive structures that had long dominated the lives of Spaniards had arrived. They further believed that the opportunity for laying the foundations of a truly emancipated society would be lost if they delayed the revolution until after the rebels had been defeated. Convinced that the State could reassert itself at anytime, they simultaneously sought to promote revolutionary changes in the rearguard while prosecuting the war at the front lines.

Tens of thousands of people participated in the libertarian collectivist experiments that sprang up throughout much of Republican territory in the first months of the war. The breadth and scope of collectivization varied from region to region. In parts of Aragón, the Levante, and Barcelona, where anarchist troops were most active, the collectives embraced both agricultural and industrial enterprises. Farms, sweet shops, bakeries, barbershops, the cinema, theatres, automobile plants, restaurants, transportation facilities and even public utilities were, in varying degrees, taken over and then administered by worker committees which were themselves affiliated to the regional federations of the unions. Nearly all collectives were improvised systems that were constructed along vaguely-defined economic models that had never been tested in peacetime, let alone during a war. Not surprisingly, then, most collectives failed to achieve the libertarians' utopian goal of bringing about social harmony and economic prosperity for Spain's most downtrodden classes.

The July revolution and civil war allowed Catalonia to experience greater autonomy than could be found anywhere else in the Republican zone. By the end of December, the Generalitat had already raised its own army, begun issuing its own currency, and begun promoting its own foreign relations with other countries. While it is true that Catalonia was never in a position to secede from the Republic, its highly developed autonomy often compelled the central government to treat the Generalitat as an ally rather than as a regional government under its sovereignty.

These developments owed a great deal to the policy of collaboration adopted by the revolutionaries of the POUM and CNT–FAI. Rather than press forward with the July revolution, the leaders of the far left decided early on to share power with their political rivals. But the revolutionaries proved to be ill-adapted to the world of politics and, as a result, they soon found themselves yielding step by step to the Popular Front parties intent on restoring a centralized government. By the spring of 1937 a boiling point was reached in the struggle between the pro-revolutionary forces and those in favour of a containment of the revolution for the sake of anti-fascist unity. During the first week of May, Barcelona became the stage for what George Orwell, in *Homage to Catalonia*, famously characterized as an inner civil war and Ken Loach reconstructed in his fiction film *Land and Freedom* (1995).

On 3 May, a police attempt to eject the anarchosyndicalists from the main telephone exchange was met by machine gun fire, and for the next few days much of Barcelona became a battlefield. On the one side stood the militant sections of the anarchist CNT–FAI and Marxist POUM, who were fighting in order to hold on to the power and authority they derived from their revolutionary conquests. On the other was an assortment of parties, including the Esquerra and the communist-controlled United Socialist Party of Catalonia (PSUC). Forces sent by the government in Valencia arrived only on 7 May, by which time the revolutionaries' resistance had been broken. The crisis ended the next day, with the victory of the anti-revolutionary parties. Apart from the physical destruction and loss of human life (an estimated 400 people were killed), these events had significant political consequences, above all, the ascendancy of the PCE and PSUC and their socialist allies within the PSOE and UGT. On 17 May, Prime Minister Largo Caballero was forced to resign and was replaced by Juan Negrín, who would govern Republican Spain until the end of the war. Known as a moderate, Negrín was willing to promote the communists' growing role in the government, and this has placed him at the centre of many post-civil war historiographical debates. Critics have vilified him as a willing tool of the communists, whereas his defenders have tended to portray him as a pragmatic politician who did his best to rebuild a government which could prosecute the war effectively.

Negrín's administration did mark a departure from the previous regime in that he wanted to use the machinery of the state to reanimate the Republican war effort, and he did not hesitate to use the full power of the state apparatuses to clamp down on the refractory elements, particularly the revolutionary forces on the left. This may have created the structural basis for greater government unity and cohesion but it also alienated various key factions in the Republican camp.

Following Negrín's ascent to power, the PSUC acted quickly to undermine the economic and social power of their political rivals, launching a Moscow-style witch-hunt against the POUM and the so-called 'uncontrollables' of the CNT–FAI. The most famous victim of these purges was the POUM leader Andreu Nin, who was secretly abducted and later tortured to death by communist agents. The anti-POUM campaign culminated in October1938, when several prominent party figures were put on trial for espionage. The special tribunal could not bring itself to convict any of the accused, but the POUM and its youth organization were forced underground.

The anarchosyndicalists did not face such persecution, but they did rapidly lose ground. Negrín excluded CNT–FAI members from his newly formed cabinet, and even in Catalonia, where the anarchosyndicalists had dominated local affairs since July 1936, there were unmistakable signs that the tide of revolution was receding. On 29 June the head of the Generalitat formed a new government without the support of the CNT–FAI, something that would have been unthinkable before the May events.

With the Nationalists marching inexorably towards victory, Negrín believed that the Republicans had no choice but to adopt a political model that promised unity and order. Because the socialist movement was hopelessly divided, Negrín knew that the PSOE and UGT were not in a position to fulfill a leadership role. By contrast, the communists had, over the course of the war, become the most powerful and unified force on the Republican side. Moreover, because he realized the extent to which Republican Spain relied on Soviet assistance to conduct its war effort, Negrín was loathe to curb communist power and influence if it meant alienating the Republic's only loyal ally. Finally, Negrín shared the communists' contempt for the revolutionary forces in the Republican camp, whom he regarded as political renegades who represented a major stumbling block to Republican unity. He therefore was prepared to turn a blind eye to the excesses of the communists whenever they resorted to heavy-handed tactics against their political rivals. In the end, this cost Negrín the good will of many Republicans, who increasingly saw him a pawn of communist interests.

The May crisis and the formation of the Negrín government also fatally undermined the unity of the libertarian movement, driving a wedge between the revolutionary elements and the more moderate leadership. A growing number of *cenetistas* were willing to endorse Negrín's approach, even if this meant closing their eyes to his anti-revolutionary measures. In the end, this cost them dearly as the chasm separating the pro-revolutionary elements from the collaborationists continued to widen during the last year of the war.

Final year of fighting and the Casado coup (1939)

At the same time as it was asserting its control over the rearguard, Negrín's government was desperately trying to reverse the Republicans' military fortunes. In July it tried to relieve Nationalist pressure in the north by mounting a major offensive on the Madrid front. The battle of Brunete, as this operation came to be known, began on 5 July when republican troops broke through Nationalist lines around the village of Brunete, approximately 19 miles west of Madrid. However, the Nationalists launched a counter-offensive two weeks later that forced the Republicans into a full retreat. By 25 July the battle had ended without either side declaring a decisive victory.

Brunete had demonstrated that the Republicans were more capable than ever of waging an active war policy, but in terms of casualties (25 000) and the loss of prime war materiel, the offensive had also proved costly to the Republican Army. Following Brunete, the Republicans shifted their attention to the Aragón front, which had remained relatively quiet up to this point in the war. In late August, Republican forces launched a series of attacks against Nationalist lines in an effort to capture the Aragonese city of Zaragoza. In the end, however, the Republican offensive sputtered out and Zaragoza remained in the hands of the Nationalists.

In the meantime, Santander had fallen to the Nationalists (24 August 1937), and despite the determined resistance of Republican troops defending the Asturian cities of Oviedo and Gijón, this remaining enclave of Republican territory in the north fell on 21 October. With the North now under their control, the Nationalists revived their drive to take Madrid. Quite unexpectedly, however, their efforts were thwarted in mid-December by yet another Republican offensive. During a particularly bitter winter storm, Republican troops attacked Teruel, a small town some 112 miles south of Zaragoza. Overcoming both the harsh elements and Nationalist resistance, they managed to capture the city on 7 January 1938. The surprise Republican attack forced Franco to suspend his Madrid operations. He launched a counter-offensive in late December, and by early January his troops were laying siege to Teruel. Exhausted and desperately in need of supplies, Republican troops held out for nearly eight weeks but had finally to give in.

After Franco's troops reached the Mediterranean on 15 April 1938, the Republican Army grew ever more desperate. Sensing that their opportunities to stop the Nationalists were rapidly diminishing, the general staff laid plans for a major offensive. The question of where to launch such an attack was answered by Franco, who had chosen to advance on Valencia rather than on

Barcelona. This made the relatively quiet Catalan front a suitable area for mounting a surprise operation. By mid-July some 80 000 Republican troops and the bulk of the Republican army's aircraft and artillery formations began gathering along the Ebro river in preparation for the last great military contest of the war, the battle of the Ebro.

On 24 July Republican commandos crossed the river, catching the Nationalists completely off-guard. Within a few days they had established a bridgehead across the river, which they used to drive deeper into Nationalist territory. But, as in previous military engagements, the momentum of their drive was short-lived, mainly due to problem of supplies. Less than a week after the battle had begun the Nationalists recovered from their initial setbacks and managed to halt the enemy: the two sides fought a gruelling battle that would drag on until mid-November, when the Republicans were finally defeated by the superior fire-power of the Nationalists. The defeat came as a terrible blow, not least because it demonstrated beyond a doubt that the Republican Army was close to collapse and that the Republicans' chances for holding out much longer were rapidly fading.

In the wake of Ebro, Negrín's government renewed their appeals to the international community for assistance. Negrín himself did everything he could to convince the Western democracies that his government was determined to fight to the end. To demonstrate that the Republic was worthy of their support, he announced on 21 September that all foreigners still serving in the International Brigades would be sent home. He kept his word and at the end of October the remaining units were honoured by a gigantic farewell parade held in the streets of Barcelona.

Unfortunately for the Republicans such grand gestures were futile. Recent events in the international arena meant that the rest of Europe was no longer interested in Spain's war. Germany's annexation of Austria (March 1938), the Anglo-Italian treaty signed in April, and the Munich Agreement signed at the end of September underscored the Western powers' continued commitment to the policy of appeasement. Even the Soviet Union, Republican Spain's only firm ally up to now, was greatly reducing its material support to the Republican cause. Stalin had all but abandoned hope of a Republican victory and had instead decided to pursue a fresh course in foreign policy, seeking to improve relations with its arch-rival, Nazi Germany. The results of this initiative were made public in August 1939, when Germany and the Soviet Union shocked the world by announcing their pact of non-aggression.

The Republicans' defeat at Ebro paved the way for the Nationalists' final offensive. By 3 January the Nationalists began their assault on Catalonia, and on 26 January they occupied Barcelona. The collapse of the regional capital sparked a mass exodus of tens of thousands of civilians and soldiers towards the French border.

Madrid, the last Republican stronghold, was left surrounded by a sea of Nationalists. Short on ammunition and weapons and with their food supplies running out, it is hardly surprising that the Republicans' will to resist was rapidly dissipating. It was against this background of deteriorating conditions that an anti-communist group of socialists, anarchists, and republican military officers led by Colonel Segismundo Casado, the commander of the Army of the Centre, decided to take matters in their own hands. Just before midnight on 6 March the conspirators took over the chief government ministries and set up a provisional government called the National Council of Defence. Anxious to put an end to what they saw as the senseless sacrifice of lives, this group believed that Franco would negotiate with them rather than with the pro-communist government. It must have appeared to many on the Republican side as a cruel irony that the Spanish Civil War was ending just as it had begun nearly two-and-a-half-years earlier: as a military rebellion against the government. For his part, Negrín was so stunned by this turn of events that he decided to leave Spain.

Back in Madrid, the communists were locked in fierce street battles with the forces of the Council of Defence. The fighting raged on until 12 March, when communist resistance was finally crushed. This enabled the Council to step up its efforts to reach a negotiated settlement with the Nationalists, but Franco had no interest in accepting their conditions for surrender. On 27 March Nationalist troops began to occupy the desolate streets of the city, cheered by their fifth columnist supporters and the chants of the war-weary citizens who were relieved that the war was coming to an end. On 1 April 1939, Franco proclaimed that his troops had 'achieved their last objectives'. Spain's thousand-day war was finally over.

IV

THE FRANCO REGIME, 1939–1975

Compared to the drama and turmoil that had marked so much of Spain's political life since 1808, the years of the Franco regime seem strangely tranquil. One might even be tempted to say that 'nothing much happened'. Such an impression, however, would be a superficial one, for beneath the staidness of political life, itself severely limited due to ongoing repression, Spain was experiencing changes as thoroughgoing and dramatic as at any time in its modern history. Only an appreciation of those changes makes it possible to understand what happened when Franco died.

The durability of the Franco regime requires that it should not be considered as a single, undifferentiated whole but be seen as having at least two significantly different periods. Antonio Cazorla looks at the first period, what he calls 'early Francoism', between the end of the Civil War and 1957. This period itself had two phases: the Falangist phase (1939–45) in which the regime emphasized its ideological affinity with fascism, and a 'Catholic' phase (1945–56) in which it responded to the defeat of fascism and the emergence of the Cold War by presenting a Catholic, more pro-Western face. Cazorla-Sánchez analyses the organization of the regime and its limited attempts to penetrate Spanish society, through both ideology and state and party structures, such as the official trade unions, youth organizations and the Sección Femenina. Economic policy changed significantly in this period, from the disaster of autarky and the idealization of peasant life to advocacy of freer markets and agricultural productivism.

These policy changes were continued and extended in what Sebastian Balfour describes as the '*Desarrollo* [development] years' between 1957 and 1975. The liberalization of the early 1950s proved insufficient, and under the guidance of a team of technocrats associated with the Opus Dei, the regime opted for full integration into the international capitalist system. The 1960s and early 1970s saw what was called the 'Spanish miracle', as Spain achieved some of the most rapid growth rates in the world and moved definitively from being primarily an agricultural economy to becoming one based on industry and services. Economic changes of such magnitude had their social and cultural consequences: mass migration, urbanization, the growth of the middle classes, and the rise of consumerism, but also the spread of social and political protest. The result was a paradox: the transformation of Spanish society, which should have been the regime's greatest achievement, produced the very tensions and dissatisfactions that made its continuing existence increasingly problematic.

While not as ambitious as the Fascist regime in Italy and the Nazi state in Germany, the Franco regime did aspire to create a new moral and cultural order in Spain. This is the subject of the chapter by Mary Nash. In fact, much of the 'new' was really old, as the foundation of the 'New Spain' was the Catholic Church and the recuperation – or imposition – of Catholic belief, morality and social practice. As important as Catholicism was, however, it was not the sole cultural marker of the New Spain: both race and language were central to Francoist definitions of Spanishness. Another crucial element was gender, as Francoism sought to impose its clearly-defined gender roles, with women relegated to the home and motherhood in order to regenerate the race. The vision was anything but innovative, but the regime did attempt to realize it through new means, especially the Sección Feminina. In the end, the new moral order failed to materialize: fewer Spaniards than ever went to Church, regional nationalisms were thriving, and instead of being the mothers to large families Spanish women were having fewer children, were moving into the work force and opposing the regime itself by joining unions, student organizations, political parties and even feminist organizations.

|16|

Early Francoism, 1939–1957

ANTONIO CAZORLA

In 1953 Franco scored two resounding international successes which further solidified his dictatorship. The first was reaching a Concordat with the Holy See, confirming the regime's legitimacy before the Catholic world. The second was the signing of the Spanish–United States Accord, which provided Spain with military and economic assistance in exchange for permitting the US to build military bases. For the regime, the real importance of the accord lay in its rehabilitation as a fitting ally in the defence of the 'free world' against communism. The framework of the Cold War made possible the reversal of the international condemnation of 1946, when the newly created United Nations had categorized the regime as 'fascist', excluding it from the international body, calling for its substitution by a democratic regime, and declaring an almost universal boycott which included the closing of the border with France and a withdrawal of ambassadors (with the sole exceptions of the Vatican, Portugal, Ireland and Argentina). But little else was done to end the dictatorship. The French border was reopened in 1948, and the UN condemnation was lifted in 1950. Spain would soon join the FAO and UNESCO and, in 1955, the UN itself.

The problem of definitions

In addition to the favourable context provided by the Cold War, international acceptance of Francoism during the early 1950s was helped by the regime's efforts to reinterpret its origins and intentions, and to adapt its institutions, language and symbols to the new external·reality. An analysis of Spain's political, economic and social evolution for the 36 years between the end of the Civil War in April of 1939 and the death of Franco in November of 1975 reveals just how spectacular these changes were. Precisely because of its endurance and the variety of phenomena which it encompasses, Francoism presents historians, political scientists and sociologists with a series of conceptual and theoretical problems which do not arise in the already complex analysis of fascist regimes which disappeared at the end of the Second World War.

By the 1960s, the ideological heterogeneity of the dictatorship itself, and the need to overcome its rigid pigeonholing as 'fascist' led to its being defined as 'authoritarian' with 'limited pluralism', thus distinguishing it from other, more accomplished, 'totalitarian' systems of social control. According to this view, developed by Juan Linz, the political 'families' that supported the regime enjoyed a scope for action denied to the losers of the war. But this analysis was criticised for, among other things, not explaining the link between the social sectors represented as a whole by the regime, and each one of the active political 'families' in particular. Other formulations have been proposed in its place – 'reactionary despotism', 'Bonapartism', 'Praetorianism' – which allude to its conservatism, its use of force to preserve the interests of the dominant coalition, and to the role of the army and the military dictator. Recent attempts to explain many essential features of the regime have stressed the personality of Franco himself.

At root, Francoism was characteristic of contemporary 'fascist regimes' that emerged from the crisis of the model of domination existing in the liberal state. Nevertheless, Falange Española Tradicionalista de las JONS (FET–JONS), the only party, did not originate with a triumphant mass political movement [see chapter 15]. Beneath clearly falangist or fascist constructs and language, the party would then and forever be subordinated to the interests of the state, of the dominant groups within it, and especially of the dictator himself, who used it as a counter-weight in the delicate balancing act between the various sectors – military, monarchists, and Catholics – which constituted the regime's real basis of support.

The survival of the dictatorship, with Franco at its head, depended upon the adaptation of that internal equilibrium – made possible only with the annihilation of internal democratic opposition and the fear of any potentially risky political change – to external circumstances. This is the underlying logic behind the different phases of the regime, which for the period under analysis are: 1) 1939–45, the 'Blue' or 'Falangist' phase, marked by a strong ideological affinity with the Axis powers and hostility towards the so-called decadent bourgeois democracies and 2) 1945–56, the 'Christian Democratic' phase, when the appearance of fascism was reduced in favour of a more moderate, pro-Western image which sought to connect with American interests and make a space for itself in the context of the Cold War. The change of government in 1957 marked the end of Christian Democratic rule, and would open the way for rule by Technocrats – with links to the Catholic fundamentalism of the Opus Dei – who carried out the liberalization of the economy which preceded Spain's 'economic miracle' of the 1960s. This change of direction, and the important consequences which followed, explain why the period known as Early Francoism is considered to have ended at that time.

The army and the Church

In 1937 the President of the Republic, Manuel Azaña, wrote that if the uprising were successful, it would lead to a traditionalist military and ecclesiastical dictatorship. To a large extent, he was right. Franco's New State found, in the ideologies of Church and Army and in the personnel provided by the officer corps and the confessional organizations, an abundance of resources for its constitution and preservation. Whatever the rhetoric of the day, the backing of arms and the defence of the most traditional interests and beliefs were always fundamental to its underlying purpose.

Unlike other generals, Franco managed to rise above the army during the war, and to hang on to its loyalty in spite of internal ideological differences within the predominantly monarchist high command. The Francoisation of the military offered ample rewards. Officers acquired an extensive hold on the state apparatus and in the private sphere. High ranking officers seized 47 per cent of ministerial posts between 1938 and 1957, took over management or ownership of large corporations, and often conducted all manner of private business with complete freedom. Officers commissioned during the war were allowed to remain in the ranks while ex-combatants and Nationalist prisoners who chose to retire were guaranteed direct entry into the state administration, the teaching profession, and the police, replacing the hundreds of thousands of civil servants purged for their ideological tendencies.

The Movement (a vague term adopted in 1945 to describe not only the 1936 uprising but also to identify the different regime's official organizations), was inspired by corporate and fascist models for politics and work but retained and empowered those persons and groups who adapted to the mental and organizational schemes of the military, and eliminated as nuisances those who did not fall into line. The influence of military thinking is also evident in other aspects of official ideology such as xenophobic nationalism and the exaltation of aggressive imperialism, as well as in the policy of economic isolation. It is no accident that between 1938 and 1957, 87.7 per cent of the highest positions in the Prime Minister's office were held by military men.

For its part, the Catholic Church enjoyed power such as it had never had in the modern Spanish state. By virtue of the 1941 agreements and the 1953 Accord, the regime turned over the regulation of public morality to the Church through specific legislation (such as the abolition of common law marriage, divorce and the right to abortion), and through censorship. More importantly, the Church shaped education policy through its control of the Ministry of Education, realizing the goal that had eluded it since the liberal revolution of the 1830s. Its domination was clearly evident in the – then elitist – secondary school system, where Catholic school enrolment tripled that of the public schools. At the same time, official subsidies, which accounted for between 1.25 per cent and 2 per cent of the national budget, contributed to the support of the clergy, and the construction or restoration of Churches, seminaries, convents, etc. In exchange, the Church legitimatized the dictatorship, doing its utmost to defend it even under extremely challenging internal or external circumstances. Out of this relationship arose a new term, 'National-Catholicism', which described the identification between civil and religious institutions and ideology.

The majority of Spanish Catholics and clergy viewed this alliance between Church and State with satisfaction. The Cardinal Primate, Isidro Gomá, picked up on this sentiment when he conferred the title of 'Caudillo' (supreme leader) upon the dictator in May 1939, sanctioning the sacred nature of his power, itself born of the 1936–39 'Crusade'. Politicians, beginning with the Minister of External Affairs, Alberto Martín Artajo, would be drawn from an elite Catholic organization, the National Catholic Propagandists Association (ACNP). This political staff would prove invaluable during the delicate shift in direction in 1945. The exception to this Catholic support (apart from broad segments of the Basque country, and to a lesser extent in Catalonia), came from those who, like Pedro Segura, the former Republican era Cardinal Primate, resented the Falangists' totalitarian aspirations.

After the war, the Catholic Church sought to reassert its position of moral authority and prestige in Spanish society by recovering the popular masses who, especially in the southern half of the country, on the Mediterranean coast, and in the large urban and industrial centres, had long before shaken off its tutelage and embraced indifference or anticlericalism. It spread its message in the schools, popular organizations (in 1943 membership in Catholic Action had swollen to more than 100 000), and the media. One of its privileges was precisely the power to maintain its own propaganda machinery outside of the Movement's monopoly. During the 1940s and 1950s it carried out an extensive campaign of public events, including pilgrimages, open air masses, the enthroning of religious images, national and international congresses, and missions. These consisted in virtual sieges of towns and cities, where baptisms, weddings and mass confessions, rosary prayers and hymn singing in the streets, the closing down of places of entertainment, etc., created a climate of religious sensationalism. In Catalonia and especially the Basque country there were campaigns of religious 're-Spanishization' that included not only the imprisonment and deportation of priests but also the purge of local religious images which had political significance. Thus in 1937, the 'Basque-Nationalist' Virgin of Begoña was carried during a surrealist Andalucian-style pilgrimage by horsemen dressed in Southern clothes singing typical flamenco tunes.

The spiritual reconquest of Spain had little success because it insisted more on outward acceptance than on inward conviction, and because the human and material resources upon which it relied were insufficient. The chronic lack of parish priests had become acute even before the Civil War, and would not begin to ease until the late 1940s. In 1953 there were still

3000 fewer priests than in 1939. But the major difficulty in the struggle against the so-called 'apostasy of the masses' arose from the identification of Church and State, which distanced the former from the bulk of industrial and agricultural workers. This is the critique that began to emerge within the bosom of the Church itself by the end of the 1940s.

The regime, the falange and Spanish society

Francoism appropriated the post-1898 reformists' use of the distinction between old politics (decadent, corrupt) and new (vigorous, reformist). The New State defined itself as breaking from a divisive, chaotic and degenerate past that, with the exception of the brief hiatus of the Primo de Rivera dictatorship comprised Spain's history for the nineteenth and twentieth centuries. The leaders of the regime wished to return Spain to her former glory of Empire and Counterreformation, of unity and uncompromising Catholicism, and the supposed absence of class struggle. Like many authoritarian regimes in Europe (Italy and Austria, for example), and in accordance with Vatican social policy, they considered corporatism to be the organizational model which would permit them to attain the ideal. This national-syndicalist model asserted that the political integration of individuals was expressed not in terms of class interest but of 'natural' arenas for action: the family, the municipality, the union or association. Direct universal suffrage was thus avoided in favour of opinions summarized from these institutions; confrontation was replaced by 'cooperation'.

The organization of the New State was a long process of adaptation to the exigencies and circumstances of the moment. Francoism was never based on a formal constitution, adopting instead a succession of laws of varying importance. This juridical edifice was begun between 1937 and 1942 by Franco's brother-in-law, Ramón Serrano Súñer. A former CEDA deputy and a friend of Jose Antonio Primo de Rivera, Serrano Súñer strove to create a strongly authoritarian and centralized state structure. After Súñer's dismissal under pressure from the army who distrusted his ambition, as did Franco himself, a group in the Prime Minister's office coordinated by Admiral Luis Carrero Blanco began to create the illusion of a rule of law. This fiction included, among other things, the creation of a rubber stamp parliament in 1942, the promulgation of the 1945 Local Authorities law governing the 'organic' election of Municipal bodies (through a combination of governmental appointment and indirect election); the promulgation, also in 1945, of the Charter of the Spaniards, a bill of rights which was applied at the government's pleasure; and, finally, the 1947 Law of Succession which, through a rigged referendum, confirmed Franco as Chief of State for life of a monarchy whose dynasty and prince were yet to be determined.

The New State claimed to have ended the endemic evil of *caciquismo*, while in reality embracing it wholeheartedly. During the war, FET–JONS welcomed tens of thousands of activists from across the political right. In areas conquered after the March 1939 Republican collapse, the military authorities decided the composition of thousands of municipal councils and dozens of provincial governments with the support of the local elites. Once the situation stabilized, the task of reorganizing public life fell to the civil governors, who began renewing the composition of town councils and provincial governments. But local and provincial Falange leaders fell outside the jurisdiction of the civil governors, creating a situation of dual power which led, during the early years, to frequent struggles for control of the party and local administrations.

The regime sought a compromise based on a mixture of repression and concessions. To begin with, in 1941 the governors were named provincial leaders of the party, thus reinforcing state control over it. Then, the more scandalously behaved groups or individuals who had not shown the regime sufficient loyalty were discarded. At the same time, corruption in local administrations, the Party and unions was permitted. Marketing controls and rationing, which lasted until 1952, offered plenty of opportunities in this regard. In addition, a rotation of local and provincial public office, worked out by the respective civil governors, was instituted. Each change of civil governor usually set off a period of consultation, inspections and, occasionally, punishments, which resulted in the seating of new town councils, members of the Courts and local union or Falange officials. The death of *caciquismo* came only with the disintegration of traditional agrarian society in the 1960s and 1970s, which occurred side by side with the emergence of a civil society. In other words, it occurred during the Francoist period but in spite of Francoism.

The single party, FET–JONS, could hardly be a strong and independent organization when the original Falange proved incapable of regulating the admission of new members, much less when its own leadership was imposed by a government which decided, for example, to designate all civil servants and career soldiers party activists. In 1940, the party militias existed in name only; the Spanish military did not want a repetition of some local version of the German 'SS' or Italian 'Blackshirts'. Of the 100 or so members of the 1942 National Party Council only 40 could properly be called Falangists; 20 were military men, 12 Carlists, and the rest assorted right-wingers. Even the office of general secretary was held in 1939 by a military officer, General Muñoz Grandes, who was succeeded by an 'old shirt' (activist from the early days), Jose Luis de Arrese, whose primary political conviction was loyalty to the Chief of State. The post was left vacant from 1945 until 1948. In the interim, it was held by the Vice-secretary General, Rodrigo Vivar Téllez, a man of such weak falangist convictions that he advised Franco to dissolve the party.

FET–JONS' survival as the only legal political organization was not due to its ability to mobilize the masses but rather to its convenience for the dictator. In addition to decorating the dictatorship with an ideological facade, it served as a counterweight to the other forces of the regime, allowing Franco to present himself as the arbiter of the New Spain, and therefore block any political project which might jeopardize his power. Without the support of the state and of the dictator himself, FET–JONS would hardly have survived.

The official unions were one sphere dominated by the Falangists but their effectiveness in gaining the support of the working class was quite limited. A number of factors attributable to the regime itself lie behind this failure: hostility of the more conservative elements of Francoism toward the effective mobilization of the working class; the scarcity of resources placed at its disposal; the slow pace of legislation; and the serious deterioration of material conditions for workers during the first 15 years of the dictatorship, which led to sporadic and illegal strikes in 1945–47, 1951–53, and 1956–58.

The official unions confined themselves to following instructions from the government. The Civil War had been unleashed precisely to stop the political mobilization of traditionally dominated social sectors; the regime had no interest in reviving it. When Gerardo Salvador Merino, head of the Unions from 1939 to 1941 and a sincere Nazi sympathizer, tried to assert the autonomy of his organization he was dismissed, accused of being a free-mason, and exiled. No high ranking falangist official dared defend him. His successor, Fermín Sanz Orrio, trod a path of absolute moderation and respect for the government until 1951, when the new National Representative for Unions, the charismatic officer Jose Solís, subjected the organization still further to the exigencies of the government's new economic policies.

Francoist unions begin with the Labour Charter (Fuero del Trabajo, 1938), copied from the Italian *Carta del Lavoro*, which put an end to the prohibition against union activities decreed by the military at the start of the war. Two laws passed in 1940 sought to end conflicts between Catholic and Falangist labour organizations. This legislation effectively created a single organization under strict state control. This Organización Sindical (OS) comprised 28 national unions which supposedly regulated all sectors of the economy. These were complemented in the agricultural sector by the Union Brotherhoods (Hermandades Sindicales) and Chambers of Agriculture (Cámaras Agrarias), which became a stronghold of landholders' interests.

For many years the OS did not truly establish itself in the provinces, particularly in smaller ones where it frequently lacked any facilities, materials, or even any clear bureaucratic structure. Given this lack of means and results, the OS could hardly aspire to the control of the regime's social project. The practically forced membership of labourers and entrepreneurs in twin, and supposedly cooperative, 'economic' and 'social' sections, the election of bottom-level union representatives (first held in 1944), and social assistance projects for workers could not conceal these shortcomings.

Between 1939 and 1942 the OS created a series of agencies with a clear social assistance mandate. Although they constituted one of the regime's more positive sides, and were innovative compared to the liberal state's negligence, their achievements remained limited. Most significant were the 'July 18' and 'Social Provisioning' projects, charged, respectively, with caring for public health (health insurance was established in two phases, between 1944 and 1947), and creating a pension system. But their development was slow and uneven, and they could not compensate for the decline in wages (which partly financed the projects) and nutrition, or combat the abysmal state of public health. By the end of the decade, confidential union reports admitted that the situation of workers was desperate and that confidence in the unions was minimal, even among amongst entrepreneurs.

Reproduction of ideology

Francoist propaganda never enjoyed the huge material resources or ambitious projects of, for example, Nazi Germany. The first major efforts at ideological mobilization were made after nationalist forces 'liberated' a locality, when military parades and huge religious processions demonstrated the restoration of the traditional order and an end to ideological dissidence. Official control of the media was extended to newspapers and magazines, which became severely reduced in number, as most provinces were left with only one or two. The largest publishing consortium, 'Movement Publications', was in the hands of FET–JONS. Its shops and presses had mostly been seized from outlawed parties and unions. The Church was able to publish its own papers, although *El Debate*, erstwhile voice of clerical and agricultural interests, was banned. The monarchists were also permitted to continue publishing their most important paper, *ABC*, although it had to accept the constitutional irregularity of Franco's rule. As for radio, only the Church managed to maintain or establish broadcast stations aside from official ones.

Propaganda efforts were aimed at conveying a homogenous image of a militaristic, clerical, folkloric, *machista* and happy country. Without doubt, its strongest internal ally was the wish of Spaniards to escape from a harsh, futureless reality. This state of affairs is partially responsible for the general acceptance of 'popular' artistic images, (fashioned, for the most part, after Andalucian stereotypes), in songs, radio programmes, and in the movies (which enjoyed among the highest public attendance rates in the world). Another constant of the propaganda campaign was the continuous exaltation of the figure of Franco, presented as a providential and exceptional man. This strategy was partially successful, not just among partisans of the regime but also among broad sectors of the depoliticized masses who, in the tradition of absolute monarchies, wished to distinguish between the Head of State – a man of peace, well-intentioned but isolated from reality – and his subordinates – responsible for the injustices and errors that were being committed.

Mass organizations played a very secondary role and always suffered from a lack of material and human resources. The body officially in charge of mobilizing young men was the Youth Front (FJ – Frente de Juventudes). Inspired by Nazi and Fascist models, it aspired to inculcate paramilitary values. In spite of the padding of official membership figures and records of events, official statistics do show that between 1943 and 1956, fewer than 30 per cent of eligible Spanish youth joined. Of these, only a minority were actively and constantly involved, and they were concentrated in the large urban centres. The Female Section (SF – Seccion Femenina) was even smaller [see chapter 18]. While the SF's work was, in many ways, remarkable, especially in the areas of rural sanitation and the recovery of folklore, it enjoyed even less state support than the FJ. Membership peaked in the early 1940s only to fall by two-thirds by 1959.

Falangist pretensions to monopolize public life were challenged by the organizations comprising Catholic Action (AC – *Acción Católica*). Reorganized in 1939, by 1950 its men's, women's, and youth branches boasted a membership of more than half a million members. The AC included organizations as diverse as the pro-Franco ACNP and the scarcely-tolerated Brotherhood of Workers (HOAC). While this latter group never had more than 5000 or 6000 active members, it produced much of the leadership of the class-based unions that were to play a leading role in the opposition to Francoism throughout the 1960s and 1970s.

Schooling was the regime's principle instrument for the political socialization of youth [see chapter 18]. To avoid any 'ideological contamination' one quarter of all teachers were fired from their jobs or suffered lesser sanctions. The zeal for ideological purity in the classroom was not matched by investment in schooling. Until 1945, the State did not spend one penny on the construction of new schools. The results of this policy were devastating: in the 1950–51 school year, approximately one million children had no school, and some 850 000 had to attend private schools because of the lack of public institutions. In 1955, the rate of elementary schooling was only 76 per cent, significantly less than in Italy, Portugal, or even Greece.

Economy: from autarchy to liberalization

The Spanish Civil War, while tragic in many ways, did not cause massive material destruction as did the Second World War. Factories and fields were largely spared, and only the traditionally mediocre transportation and communications systems were seriously damaged. On the other hand, machinery and stockpiles suffered critically from lack of maintenance or replacement and established commercial relations were seriously altered. Under these circumstances, the logical response would have been to invest aggressively to reestablish agricultural production, rebuild basic infrastructure, support industrial recovery, and seek to reestablish internal and external business contacts.

Such a policy would have allowed Spain to take advantage of its neutrality in the Second World War, as did countries like Portugal, Sweden, Switzerland or Turkey. Nevertheless, this did not occur, and for two reasons.

The first was that the New State opted for a policy of highly protectionist economic self-reliance, following policies initiated by Primo de Rivera, which meant that trade was neglected and that Spanish industry became increasingly uncompetitive. At the same time, a complicated, inefficient and corrupt system of intervention and control of raw materials and products was adopted, which completely distorted the market. This stimulated a parallel economy and the strangling of private initiative. To these factors must be added limited public investment (partly the consequence of a restricted, unjust and irrational system of taxation) and internal demand constricted by starvation wages which oscillated between 40 and 70 per cent of those before the war. This was caused by spiralling inflation which peaked during the 1940s, and because of the utterly wretched wages paid by agricultural day-labour contractors (see table 16.1).

Table 16.1 Real wages in industry and agriculture 1939–1950 (Level 100=1936)

Year	Industry (Sabadell, Catalonia)	Agriculture (Córdoba, Andalucia)
1939	48	–
1940	43	82
1941	–	73
1942	28	72
1943	39	74
1944	71	73
1945	72	72
1946	55	63
1947	50	60
1948	60	56
1949	66	53
1950	65	56

Source: Carme Molinero and Pere Ysas, 'Patria, Justicia, Pan'. Nivell de vida i condicions de treball a Catalunya, 1939–1951 (Barcelona, La Magrana, 1985) p. 196; Juan Martinez Alier, La estabilidad del latifundismo (Paris, Ruedo Ibérico, 1968), p. 27

The second great obstacle to the country's renewed economic take-off was its foreign policy, which was initially oriented entirely towards the Axis. The expectation that this would be rewarded in Hitler's new world order led

Madrid to reject repeated offers of Anglo-American financial aid and to restrict trade with countries within their sphere of influence. When the United States launched the Marshall Plan in 1947 Franco's regime paid the price. In this manner, the New State's foreign policy became key to the economy's lasting downturn, while its economic policies accounted for a good deal of its structural problems. The regime's response was to sit tight, to blame external forces – from Marxist conspiracy to lack of rain, and, of course, the war – and to step up economic planning based on autarchic, forced industrialization.

Agricultural policy

In 1939 Spain was a fundamentally agricultural country with 52 per cent of the active population employed in this sector. Apart from causing appalling hunger, the paralysis of factories, mines and even of the service sector not only kept the population in the rural areas but also provoked people to return to the countryside where finding work, food and support was easier than in the destitute cities. Between 1935 and 1940 the active rural population increased by 700 000 people (something unparalleled in the history of Europe), the same number lost by industry. On the other hand, the destruction of agricultural machinery and, above all, the drastic reduction in replacement parts and in the use of chemical fertilizers and pesticides, the importation of which were neglected by the government, so reduced production as to make the use of technologies and systems of production long abandoned as inefficient, either necessary or worthwhile. In addition, export agriculture (mainly citrus fruits, grapes and wine) suffered, as did the whole commercial sector, because of unrealistically high exchange rates set for the peseta. The myth of a strong currency as a show of external prestige was very deeply rooted in Franco's extremely simplistic economic thinking.

Throughout this period agricultural policy was strongly guided by ideology and the desire to compensate those segments of society which had supported the 18 July revolt. The regime's 'ideology of peasant sovereignty' saw city and country as morally counterpoised: the former was the symbol of national corruption through liberalism, Marxism and anarchism, while the latter was the cradle and keeper of Spanish virtues embodied in Catholicism, patriotism and private property.

One of the cornerstones of the Francoist rural social project was agrarian counter-reform. This was carried out mainly during the war and later sanctioned by the authorities. With the support of the Falangist militia and the army, former landlords seized land that had been subject to the Republic's agrarian reform. This extremely violent counter-reform not only destroyed the social labour of the Republic, handing back 6.3 million hectares, but also permitted the appropriation of lands, livestock, machinery and other goods belonging to persons from the Republican camp.

In 1939 the New State created the National Settlement Institute (INC – Instituto Nacional de Colonización) which was supposed to carry out the Falange's agrarian reform, seek technical improvements in agriculture (essentially expanding irrigation), and pursue greater 'social justice' through the distribution of land. But it was not until the appointment of a competent Minister of Agriculture, Rafael Cavestany, in 1951 that the INC realized any practical achievements. Until 1950 only 10 000 hectares had been colonized; a further 200 000 were added over the next 10 years. But these projects were implemented primarily to bring technological improvements to the countryside, for the benefit of the owners of large, now irrigated, holdings, and only secondarily to reform the structure of land tenure. Whereas some 225 000 families had received land between the electoral victory of the Popular Front and the outbreak of the Civil War (February–July 1936) fewer than 50 000 peasants had land distributed to them between 1939 and 1975.

The second mainstay of the agricultural policy was the defence of grain producers' interests. The ranks of the victorious army consisted of a large mass of grain producing Castilian peasants, most of them smallholders. As for the large landholders of Andalucia and Extremadura, they had been among the strongest enthusiasts of the military uprising. In order to defend the parallel, though unequal, interests of both groups, and to guarantee market prices, the National Wheat Service (SNT – Servicio Nacional del Trigo) was created in 1937.

The SNT began badly. Estimating a surplus in grain production, it recommended reducing the area under cultivation. It soon became evident, however, that the harvest was insufficient. The SNT decided to intervene, paying producers prices below those on the open market. The producers' response was to throw themselves in increasing numbers into the black market (*estraperlo*). The SNT countered with yet more mechanisms for intervention, provoking a spiral whereby every attempt to reduce the black market resulted, paradoxically, in its growth, to the point that quantities sold on the parallel market during the 1940s exceeded official sales. (The black market in grains only began to be brought below 30 per cent of the total with the 1953–54 harvest.) Similarly complex and bureaucratic intervention was extended to most agricultural products, creating the same problems of parallel markets, administrative corruption and inefficiency.

Industrial policy

The benefits of the dictatorship's economic policies for Spanish industry – the importation of machinery, low wages, exclusive markets, the strengthening of banks closely associated with the regime – were more than outweighed by the disastrous consequences of low demand, bad public sector investments, and autarkic controls on the supply of staples, domestic and external businesses transactions and foreign currencies. Between 1940 and 1950 (when pre-war levels began to be recovered), these policies produced a record of industrial stagnation unequalled in contemporary European history. This alone explains the backwardness of Spanish industry in relation to surrounding countries, where the end of the Second World War brought rapid economic expansion (see table 16.2).

Table 16.2 Comparative GDP of Spain, Italy and Portugal, 1940–1953 (Level 100 = 1929)

Year	Spain	Italy	Portugal
1940	72	122	144
1941	74	121	162
1942	80	119	153
1943	80	108	157
1944	92	88	155
1945	77	67	149
1946	82	90	161
1947	82	106	176
1948	86	112	178
1949	79	120	188
1950	84	130	193
1951	91	140	213
1952	108	144	218
1953	103	157	226

Source: Jordi Catalan, 'Reconstrucción, política económica y desarrollo industrial: tres economías del sur de Europa, 1944–1953', in Leandro Prados de la Escosura and Vera Zamagni (eds), *El desarrollo económico en la Europa del Sur* (Madrid: Alianza, 1992), pp. 392–3

With the exception of military spending (on average 53.5 per cent of total expenditures between 1940–45), the public demand for goods and services was scarce. In fact, the state spent even less on infrastructure than did the Republic, even after war had especially devastated this sector! The most significant investment of this type was the nationalization of the practically bankrupt rail companies in 1943. Private investors were paid about two billion pesetas but the new company, RENFE, was left chronically decapitalized.

A key element of industrial policy during these years was the creation in 1941 of the National Industry Institute (INI – Instituto Nacional de Industria), fashioned after Mussolini's IRI. The INI was assigned the role of investing in areas were private initiative had either failed (nationalizing bankrupt businesses), or had never operated (creating new companies). In this sense, its policy of investment in profitable networks and industries helped, in the long run, to eliminate the chronic stranglehold on the energy and steel sectors, and has been considered key in the take-off of industry. At the same time, its autarkic orientation, bent on seeking self-sufficiency without regard for the costs and benefits of investments, led to the misallocation of scarce resources. It also encouraged the creation of protected businesses with poor levels of production and incompetent management, whose future insertion in a more open economy would prove problematic.

The strength of the banking sector was another important factor in the industrial take-off of the 1950s. Five large banks enjoyed a legally-mandated oligopoly free from foreign competition. Their reserves increased with the savings generated by agriculture – to a great extent in the black market – and with regressive fiscal measures that taxed consumption far more heavily than income or inheritance. In addition, savings offices, which were closely linked to the Church, grew, capturing during these years of tremendous material hardship the tiny deposits made by the lower classes, including those generated by the pawning of personal belongings.

Reform and economic liberalization, 1951–1956

By the end of the 1940s, the autarkic model was completely exhausted, but Franco and his most intimate collaborators agreed to reform it only with great reluctance. This is the context for the 1951 change of government that, in the midst of serious strikes and public transport boycotts in Barcelona, Bilbao and Madrid, sought to reinvigorate the choking economy. This was achieved through a reformulation of agricultural policy: self-sufficiency was abandoned in favour of greater productivity, economic intervention mechanisms were partially dismantled in favour of a free market, private enterprise was facilitated to the detriment of state ventures, and greater fiscal conservatism (including the reduction of public spending) was adopted. Also of key importance were the arrival of the first US credits in 1949, which opened the way for importing capital goods and inputs, and of the aid given in exchange for military bases (amounting to some $625 million between 1951 and 1957). With these measures Francoism embraced the liberal capitalist ideology, scorned only a few years earlier as obsolete and corrupt.

The 1951 change of course also implied an abandonment of the ideology of 'peasant sovereignty', the glorification of (supposedly) traditional rural values, in favour of agricultural productivism. The new Minister of Agriculture, Rafael Cavestany, pushed for a completely new course, removing rigid production controls, raising prices and increasing productivity, relaunching settlement and public investments, and updating agricultural legislation. The recovery was immediate and widespread hunger disappeared, but pre-war levels of production of several key products and nutritional levels were not achieved until the latter half of the decade. At the same time, a huge rural exodus was unleashed, mainly affecting impoverished day-labourers who sought to improve their lot in the new industrial areas. The arrival of more than a million rural immigrants during the 1950s completely overwhelmed urban service networks, causing serious social problems (housing, health, education, etc.) which the authorities were incapable of handling.

Although the measures adopted from 1951 onwards proved successful, their limited nature soon began to restrain the economic recovery. Incomes were kept low and were unable to absorb growing industrial production. Agricultural prices shot up, dragging along wages, which had to be increased in 1954 and twice in 1956. This added to the economy's inflationary tendencies, against which no decisive measures were taken because of opposition from Falangist ministers of Labour and the Movement, who were trying to curb labour unrest. With increases in imports not balanced by exports, foreign currency reserves entered into a critical phase. With the instability of the peseta, capital increasingly fled. The situation called for radical change.

Repression

One the most characteristic features of early Francoism was a violence whose extent and intensity impressed even the leaders of fascist Italy and Nazi Germany. The New State was particularly effective in its repression of political opposition, a task to which it devoted more material, legal and human resources than any other regime in Spanish history. The duration and the number of people affected by Francoist violence destroyed any possibility of rebuilding the forces defeated during the war. Their leadership was eliminated and their supporters terrorized.

Repression was carried out both legally and extralegally. Legal means included laws (Political Responsibilities, 1939; and Repression of Masons and Communists, 1940) that retroactively criminalized what had been legal political activities, and an interpretation of the Code of Military Justice whereby the very people who had opposed a military revolt were found guilty of rebellion. Public institutions suffered purges which resulted in the expulsion of those workers and public servants hostile to the regime. These laws, together with the resulting legal proceedings, succeeded in creating widespread insecurity. Guarantees of any defence for those accused (usually of nothing more than exercising or defending civil rights), were scarce. Wholesale war trials and courts martial, blanket accusations, lack of counsel for the defence, missed procedural deadlines, and summary sentences were the rule. Some 28 000 people were executed after the war, most of them before 1941. In addition, hundreds of thousands of people were given lengthy jail sentences, stripped of their professional credentials, exiled, fined, etc. Imprisonment often implied a death sentence because the jails were overcrowded and unhealthy, and mortality rates among inmates were extremely high. Other prisoners ended up in forced labour gangs working on various public projects, among them Franco's favourite scheme, the famous Valley of the Fallen.

Extralegal repression, which continued with impunity, was carried out as much by private individuals as by the members of the police, the army or the Falange. In the first case, local notables sought revenge for past effronteries. In the second, police investigations were accompanied by torture, beatings, coercion and murder, occurrences which were particularly frequent when dealing with guerrilla fighters or fugitives.

Fear, legal defencelessness and a lack of any truly representative popular organization prevented the working population and the liberal-minded middle classes from protesting openly against the deterioration of living conditions or the corruption and inefficiency of the authorities. The 1940s are engraved in popular memory as the 'Years of Hunger' with associated images: low wages, ration queues, expensive and adulterated food, rich blackmarketeers, infectious diseases, lack of transport, of petrol, etc. Estimates put the number of deaths due to disease and hunger between 1939 and 1945 as high as 200000. This is the Spain described by Camilo José Cela in *La Colmena* (The Beehive), a novel which could only be published in Buenos Aires in 1951. Death from starvation in the sprawling urban slums and in the shanty towns was a daily fact of life.

Repression extended into the cultural sphere in an attempt to put an end to ideological and national plurality in Spain. The publication or use of Catalan, Galician, and Basque in commercial and official arenas was prohibited, and their status was downgraded to that of 'dialects'. Meanwhile, Castilian became the language of the 'Empire', the only true language for Spaniards (regardless of what Spaniards themselves thought of it). At the same time, artistic creativity suffered the loss – through death, exile or self-censuring – of most of the writers, painters, sculptors, musicians and academics who had developed a veritable second Golden Age of Spanish culture in the two previous decades. These artists swelled the ranks of the so-called Spain in Exile which established itself in France and, above all, in the Americas.

Opposition

After losing the war, political parties and unions were left internally divided and in serious confrontation with each other. The great split was between the Communist Party and its allies in the Negrín government and everybody else, most of whom had supported the coup by Colonel Casado. This dispute was taken up in the heart of the political parties, especially the PSOE which ended up fractured into three main groups. The placing of personal and ideological differences before the common struggle against the dictatorship was common to Spain in Exile and was decisive in preventing the formation of a unity government that might have been recognized by the Allied forces during the Second World War. When such a government appeared in 1945 it was already too late to take advantage of the defeat of fascism. The Cold War soon imposed its own geostrategic logic, rekindling ideological differences in the Spanish opposition.

Another of these organizations' grave errors was to cling to republicanism. Their aspiration to reestablish the state born in 1931 failed to recognize the true balance of power within and outside of Spain, and prevented an alliance with the monarchists, who, at the first sign of an Axis defeat, began to seek a replacement for Franco and the Falange that would preserve their basic interests. This was the framework for Don Juan de Borbón's Lausanne Manifesto (1945), which called for the restoration of a democratic monarchy. By the end of 1946 monarchist military conspiracies began to weaken, thanks in part to Franco's cool bloodiness in dealing with them. In 1948, a meeting held on the high seas between the Caudillo and Don Juan ended with the agreement that Don Juan's son, Juan Carlos, would return to Spain to study and, it was understood, to prepare himself to be king.

Around the same time, the clandestine efforts at reorganization inside the country had ended in unmitigated failure. With their leaders in prison, the reconstruction of the CNT and UGT, which had managed to regroup to a surprising extent by 1945, was aborted. The discrepancies between the leadership in exile and their efforts to impose their authority inside – sometimes violently in the PCE's case – and their usually mistaken analyses of the situation, contributed to a further wearing down of the resistance. By the end of the 1940s, the majority of the militants chose to abandon the struggle. The certain prospect of ending up beaten or executed was no longer compensated for by the waning hope that the democratic powers would decide to finish Franco off. The strikes in the years that followed were more the spontaneous explosions of a desperate populace than the work of the organized opposition.

Political resistance during early Francoism was followed by the organization of armed guerrilla groups. These emerged spontaneously during the Civil War, as individuals and units were left stranded by Franco's advancing army. After the defeat, many soldiers refused to lay down their arms and took refuge in the mountains. The composition and leadership of these resisting groups was completely heterogeneous, in powerful contrast to the factionalism reigning amongst those in exile.

This phase of clearly defensive guerrilla warfare lasted until 1944–45. Despite having ample support among some sectors of the peasantry, guerrillas never managed to liberate any zones and were relentlessly hounded by the army and the Civil Guard. Its most spectacular operation, the invasion from France of the Aran valley late in 1944, ended in dismal failure. The regime reacted strongly against the actions of the guerrilla forces, stopping at nothing in order to destroy them. Reprisals against those accused of helping them were so severe and merciless that support among the civilian population was undermined. By 1951–52 there were virtually no resistors left in the mountains but, incredibly, a few carried out isolated urban actions in the early 1960s.

A new opposition to Francoism would eventually emerge with a leadership, tactics and circumstances incubated throughout the 1950s. Key among these was the infiltration of official unions. In the midst of anticapitalist rhetoric and Falangist plans for unions it was possible to develop a practical underground struggle which was very far from the exiles' analysis of the imminent collapse of the regime. The 1951 strike in Barcelona, launched from the official union's own offices, was an early test of these tactical possibilities. In addition, a new and unexpected element in the fight against the dictatorship was the presence of students: in 1956 they were at the forefront of the disturbances and protests in Madrid. For the first time Francoism was confronted with the fact that it could no longer count on the unconditional support of the whole of the middle classes nor trade on their fear of political strife. In the Basque country and in Catalonia the new opposition had a strong nationalist component. From these forces, from disenchanted monarchists and more moderate Catholics would emerge the groups whose pressure on Francoism would accelerate its internal disintegration in the years to come.

17

The desarrollo years, 1955–1975

SEBASTIAN BALFOUR

Between the mid-1950s and the early 1970s, Spain underwent social, economic and cultural changes far deeper and more rapid than at any other period in her history. This transformation affected every Spaniard and penetrated to the remotest corners of the country, uprooting people and overturning customs, values and social relations. For many, it cannot have been a pleasant experience. Families were torn from their homes in the rural areas and agrarian towns, separated from each other and thrown into unfamiliar and sometimes degrading environments in Spain or abroad. At the same time, however, the living standards of Spaniards rose to a degree never known before and people acquired levels of knowledge and skills which had been unthinkable for earlier generations. Social and economic change both stimulated and was accompanied by a revolution in values. As Spain modernized, her people increasingly adopted urban, secular and democratic values. However, Spain's political regime, though it briefly attempted a highly circumscribed *apertura* (opening) in the late 1960s, remained rooted in the reactionary values of the Civil War.

Economic modernization (or *desarrollo*) without cultural or political change was a fundamental objective of the Francoist dictatorship. The autarky imposed on Spain at the end of the Civil War was an attempt to lay the basis for the accumulation of capital in isolation from the world economy, but the failure of this model was patent by the late 1940s. While countries with similar socio-economic structures, such as Italy, were beginning to enjoy industrial take-off thanks in part to the European Recovery Programme (otherwise known as Marshall Aid), Spain's economy was still backward. The crisis of the late 1940s forced the regime to reassess its policies of autarky, but the timid liberalization of the early 1950s proved insufficient, as waves of strikes and student mobilizations demonstrated. The Church was also showing the first manifestations of opposition to the cause it had adopted passionately in the 1930s. Among the military, who tended to favour a restoration of the monarchy, there were rumblings of discontent about the hegemony of the Falange. The threat all these events posed to the continuation of the regime persuaded a reluctant Franco to demote his falangist advisors and reshuffle the cabinet in 1957, allowing a new layer of neo-liberal technocrats closely associated with the Catholic lay organization, the Opus Dei, to seek to implement a distinct economic path towards development.

Their most radical proposal was the dismantling of autarky and the opening up of the economy to the economic boom of the West. Their aims were not fundamentally different from those of the founders of the regime in that the new strategy would not entail any liberalization of politics or society. Indeed, it was believed that the benefits of economic growth and the rise of consumerism would help to legitimize the regime and outweigh the risks of the penetration of foreign values of democracy and pluralism. The regime would continue its practice of political repression and the propagation of regressive nationalist values through education, censorship and cultural policies. In short, this new policy entailed not so much the reversal of autarky but the pursuit of the same objectives by other means.

The transformation of the economy

The ground for greater economic contact with the West had been prepared since the late 1940s by the increasing and unavoidable recourse to loans from the United States, commercial agreements with France and Great Britain and Spain's incorporation into the Cold War network of Western international institutions. In the 1953 Pact of Madrid, in particular, Spain had gained extensive economic and military aid from the US in exchange for the American use of military bases on Spanish soil. By 1958, Spain had become part of the United Nations, the OEEC, the International Monetary Fund and the World Bank, amongst other organizations.

The severity of Spain's economic crisis at the end of the 1950s finally persuaded Franco and his closest advisors into accepting the programme of the technocrats. Through the Stabilization Plan of 1959, the government carried out an immediate semi-liberalization of the economy. The peseta was devalued by 50 per cent, restrictions on foreign investment were lifted, a range of government subsidies were withdrawn in an attempt to reduce the Public Sector Borrowing Requirement and the prices of many goods and services were raised. Simultaneously, in an important move to open up the economy, exchange rates were unified, giving the peseta a fixed value on the international exchange and making it a convertible currency.

The immediate effect of the Plan was to provoke a recession in the Spanish economy that lasted until 1961. Thereafter, until the energy crisis of 1973, the economy experienced a spectacular rate of growth that was higher during most of this period than in any other country in the West and for a period of more than twice that of the European Community. From a predominantly agrarian society on the fringes of Europe, Spain became an industrialized urban and consumer society largely integrated into Europe.

The engine of this growth was the economic boom of the Western economy in the 1960s and the early 1970s. Foreign investment poured into Spain, attracted by a largely untapped market full of potential for expansion and by the favourable conditions offered by the Spanish government, such as subsidies and a low-paid and ferociously regimented workforce. It introduced into Spain technologically advanced industries dominated by multinationals in sectors such as engineering, chemicals, steel, shipbuilding and pharmaceuticals. This new industrial structure was superimposed on a network of small companies, many of which survived or indeed emerged during the decade thanks to continued state protection. The presence of leading multinational firms ensured high levels of productivity and reinvestment in technology and capital goods. As a result, the participation of Spanish industry in the gross domestic product rose from 25 to 40 per cent in one decade.

Spain also benefited from the economic growth and rising living standards in Europe in other ways. Attracted by her sun, beaches and cheap services, tourists began to flood into the country. Between 1959 and 1964, their number rose from 4 million to 14 million and earnings from tourism increased in the same period from 129 million to 919 million dollars. Shortages of labour in booming Europe also encouraged thousands of Spaniards to emigrate there after their precarious wages in the agrarian sector were thrown into jeopardy by the restructuring of the Spanish economy following the Stabilization Plan. Between 1960 and 1973, over one and a quarter million Spaniards, some 8 per cent of the active population, emigrated to Europe, most of them assisted by the Spanish Institute of Emigration. Their remittances to Spain in the same period totalled as much as $5 billion.

Foreign investment, tourism and emigrant remittances provided the invisible exports that helped to finance Spain's trade deficit. The growth in domestic industry entailed the massive import of technology, capital goods, raw materials and energy resources unavailable in Spain. Although the agricultural sector was successfully restructured to respond to consumer demand from Europe, rising export earnings still fell far short of the cost of imports. The resulting balance of payments deficit, therefore, was largely covered by the remarkably high level of invisible earnings.

Perhaps the most dramatic change in the economy took place in the countryside. The state's partial abandonment of the price-fixing of foodstuffs and the protection of traditional produce led to a crisis in the agricultural sector. Labourers and small farmers were forced to abandon the countryside and seek work either in the industrial centres or abroad. At the end of the 1950s, agricultural workers had represented 40 per cent of the total workforce; by 1975 they were less than 14 per cent of the active population. The crisis in the early 1960s led to the restructuring and mechanization of agriculture. In 1960, there were about 57000 tractors in use on the land; by 1970, their number had risen to just under 260000. Land use also changed. One of the most widespread crops, grain for domestic consumption, gave way to the expansion of the fishing, wine, fruit and market garden sectors, above all for export. By the early 1970s, nevertheless, agriculture accounted for only 10 per cent of gross domestic production.

Migrants from the countryside found work not just in industry but also in the tertiary sector. Many were absorbed into the construction and tourist industries, both of which were burgeoning in response to migration to the cities and the expansion of tourism. They were thus incorporated into the consumer market, helping to raise demand as their living standards rose. The growth of both industry and tourism led to increasing efforts to develop Spain's infrastructure, such as roads and hotels. The completion of these projects was usually imbued with political meaning. Franco was often deployed cutting ribbons to open public buildings or dams. Besuited and aged by the mid-1960s, he had become more of a figurehead than a political leader.

Regime apologists attributed the extraordinary growth of the economy to their own management. With the Stabilization Plan, the government had abandoned the planned economy of the autarky and had adopted a form of *dirigisme*, or indicative planning borrowed from the French model. Government intervention provided public investment to build the infrastructure that private capital required. It was also intended to reduce distortions and regional inequalities in economic growth. The policy, it was repeatedly claimed, was carried out in a series of Development Plans.

In reality, however, much of the economic growth in Spain was unplanned. Far from creating 'poles of development' in hitherto lesser developed areas, industrial growth was increasingly concentrated in traditional areas: the Madrid region, Catalonia and the Basque Country. By 1971, five provinces, Barcelona, Madrid, Vizcaya, Valencia and Oviedo, accounted for over 43 per cent of national production.

Nevertheless, the Franco regime attempted, in a small measure, to compensate for the growing regional disparities exacerbated by the concentration of industry and production in general in a few regions. Thus between 1968 and 1973, ten of the poorest regions were net beneficiaries of public funds through official credits, public sector investment and social security, which were raised at the expense of the richest regions. To this effect, Catalonia contributed an average of 12.24 per cent and the Basque province of Vizcaya some 12.11 per cent of their revenue over this period while at the other extreme, Extremadura received 13.35 per cent more than it earned. However, income differentials between regions were also reduced considerably by the migration of low-income workers to areas where better-paid work was available.

Moreover, the initial gesture of economic liberalization between 1959 and 1961 gave way to the traditional Spanish model of patronage and protection.

Government ministers and officials reimposed tariffs and distributed credits and tax concessions to firms with which the regime maintained close contacts based on ideology, friendship or nepotism. This practice allowed the emergence of domestic monopolies and oligopolies. At the same time, the economy became increasingly dependent on foreign capital and the import of raw materials, energy products and technology. Between 1960 and 1973, over 20 per cent of gross industrial investment came from Europe and the United States.

However, when oil and certain raw materials rose in price in the early 1970s, Spain's balance of trade began to deteriorate, leading to rampant inflation. The economic crisis of 1973–74 was a contributory factor in the political crisis of the regime. In the longer term, the lack of rational planning and regulation also contributed to severe environmental damage and health hazards to urban-based populations. In new industrial areas, smoke, chemical emissions and toxic waste polluted the environment.

The transformation of society

Economic development led to a transformation of Spanish society. The most striking change was the growth of urban classes and the decline of rural life. Between 1951 and 1970, some 3 million people left rural areas to work and live abroad or in the industrial centres of Spain. The concentration of the population in the latter was such that by the beginning of the 1970s, over 25 per cent of the total population lived in Madrid, Barcelona and Vizcaya, areas which accounted for less than 4 per cent of the total surface of Spain. The migrants left behind them depopulated villages inhabited mainly by older generations, some of which ended up as ghost villages. The great movement of people from the countryside to the city contradicted one of the most characteristic features of the regime's ideology, the glorification of traditional rural life in Spain.

Urban growth in the areas of expansion was largely unplanned. Huge estates were built on the fringes of cities to accommodate some of the new inhabitants but their construction was characterized by speculation, the absence or lack of application of controls and frequent corruption. The quality of the new housing tended to be very poor. Although vast building programmes were carried out in the 1960s, housing standards in all of Spain remained low in comparison to other European countries. An official survey in 1968 revealed that 34 per cent of households in Spain had no running water and only 37 per cent had a bath or shower, 18 per cent hot water and 6 per cent central heating. Estates on the outskirts of the cities were often overcrowded and the surrounding environment neglected; building rubble lay strewn in the area, street lighting was inadequate, parks and leisure facilities were rare. Local services, such as transport and medical facilities, also tended to be sub-standard or distant.

Beyond or between the dormitory suburbs lay vast and illegal *bidonvilles*, built by migrants who could not afford or were waiting for flats in the estates. The inhabitants of these slums were barely integrated into the surrounding society. In one slum on the outskirts of an industrial suburb of Barcelona, a whole village from Andalucia had settled, retaining some of its old customs and' structures, such as a mayor responsible to no one but the erstwhile villagers.

On the other hand, growth and development led to considerable improvements in health, nutrition and education. Mortality rates dropped among both adults and infants. Food consumption per inhabitant increased dramatically. During the 1960s, the average annual consumption of meat rose from just under 20 kilos per inhabitant to over 45 kilos and citrus fruits from 14.3 to 24 kilos. During the same period, educational standards rose even more strikingly. Over 14 per cent of the population had been illiterate in 1950. By 1975, this had fallen to under 9 per cent, of whom almost half were over 55 years of age. As for the younger generations, 90 per cent of the school age population were undergoing compulsory education by 1970. During the 1960s the university student population rose three times.

The mass migration of rural inhabitants to cities in Spain and abroad led to an important shift in social structure. The number of agrarian smallholders and labourers fell sharply while industrial and service-sector workers rose correspondingly; in 1960, some 42 per cent of the active population were engaged in agriculture and fishery and 57 per cent in industry and services. A decade later, only 29 per cent were involved in the first and as many as 71 per cent in the second. The increased rate of urbanization and the development of the service sector also led to an expansion of the professional middle classes.

Yet the geographic mobility described above was not matched by social mobility in the period under discussion, despite improved educational standards. The only significant occupational change took place in the status of women, many of whom were incorporated into the labour force. By 1971, some 28 per cent of women worked outside their home. Nevertheless, this figure was far below that of more developed countries in the north, such as Britain and Germany, where some 50 per cent of women held jobs in the same year. The most important difference lay in the continued traditionalism of the role of married women in Spain [see chapter 18].

Another important indication of the changing social structure was the different patterns of consumption. As rural migrants became integrated into consumer society and living standards improved, there was an overall rise in the family consumption of those commodities and services outside essential personal and household goods. Their part in total family consumption rose from 18 per cent in 1960, to over 27 per cent in 1971, despite the relative rise in housing costs. The most obvious symbol of consumerism was the television. By 1974, almost 70 per cent of homes in Spain possessed a TV set. Another sought-after consumer durable was the car and in that same year, one in nine inhabitants owned one.

The transformation of values

Value-systems were a battleground for the regime. The residual legacy of the Second Republic and the risks posed by economic modernization encouraged the intense promotion of values such as cultural nationalism, which excluded regional identities outside the traditional power centre of Spain, as well as a fundamentalist Catholicism and an authoritarian, paternalist system of politics. Economic development, however, generated a range of values and attitudes which increasingly conflicted with those of the regime.

The most striking change took place in the moral and political stance of the Church. Most of the hierarchy had ardently supported the Nationalist uprising as the defence of traditional Catholic Spain threatened by atheism and communism. Beginning in the early 1950s, however, sections of the Church began to disengage themselves from the regime. This was the result in part of the contradiction between the Church's rhetorical commitment to the poor and needy and its support for a regime that was protecting the interests of the rich. The most critical voices in the Church were the lay organizations set up after the Civil War amongst rural and urban workers and Catholic youth. The flight from the countryside had concentrated the Church's clientele in urban areas and the social views of the young priests were increasingly shaped by the problems posed therein to the working classes.

Another powerful influence contributing towards the growing dissatisfaction with the regime was the reemergence of regionalism in the Basque Country and Catalonia which had traditionally been strongly Christian Democratic. The Spanish Church was influenced above all by the radical changes taking place in the world-wide Catholic movement which were expressed in the Second Vatican Council (1964–65). By the late 1960s, inspired by a liberal Vatican, a new generation of Spanish bishops began to challenge the association of the Church with the regime. The new position adopted by Catholic leadership entailed a respect for democracy and pluralism and a defence of the interests of the poor and exploited. In 1971, the Church decided to ask forgiveness from the Spanish people for its role in the Civil War and in 1973, the Spanish bishops demanded the separation of the Church and the State.

The Church played an important role in the reshaping of social attitudes towards the regime because Spaniards were still predominantly practising Catholics. A survey in 1974 found that although some secularization had occurred among workers and above all students, as many as 89 per cent of interviewees declared themselves to be Catholic and 95 per cent to be baptized. However, Catholicism was increasingly seen as a personal belief rather than a politically-linked ideology, as it had been practised in the early period of the dictatorship. A more important cause of the transformation of values was the increasing contact with developed and democratic Western societies through imported television programmes, films, advertisements and social intercourse with tourists and with immigrant members of the family on holiday in Spain or returning home permanently.

Endogenous factors also contributed to the transformation of values in the 1960s and early 1970s. Urbanization and the corresponding marginalization of agrarian cultures, the decline of rigid hierarchies of class and status and the greater mobility of the population all led to greater cultural homogeneity and the development of concepts of citizenship, tolerance, social dialogue and negotiation. These urban, democratic values replaced the more personal and differentiated ones characteristic of life in small villages. Thus, a rural migrant confessed in an interview that he had found it difficult for a while after his arrival in the city to suppress giving a spontaneous greeting to all the passers-by whenever he emerged from the underground station.

The rise of protest

The transformation of Spanish economy and society and the tensions thrown up by Spain's modernization generated a range of new forms of agitation mainly in urban, industrialized areas. The process of change sharpened the contradiction between society and a state rooted in the reactionary ideology of the thirties. The authoritarian structures of the regime were increasingly unable to respond to the needs of a more complex, mobile, educated and pluralist society. As a result, social and cultural protests were progressively channelled into political agitation or took on a more overt political profile.

The sector of society that most challenged the regime was the working class. The wave of strikes that surged through Spain from 1962 was part of a wider pattern of labour protest that swept across Europe in the 1960s. These conflicts embraced not just traditional sections of workers but also new groups of white-collar employees created by socio-economic and technological change. The roots of the new militancy were the expectations and confidence generated by the post-war boom and the growing pressure of inflation. To this was added the problem of the Spanish centralized, authoritarian and paternalist system of industrial relations based on the fascist-inspired Vertical Unions.

The new technologies introduced into production from the end of the 1950s required the transformation of this system into one based on collective bargaining at both sectoral and factory levels. The Law of Collective Agreements promulgated in 1958, however, proved yet again that the measures undertaken by the regime to adjust to modernization helped to undermine the legitimacy of its industrial relations model. Bargaining in factories encouraged the development of democratic structures at shop-floor level and higher; it also educated and empowered workers in the practice of democracy. The clandestine organization which emerged in workplaces throughout Spain was the Workers' Commissions, dominated by militants of the Communist Party.

Given the developing strength of shop-floor organizations, repression ceased to be an effective means of controlling working class discontent; on the contrary, it only generated further protest. Although strikes were officially prohibited, their numbers increased dramatically: while in 1963 there were 777 strikes, the number had risen to almost 1600 by 1970. Labour protests overflowed into the surrounding neighbourhoods and workplaces, taking the form of solidarity movements and mobilizing more and more sections of the population.

One of the most powerful agitations influenced by labour protest was the neighbourhood association movement. This grew above all in estates built on the periphery of cities to accommodate the waves of immigrants from the countryside. The increasing confidence and organizational abilities of workers encouraged the orchestration of collective protest against the appalling conditions on many of these estates. The legitimacy of local Francoist government, characterized by corruption and patronage, was undermined by these movements. At the same time, their protest helped to generate concepts of citizenship, participation and political ideas.

Another section of society which took on the regime was the students. Like the workers, their protest emerged out of the modernization process. Universities changed from elite institutions to mass centres of higher education characterized by new cultures and preoccupations. Though student unrest in the 1960s was in part the expression of the generational contradictions of post-war society in Europe and elsewhere, it was also a response to the immediate conditions of university life, especially the lack of internal democracy. The first outbreak of protest against the undemocratic, official Falangist union in 1956 was followed by mass campaigns which led to its dissolution in 1965. Further agitation attempted to replace it by democratic students' unions and was marked by strikes, demonstrations and violent clashes with police, occasioning frequent closures of campuses, the arrest of hundreds of students and in 1969, the declaration of a State of Emergency throughout the country.

The radical political culture that developed in many universities challenged not just the university system, but the regime itself. The 1960s' and early 1970s' generation of students represented a future elite strongly opposed to Francoist society and closely identified with democracy. Their struggles spilled over into the streets of the main cities, evoking brutal responses from a regime unable to satisfy their demands, and generating a widespread movement of solidarity among other citizens.

The regime was also defied by burgeoning regional nationalisms. After the Civil War, it had imposed on Spain a single national identity based on the

Castilian language and on the centralist, Catholic and imperial myths generated by the Spanish right. As economic and social modernization began to transform Catalan and Basque society, regional rights there became the focus of the widespread demand for democracy. In Catalonia in particular, the struggle for Catalan rights forged a sense of cohesion and shared identity across barriers of class and even to some extent across linguistic and cultural differences. Amongst many migrants who had settled in the region, most of whom had not learnt Catalan, regional claims such as autonomy were perceived as an instrument of social advancement.

Amongst Catalans, regional nationalism was a widely diffused movement rallying the local Church, workers, students, intellectuals, professional and lower middle classes and even supporters of the Barcelona football team. The creation in 1971 of the clandestine movement for Catalan rights, the Assemblea de Catalunya, brought together a wide range of political, social and cultural organizations. As in the first quarter of the century, Catalanism attracted thousands of people because it was identified as a modernizing and democratic project linked to European models, as opposed to the reactionary and nostalgic projection of Spanish nationalism by the Francoist state.

Basque nationalism, on the other hand, was characterized by a more inward-looking and separatist ideology. The wave of migrants from other parts of Spain into the industrial areas of the Basque Country heightened the insecurities of an already exclusivist national identity. Regional protest in the Basque Country took a violent and clandestine form after the creation of the terrorist organization ETA in 1959. Between 1968 and 1975, when ETA was at its most active, 47 people associated with the regime and its repressive apparatus were assassinated, including in 1973, Franco's Prime Minister, Admiral Luis Carrero Blanco. ETA also carried out a series of kidnappings and bank raids to which the regime responded by increasing its repressive measures throughout the region. Despite its violent nature and the barriers of its exclusive nationalism, ETA became a symbol of resistance against the authoritarian and centralist state amongst democratic opinion throughout Spain. The Burgos trial of ETA members and sympathizers in 1970 generated a widespread movement of solidarity in the Basque Country which transcended support for separatist demands.

The political opposition and social protest

Social protest in the 1960s was not launched or controlled by the political opposition, though their militants played a crucial role in its organization. It was a result of the contradictions of modernization and was exacerbated by the failure of the regime to adapt political structures to social realities. However, a new political opposition, as well as new democratic traditions and ideologies, arose out of the agitation of the 1960s. By 1950, the clandestine organizations of two of the dominant left-wing movements in the

1930s – the Socialists and the anarchists – had largely been dismantled by repression. Although the Socialists retained considerable residual support in industrial areas such as Asturias and the Basque Country, they failed to engage, in their clandestine work and propaganda, with the grievances thrown up by the new socio-economic conditions. It was only in the early 1970s that new Socialist groups emerged within Spain more attuned to the realities of modernization than their long-exiled leadership.

Of the traditional organizations of the left, only the Communists were able to build a new social base by relating to the immediate problems of workers, students, immigrants and others living in the new and poorly equipped estates. Having renounced the guerrilla struggle of the 1940s, they encouraged their militants to play a leading role in establishing the Workers' Commissions, in organizing labour and urban protest and in mobilizing solidarity movements. The Communists had initially believed that the growing social discontent of the late 1950s signalled the imminent fall of the regime. However, their attempt to bring this about in 1959 by mobilizing mass protest through clandestine propaganda was a complete failure. The Communist Party then adopted the strategy of 'national reconciliation' (known later as Eurocommunism), a reformist road towards democracy in which elites such as the bourgeoisie and a more progressive section of the military would continue to exercise considerable influence.

Alongside them, new and more radical organizations emerged, especially in the universities, which were closely linked to the revolutionary left in Europe. Despite its considerable growth and influence, however, the political opposition in the 1960s and early 1970s was unable to create a common programme uniting all organizations opposed to the regime and thus embodying an alternative to it. This failure was the result largely of the Cold War divisions in the left and the different agendas for political change in Spain.

Modernization and the Franco regime

The transformation of Spanish society had a paradoxical effect on the regime. On one hand, it was able to strengthen its claim to legitimacy on the grounds that Spain was experiencing unprecedented economic growth and a rise in living standards. On the other hand, the demands and contradictions generated by this transformation were increasingly difficult to contain within the structures of the dictatorship.

As part of an effort to change its image, the regime had attempted, at the end of the 1950s, to shed its fundamentalist identity associated with the Spanish fascists, the Falange. Franco announced that he had embraced the concept of monarchy, though he was too reticent to define when this succession would take place. The dictator and his advisors were careful to maintain the alliance of elites which had supported the 1936 uprising by the

careful balancing of interests and representation in his regime of the different
'families' that it constituted. In the early 1960s, however, they were also
concerned to begin incorporating some of the new social forces in Spain,
which were emerging out of the process of modernization, without undermining the principles of the dictatorship. The means that were chosen
represented a purely superficial renovation of the institutions of the regime.
A very limited form of elections was introduced into the state trade unions,
the Vertical Syndicates. A highly restrictive Law of Associations was passed
in 1964, allowing the legal constitution of opinion groups which respected
the principles of the regime, and a Press Law was promulgated in 1966 that
in practice permitted the expression merely of timid and indirect criticisms of
institutional arrangements in Spain.

The ambiguities of the future character of the regime became evident in
the debate on the monarchy and the modernization of institutions. The
families of the regime were evidently divided between those arguing for a
limited *apertura* and those insisting on the permanence (or immobilism) of
Francoist structures. However, the Organic Law of 1967 enshrined the rule
of the dictatorship, its reliance on organic democracy and the confessional
nature of the state. The nomination in 1969 of Prince Juan Carlos as Franco's
heir and the future king did not resolve these ambiguities which were only
temporarily reconciled by the unity of support for Franco.

One of the most repeated claims to the legitimacy of the regime was that
it had brought social peace to a country previously torn by bitter conflict.
This claim was increasingly tested by the rising level of agitation after 1970,
whose main protagonists were striking workers, ETA activists, university
students, Catalanists and a progressively critical independent press. The
challenge of the regime culminated in the spectacular assassination by ETA
at the end of 1973 of the recently nominated Prime Minister Luis Carrero
Blanco. His replacement, shortly afterwards, by another old hard-liner, Arias
Navarro, led to a shallow attempt to open up the regime to political
associations which was blocked by the Francoist right, soon nicknamed 'the
Bunker' by the oppositionists. Instead of *apertura*, the regime resorted to
repression, including the execution of anti-Francoist terrorists and the use of
martial law to quell strikes.

The inability of the regime to open up in response to a changing society
culminated in the crisis of 1974–75 when protest became widespread across
the country. Franco's illness, which ended in his death in November 1975,
was symbolic of the terminal decline of his regime. The speed of the demise
of the dictatorship after Franco's death was a measure both of its alienation
from a society transformed by modernization and of the strength of forces
for political change.

|18|

Towards a new moral order
National Catholicism, culture and gender

MARY NASH*

National Catholicism, together with national syndicalism and the military, were the pillars of Franco's authoritarian regime which came out of the Civil War of 1936–39. Initially, the single official party, the Falange, formulated a view of 'national syndicalism' that attempted to give a fascist mode to the political dictatorship based on a corporativism whose spine was a 'vertical' compulsory syndicate of workers and employers. The decline of the Falangist character of the regime in the early forties and the growing exclusion of Falange leaders from political power led to a weakening of Francoism's more fascist components, particularly with the changes in international politics by the end of the Second World War.

In contrast, National Catholicism was the unchanging foundation of the political order reigning in Spain between 1939 and 1975. National Catholicism can be defined as a Spanish essentialism based on Catholicism. On this view, the country had reached the peak of its greatness and power in the sixteenth and seventeenth centuries, when both its internal and foreign policies were geared to the defence of Catholicism against Protestantism and Islam. This theocratic vision at first provided the regime with ideological legitimacy and cultural cohesion; later it provided political ideals. The construction of a new moral and cultural order was a crucial goal of the triumphant Nationalists, ·who sought to discredit the democracy they had defeated by claiming that the Second Republic was a repository of both political and cultural decadence. Gender and cultural factors played a prominent role in this defamatory account which attributed the moral degeneracy of the democratic regime to changes in traditional cultural and religious values, increased secularization and the spread of irreligiosity, the emancipation and changing status of women and the degradation of the family.

* I am obliged to my research assistant Javier Florensa.

Church and State: a mutually beneficial relationship

From the very beginning of the Civil War, the political support of the Catholic Church played a definitive role in the articulation of the Francoist dictatorship. Franco combined the task of 'National Reconstruction' with that of 'Catholic Reconstruction' while the Church hierarchy backed the fundamental agenda of the new political system. The strong Catholic component of the political–military system of the dictatorship was an overriding feature of the 40 years of the Franco regime, quite different from German national socialism and Italian fascism. The political collaboration of the majority of the Church hierarchy lasted until the decline of the Franco regime and the development of political opposition among some dissident, progressive catholics in the late 1960s. By then some members of the catholic social and labour movements such as the Hermandad Obrera de Acción Católica (HOAC) expressed open opposition to the dictatorship, while progressive priests offered Church spaces as forums for the wider political opposition movement to Franco.

The relations between Church and State took the form of a symbiosis in which the hierarchy gave its imprimatur to a regime which, in turn, created a confessional, Catholic state that placed the absolute defence of Christian values and morals as a key agenda. National Catholicism became the guiding feature that united the interests of the *Patria* and Religion. Although during the Civil War some members of the Church hierarchy such as Catalan Cardinal Vidal y Barraquer opposed the repressive policies of the Francoists, the new dictatorship was, from the beginning, seen by the Church as an effective mechanism to achieve the re-evangelization of decadent Spanish society. For its part, the Vatican conceded significant privileges to the *Caudillo*, such as the right to name candidates to bishoprics (1941) and the blessing of his regime as the perfect model of a Catholic polity This mutually beneficial relationship took concrete form in the 1953 Concordat. This recognized Apostolic Roman Catholicism as the religion of the state and provided significant economic concessions to the Church. In addition, the teaching of religion and control of the educational system were guaranteed as its prerogative, and the Church was allowed to maintain its own, independent, press and radio network.

The Church also promoted the presence of Catholics in the political arena. The notion of the fusion of interests between Church and State was clearly voiced at an early date by Cardinal Gomá when he proclaimed that 'Ecclesiastical hierarchy, civil hierarchy and Christian people, all united by charity and love, constitute this member of the Mystical Body of Christ called Spain'. And, prominent Catholic politicians such as Alberto Martín Artajo, Minister of Foreign Affairs in 1945, contended that service to God, *Patria* and Church were one and the same, thus espousing the view of the identical interests between Church and State. National Catholicism as an ideology systematically promoted the idea of the identity between the 'essence' of Spanish nationality and catholicism.

National Catholicism was the instrument intended to provide stability and unity through the restoration of a common religious identity in the context of fractured post-war Spain. This goal of returning to Baroque Christianity based on pastoral action and Church politics was divided, none the less, on the issue of the need for a theocratic agenda that subordinated political interests to those of the Church or that of a clearer separation between Church and State with mutual collaboration between both institutions. Of course, Franco's agenda clearly defined National Catholicism as a political instrument geared towards the enhancement of the goals of his regime. These differences in the agenda of Church and State led to some manifestations of tension during the long period of the dictatorship. However, until the late 1960s, collaboration between both led to the effective consolidation of National Catholicism as the backbone of the Franco regime.

Religion and cultural values

The Catholic dimension of the Franco regime went beyond mere political support from the Church. National Catholicism espoused the crusade for moral regeneration, the recuperation of Christian ideals and the restoration of the traditional family as the primary social unit of Spanish society.

The recuperation of the authentic Spanish Catholic past and its values were significant features in state policies driven by the need to undermine all the cultural and social advances of the Second Republic. Francoist discourse was not innovative. It drew on two distinct but related sources: 1) traditional, 'integrist' Catholic ideas, the reactionary, anti-modern attitude born as a response to the French Revolution and which culminated with Pope Pius IX's 'Syllabus of Errors' (1864) and 2) the indigenous, Spanish counter-revolutionary tradition of 'Throne and Altar' embodied in Carlism and, on a more elevated intellectual plane, the thinking of Marcelino Mendez Pelayo. To these two traditions, fascism and the experience of civil war added their own touches. The new cultural code that was applied after 1939 was articulated on the basis of exclusion, not reconciliation. National Catholicism conflated religious with moral values and cultural norms, and all aspects of Spanish life were made subject to this all-encompassing cosmovision. The result was an implacable moral order that made everything subordinate to the needs of God and the Fatherland.

National Catholicism was the vehicle for cultural and political indoctrination from childhood to adulthood. The Church-controlled school system guaranteed the dissemination of Catholic doctrine. According to law, teaching was based on Catholic doctrine, while of course, religion was an obligatory subject. Not only Catholic dogma, but also religious imagery, iconography and rituals shaped the education, culture and cosmovision of all Spaniards throughout their life. The Church had thus succeeded in reversing the liberal revolution of the 1830s and 1840s. José Pemartín, one of the leading ideologues of National Catholicism, openly spoke of the effectiveness in harnessing popular Church cults to political interests: 'Think of our ... Cult, the most magnificent and marvellous on earth; our processions and pilgrimages, fiestas, saints' celebrations, May stations and splendid processions at Corpus, Holy Week; think of fascist Spain, the State has to live ... much more intensely with all the people.' Franco himself made maximum use of religious rituals and imagery, such as the recurrence to the famous arm of Saint Theresa of Avila to enforce his image of authority and divine legitimacy.

The disappearance of significant cultural elites of the 1930s produced a rupture with the flourishing cultural world of the Second Republic. The systematic condemnation and censorship of the cultural traditions of the 1930s gave way to a barren landscape that the creation of new institutions such as the Instituto de Estudios Políticos, the Instituto Nacional del Libro and, above all, the Opus Dei-controlled Consejo Superior de Investigaciones Científicas did little to improve. Until the early 1960s Spain lived in a void imposed by a fierce censorship that impeded access to European cultural trends.

In an inquisitorial fashion, the censors of State Security examined books for manifestations of attacks not just against the political regime and its institutions but also for any challenge to Catholic dogma, morals, or the clergy. Although criteria for censorship were vague and changing, they covered a wide range of political, religious and moral views. Political censorship could range from the prohibition of mentioning football players of the Republican period to the suppression of all political and cultural references to the democratic Republic. Moral and religious criteria were more diffuse although intertwined. Any challenge to the Catholic Church, ecclesiastical hierarchy or religious institutions as the depository of human and divine values was immediately banned.

Much of the censors' energies were devoted to erasing references to sexual morals that challenged the prudery and modesty central to the prescribed codes of moral conduct. Indecorous language disrespectful of traditional standards was also eliminated. Traditional moral values also led censors, for instance, to bowdlerize US movies, turning lovers into husbands or girlfriends into wives and generally providing filmgoers and readers with a stultifying prudishness that permeated Spanish society. Writers practised self censorship in order to avoid official prohibition of the publication of their works. The 1964 Press Law provided a more lenient mode of censorship by suppressing the mandatory consultation of all works by the censor board prior to publication except in some specific cases, leaving it up to the initiative of publishers and writers to censor books proactively.

The cinema was also an important instrument of propaganda. In the decade or so after the Civil War, Francoist film makers developed five basic genres: historical, religious, heroic, folkloric and documentary films. Historical and religious productions, such as *Alba de América, La Leona de Castilla* and *La Reina Santa,* among many others, evoked a triumphant, imperial past with a strong Catholic identity. The more recent triumph of the Civil War was glorified in films such as *Raza* (1941) for which Franco himself wrote the screenplay under a pseudonym, and Spanish–Italian co-productions such as *Frente de Madrid* and *Sin Novedad en el Alcázar.* In 1942 it became mandatory to project NO-DO, documentaries exalting Franco and the regime, before films shown in all cinemas. This practice continued until a year after Franco's death.

As early as 1938 film censorship was established under the Ministry of the Interior. Distributors were obliged to present all films for prior control before being shown at the cinemas. In 1944 *Casablanca* was banned on the alleged grounds that it discredited several countries at war, while in later years films such as Fellini's *La dolce vita* (1959) and Ferreri's *La Grande Bouffe* (1974) were also banned as immoral. However, by the 1970s, hundreds of Spaniards were crossing the French border to view the forbidden films in the cinemas of Perpignan and, after the Revolution of April 1974, in those of Lisbon.

The 1960s brought changing cultural dynamics, an air of greater freedom that was, however, often an illusion, and a number of cultural changes with respect to the early years of the regime. Changing government policies leading to economic development ended the extreme cultural isolation of the country and wider concessions in cultural policies. Manuel Fraga Iribarne became Minister of Information and Tourism, charged with initiating the liberalization of the regime in the cultural arena, and laws he sponsored gradually gave rise to the publication of books hitherto banned, to greater tolerance in the projection of films and to a lesser degree of censorship in the press.

Spanish society slowly became more permeable to European and North American cultural developments. Economic development, mass tourism and greater cultural tolerance provided a contrast to the traditional cultural paradigms of National Catholicism. Although the clergy warned about the damaging moral effects of such international encounters, Spanish men and women avidly consumed films from Hollywood without necessarily challenging the political basis of the regime. The culture of evasion promoted by official institutions combined traditional leisure outlets such as bullfighting with more modern mass media venues such as radio series, football and later, television. Despite greater tolerance and a weakening of the brutal repression of earlier years, the new cultural messages did not provide a critique of the regime. The generalization of the culture of evasion played a significant role in the political demobilization of opposition to the dictatorship while hiding the continuity of ideological control and repressive policies. In the 1960s and early 1970s the austerity and abstinence of post-war Spain gave way to greater consumption, changing values and cultural demands, in a society experiencing economic development and international integration.

Race, religion and language: markers of a cultural identity

Francoism shared with fascist regimes at least one significant rhetorical feature: the importance it attributed to race and the imperial past. All this was epitomized in a single word: *Hispanidad*, the idea that there existed a world much larger than Spain itself defined by Spanish language, culture and values. This world included the former colonies, especially in America, where it confronted the immense power of 'Anglo-Saxon', Protestant, materialist culture.

Writing in 1944 in the semi-official *Revista Internacional de Sociología*, the demographer Javier Ruiz Almansa emphasized that cultural imperialism through the elaboration of a universal Hispanic culture in Latin America and North Africa would be a major contribution to the civilization of the West. In the falangist years of the regime, the discourse of *Hispanidad* espoused utopian ambitions that went beyond the boundaries of national interests and attempted to recover for Spain a role in international politics. This was expressed in an imperialistic rhetoric that evoked the greatness of sixteenth century Spain. Of course, given the feebleness of Franco's Spain, such ambitions were nothing more than vain illusions, and they were abandoned after 1945.

As insignificant as they were in terms of actual foreign policy, domestically these references to race and empire were decisive. The Francoist construction of national identity required the establishment of cultural markers which excluded the 'anti-Spain', the 'un-Spanish other'. Above all else, Spanish identity was constructed around cultural identity, the Castilian language, culture and traditions. This cultural representation provided a symbolic foundational myth for Spanish society that not only differentiated Catholic Apostolic Spain from the religious decadence of the other beyond its borders, but also provided the internal differential markers of the Castilian language and cultural traditions that excluded the internal others: laic or 'un-Christian' Spain, freemasons, Catalans and Basques, from the national community.

Even when Francoist rhetoric included references to race, it understood this word in cultural rather than biological terms and did not propose eugenics policies. The weight of the Roman Catholic Church and the ideology of National Catholicism impeded the development of a racial discourse based on biological differentiation. The common religious and cultural identity of the Spanish race called on models of Saints of the *Reconquista* and baroque imperialism to guide the path of Spain through the development of a unitary Spanish identity that would annul any regional or national differences. The unity of Spain had already been established in the sixth century, with the 'conversion' of Reccared to Catholicism, and confirmed through the reconquest of the country from the Muslims beginning in the eighth century and the expulsion of the Muslims and Jews in the sixteenth century.

Franco's racial discourse was culturally construed as an integratory centralist model that attempted to annul regional differences which had developed during the Republic with the creation of autonomous governments in Catalonia and the Basque Country. Language and culture were thus key features in establishing the markers of the Spanish race. Franco resorted to a unitary model of Spain which would weaken nationalist traditions in Catalonia and the Basque Country while providing an authentic Spanish culture and identity based on Castilian traditions, language and culture. Of course, this unitary scheme was grounded on a systematic repression of nationalist identity and culture in Catalonia and the Basque Country.

This explains why, together with the opposition of the labour and student movements, nationalist protests were a significant feature of the anti-Franco movement which began in the late 1950s. The defence of the Catalan language and cultural traditions against the imposition of the 'language of the Empire' – Spanish – and the demand for the recuperation of political autonomy were significant features of the democratic resistance movement for political freedom in Catalonia. Similar demands were also expressed in the Basque Country; however, after the foundation of ETA *Euskadi ta Askatasuna* (Basque Country and Freedom) in 1959, recourse to violence together with pacific resistance characterized the strategies adopted by the Basque opposition movement. Cultural resistance in both regions played a crucial role in the opposition to the dictatorship in the 1960s and early 1970s.

Gender identities and the Sección Femenina

The codification of new gender identities was another cornerstone in the construction of the 'New Spain'. In the post-war years male gender models were those of outstanding soldiers and fighters, exceptional figures that transcended daily life. The image of the warrior-monk shaped around a combination of *conquistador* and the founder of the Jesuits, Saint Ignatius de Loyola, and combining courage, virility, religiosity and military values, became the prototype of role models for young Spanish males.

In contrast, gender identity for women was constructed very differently. The dictatorship reversed the egalitarian principles and progressive legislation of the Republic and endorsed the traditional view of the Catholic Church that proclaimed women's sacred duty to motherhood and family. Turn of the century gender and religious discourses were recuperated to reinforce gender role models for women as mothers and housewives as the regime urged women to submission, docility, and unquestioning obedience to the traditional tenets of domesticity.

Vigorous defence of the family was a also a primary goal of the·Franco state, as well as a key to maintaining women in a subordinate status. National Catholicism reestablished a highly structured patriarchal family that redefined the role of women as the traditional *perfecta casada*, the perfect married lady, submissive spouse and mother lovingly devoted to the needs of husband, children and home. Women's primary social function was motherhood, hence their aspirations to work, education and self-betterment, social activity or emancipation were rejected as a threat to their biological destiny as breeders of the nation's future generations. Women could only be politicized by the notion of fulfilling a common female destiny based on their reproductive function. As Pilar Primo de Rivera, leader of the Sección Femenina, the official Francoist women's organization stressed, women's inevitable and total destiny was maternity, a mandate she qualified as 'a biological, Christian and Spanish function'.

As conscription and military service provided a framework for inculcating the codes of the new regime in young men, the obligatory social service training for all women under the Sección Femenina provided preparation and indoctrination for young adult women. Originally created in 1934 and run by Pilar Primo de Rivera, sister of the Falange's founder, Jose Antonio, the leaders of the Sección Femenina broke, in practice, with the norms of domesticity as many were not married and were active in the public arena, albeit in subordinate roles. However, the Sección Femenina attempted to indoctrinate and mould all young Spanish women to accept their role as 'angels of the home' and motherhood as their primary social function. Although women were permitted to be educated, the system transmitted differential educational gender models that socialized girls in the virtues of docility, submission, and self-sacrifice.

Despite growing from 56152 members in 1940 to 490155 in 1949, the Sección Femenina never achieved membership levels comparable to those of women's movements in Nazi Germany or Fascist Italy. In 1969, it claimed to have some 400000 members and run a vast range of cultural, educational and training programmes across the country. Its 400 training centres taught 95000 women each year, and it also ran 32 nursery schools and some 650 cultural circles which provided activities such as music, drama and library services. It also had 62 Cátedras Ambulantes, peripatetic instructors, who provided rural women with educational, cultural and home economics programmes. Sección Femenina propaganda was also transmitted through the media: radio, films and publications such as *Teresa*, *Consigna* and *Bazar*, each directed at different age groups.

The gains of suffrage, political rights and the social achievements for women under the Second Republic were systematically obliterated. Given the prevalence of the idea that it had been precisely women's aspirations to social advancement, female emancipation and economic independence that had been crucial in drawing women away from their natural biological mandate of reproduction, many propagandists advocated restrictions on female access to work outside the home. In an attempt to increase the number of children among working families, numerous policies were developed to dissuade women from such work expectations. In 1938 the Fuero del Trabajo (Labour Charter), the major legal statement on work, declared that the State 'will free married women from the workshop and the factory'. This norm was strictly applied in state and para-state firms, and somewhat less rigidly in other sectors, with the aim of excluding married women from the labour market. In the 1960s, economic development required the presence of female workers in the labour market, thus leading to a revision of existing legislation that provided women with greater access to waged work. In July 1961 the law on 'Political, Professional and Labour Rights of Women' recognized equal rights between men and women in political activities, professions and work. Although an advance over existing legislation, it was couched in a rhetoric that stressed an ancillary role for women in the family economy. It also established some professions, such as the judiciary, as off-limits to women. Moreover, despite the recognition of the principle of equal pay for jobs of equal value, acute wage discrimination continued and occupational segmentation was a significant characteristic of the female labour force. Discriminatory labour practices against women were not officially eliminated until the 1976 Law on Labour Relations.

Family and home: the expansion of the race

The state played a decisive role in the rehabilitation of the family and accorded it a central place in its social construction of a new Spain. The revitalization of the Christian family was considered essential for population growth and the re-evangelization of Spain. The family was the primary unit of society, a basic cell in the body politic of the state and the Christian community. Some racial hygienists such as A. Vallejo Najera also claimed that the goal of the New Spain was the creation of a super talented Spanish race. One of the major legal statements of the New State, the Fuero de los Españoles, declared that the family was a natural institution with specific prerogatives and rights which went beyond the boundaries of human law. The status of the family as the prime unit of social organization was complemented in the Fuero by a declaration of the indissolubility of marriage. In March 1938 a law abolished the 1932 Republican Law on Civil Matrimony while the 1932 Divorce Law was repealed in September 1939, leaving many marriages that had been contracted during the Republic open to legal contestation.

Women were particularly affected by the new family legislation, for not only did it imply the advocacy of a stable Catholic family but also the reconsolidation of a patriarchal family unit where women held a subordinate position. Family legislation starkly confirmed male superiority, the wife's dependence and her loss of legal authority over their children, measures which lasted for the forty years of the Franco dictatorship. Many of these measures were not original but reverted to the 1889 Civil Code in force until the introduction of egalitarian legislative reforms during the Second Republic.

In the 1940s and early 1950s pronatalist policies were another significant feature of the Franco regime. Pronatalist thought generated a view of women basically as mothers or potential mothers. Women were politicized through the notion of a common female destiny based on their reproductive capacities. Female sexuality, work and education were regulated in accordance with this social function, while motherhood was idealized and considered as a duty to the Fatherland. Franco associated national power with the numerical superiority of a growing population that would eventfully lead to the empowerment of Spain in international politics. Pronatalist policies had a clear political reading as an essential mechanism towards providing a vital population growth that would ensure Spain as a powerful nation. In the postwar period the spectre of population decline became a major concern because of war deaths but more significantly because of the growing obsession by demographers and sociologists with declining birth rates in earlier decades.

Rejected in a rhetoric that chastised the moral decadence of the Republican period, birth control was repudiated: in 1947 the Catholic ideologue Severino Aznar denounced it as the 'leprosy of neomalthusianism'. The state moved energetically to criminalize abortion and the use or advertising of contraceptives. The preamble to the Abortion Law of January 1941 raised voluntary abortion to the rank of 'a social crime ... which prevents many thousands of Spaniards from being born annually'. Abortion went against the social interests of the state whose duty was to preserve and conserve the race and thus all potential population. For the same reasons the Abortion Law also made it a crime to advertise or sell contraceptives.

The Abortion Law was very comprehensive in its stiff criminalization of all those who either performed abortions or provided contraceptives. Gender differentiation was present in the penalization of abortion as the women involved were given somewhat more lenient sentences, although they, too, were sentenced to imprisonment. The acceptance of the double standard in sexual behaviour was implicit in the Abortion Law insofar as it contemplated greater leniency if an abortion had been performed in order to avoid the 'dishonour' of the woman, a circumstance that had been admitted in former Penal Codes. The greater admissibility of an abortion in the case of a non-married woman is significant in the context of a rigid gender code that saw the legitimization of women's natural biological destiny exclusively within the institutions of the family and religious marriage. Sexual behaviour which deviated from the norm was not admitted and indeed many of the propagandists of the 'National Revolution' saw themselves as moral regenerators engaged in the purification of public morality.

Other policies sought to encourage couples to have more children. Various measures provided for family allowances, *premios de natalidad* (birth prizes) and certain concessions for specially large families, the *familias numerosas* which were offered specific protection and were often evoked as models to be followed. In 1943 large families were defined in two categories: from four to seven children in the first category and of eight children or more in the second, with an honorary category of 12 members or more. Members of large families were allowed numerous fringe benefits graded according to their category. These ranged from transport and school grants to tax exemptions, credit facilities, access to housing and sanitary assistance. Family allowances in July 1938 and family bonuses in June 1945 affected a much wider section of the population. Both represented a clear support of paternity through income supplements. Family allowances were conceived as a supplement paid directly to the male breadwinner and they reinforced the figure of the *jefe de familia*, the male head of the family, the patriarchal figure who was to be linked with the authoritarian figure of the *Caudillo* and Head of State, Franco. The annual concession of prizes to the *familias numerosas* in the different provinces of Spain (ranging usually from over 14 children) on Saint Joseph's Day (19 March) came to form part of the propagandist ritual attached to the figure of Franco even when pronatalism was no longer a major official policy.

Despite this concerted drive, the regime did not realize its demographic goals. Unlike other immediate post-war periods in other countries, there was not a 'baby boom' in Spain in the 1940s. The general rhythm of population growth was maintained because the decline in infant mortality exceeded the steady decline of birthrates in the first decade of the regime. Family survival in the harsh circumstances of rationing, scarcity, unemployment, housing problems, deficient sanitary services, severe economic difficulties and relentless repression led women to ignore pronatalist urgings and resort to home remedies, quacks, doctors or midwives in order to abort when methods of birth control failed. Demographic patterns did not start to change until the mid-1950s. Population growth occurred when the dictatorship had long desisted in its pronatalist policies. The growing economic development in the 1960s achieved what repressive policies were unable to do. Greater prosperity and wider economic expectations for the Spanish people led to changing patterns in birthrates and, ultimately, to an increase in the population.

Conclusion

The Franco regime's discourse of order, religion and family was nothing new, and it resonated with many Spanish women, especially in rural areas and small towns, where conservative traditions and connection to the

Church remained strong. The regime did break new ground, however, in attempting to use a 'modern' institution, the Sección Femenina, to spread its view of what constituted proper womanhood.

Despite all the repressive legislation and systematic indoctrination by the Sección Femenina, many Spanish women refused to behave as they were told. They were active agents in the resistance movement against Franco, in trade unions, student organizations, community associations, feminist organizations, political, cultural and nationalist groups. They fought for political rights and freedom and challenged the cultural values of the 40 years of dictatorship. In the process, they also pursued a feminist reawakening that linked democratic rights and culture with women's emancipation.

THE DEMOCRATIC
MONARCHY, 1975–1996

In many ways, the period that followed the death of Francisco Franco in November 1975 was the most amazing of all. Franco and his supporters had bet the future on a combination of economic development and political immobilism, but as the dictator endured his long death agony its success was very much an open question. Spain was hit hard by the international economic crisis that began in 1974, and strikes, student demonstrations and terrorist violence became ever more prominent parts of the landscape. At the same time, the institutions of the regime, and especially the armed forces, remained solid, and the dictator's hand-picked successor, Prince Juan Carlos, assumed his place as Head of State immediately. What happened next surprised everyone.

Less than a year after the dictator's death, the Francoist Cortes effectively committed suicide by passing a Law of Political Reform that proclaimed popular sovereignty and called for democratic elections. Eight months after that Spaniards voted in free democratic elections which included even Franco's *bete noire*, the Communist Party. A year and a half later, they overwhelmingly approved the democratic Constitution of 1978 which, among other things, opened the door to widespread regional autonomy. The approval of the Constitution ended the period of political consensus. The years that followed were marked by the collapse of the governing party, UCD, an attempted military coup and, in October 1982, the massive electoral victory of the Socialist Party, an event that marked the full consolidation of the democratic monarchy.

Paloma Aguilar describes and analyses Spain's transition to democracy in her chapter. She emphasizes that the transition occurred in an improvised way, without any preconceived plan, and that its successful outcome was very much the product of negotiation between a government seeking reform and an opposition determined to return the country to democracy. And while both the internal and international circumstances were more favourable than those which had faced the Republic in the 1930s, there were serious obstacles, especially Basque terrorism and the attitude of the army.

Given Spain's long history as a highly centralist state, perhaps the most striking feature of the Constitution of 1978 was its recognition of the 'historic nationalities' in Galicia, the Basque Country and Catalonia and its extension of autonomy to the country as a whole. Where the Second Republic created only two autonomous regions, the democratic monarchy has created a quasi-federal 'State of the Autonomies' with 17. How this happened and what it has meant for Spain's subsequent political life are the subjects of the chapter by Xosé M. Núñez Seixas. Regional nationalisms are more numerous and stronger than ever before, but even in Catalonia and Euskadi most people combine this with self-identification as Spanish in a form of 'dual patriotism'. As individuals balance these two identities, the political system is the site of an open-ended and ongoing negotiation between national and regional governments that makes the 'state of the autonomies' a perpetual work in progress.

The Socialist Party came to power in 1982 with an absolute majority and amidst great popular expectation. They won three more elections: 1986, 1989 and 1993, each time with fewer votes and the last time without a parliamentary majority, before finally – and barely – losing to the conservative Partido Popular in 1996. Santos Juliá assesses this 'Socialist era' in the final chapter of the book. During 13 years in power, Felipe González's governments achieved much, especially eliminating the spectre of military coups, modernizing the nation's infrastructure and taking Spain into the European Union. At the same time, there were significant failures, such as the intractable problem of massive unemployment and the lengthening list of scandals that marked their last years in office. Success and failure, 'light and darkness' is how Juliá characterizes the record of the Socialists, while warning that it is far too early to consider such an assessment anything but provisional. The Socialist era ended in March 1996, when the conservative Partido Popular narrowly defeated the PSOE in a national election and came to power as a minority government supported by Basque and Catalan nationalists.

|19|

The opposition to Franco, the transition to democracy and the new political system

PALOMA AGUILAR

The behaviour of the political and social actors in the first years of democracy in Spain, and especially the policy of agreement and consensus that marked the transition, can only be understood against the backdrop of the major activities undertaken by the various groups within the opposition to Franco. These opposition forces emerged and evolved slowly and with great difficulty. This is not surprising when we recall that the dictatorship was based on total victory in a civil war and that its opponents had either gone into exile, especially in France and Mexico, or had been the objects of an intensive repression that had liquidated any trace of organized dissidence.

Forces of opposition

The opposition that was based outside the country never managed to act with much unity or coherence. The combination of their scant resources and the minimal cooperation they received from certain countries and international organizations, resulted in their failing to realize their primordial goal: the overthrow of the Franco regime. In addition, the rift which, over time, emerged between the nascent internal opposition and its counterpart outside the country proved an obstacle to coordinating the two fronts of the struggle.

While the exhaustiveness of the regime's persecution of the forces that defended the defunct Second Republic made the task of the political opposition enormously difficult, there can be no doubt that the confrontations and divisions among those forces also contributed to their fragility. The tensions produced during the years of the Republic and the Civil War both among and within the parties and unions only deepened during the first years after the war. There were mutual accusations of having destabilized the Republic, of having lost the war and, as a consequence, of being responsible for the dictatorship. All this explains why the Communists remained isolated from the rest of the opposition until the 1960s.

The first attempts to overthrow, or at least destabilize, the regime from without came from a number of isolated guerrilla groups, known as the *maquis*, who took to the mountains after having carried out attacks of varying magnitude against the security forces. Most of the *maquis* were organized by the Communist Party (PCE), which sent them across the French border throughout the 1940s. Their activities lacked both coordination and resources, and given the fear of reprisals they did not receive the logistical support they needed from nearby villages. *Maquis* activity was all but non-existent by the end of the 1940s and a few years later the PCE decided to end its strategy of trying to overthrow the regime by armed struggle.

One of Francoism's principal characteristics was its ability to adapt itself to changing circumstances, the most concrete example being its extraordinary skill in taking advantage of the Cold War climate that dominated the United States and Europe. But it was not this external context alone that impelled the regime to introduce institutional changes; the catastrophe produced by its own economic policies was equally compelling. Thus, after a period of international isolation, economic autarky and severe political repression, the regime altered its approach. And once it began to relax its repression, albeit slowly and irregularly, during the 1950s and undertake some political liberalization in the 1960s, various protest movements began to emerge. At first these were sporadic and uncoordinated, but with time they became capable of carrying out organized collective actions with some regularity.

These first protests were basically economic, usually demanding specific workplace measures or protesting against the high cost of living. For example, in 1951 an increase in fares produced important public transport strikes in Madrid and Barcelona. Even though such actions did not threaten the regime's survival, its intransigence in responding to them facilitated the transformation of merely economic demands into political protests. On a number of occasions this process began with collective requests to have workers who had been fired for taking part in illegal protests restored to their jobs. Labour amnesties quickly became a clearly political issue accompanied by demands for various other rights.

These labour conflicts were closely connected to protests by students, and both labour and student leaders frequently belonged to clandestine opposition parties. The first important student protests took place in 1956 and were largely the result of a new generation of students who had not participated in the Civil War, a significant number of whom had been socialized in values distinct from those promoted by the regime. These discordant influences came in part from their families and in part from having attended schools which had taught them tolerance and respect for pluralism. That Francoism was authoritarian but not totalitarian made possible this transmission of alternative values in the private sphere, whose spread would have an increasing impact on public life. Finally, this generation's contact with more liberally-minded professors, a number of whom had sympathized with the Falange, who made available to them books that were persecuted by Franco-ist orthodoxy, helps explain the climate that developed in a number of Spanish universities in the mid-1950s. From that point on, the opposition to the dictatorship began to organize, slowly but continuously.

The rapid economic growth and subsequent social transformations also brought notable changes to Spanish society [see chapter 17]. Moreover, as the regime enjoyed increasing foreign recognition and began to open up, Spain became the destination not only for tourists but also for books and periodicals that brought new ideas. At the same time, Spaniards had greater opportunity to travel abroad. The regime had attempted to isolate Spain from foreign influences, but this was no longer possible. Some of the changes were reflected in new cultural productions, especially in literature and cinema, which, in turn, helped create an atmosphere ever more suited to the development of democratic values. This is not to say, however, that this process of economic, social and cultural modernization prevented the survival among some sectors of the population of the regime's authoritarian values. While surveys showed that some Spaniards valued the maintenance of peace and order above all, an ever increasing number sought more democratic values such as liberty and justice. The struggle between authoritarian and democratic culture lasted until the transition, and only with the arrival of democracy did the latter defeat the former. The authoritarian mentality did live on, albeit in a dwindling percentage of the population.

Rebuilding a civil society dismembered by a devastating war and a brutal dictatorship was a slow and difficult process which began with the emergence of small bubbles of liberty that began to develop on the margins of the regime. Workers and students made themselves heard in 1962, and from then until repression was stepped up in 1969 they staged intermittent acts of public protest. Both adopted the strategy of infiltrating the official institutions of the regime, the Spanish Union of University Students (SEU) and the vertical unions of the Organización Sindical (OS). In this way, clandestine political groups progressively took control of much of the labour and student movements.

Workers and students were not the only ones who had begun to challenge the regime. There were even groups which had initially supported the Nationalist uprising and the dictatorship but who quickly felt themselves cheated and became critical of the regime. There were the monarchists, some of whom had been sent to Munich in 1962 to meet with the opposition in exile. This meeting was a turning point in the history of the opposition to Franco: for the first time the opposition and 'semi-opposition' within the country talked and were even prepared to make significant agreements with the exiles, who little more than 20 years earlier had been their enemy on the battlefield.

Dissident voices also began to emerge within the Catholic Church. This process of distancing itself from the regime had been proceeding for a number of years, but the celebration of the Second Vatican Council in 1964–65 brought it to the surface. From that point on the Church began to defend religious liberty and its separation from the State, a development which was deeply upsetting to certain sectors of the regime and to Franco personally. It is important to note that significant numbers of young priests had long been in contact with the socially marginalized in the outlying districts of the large cities where they had their parishes. This first-hand experience of social reality, along with their belonging to a new generation, made these priests open to political militancy and solidarity with the political parties and neighbourhood organizations that undertook collective protests during the 1970s.

Meanwhile, the clandestine parties had begun to reorganize, lead a range of protests and become visible in the daily lives of Spaniards. The most important were the Communists, who dominated the clandestine union Comisiones Obreras (CCOO) and the Socialists, but until the 1970s they remained internally divided and at loggerheads with each other. In 1975, the year of Franco's death, the main opposition forces were divided into two large coalitions: the Junta Democrática led by the PCE and the Plataforma para la Convergencia Democrática led by the PSOE. It was only in March 1976 that they came together in the Coordinación Democrática, and this gave them greater influence and visibility in negotiating with the government. For their part, in July 1976 the unions also created a single organization, the Coordinadora de Fuerzas Sindicales, although the anarchosyndicalist CNT, now much less significant than it had been in the 1930s, chose not to join.

A final focus of opposition were the nationalist organizations in Catalonia and the Basque Provinces, frequently supported by leading local figures in the Catholic Church [see chapter 20].

The transition

Franco died in November 1975, and the mechanisms which he himself had put in place to secure the succession did their job. Only two days after Franco's death Juan Carlos was crowned king. The new monarch gave a speech whose ambiguity bothered many: stating his loyalty to the Ancien Regime while seeming to leave open the possibility of bringing into political life groups which had been excluded from it since 1939. His insistence on being 'the king of all the Spaniards' was interpreted by reformers within the regime as a hint to the most moderate part of the democratic opposition, although at the time there was not the slightest suspicion that the process would produce such a solidly democratic outcome. In spite of how it may look from our perspective, and in spite of how some political personalities self-interestedly want it to appear, the transition was strewn with difficulties and uncertainties. Far from there being a preconceived plan, the path was full of improvisation.

The first weeks, and even months, were marked by the institutional inertia of Francoism. It is undeniable that the ideological influence of the regime was considerably diminished and that a majority of the population wanted Spain to enjoy a political system like those in the advanced countries of Europe. At the same time, the administrative structure built during the dictatorship was very solid, especially as it had long favoured professionalism over ideological purity. On the other hand, the majority of the population, made wary by the traumatic experience of the Civil War, did not seem disposed to have the coming changes made in a radical way that might threaten their much-appreciated stability. If democracy were to finally come to Spain, it could not arrive in any old way, since the vague threat of a military coup hung over any transition that was not sufficiently gradual. Pieces of the old system that were incompatible with the new had to be replaced with extreme caution so that those who retained political power and the security forces would not feel threatened and thus obliged to intervene.

The formal process of change was initiated from within the regime, by members of the political elite who, in spite of having held high office, saw the need of reaching an agreement with the democratic opposition and containing the displeasure that such negotiations would inevitably produce in the most conservative sectors of the regime. In a climate of significant popular mobilization, the government had no choice but to enter into conversation with the opposition parties, even when that mobilization was not supported by the most representative part of the opposition. But it was not only the pressure from this long series of strikes and demonstrations which explains the government's desire to take the country down the road of modernization or to negotiate with the opposition. We must remember that this was the only sensible approach if Spain were ever to become part of the European Community. In any case, the government had to bring to an end this mobilization which not only irritated the security forces but also created an atmosphere of profound instability that was not the least advisable during the deep economic downturn triggered by the 1973 oil crisis.

Franco's last prime minister, Carlos Arias Navarro, and his cabinet, all remained in office after the dictator's death. The king confirmed Arias in his position on 4 December and the next week he appointed a new cabinet which included a number of reformers such as Manuel Fraga, José María de Areilza and Antonio Garrigues. They immediately had to deal with an unprecedented wave of strikes and demonstrations. The police intervened with their usual brutality, causing numerous injuries and some deaths. All this brought into question both the will and the ability of the government to direct the process of change toward a satisfactory outcome. Neither those who wanted to keep the regime unchanged nor the genuinely democratic reformers were happy; the opposition, who were the targets of its repression, even less so.

Opposition political parties remained illegal and the much-desired amnesty of political prisoners had yet to be proclaimed.

Meanwhile, besides demonstrating their capacity to overcome the disagreements that had divided the Spanish left for decades, the leaders of the opposition had provided numerous examples of moderation. After the repression of demonstrations in Vitoria in March 1976 had caused a number of deaths, the opposition created a single front, the Coordinación Democrática. In the months that followed, the unified opposition would successfully convoke a series of demonstrations at which ever larger numbers of people demanded amnesty. The strategy of the new coalition was to achieve a 'democratic rupture', but the conversations between its leaders and members of the government betrayed a dissonance between its frequently radical rhetoric and its moderate actions. In the end, rhetoric would adapt to practice, with the result being the adoption of a new goal: the 'negotiated rupture' (*ruptura pactada*).

For its part, the monarchy made gestures of conciliation to certain sectors of the opposition as well as of tolerance of the historic nationalities. It was highly significant that the first official visit of the king and queen, in February 1976, took them to Catalonia. In June of that year, Juan Carlos made an official visit to the United States where, for the first time, he declared himself in favour of establishing a democracy in Spain and described Arias Navarro's government as 'an unmitigated disaster'. Around the same time, a Law of Associations legalizing political parties, except the PCE, was approved. Two days later, however, the Cortes rejected proposed changes to the Penal Code, thereby gutting the law it had so recently passed. This was further evidence of the government's inability to deal with the pressure from Francoist hardliners, known as the 'bunker'. In this context of political paralysis and popular mobilization the king dismissed Arias Navarro. His replacement was not one of the well-known men whose names had been discussed in the press, but a young Francoist bureaucrat named Adolfo Suárez.

For many, the appointment of Suárez was both irritating and perplexing. The democrats associated him with the Falangist family of Francoism, while the regime's reformers did not believe that he had sufficient political weight to carry out the complex and delicate task before him. Within a few days Suárez named a cabinet marked by the presence of a new generation of reformers, many of whom had experience in the state administration and were close to the Christian Democrats. This new cabinet appeared anodyne to many but it very quickly showed itself to be much more open to democratization than its predecessor. One of its first decisions, taken less than a month after taking office, was to make key changes in the Penal Code and approve an amnesty for political prisoners. Although judged insufficient by some sectors of the opposition, the amnesty was accepted by many as the most generous possible under the circumstances. (The law was extended to include even politically motivated killings in October 1977, after the first democratic elections.)

The new government undertook a dialogue with the leading figures of the opposition, with whom it could deal more easily than with the most recalcitrant sectors of the army and the 'bunker'. Suárez wanted to test the reaction of both sides to a project for political reform that would bring the Francoist regime to an end. The left opposition was prepared to negotiate, but it continued fostering a climate of social mobilization by which it demonstrated both its desire to lead the process of change as well as its refusal to accept a project designed by a government that lacked democratic legitimacy. Nevertheless, the government continued with its plans and drafted the Ley de Reforma Política. Through a combination of pressure and political skill it got the Francoist Cortes to approve the law on 18 November 1976 and thereby dissolve itself. A referendum was held on 15 December and even though much of the opposition called for abstention, the law received massive support – 94.1 per cent of the votes cast with 77.1 per cent of the electorate participating. Among the most significant features of the Law of Political Reform were the recognition of popular sovereignty, the protection of a series of rights and freedoms and the creation of a bicameral legislature to be elected by universal suffrage.

Discussions between the government and the opposition began again immediately after the referendum. The goal was now much more clearly defined: to prepare democratic elections to be held in 1977. Even so, the new year brought uncertainties and complications that would generate serious new tensions. On 24 January a group of right-wing terrorists attacked the Madrid offices of some labour lawyers close to the PCE, killing five people. This brutal episode gave the Communists the opportunity to try out their new moderate rhetoric. The victims' funeral turned into a mass demonstration and marked the first occasion since the Civil War on which a large number of Communists publicly displayed their red flag with the hammer and sickle, but more significant was that the marchers accompanied the caskets in silence instead of shouting slogans. This gesture of moderation was not forgotten by Suárez, who did not delay in rewarding the party.

Throughout February most opposition parties requested registration in the Register of Political Parties. In most cases this was not problematic, but the government had sent the PCE's file to the Supreme Court which in turn sent it back on the grounds that the question was not within its competence. Then on 9 April, in the midst of the Easter holidays, Suárez decided to legalize the PCE if it promised to accept the monarchy and the flag. This decision caused considerable disgust on the right, and especially in the Armed Forces, but in the end the Supreme Council of the Army announced that it would accept the government's decision even though it did not agree with it. The legalization of the Communists removed an important stumbling block and helped to give full democratic legitimacy to the elections held on 15 June 1977, the first since 1936.

A few months earlier the main leaders of the opposition in exile had begun to arrive in Spain. The conflict between the exiles and the internal opposition had been greatest in the Socialist Party, which was divided in two: a 'historic' party, which included the old leaders, and a 'renewed' party led by Felipe González that kept the old name and symbols and managed to absorb most of the small socialist and social democratic parties that had emerged over the years. The PCE also suffered this conflict between the exiles and those inside Spain, although in its case it was the internal leaders who felt marginalized as the leadership of the party went to returning exiles such as Santiago Carrillo and Dolores Ibarruri.

The right organized itself around seven men who were well known because they had held important positions under Franco. As quickly became evident, the democratic convictions of some of them were dubious at best. The internal heterogeneity and the excessive 'personalism' that marked the Alianza Popular (AP), as well as its defence of what it called the 'positive legacy' of Francoism meant that the party received little support at the ballot box. The dictatorship was still too close and AP evoked it too strongly for Spaniards to accept its democratic credentials.

The centre of the political spectrum was occupied by the Union of the Democratic Centre (UCD), which enjoyed the support of the leading members of the government, the prime minister among them. UCD was an extremely fragile coalition comprising a number of political currents, the most important of which were the liberals, Christian Democrats and social democrats. There were also a number of individual 'notables' who had their own political projects and who enjoyed varying degrees of support. This heterogeneity lay behind the multiple crises that confronted the UCD during its brief but intense history, but it was not apparent until it confronted such difficult issues as divorce and education.

The first elections and the Constitution of 1978

The first democratic elections were held in June 1977. Over three-quarters (78.7 per cent) of those eligible cast their ballot with the following result: UCD 165 seats; PSOE 118; PCE 20 and AP 16, with the remaining 31 seats spread among various other parties, the regional nationalists among them. The vote revealed the moderation of an electorate which spurned the extremes in favour of those parties closest to the centre of the ideological spectrum. The winning party, UCD, had been able to transmit the message of moderation and conciliation that Spanish society apparently wanted at that moment, but it also enjoyed other advantages, most notably the leadership of the increasingly charismatic Prime Minister Suárez.

The entire political process was conditioned by the profound international economic crisis provoked by the oil crisis of 1974. Spain had been especially hard hit but the Franco regime had not dared adopt the restrictive policies that were called for. This initial delay was compounded by the fact that from Franco's death until the election of June 1977 the overwhelming priority of

Spain's political leaders had been the political transition. All this deepened the economic crisis and made it absolutely necessary to have the cooperation of the unions in an austerity policy to control the spiralling inflation and permit greater growth. The so-called Moncloa Pacts represented the attempt to achieve this end: in exchange for a series of political rights and promises of tax reform, the unions accepted limits on wage increases and public spending. These agreements were signed in October 1977 by the government and all the political parties, although AP refused to agree to their political aspects.

The international context was certainly more favourable than that which had faced the Second Republic in the 1930s. Spain was struggling to end the international isolation it had suffered for much of the Franco period, and one of the first decisions taken by the newly-elected Cortes was a unanimous request to be admitted to the European Economic Community (EEC). The economic, political, social and even cultural conditions of the country had changed markedly over the previous four decades and most of the issues that had undermined the Republic had ceased to be problems. The religious question no longer produced irreconcilable confrontations. Indeed, the Church had radically changed its strategy: under the Republic it had intervened in political struggles and further poisoned the political atmosphere, but during the transition it remained aloof from the partisan conflict and frequently helped political actors to achieve a consensus. Even so, the hierarchy put severe pressure on the UCD when the parts of the Constitution dealing with divorce and education were being drafted.

On the other hand, one of the principal problems of the 1930s, the structure of the state and the demands of regional nationalists, remained – and had been exacerbated by the repressive policies of the dictatorship. The greatest problem facing the leaders of the transition, and their successors 20 years later, ETA terrorism, originated during the Franco years and worsened during its death rattle and the beginning of the transition. Between 1978 and 1980 alone these Basque separatists killed 239 people, but ETA was not the only organization that resorted to violence: another 88 people fell victim to terrorists on both the left and right during those three years. The fact that numerous scholars of the later changes in Latin America and Eastern Europe have made the Spanish transition a model should not lead us to forget that the process was neither easy nor especially peaceful.

Catalan nationalism did not prove nearly so problematic. The Generalitat, the regional government created during the Republic, was reestablished in September 1977 and Josep Tarradellas, its president in exile, who had had a series of conversations with Suárez and the king, was named its president. Nevertheless, the government refused to recognize the legitimacy of the Republic by recognizing the autonomy statutes it had passed in the 1930s, insisting that any regional autonomy should derive from the new Constitution and not from the still highly controversial Republic.

The president of the Basque government in exile, José M. Leizaola, was also in contact with the Suárez government and after negotiations between the government and Basque members of parliament the Consejo General del País Vasco, led by the veteran Socialist Ramón Rubial, was created in December 1977. Three months later the Junta of Galicia was established. Following the inauguration of these pre-autonomy institutions other regions began to demand similar treatment. Thus, even before the Constitution was approved, pre-autonomy was spreading across the country, albeit provisionally [see chapter 20].

In its first session the new Cortes decided that it would give Spain a new constitution and in August a 36-member Committee for Constitutional Affairs was created. This committee designated a seven-person panel, three from UCD, two from the PSOE (which yielded one to the Catalan and Basque nationalists) and one each from the PCE and AP, to draft the document. The small size of the committee, plus the fact that it worked in total secrecy, facilitated agreement and protected the general political climate from inevitable tensions. The first draft was made public at the beginning of 1978 and debated until June, first in the Constitutional Committee and then in the parliament itself, before being approved on 31 October 1978. The new Constitution was very much the product of consensus, but there were some moments of tension and the slow pace at which the discussions proceeded left an impression of political paralysis. In the end, the PNV did not endorse the final text because it did not recognize some nationalist demands.

The Constitution was put to a referendum on 6 December and was endorsed by 87.8 per cent of those who voted. However, barely two-thirds of those eligible, 67.1 per cent, did vote, and the very high abstention in the Basque Provinces (51.5 per cent) was particularly notable.

The Constitution proclaims Spain to be a parliamentary monarchy. It recognizes the existence of the Spanish nation while guaranteeing the right of autonomy to the 'nationalities and regions that comprise it'. The Constitution is also characterized by the difficulties it puts in the way of later reform. It sets out in great detail the rights and freedoms to be enjoyed by Spaniards but it is very unclear when it comes to delineating the respective jurisdictions of the national and regional governments. Finally, it provides the Executive with great stability by setting demanding standards for toppling a government through a vote of non confidence.

The end of consensus, 1979–1982

Most scholars agree that the approval of the Constitution marked the end of the transition and the beginning of what has become known as the period of democratic consolidation. This too had its share of difficulties. To begin with, by early 1979 the economic crisis had become particularly alarming. The rate of growth plummeted, both inflation and unemployment continued to rise steadily, and a new energy crisis had made the situation even worse. The Moncloa Pacts had clearly failed to ameliorate a catastrophic economic situation.

On another front, the policy of consensus followed by the major political parties broke down early in 1979. This was both logical and expected. With both the second general election and the first municipal one to be held that year, the parties would have to begin to compete openly with each other. The policy of negotiation and agreement that had marked the transition had not permitted them to present their differences to the electorate fully. The fact that no party had managed an absolute majority in 1977 was a further incentive for them to compete.

This was also the period in which significant tensions began to emerge within the most important parties. Its brief experience of government had produced the first fissures in UCD, and these would only widen as time passed. For their part, in 1978 the Communists had endured a strident three-sided internal debate over the desirable degree of internal democracy and the party's position on Eurocommunism. Santiago Carrillo's line of defending the latter but not the former won out. The Socialists' turn came later, at the 28th Party Congress in May 1979. As had their Communist counterparts, Socialist leaders had felt it necessary to eliminate some of the ideological baggage of the past. Felipe González proposed eliminating 'Marxism' from the party's ideology but the congress approved a motion defending Marxism along with other revolutionary aspects of its programme. González's response was to resign as General Secretary, provoking a crisis which ended only after an Extraordinary Congress in September reelected him by an overwhelming majority.

The results of the elections of March 1979 were similar to those of June 1977, although the rate of abstention had grown markedly. The right did worse, the PCE and the regional nationalists slightly better. The result of the municipal elections held in April were disappointing for the two main parties of the left but they were then able to develop agreements which brought them to power in a majority of municipalities.

The year of 1979 also brought other problems. Social conflict reached its highest level, while terrorism claimed its greatest number of victims between 1979 and 1980. An already delicate situation was deteriorating rapidly. The economic crisis was taking on truly worrying dimensions, but that was not all: the chasm that separated the complexity of the problems from the evident inexperience of those in power was visible to everyone.

The 1980s began with the sharpening of the crisis within UCD. To start with, 1980 was the year of spectacular resignations and the flight of deputies: the party's parliamentary delegation shrank while its popular support sank and that of the opposition, and especially the PSOE, jumped. In May 1980 the Socialists brought a motion of non confidence and although it failed, the debates between the two party leaders were followed attentively by a public which could observe both the deterioration of Suárez's leadership and the consolidation of González's. The party's fortunes were further diminished by its erratic policies on autonomy, and in the first regional elections its support collapsed while the Catalan and Basque nationalists prospered.

The armed forces continued to be a significant political player and they further complicated the situation. They were still the armed forces of the Franco regime and they were the ones on the receiving end of terrorism. In addition, their tremendous conservatism made them especially sensitive to what they considered an intolerable climate of social disorder. They were also angered by the spread of regional autonomy, which they saw as a danger to the 'unbreakable unity of the fatherland' they were sworn to defend. Much of the high command had had the Civil War as their formative experience and their democratic convictions were tepid, to say the least. As the ultra-right press of the period makes clear, many of them did not hide their affection for Franco's dictatorship nor their desire to take control of the situation. At the end of 1980 a number of high-ranking officers were arrested for their involvement in a planned coup which became known as 'Operation Galaxia', but to avoid antagonizing the army the conspirators received very light punishments. They certainly did not discourage further plots: on 23 February 1981 a number of those involved in 'Operation Galaxia' joined other soldiers and Civil Guards in assaulting the parliament and holding its members, and by extension the country as a whole, hostage for almost a full day. The king, who is commander in chief of the armed forces, played a crucial role in getting the rebels to surrender. His appearance on television ordering his subordinates to back down gave a major boost to the monarchy, which has become one of the most highly valued political institutions in the country.

The day that Lt.-Col. Antonio Tejero and his armed followers burst into the parliament the deputies were voting to approve Leopoldo Calvo Sotelo as prime minister. Suárez had resigned a few days before in the face of his inability to control the situation. The main effect of the attempted coup was to revive, at least temporarily, the earlier spirit of consensus and moderation. Calvo Sotelo did become prime minister, but he was unable to end the chaos within UCD as one deputy after another left to join other parties.

The most important actions of the Calvo Sotelo government were the trial of the perpetrators of the coup, the signing of a new agreement on employment, the treaty which took Spain into NATO and, above all, the partially successful attempt to deal with the autonomy question. Faced with the ongoing crisis in his party, Calvo Sotelo dissolved parliament in August 1982. Elections were held in October and the Socialists won an absolute majority. Just as the approval of the Constitution had marked the end of the political transition, this first changing of the political guard is generally considered to be that which marked the full consolidation of Spanish democracy.

|20|

The reawakening of peripheral nationalisms and the State of the Autonomous Communities

XOSÉ M. NÚÑEZ SEIXAS

After General Franco's death in 1975, the unsolved national question emerged as even more significant than it had been before 1936. Catalan, and especially Basque, nationalism enjoyed greater support than during the Second Republic. Galician nationalism was also present, albeit much weaker, at least until 1989. The delegitimization of Spanish nationalism also made it possible for new nationalisms to appear. Some, like Andalucia and Valencia, could call on historical and ideological traditions from before 1936, while others, for example the Canary Islands, could not. The generalization of home rule to all regions of the country contained in the 1978 Constitution also provided new opportunities for political elites and opened the door to the emergence of new regionalisms.

Peripheral nationalisms under the Franco regime

From 1939 on, Spanish nationalism was monopolized by Catholic–traditionalist discourse, with the addition of some fascist touches (see chapter 18). This Spanish nationalism proved unable to impose itself beyond the sphere of public life, and hence did not uproot the social acceptance of hidden peripheral nationalisms in some regions. In trying to impose a single state language the regime undertook a conscious repression of languages other than Castilian, although it was possible to publish literature in Catalan, Galician and Basque under severe censorship. State oppression was perceived in some areas, particularly in Catalonia and Euskadi, as a kind of 'Spanish occupation'; thus the Francoist regime had the unintended consequence of reinforcing the social and political cohesion of the Catalan and Basque nationalist communities, whose durability was assured by family and other private networks. In the case of Galicia, the Civil War interrupted a dynamic of social expansion of the nationalist movement, which then proved unable to withstand the long years of dictatorship: the number of Galician nationalist activists remained very limited, and after 1950 they focused on cultural resistance.

State repression and the survival of the peripheral nationalist legacy, together with the partial failure of 'authoritarian nation-building' made it possible for Catalan, Basque and also Galician nationalisms to remain alive, although silent, during the 1940s and 1950s. After 1950 the main character-istics of peripheral nationalist movements changed, in accord with the deep transformations experienced by Spanish society: modernization, industrial-ization, and new waves of internal migrations towards the Basque Country and Catalonia. There were also important ideological mutations within these movements. In Catalonia there was a reconversion of previously existing Catalanism into a new doctrine clearly influenced by Social-Catholicism and Christian personalist thought under the protection of some sectors of the Catalan Church, which favoured the anti-Francoist mobilization of Catho-lics, and left-wing Catalanist groups.

From the beginning of the 1960s onwards, the influence of Marxist–Leninist ideology on the younger generation of nationalist activists, together with the popularity of doctrines of 'internal colonialism' in Europe and the example offered by third world liberation movements, caused the emergence of new ideologically distinct nationalist parties, especially in Galicia and the Basque Country. These new organizations included the Galician People's Union (UPG), the Catalan Liberation Front (FAC) or the Socialist Party of National Liberation in Catalonia (PSAN). Basque Country and Freedom (Euskadi Ta Askatasuna, ETA), which was founded in 1959, evolved in similar directions. This influence also took place among some currents within the Canary Islands' left-wing, which proceeded to interpret the peripheral situation of the archipelago in colonial terms, thus giving rise to a new peripheral nationalist movement, although one whose influence lagged far behind the three 'historical' ones.

The virtual monopolization of Spanish nationalist discourse by Francoism and the antidemocratic right had further significant consequences for the whole spectrum of Spanish nationalism, particularly when it was forced to present a democratically legitimized face in the last years of Francoism and during the democratic transition. All forms of Spanish nationalism lost legitimacy, identified with the defence of old postulates advocated by Francoism. Partially as a result of this, the left-wing opposition moved towards federalist positions, and even acceptance of peripheral nationalist claims. As a consequence, the 1960s and 1970s were a period of uncertainty over how to articulate the future democratic state territorially. The Spanish Communist Party (PCE) followed the strategy of theoretically supporting nationalist claims, which was in part motivated by its need to compete with some left-wing regional parties. The PCE Congress of 1975 adopted among its resolutions the demand for recognition of the right to self-determination for the Basque Country, Catalonia and Galicia. And the Socialist Party (PSOE), at its 1974 and 1976 Congresses, also affirmed the right of self-determination for 'Iberian nationalities', while expressing its preference for a federal state. PSOE's openness towards peripheral claims also allowed it to absorb almost all the regional socialist parties which had emerged since 1950s.

Peripheral nationalisms and the democratic transition

The national question was one of the factors which most influenced the democratic transition. Some of the majority parties and currents within peripheral nationalist movements played an important role in that process; in several cases they displayed a high level of political pragmatism, particularly the Catalan nationalists, who took a very active part in the shaping of the new Constitution. The reestablishment of democracy produced an ambitious attempt to achieve a consociational solution to the satisfaction of peripheral nationalist demands.

During the early 1970s, the pressure exerted by the democratic opposition in certain regions increased greatly. This was particularly noticeable in Catalonia, where in 1971 a multi-party platform (Assembly of Catalonia) was set up to advocate a common programme, which included political amnesty, democratic freedoms and the restoration of the home rule statute of 1932. A similar programme was adopted at the end of 1975 in the Basque Country, Galicia and Valencia, although in these cases there was not always the same level of consensus as in Catalonia, so that the peripheral nationalist parties tended to go their own way. In the Basque Country, the first half of the 1970s was marked by the virulence of ETA's terrorist activity and also by the strong repression carried out by Francoist police, which, after the Burgos trial of 1970 and the killing of Admiral Carrero Blanco in 1973, made ETA appear as a kind of incarnation of the Basque Fatherland's 'heroic fight' against the dictatorship. This seriously damaged the legitimacy of the Spanish state in the Basque Country and paved the way for the difficulties of integrating Basque nationalism into Spanish democracy after 1975. (ETA's terrorism did not end in 1975, and has claimed more than 800 victims.) Demands for autonomy were also put forward by anti-Francoist opposition in other regions, such as Valencia, Aragón, Asturias and the Balearic Islands, though their impact was much weaker. The timid offers of administrative decentralization which emanated in 1976 from the post-Francoist government headed by Carlos Arias Navarro were soon overcome by the pressure of the left-wing and peripheral nationalist organizations.

The support that peripheral nationalisms enjoyed, particularly in Catalonia and the Basque Country, was clearly displayed in the results of the first democratic parliamentary elections held in June 1977: Catalan nationalists reaped 26.9 per cent of the vote in their region, their Basque counterparts

39.3 per cent. The polls also demonstrated the persistence of Galician nationalism (6.7 per cent), the emergence of a new, leftist Andalucian regionalism and of a recently constituted Canary Islands' nationalism. It became clear that full political democracy would permit peripheral nationalist movements to enjoy a marked consolidation.

Moderate Catalan nationalism incorporated new ideological ingredients, such as Christian Democracy and even social democracy. The main nationalist party, Democratic Convergence of Catalonia (CDC), was founded in 1974 under the charismatic leadership of Jordi Pujol. In 1978 it merged with the Christian-Democratic party Democratic Union of Catalonia (UDC) to form the highly successful electoral coalition Convergence and Union (Convergència i Unió, CiU), which has won all regional elections since 1980. These Catalan nationalists are characterized by strong pragmatism, aiming at the largest possible degree of self-government within the framework of the Spanish state and the European Union. For this reason, CiU abandoned independence to advocate full development of regional devolution to Catalonia. Political autonomy must be constantly 'deepened', although they never specify the final point. The model preached by CiU leaders seems to be a kind of bilateral relationship structure between Catalonia and the rest of Spain, although CiU also keeps alive the historic vocation of moderate Catalanism towards 'active intervention' in national politics, as evidenced in their support of the minority Aznar government after 1996.

In the Basque Country, peripheral nationalists recovered their social and electoral hegemony after 1977. Indeed, their political support was much greater than during the 1930s. Nevertheless, the support for Basque nationalist parties is very fragmented and nationalist electoral results vary a great deal in each of the Basque provinces: nationalists are hegemonic in Guipúzcoa and Vizcaya, while they are a significant minority in Alava and especially Navarre, which is an autonomous region of its own. Within each province, there are strong variations between rural and urban working-class and Spanish-speaking and Basque-speaking areas: urban and Spanish-speaking districts tend to be less nationalist.

Basque nationalism is divided into two basic camps. On the one hand, the traditional Basque Nationalist Party (PNV), founded in 1895, which belongs to the Christian Democratic International, remains faithful to Sabino Arana's original legacy, but reinterpreted in a more modern form. The main emphasis is now put on the Basque language as the basis for the existence of a Basque nation, even though Basque is spoken by only a quarter of the population. The PNV preaches a broad social reformism corresponding to its inter-class base, but it is also characterized by a permanent tension between a far-reaching independentist discourse at the ideological level and a constant political pragmatism at the strategic level. Although the PNV has never given up the possibility of achieving self-determination for Euskadi in the short term, it is also clearly in favour of exploiting the Autonomy Statute in place since 1979. The PNV merely observes, but does not explicitly endorse, the Spanish constitutional framework, and sometimes expresses its preference for a kind of bilateral confederation between the Basque Country and the Spanish Crown, as a return to the political situation prior to the abolition of the *Fueros* by the liberal State in 1839.

The second group within Basque nationalism, the so-called 'patriotic left', constitutes a broad social movement clearly linked to the terrorist organization ETA, whose political branch since 1978 is the coalition People's Union (*Herri Batasuna*, HB). ETA's and HB's programmes are condensed into a set of slogans: self-determination and total independence for Euzkadi, socialism and 'reunification' of all Basque territories, including Navarre and the French Basque Country. The 'patriotic left' considers the constitutional monarchy to be as much the 'oppressor' of their Fatherland as was the Franco regime. Attempts at building nationalist alternatives which could shape a sort of 'third road' between PNV and HB have had minimal success. One branch of ETA relinquished violence at the end of the 1970s and gave rise to a new party, Basque Left (*Euskadiko Ezkerra*, EE). It moved from initially secessionist and anticonstitutional positions to more moderate and autonomist ones but never surpassed 10 per cent of the vote and finally disappeared in 1993, being absorbed by the PSOE. Basque Solidarity (*Eusko Alkartasuna*, EA), a party born in 1986 from a split in the PNV around the former *lehendakari* (head of the regional government) Carlos Garaikoetxea, saw its influence dwindle during the 1990s, as its electoral percentages decreased from 15.8 per cent to 9 per cent. Both parties were unable to overcome the fundamental cleavage between PNV and HB. In any case, since 1977 the PNV has remained the major political organization in the region, receiving between 27 per cent and 30 per cent of the vote.

The significance of openly secessionist parties is very different in Euskadi to that in Catalonia. The violent secessionism represented by HB peaked at the end of the 1980s with around 18 per cent of the vote, and its support decreased slowly but continuously afterwards. In polls taken between 1994 and 1996, HB reaped from 12 per cent to 14 per cent of the vote, less than in Navarre. In Catalonia, separatist options were totally marginal in electoral terms between 1977 and 1992, although some minority tendencies within CiU confessed to favouring independence. Nevertheless, secessionists maintained some degree of support through their influence in social movements, such as Crida a la Solidaritat (Appeal to Solidarity). After 1992 the Catalan independence movement received a new impulse from the reinforcement of the old Catalanist party, Republican Left of Catalonia (ERC), which fell under the control of a secessionist group originally from the Crida. In spite of a spectacular propaganda campaign in 1992, when the party achieved 8 per cent of the vote in the regional elections, its electoral increase since then has been quite modest, and in the November 1995 regional elections it received only 9.4 per cent of the vote.

In Galicia peripheral nationalism retains a lower profile, and has yet to surpass 26 per cent of the vote in any election. The reasons for this weakness, apart from a less favourable historical tradition, lie in the extreme fragmentation and instability of the political spectrum of Galician nationalism, which has undergone several splits and party changes; the radicalization of nationalist demands in the transition period; and the great difficulties in consolidating any moderate right-wing nationalist organization in this region, that have been aggravated by the regionalist turn taken by the right-wing Popular Party (PP) since 1980. Thus, the political expression of Galician nationalism has been overwhelmingly monopolized by the left, mainly by two tendencies: the Marxist–Leninist left, eventually called Galician Nationalist Block (Bloque Nacionalista Galego, BNG), and the reformist socialist and democratic left, represented by the Galician Socialist Party–Galician Left (PSG-EG). The latter current was subsumed into the former at the beginning of the 1990s allowing the BNG, as the sole remaining and increasingly moderate nationalist organization, to achieve significant results, including 18.8 per cent of the vote in the regional elections of 1993 and 24.8 per cent in 1997.

The level of votes for peripheral nationalist parties in Euskadi, Galicia and, especially, Catalonia vary from national to regional elections, as Table 20.1 shows.

Table 20.1 Electoral results of peripheral nationalist parties in Euskadi, Catalonia and Galicia (% of valid votes)

Parliamentary elections (1977–96)							
	1977	*1979*	*1982*	*1986*	*1989*	*1993*	*1996*
Euskadi	39.3	50.6	54.5	54.9	59.4	48.5	46.5
Catalonia	26.9	20.2	26.2	34.5	35.1	36.9	36.8
Galicia	6.7	11.2	4.6	11.9	9.5	13.9	13.1

Regional elections (1980–95)						
Euskadi	*1980*	*1984*	*1986*	*1990*	*1994*	*1998*
	65.2	65.6	67.9	66	55.5	54.6
Catalonia	*1980*	*1984*	*1988*	*1992*	*1995*	*1999*
	36.6	51	49.6	54.4	50.1	46.4
Galicia	*1981*	*1985*	*1989*	*1993*	*1997*	
	12.7	24.7	26.9	22.3	25.1	

Peripheral nationalists do significantly better in regional and municipal elections than in national parliamentary elections, where electoral participation also increases.

Peripheral nationalist movements also extend their influence to other spheres of civil society, as well as in the areas of culture and labour relations. They have contributed decisively to enhancing the status of the Catalan, Basque and Galician languages, which are co-official in their respective territories. Autonomous regional governments, particularly the Catalan and Basque ones, have pursued a linguistic policy which seeks to restore non-Castilian languages to equal level with Spanish. Educational policy has been the main instrument of 'renationalization' and also sometimes a source of conflict. Peripheral nationalisms also maintain a strong degree of influence in labour relations. In Catalonia there is no specific nationalist trade-union, though the Catalan branch of Workers' Commissions (CC.OO.) displays a strong sympathy for Catalanism; in the Basque Country, nationalist trade unions constitute the majority of labour representatives and in Galicia they occupy third place.

New peripheral nationalisms have emerged in other regions. The political influence of this group of minority nationalist movements has remained very limited, and their ideological definition is sometimes a mixture of regionalist proposals and imitation dynamics caused by a 'domino effect' emerging from Catalonia, Euzkadi and Galicia. Apart from Navarre, where Basque nationalism collects around 15 per cent of the vote, we can mention three main groups of 'minor' peripheral nationalisms. The first one is composed of more or less openly pan-Catalanist nationalist parties in the Catalan-speaking Balearic Islands – today represented by Mallorcan Union (Unió Mallorquina) and Socialist Party of Mallorca (Partit Socialista de Mallorca), whose joint electoral results at the 1995 regional elections were 17.56 per cent, and in Valencia, where political nationalism has been much less successful. There the most important organization has been the left-wing Valencian People's Union (Unitat del Poble Valencià), which obtained less than 4 per cent at 1995 regional elections.

The second group is composed of those minority movements which seek to promote a newly-fashioned national identity based on declining local languages such as Asturia and Aragonese: the Partiu Asturianista and the Aragonese Assembly (Chunta Aragonesista). Their cultural proposals, particularly in the Asturian case, have found some echo in the regional governments, which have implemented measures to promote these languages.

A third group are those nationalist movements which are not based on any claim of cultural and linguistic difference, but whose electoral success has been greater thanks to their ideological ambivalence, which makes them closer to the 'autonomic regionalisms' which will be mentioned below. Here two movements stand out: the Andalucian, represented by the Partido Andalucista which obtained 6.9 per cent of the vote in 1996, and the Canary Coalition, with 36.18 per cent in the 1995 regional elections and 25.1 per cent and four deputies in the 1996 parliamentary elections.

The 1978 Constitution and the State of the Autonomous Communities

The Constitution of 1978 established a complex framework that combines the conception of Spain as a single political nation with the existence of autonomy statutes granted to all regions: the so-called State of the Autonomous Communities, a decentralized structure, composed of seventeen 'autonomous communities' which reassembled the existing fifty provinces. In many cases they clearly overlapped with the previous 'historical regions' (which had had no administrative recognition whatsoever during Francoism). Autonomous communities are not equal in size, population or economic weight, nor do they always correspond to the historic regions: thus, the national capital, Madrid, became a uniprovincial community, as did the provinces of Santander, which was transformed into Cantabria, Logroño, which became La Rioja, and Murcia. Most autonomous communities were implemented on the basis of the so-called 'Pre-autonomies', provisional representative bodies which were constituted in 1976 and 1977, before the Constitution was ratified. Between 1979 and 1983 all of them elaborated their own home rule statutes.

The Constitution created two groups of autonomous communities. The so-called 'historical nationalities': Catalonia, the Basque Country and Galicia, which had approved a home rule statute by referendum prior the Civil War, and the rest. The application of this structure to the whole of the national territory was the result of a political agreement among the different political actors involved in drafting the Constitution. Basque and Catalan nationalists pressed for self-government for their communities within the framework of a multinational state which could adopt a federalized or confederalized structure. This claim was unacceptable to the right-wing parties, mainly composed of 'reformists' coming from the Francoist state apparatus, including much of the party which led the first phase of the democratic transition, the Union of the Democratic Centre (UCD) and was especially unacceptable to the People's Alliance (AP) headed by former Franco minister Manuel Fraga. They were not ready to accept that Spain cease to be considered a single nation and would tolerate nothing but a mild administrative decentralization. In theory, the left advocated a federal solution. Nevertheless, UCD was eager to achieve a compromise with moderate Catalan nationalists, so the decision was made to extend the right to autonomy to all regions while establishing different routes to, and levels of, home rule. In this sense, the new State of the Autonomous Communities is a typical product of the complicated agreements which made the Spanish transition to democracy possible. Sovereignty was kept by the Spanish state, which transferred broad powers to the autonomous communities, including legislative and executive authority in areas such as agriculture and fishing activities, transport, culture and education, public health, tourism, and commerce. At the same time, the central state maintained legislative pre-eminence in many other areas as well as the capacity to collect all taxes (with the exception of the exemption enjoyed by the Basque Provinces and Nav-arre, the 'Economic Agreements' dating back to 1878).

The 1978 Constitution was ambiguous in defining certain crucial con-cepts. On the one hand, it affirmed that Spain is the sole existing Nation, and hence the sole collective entity enjoying full sovereignty; but on the other hand, 'nationalities' and regions were also recognized, while the difference between a nationality and a nation was not clearly established. Two different paths for achieving autonomy were also delineated. The 'fast track' defined by Article 151 was reserved for the 'historical nationalities', who were joined later by Andalucia, while Article 143 defined a 'slow track' for the rest of the regions. In practice, Valencia, Navarre and the Canary Islands advanced far more rapidly than the other 10 and by the late 1990s were practically at the same level as the 'first class' communities. By mentioning the existence of 'historical nationalities', the Constitution's authors intended to satisfy peripheral nationalist demands that the new territorial structure of the state should explicitly display recognition of the 'qualitative' historical, cultural and social peculiarities of some specific territories.

Basque nationalism in its majority did not accept the framework drawn up by the 1978 Constitution: the 'patriotic left' and even the PNV rejected it because of the failure to recognize 'historical rights' in a form which affirmed Basque sovereignty. This caused what has been called a 'legitimacy deficit'. The majority of Basque voters (55.5 per cent) abstained in the Constitutional referendum held in December 1978, following the recommendation issued by PNV. The posture of Catalan nationalists was very different: they took part in shaping the Constitution and recommended a 'yes' vote. Two-thirds of those eligible voted and 90 per cent voted 'yes'.

Strong criticisms were directed at 'Part VIII' of the Constitution by conservative leader Manuel Fraga and were sustained in the following years by AP. For example, it opposed the term 'historical nationalities' and was reluctant to accept bilingualism in certain autonomous communities. Feder-alism as a final goal endured among some currents of the Socialist party and the rest of the left, especially among the ranks of Catalan socialists and (post)-Communists, who repeatedly insisted upon a 'federalizing interpreta-tion' of the 1978 Constitution.

The State of the Autonomous Communities contained several ambiguities requiring permanent bargaining among the political parties, the central state and regional governments. The jurisdictions of the levels of government were not closely defined. Among the many details regarding the financing of the new system that were not resolved, the most important was the absence of an efficient mechanism for transferring resources from richer to poorer regions. There was no provision for the creation of a parliamentary forum for cooperation and coparticipation in the government's tasks by the autono-mous communities. Nor was there provision for the participation of the autonomous communities in the making of Spain's European policy after the country joined the EEC in 1986. These deficiencies made the system heavily dependent on short-term agreements and negotiations between the central government and the nationalist parties. For this reason, the need to achieve a definitive 'rationalization' and completion of the autonomic process became one of the major political problems after 1978, especially following the failed military coup of 23 February 1981. Several attempts to do so failed: the 1981 Law for the Harmonization of the Autonomy Process was fiercely opposed by peripheral nationalisms and declared partially unconstitutional by the Constitutional Court on the basis that the Madrid government's claim that all autonomous communities should be granted a similar level of responsibilities was not included in the Constitution which, on the contrary, assured regional 'asymmetry'.

Indeed, the rather artificial development of regional administrations between 1980 and 1990 generated further problems. State and regional administrations often overlap while public expenditures have risen due to the frequent borrowing by the regional governments. New administrations created a new political opportunity-structure for regional elites which have since been forced to justify their existence by a permanent vindication of further self-government, even, as in La Rioja and Cantabria, inventing a new collective identity.

The emergence of 'autonomist regionalisms'

The real reinforcement and proliferation of new regionalisms took place after the spectacular collapse suffered by UCD in the 1982 parliamentary elections. With the right unable to seriously challenge the PSOE, the sole method of survival for many of UCD's regional elites raised the banner of regionalism. This dynamic provoked either the reinforcement of autonomic regionalisms, the best example being the Aragonese PAR, or the emergence of new ones, such as La Rioja's Party (PRP), the Independent Canary Islands' Grouping (AIC), later on subsumed into Canary Coalition (CC), and the Valencian Union (UV). The ideological principles sustained by these organizations are rather vague, although most of them are clearly conservative. The most traditionalist among them, such as the Navarrese UPN, appeal to the legacy of Carlism and to the maintenance of the ancient *Fueros*, while advocating a view of the Spanish nation based upon 'regional freedoms'. New regionalists proved to be pragmatic improvisers. Where they assumed regional power, usually in coalition with all-Spanish parties, they undertook the task of promoting regional identity from above, sometimes imitating mimetically the strategies outlined by Catalan or Basque nationalists. At the same time, they attempted to set up little welfare states, particularly in the decade after 1982, a period characterized by increasing public expenditures.

Public expenditure by autonomous communities tripled between 1986 and 1992 and the number of civil servants they employed increased tenfold between 1981 and 1991.

Table 20.2 Election results of regionalist parties in some autonomous communities, 1983–95 (only regional elections) (% of valid votes)

	1983	1987	1991	1995	1999
Aragón	20.64	28.48	24.68	20.46	13.29
Valencia	–	9.24	10.41	5.72	4.00
Navarre	23.51	31.18	34.95	49.90	49.45
La Rioja	7.52	6.49	5.38	6.66	5.75
Cantabria	6.77	13.29	6.36	14.63	13.51

Note: The following parties are taken into account: for Aragón, Partido Aragonés (PAR); for Valencia, Unión Valenciana (UV); for Navarre, Unión del Pueblo Navarro (UPN), Convergencia de Demócratas Navarros (CDN) since 1995; in 1995 UPN stood in coalition with the Popular Party (PP). For La Rioja, Partido Riojano Progresista (PRP); for Cantabria, Partido Regionalista de Cantabria (PRC).
Source: *Historia 16*, n. 200 (1992), and *El País*, 29 May 1995.

The multiplication of 'regionalisms' also reflects the persistence of the legitimacy problems of Spanish nationalism. In fact, several autonomic regionalisms are peculiar forms of Spanish affirmation. They seek less problematic ways of expression and, in many cases, challenge neighbouring peripheral nationalisms. Thus, UPN in Navarre and Alavese Union (UA) are the main representatives of anti-Basque nationalism in their territories, while UV and PAR are strongly anti-Catalanist.

The increasing dynamic of self-affirmation of regional identities promoted by autonomic administrations helps explain some of the disputes which have arisen sporadically between different regions, and also the constant necessity for regional elites to justify their own power position by demanding equality of treatment with the 'historical nationalities'. Thus the regional governments of the 'slow track' autonomous communities often harp on the comparative disadvantage in treatment by Madrid and seek to obtain as great a level of power as the 'historic nationalities'. Regionalist parties such as the PAR, CC and even UPN feel they must increase their pressure by rhetorically upholding new peripheral 'nationalisms' which aim at transforming their regions into 'nationalities', and have insisted on the necessity of further developing the principle of subsidiarity and of reinforcing the role to be played by the regions within the European Union. Not even the major national parties (PSOE and PP) have been able to escape the pressure exerted by their regional branches, which see themselves forced to demand full devolution to the 'slow track' autonomous communities. This led PSOE and

PP to conclude an agreement concerning equality treatment for all autonomous communities in the near future in 1992.

The evolution of the State of the Autonomous Communities

After 1981 rationalizing the implementation of the State of the Autonomous Communities became a constantly repeated slogan, but little was achieved. By the 1990s several steps were taken to remove some of its deficiencies.

First, thanks to the 1992 'autonomic agreement' between PP and PSOE which obligated them to accelerate the transfer of powers to the 'slow track' communities, and to the PSOE's 1993 commitment to further facilitate such transfers to the 'first class' autonomous communities, a determination to achieve maximum powers took hold among all regional administrations. Overall homogenization is nearly impossible, because of the persistence of the 'Economic Agreements' in Euskadi and Navarre, and the wider competencies enjoyed in matters such as the police by Euskadi, Catalonia and to a lesser extent Galicia. Moreover, the health system, which is one of the most complex areas to be transferred, was not initially included within the 'autonomic agreement'. In order to reach the best homogenization possible, a clear-cut differentiation of competencies between the central state and the autonomous communities was established in 1993, although it was not comprehensive. Besides the 'untransferable' competencies exclusive to the central state (international relations, foreign trade and tariff policy, justice, overall economic policy and planning, defence, etc.) and those which were 'easily transferable', there were some which were theoretically 'untransferable' but which article 150.2 of the Constitution permits to be delegated. These were the focus of much of the conflict between regional governments and the state.

Second, mechanisms for assuring financial co-responsibility among the autonomous communities began to be implemented. In 1992-93 a new agreement in principle was reached which implies the granting of 15 per cent of regional income taxes to the autonomous communities, along with the capacity to collect it directly. There were dissidents, particularly the poorest regions (Extremadura, Galicia and Castile-León), which felt that this concession favoured the richest communities. The situation changed in 1996 when CiU pushed the new PP minority government to adopt a further formula of financial decentralization to enable the autonomous governments to collect up to 30 per cent of certain taxes themselves.

Third, from 1993 on the possibility of making the Senate into a chamber of territorial representation like the German Bundesrat was accepted by practically all parliamentary groups. This would provide for more active participation of regional governments in the legislative activity and political decision-making of the state, although it would require amending the Constitution, a move without precedent. A first attempt was the creation in 1993 of a General Commission of the Autonomous Communities in the Senate, with participation of representatives of all regional governments. Nevertheless, such fora face the reluctance of peripheral nationalists, particularly the Basques, who seek a 'satisfactory' degree of recognition of the historical and cultural uniqueness of the 'historical nationalities' to fully take part in these institutions.

Fourth, after 1994 the central state made limited progress in involving the autonomous communities in the Spanish delegation to the European Union. However, progress in this field has been limited. Among the first measures adopted was the commitment of the central government to consult the autonomous communities about their views on European policy issues, as well as to set up a forum (the so-called 'Sectorial Conferences' (*conferencias sectoriales*) to allow the regional governments a voice in Spain's European Policy.

A good sign of the increasing political consolidation of the State of the Autonomous Communities, as well as of the larger experience accumulated by the political elites, is the continuous reduction since 1988 of the number of laws which have been appealed before the Constitutional Court, either by the central state or by the regional governments: from 131 in 1985 to 37 in 1990 and none in 1994. Many other problem areas are still far from being solved. One is the rationalization of the central state bureaucracies which are still functioning in the autonomous communities: many of them have practically no functions. In this sense, the maintenance of the figure of the Civil Governors was a matter of dispute until 1997. Another question is the role played by the municipalities, whose lack of resources has led municipal representatives to demand more income.

The imprecision of the new structure has led to a permanent tension between the demands of the diverse 'autonomic regionalisms' for achieving equality with the 'historical nationalities' and the wish of peripheral nationalists to have their qualitative differences translated into larger competencies. The latter regard any equality of treatment with the rest of the autonomous communities as a denial of what they consider to be the legitimate basis for their claims of self-government: being distinct *nations*. For this reason, they are not comfortably settled within the State of the Autonomous Communities, but accept the present situation as the lesser evil. However, here the pragmatism of the Catalan CiU has to be contrasted with PNV's permanent reluctance to participate with other communities in any common fora. In this sense, peripheral nationalists reject the proposals voiced from the left about transforming the present State of the Autonomous Communities into a federal State, but would accept the transformation of Spain into a multinational federation based on three or four clearly defined 'national' entities (Euskadi, Catalonia, Galicia and the rest of Spain).

Spanish nationalism since 1978

The new territorial framework drawn up by the 1978 Constitution also forced Spanish nationalism to redefine itself. Spanish nationalism since the end of Francoism may be characterized by two constant features: the search for a new identity and a new democratic legitimacy and its confrontation with the peripheral nationalisms.

Right-wing Spanish nationalism clearly suffers from legitimacy problems inherited from Francoism and the long interruption of what had been a tradition of liberal-democratic Spanish nationalism before 1936. It remains marked by its permanent opposition to peripheral nationalist claims, although after about 1985 its messages were quite contradictory. On the one hand, the political praxis of the PP in Galicia and the Balearic Islands, where the party has governed since the early 1980s, is characterized by the implementation of a moderate defence of peripheral languages and culture and the promotion of the sentiments of regional 'autonomic' identity. The Galician PP, for instance, has advanced a new formula which seeks to combine Spanish loyalty with reinforcement of regional identity: 'self-identification', something like the conscious pride of being Galician and loving the language and traditions of the region, combined with the promotion of a folklorist and popular culture. But this policy is counterbalanced by that followed until 1996 by the same party in Euskadi and Catalonia, where confrontation with the peripheral nationalists and the exploitation of the language conflict was frequent.

Nevertheless, right-wing democratic nationalism has changed, symbolized in the 'recovery' of the historical legacy of Republican reformism from the first third of the twentieth century, including the reclamation of the figure of Manuel Azaña by conservative intellectuals. Moreover, the democratic right has fully accepted the system of the autonomous communities. A good example of this is the formula of 'single administration', proposed by Manuel Fraga, conservative president of the Xunta of Galicia and former Franco minister. It consists of full devolution to the regional administrations and elimination of any overlapping functions between the central and regional spheres of government. This would serve to deepen the State of the Autonomous Communities as well as to put a definitive brake on increasing self-government demands from peripheral nationalists. However, the democratic right does not recognize the existence of some regional differences at the institutional level: the PP advocates full homogenization of power competences for all autonomous communities, in spite of accepting the existence of 'linguistic and geographical' peculiarities in certain regions.

Since the mid-1980s, the left has increasingly recovered a form of Spanish nationalist discourse which can be traced back to the traditions of Spanish regenerationism and liberal republicanism in the first third of the twentieth century, and which incorporates appeals to 'modernity' and the full integration into the EU. This discourse contains many variants, but it aims at combining belief in the existence of a Spanish *political* nation with the recognition of different cultural nations which would make Spain a 'nation of nations'. Jürgen Habermas' concept of 'patriotism of the Constitution' enjoyed a large audience among intellectual circles on the Spanish left. This definition raises little enthusiasm among peripheral nationalists and other currents from the left, particularly in Catalonia, which claim that Spain is a multinational state and should be defined as such.

The enthusiastic 'Europeanism' of Spanish nationalism can be seen as a sort of escape forwards by diluting Spain's nationality problems within the political and economic life of the EU. Nevertheless, this approach is shared by most peripheral nationalist parties, which regard the reinforcement of the authority of Brussels as a kind of counterweight to Madrid. Spaniards have remained among the most fervent supporters of the European project.

Others on the left remain loyal to the Jacobin legacy of Spanish left-wing nationalism prior to 1936. They uphold the need for a strong central state which should serve as an instrument of social reform and criticize peripheral nationalisms, which they accuse of a lack of solidarity and of discriminatory cultural and language policies. These people include the PSOE's left-wing trend, represented by its former vice-president Alfonso Guerra, and certain regional leaders such as Extremadura's president J.A. Rodríguez Ibarra, as well as certain groups within the PSOE's Basque and Galician branches, which appeal to the tradition of municipalism and, the defence and strengthening of the autonomy of the municipalities as a basis for efficient decentralization instead of a further regional devolution.

Conclusion: on the road to federalism?

The following trends in the development of the Spanish State of the Autonomous Communities should be stressed:

The system established by the Constitution of 1978 and further developed since then, has shown itself to be flexible enough to provide an adequate framework for resolving the territorial tensions of the young Spanish democracy. Nevertheless, peripheral nationalisms continue to demand further reforms which should recognize the state's multinational character by bestowing more power and further self-government on Catalonia, Euskadi and Galicia. The differences between Basque and Catalan nationalism in this respect are remarkable. The main Basque nationalist parties claim the right to self-determination, which is occasionally presented as a possible solution to ETA and to the so-called 'Basque conflict'. The Catalan CiU prefers a 'generous' interpretation of the present Constitution which would take into account the Catalan *peculiarity*, with Quebec's status within Canada as a possible model. Even the sporadically repeated proposals of the Spanish left for federalization of the present system cannot escape the division between those who advocate an 'asymmetrical federalism' which should take into account cultural and 'national' differences and those who support the conversion of the 17 autonomous communities into equal federal states.

Secessionism, even in Euskadi and Catalonia, has only minority support, between 25 and 33 per cent in the most optimistic opinion surveys. Peripheral nationalists face the dilemmas posed by the practical application of the principle of self-determination in the short term. These dilemmas are especially stark in the Basque case, since a referendum concerning the possibility of independence for all Basque territories (including Navarre) would probably have very different results in each of them, not to mention the possible confrontation between Basque and Spanish nationalists inside Euskadi. Basque and Catalan nationalists are perfectly aware of the fact that they do not enjoy any undisputed hegemony for the time being.

The reason for this is simple: there is no direct correlation between peripheral nationalists' election scores, national consciousness and support for independence, as is also the case in Quebec, which has a long history of voting for one party in provincial elections and another in national ones. This also deactivates the intensity of peripheral nationalist claims. Another factor which leads the majority tendencies of peripheral nationalisms towards consociational solutions is their institutionalization: since the beginning of the 1980s both Catalan and Basque moderate nationalists have controlled the regional government, a fact which fosters wider political pragmatism. PNV and CiU control significant public resources and (especially CiU) are forced to play a key role as 'third parties' in the shaping of parliamentary majorities in Madrid.

A third factor is that collective identities in Spain are multiple and heterogeneous. While traditional vehicles of Spanish national cohesion, and especially anything that refers to any unanimously accepted *national* symbolism, are weaker than in other countries, sociological studies and several opinion surveys have demonstrated that even in Euskadi and Catalonia a peculiar form of 'twofold patriotism' predominates: the shifting coexistence in the same person of identification with the peripheral nationality along with a feeling of solidarity or identification with Spain as a whole. Opinion polls reveal that those who feel Basque, Catalan or Galician *and* Spanish, for example, constitute the majority of the regions' population.

It appears that Spain has arrived at a 'historical balance' between Spanish and peripheral nationalisms. Twofold patriotism is the predominant situation in Catalonia, Euskadi and Galicia, but this does not mean that this balance is uniform and unchangeable. The collapse of the democratic system, a hypothetical sudden loss of legitimacy of state institutions, or a far-reaching social and economic crisis might have unpredicted consequences on the level of national allegiances and nationalist tensions. The consolidation of the State of the Autonomous Communities within the framework of the European Union remains a matter to be settled definitively.

|21|

The Socialist era, 1982–1996

SANTOS JULIÁ

On 28 October 1982, in the midst of great popular expectation, the Spanish Socialist Workers' Party (PSOE) won an absolute majority in the general elections which had been called at one of the most delicate moments of the then still young and fragile Spanish democracy. The economy had not yet recovered from the worst of the economic crisis that had begun in 1974: GDP was stagnant, inflation remained stuck at 14 per cent per year and unemployment had risen steadily to 16.5 per cent. Nor was there any shortage of political tension. ETA terrorist attacks had reached a pinnacle in 1980 and 1981, when almost 200 people, several army generals among them, had been killed. In the midst of all this, the abortive coup of February 1981 was still fresh in everyone's mind, especially when a new plot was discovered and three senior officers were arrested just before the election. The disintegration of the UCD, which had governed since 1977, and the crisis of the Communist Party had seriously affected the stability of the party system and added to the sensation that the country faced a serious political crisis. There was, therefore, a very strong desire among the vast majority of Spaniards to explicitly reaffirm their faith in democracy. All this gave the 1982 election a special dimension, and made it much more than the routine exercise of a democratic right. The election had to consolidate the system established in 1977 and 1978 and put paid to the notion that high rates of abstention indicated little faith in democratic institutions.

The 1982 election succeeded in further legitimizing Spanish democracy and marking the end of the transition. The growth in the abstention rate was reversed, as 79.1 per cent of the voters turned out, compared to 68.1 per cent in 1979, and the number of ballots cast increased from 17.9 million to 20.9 million. The PSOE received 10.12 million votes, 4.6 million more than in the previous election. Of these new Socialist voters, 2 million were new voters, 1.2 million had previously voted UCD, 1 million Communist and 500000 had voted for other parties. The PSOE established itself as a 'catch all' party which could attract votes from a broad spectrum and won a comfortable parliamentary majority, as the following table shows. The Socialists also triumphed handsomely in the regional and municipal elections held in May 1983. Nationalists held their own in Catalonia and Euskadi (CiU and PNV respectively), but elsewhere the Socialists took control of town halls and regional governments across the country, with the only exceptions being Cantabria and the Balearic Islands.

Table 21.1 October 1982 election results

Party	Votes	%	Seats	%
PSOE	10 127 092	48.43	202	57.71
AP–PDP	5 548 335	26.53	107	30.57
UCD/CC	1 393 574	6.66	11	3.14
PCE–PSUC	846 802	4.05	4	1.14
CDS	604 309	2.89	2	0.57
CiU	772 728	3.69	12	3.42
PNV	395 656	1.89	8	2.28
HB	210 601	1.00	2	0.57
ERC	138 116	0.66	1	0.28
EE	100 326	0.47	1	0.28

The Socialists' became the first party in Spanish history to win an absolute majority without using electoral manipulation, and their popularity was due to several factors: the disintegration of the UCD, which had governed since 1977; the crisis of the Communists, the cohesion of the PSOE around a strong and charismatic leader, and their sweeping programme, ambiguously entitled 'For Change', which promised to put a halt to rising unemployment and create 800 000 jobs. The Socialists had also spoken about modernizing the structures of production, helping small and medium enterprises, combating tax fraud, and strengthening state-owned industries through a process of 'reconversion' that would lead to new jobs as well as training workers who became redundant. They also promised a just society, with improvements in education and in health and social security systems, a modernized state administration and improved public services; they preached the ideals of freedom, public security and greater autonomy in foreign policy. In short, they presented themselves not only as a party ready to develop classical social-democrat ideals in order to attain growth, but also as a force that would consolidate democracy and tackle so many of the questions which, historically, the Spanish state and Spanish society had been unable to resolve: a more competitive economy, political and administrative decentralization and the modernization of the armed forces.

A government that governs

A moral message accompanied this undertaking to bring about change without revolution: the Socialists presented themselves as the bearers of a new political ethic, the pioneers of a moral regeneration of state and society. The eventual composition of the government bore no surprises. It was a young cabinet, the average age of which was about 40, made up mainly of high-ranking civil servants, armed with the conviction that they had an important historical mission to fulfil and that they possessed the moral superiority necessary to carry it out. It was a government that was strongly united around the figure of an extremely popular Prime Minister. It was a government of the Prime Minister, more than of the party, which had no say in its formation. It was therefore only logical that it should adopt a style that reflected the knowledge that it enjoyed a very comfortable parliamentary majority and was faced with no factions led by figures of any note, who would have to be consulted in order to secure pacts necessary to govern. This meant that one of the important features of the transition, constant negotiations among the different political forces, disappeared once the Socialists got into power. They were bent on showing the country that at last there was a government ready to govern and capable of so doing; in short, that they were a government with power and authority.

With a strong government and a highly disciplined party, the Socialists found themselves in the best possible position to develop a programme of reform, through fundamental laws (*leyes orgánicas*) and agreements with social forces, pressure groups and the so-called factitious powers, notably the army, the Church and the banks. Of course, such policies could not be carried out without a gradual shift towards the centre. The utter confusion and chaos into which the Communists had been thrown, coupled with the lack of a real alternative on the right, contributed to this. A tone of moderation began to tinge not only the definition of the PSOE as a party, but also the policies that it began to implement, as well as the aura in which the entire government was gradually shrouded. Socialist propaganda was careful to present Prime Minister González calming and encouraging the business class, attending military parades or in relaxed conversation with the head of the Catholic Church.

A concerted effort was therefore made to implement new reforms, with a very heavy emphasis placed on the consolidation of democracy without in any way offending the traditional powers. This was very evident in economic policy, which aimed, from the outset, to contain and reduce inflation, boost the economy and control excesses prior to and as a base for the creation of employment. The first Minister of Finance, Miguel Boyer, and the Prime Minister himself, tried to instil the necessary confidence in the business class, anxious to assure them that Spain now had a government capable of carrying out a policy of stabilization before contemplating salary increases above productivity and inflation. The first effect of this policy was that inflation fell

6 points in three years, from 14.2 per cent in 1983, to 8.1 per cent in 1985. Salaries only grew in tune with the expected level of inflation, although another half a million jobs were lost. The 10.6 million people employed in 1985 was the lowest number in the recent history of the country. The first measures sought to reduce the 'rigidities' that Francoism had introduced into the labour market by making it difficult and very expensive to dismiss workers. The reform of the Estatuto de Trabajadores in 1984, which introduced new types of labour contracts and made it easier to dismiss employees, resulted not in the creation of net employment, but in a dual market: areas of instability for those entering the market for the first time and lifelong stability for those with fixed, indefinite contracts.

As far as national security was concerned, the government proceeded with the kind of caution that was to be expected after the recent aborted military coup. A new law for the army envisaged the reduction by almost 25 per cent of the 23 000 generals and senior officers as well as a reduction by almost 6 per cent of junior officers. As had happened with the Republic, the objective was to reduce the size of the army in order to make it more efficient and effective, as well as more directly subject to civil power. The Ley Orgánica de Defensa y Organización Militar of January 1984 converted the General Staff into an organ of military advisors directly responsible to the prime minister, the government and the minister of defence. The internal structure of the Ministry of Defence was reformed so that the army, the navy and the air force became one single unit, directly responsible to a sub-secretary of state while in military matters, they were responsible to the chief of the armed forces, who was described as 'the minister's right hand man'. The idea of a military power with full autonomy for defence matters was therefore shelved, in favour of civil predominance, as was clearly reflected by the sacking of certain high ranking officers who made highly critical statements about these changes. The spectre of the military coup therefore vanished from the Spanish political arena for the first time since the beginning of the transition.

The idea of a firm pact with certain institutions also informed many of the reforms in education, an area of major conflict with the Church, which historically had dominated private education. The new cabinet initiated its reforms to primary education via the so called Ley Orgánica del Derecho a la Educación, which recognized the existence of private and public schools and also introduced the concept of public funding for private schools. Education in such schools became free and students had to be admitted according to geographical proximity. In addition, such schools were now run by a system of collective administration. Heavily criticized by the right and by private education federations, this law was well received by the Episcopal Conference, which saw in it a continued guarantee of the generous state sums – over 100 billion pesetas in 1982 – that private education had always received even though previously there had been no legal stipulation to that effect. The majority of religious-run primary schools were now subsidized and have remained so. Having dealt in this way with the traditional conflict with the Catholic Church, the government also sought to avoid conflict over another issue, abortion. It decided to allow it only in cases of serious danger to the life and health of the mother, of rape, or of deformation of the foetus.

In the field of Justice, the Ley Orgánica del Poder Judicial gave Parliament the power to elect all 20 members of the top judicial body, the Consejo General del Poder Judicial, not just eight as established by the 1980 law. A subsequent ruling by the Tribunal Constitucional deemed that this was unconstitutional and warned of the danger of electing members to the Consejo according to the political composition of the parliament. As time has shown, the court did point to a very crucial factor: the system of quotas has prevailed over other criteria in electing members of the Consejo. In addition, in a very short space of time, many new and young judges appeared on the scene through the system of state exams and parliament approved many of the laws envisaged in the Constitution, such as the laws of rights and freedoms of foreigners, Habeas Corpus, the right to meeting and trade union legislation.

While they developed such laws aimed at consolidating democracy, the Socialists continued something that had been initiated by the UCD governments: an increase in public spending. After the austerity measures, there was a major thrust towards tax increases and a more efficient system of tax collection, especially with regard to salaries. The idea behind such an increase was to face the problem of the increase in public spending, which, between 1973 and 1985, grew from 22.7 per cent to 42.5 per cent of GDP and reached 49.7 per cent in 1993. In so doing, in just a few years, Spain had closed the gap that had always separated it from other European states, although the system adopted – increased taxes – probably served to increase the level of tax fraud and gave rise to a very significant submerged economy, problems which the government confessed its powerlessness to resolve.

But not only did Spain have to close the gap that separated it from the welfare states: in doing so it had to be careful to satisfy the aspirations of the various autonomous communities that make up the Spanish state. In addition to redrawing the political map of the country, it was necessary to give some real functions to the new autonomous governments, a particularly thorny issue as far as Catalonia and the Basque Country were concerned. The Socialists had to decentralize state spending as well as increase the national budget. Decentralization took the form of massive transfers to the regional governments: over 20 per cent of the national budget in 1988 and 25 per cent in the mid-1990s. After no end of conflict and negotiations, parliament passed an organic law for the financing of the Autonomous Communities so that apart from a notable increase in social spending, one of the most salient features of the socialist years was a no less significant reduction in the proportion of expenditure that the central government had at its disposal. This is a feature which makes Spain strongly resemble a federal state.

Having reassured the business class, been careful not to offend the

Church, made sure the army was firmly under control and addressed the most pressing needs of the autonomous regions – four of the major stumbling blocks of the Republic – the Socialists extended their centrist thrust to foreign policy. The PSOE had carried out a very strong anti-NATO campaign in October 1981. Felipe González had even said that if Spain had entered the Alliance via simple parliamentary decision, it could also leave it in the same way. The first measure of his government was not, however, to prepare such an exit but the very opposite. It sought immediately to consolidate Spain's presence within the Alliance. While the country awaited the referendum, another socialist election promise, the government started to defend a position completely opposed to the one held by the PSOE while it was in opposition. Pressure from the USA and other European countries, the importance of remaining in NATO as a stepping stone towards entry into the EEC and the establishment of closer links with the Alliance were the factors responsible for a change from an attitude of 'comprehension' to a series of ambiguous but increasingly favourable declarations about remaining within the Alliance. From the autumn of 1983 onwards, Felipe González never tired of warning that it would be unwise to leave the Alliance at a time of great tension between the two super-powers.

The decision not to leave NATO, along with two other major issues, reflected the course that the government's foreign policy was going to take: the strengthening of relations with the United States and the acceleration of negotiations for Spain's entry into the EEC. The first led to the ratification, in April 1983, of the General Agreement on Friendship, Defence and Cooperation between Spain and the United States, which revised the Bases Treaty of 1953. As far as the second issue was concerned, the government took special care to improve the tense relations with France which had marked the previous years, especially after Spain's request to join the EEC had been paralysed when French president Valery Giscard d'Estaing put a halt to the negotiations until the thorny issue of financing was resolved. In keeping with this new spirit and thanks to the Italian presidency, the negotiations received a great push during the first quarter of 1985. At the end of March, one day before the Council of Europe meeting, the Spanish delegation, headed by Foreign Minister Fernando Morán, announced, with as much joy and satisfaction as fatigue, that the negotiations were over. Soon after, on 12 June, first in Lisbon in the morning, then in Madrid in the afternoon, the European Community formally extended its borders to Spain and Portugal.

The formal entry of Spain into the European Community on 1 January 1986 provided Felipe González with the opportunity he needed to announce the promised referendum on NATO. With great skill and no less risk, he presented the referendum as a manner of consulting the country on a decision that had already been taken. The terms proposed in the referendum question were: abstention from the full military structure of the Alliance; the prohibition to install, store or introduce nuclear arms into Spanish territory and the gradual reduction of the US military presence in Spain. If the answer was 'no', Spain would not leave NATO, but González would resign in order to allow someone else to 'administer' the result of the referendum. This virtual plebiscite served to sway a significant portion of the population – which, according to polls, seemed undecided – into saying 'yes', even though throughout the campaign and even just prior to voting, it had maintained that its answer would be 'no'. Of the 29 million Spaniards eligible to vote, only 27.2 per cent actually did. 11.7 per cent said 'yes' and 9.05 per cent said 'no' with 6.54 per cent casting blank votes. Although it was not an overwhelming victory, the Prime Minister came out of it sufficiently confident to dissolve parliament and call general elections.

Four years after coming to power, things could not have looked better for the government: the Socialist party had accepted important modifications to its programme and maintained strong internal unity. In the political arena, the Socialists were still very much the dominant force, since the right was still very much a victim of a leader who was still too strongly associated with Francoism. The worst of the economic crisis was over and a period of great activity and expansion, characterized by an annual rate of growth of 4 per cent until 1991, was about to begin. Unemployment had also improved, with some two million jobs having been created between 1985 and 1990. There were no problems with the financial and business world, which was kindly disposed towards a government that had tackled the crisis with rigour and seriousness; and the spectre of military coups seemed to have disappeared forever, with the army, for the first time, completely subjected to civil power. The Church had ceased to be a problem and the nationalists, except for the persistence of Basque terrorism, had found new and valid grounds for their political demands. Though many promises had been broken and others – such as the modernization of the civil service, an issue which they simply lacked the courage to tackle, had been put off – Spain was now in Europe, the realization of the impossible dream of liberals and the enlightened alike. And, furthermore, not everything could be done in just one term of office. In the words of the Prime Minister, Spain would need 25 years of a socialist government to become a truly modern nation.

Slow and steady decline

It was hardly surprising, therefore, that the Socialists repeated their success of 1982 in the 1986 elections, though not with the same kind of expectancy and with far fewer votes than in 1982. In contrast to the crisis being experienced by social democratic parties in Northern Europe, and to the growing difficulties of their southern European counterparts, the PSOE stood out as the only socialist party in Europe with an absolute parliamentary majority, ready and able to start another four year term, though with their parliamentary majority reduced. This time they had won 8.8 million votes, 1.2 million and 4 percentage points fewer than in 1982. But they were still far ahead of their closest rival, the Alianza Popular, which trailed them by 18 points. This led to the resignation of its leader, Manuel Fraga, and marked the beginning of a period of uncertainty during which a new leader was sought. It was not until 1990 that the party was renamed the Partido Popular (the Popular Party) and José Maria Aznar elected leader.

This second triumph could not conceal the first open rifts within the 'socialist family', which resulted in a break with the UGT, which historically had always been closely linked to the PSOE. Until then the union had been willing to accept the government's stiff policies and had decided, at its June 1983 congress, to go along with only moderate salary increases. But even then, there had been very clear signs of discontent at the manner in which the government had gone about the implementation of its economic programme without previously consulting the union. The length of time taken to introduce the 40 hour work week, the plan for greater flexibility in the labour market, which envisaged more temporary contracts and the conflict brought about by 'industrial reconversion' were the first visible signs of differences between the unions and the government. As early as 1984, UGT general secretary Nicolás Redondo had made no secret of his disappointment and bitterness: the union had been a victim of the government, which it accused of extreme high-handedness and of having succumbed to the whims and fancies of the aristocracy. The government, in reply, dismissed the unions as archaic in their outlook and added that they knew nothing about macroeconomics.

But there was still no threat of definitive rupture. Throughout 1984 the UGT maintained its policies of negotiation, the fruit of which was the signing with the government and business associations, but without the Comisiones Obreras, of the Economic and Social Agreement. However, the double pressure that resulted from the government's economic policy and the confrontation with the rival union pushed the UGT leaders further and further away from a government of which they became more and more critical. In July 1985, Nicolás Redondo could not conceal his bitterness at the pension reform project, which he viewed as the culmination of a hostile offensive against the rights that the working class had fought long and hard to obtain. Now, social security was in danger and this was something that the UGT simply was not going to tolerate. 'We can't accept the manner in which negotiations have been carried out, neither can we accept the reform in itself', said Redondo, underlining something in which he believed profoundly: to ask for help, one has to negotiate. 'But to our great surprise and dismay we have encountered a series of decisions made and policies implemented without being previously consulted.'

Once the recession was over, the unions vainly attempted to have a say in the government's economic policy, now being dictated by the new Finance

Minister, Carlos Solchaga. The fact that they belonged to the same socialist family; the personal friendship between Felipe González and Redondo; and the firm belief that they had been deceived, further strained relations between the PSOE and the UGT. The final straw was the approval of the Youth Employment Programme, which the unions considered to be detrimental to employment. It was a relatively minor affair that eventually sparked off massive mobilization against the government just when the economy was growing at its highest rate and when more jobs were being created than ever before. The general strike called on 14 December 1988 was an unprecedented success: the entire country was shut down, an event which many analysts saw more as a moral protest against a style of government than against policies considered wrong or misguided.

The government called general elections in October 1989, which the PSOE again won, though this time with 900 000 fewer votes, and with only one seat more than the number it needed for an absolute majority. This seemed to confirm the decline which had been in evidence since the municipal elections of 1987, but given that the major opposition party remained immersed in the crisis into which it had fallen since 1982, it could not be considered a serious alternative. Even so, the first signs of socialist weakness were very clear. Though still the major force in towns and municipalities of fewer than 50 000 people, they had already lost their absolute majority in the big cities, and the youth and more 'educated' voters had already turned their backs on them. The honeymoon they had enjoyed for such a long time with public opinion was drawing to a close, though the electorate did not seem overly anxious to vote for their rival. The results of those elections, which allowed the Socialists to govern for a third consecutive term without having to seek parliamentary support, had to be attributed largely to the reluctance of the electorate to vote for a party which appeared to be situated too far to the right – for many, the extreme right – of the political spectrum.

This very narrow socialist victory could be attributed to the same factors that had provoked the general strike: growing discontent with the government, as much as with its policies. Since 1982 the PSOE had governed virtually without opposition, with a legislature that was active in passing legislation but not in its mission of controlling the government, and with a party that was disciplined and unified and in which any critical voices were swallowed up in the self-satisfaction of the majority. In control of the state radio and television and riding the euphoria of an economic boom, the Socialists believed that they were in power to stay and acted as if the laws that they had passed on party financing did not apply to them.

That same year, 1989, the Juan Guerra scandal came to light. Juan Guerra, the deputy Prime Minister's brother, was accused of insider dealing and other irregularities in his capacity as his brother's 'assistant' in Seville. It was also discovered that he had, for some time, occupied an office at the headquarters or the regional government of Andalucia, though he had no official governmental position. It was also discovered that during that period he had become exceedingly rich. Alfonso Guerra's speech in parliament, in which he openly defied the opposition and threatened to reveal other scandals, only made things worse.

Juan Guerra soon appeared as a symbol of a whole system in which insider dealing, the use of privileged information, the receipt of commissions, payments for reports that did not exist and, most of all, the mixing of private business affairs with public responsibilities, had been common practice. As would later be revealed, parties had resorted to illegal methods of financing in order to meet the increasing costs of modern politics and this had given rise to the proliferation of clients and friends of high-ranking public servants who took advantage of their positions to serve their own private interests. As far as the PSOE was concerned, it came to light in May 1991 that a company called Filesa had been constituted precisely to finance the party. There was subsequently a long and drawn out legal process and court hearing, during which time the party executive lived under the cloud of institutionalized corruption that benefited the party as well as the networks of clients and families which had been built up around such illegal practices. In March 1993, an official report from the Ministry of Finance revealed that Filesa had received over one billion pesetas as payment for reports that never existed, in order to pay PSOE bills.

The Guerra and Filesa cases and other minor scandals brought to light the existence of practices of illegal financing for personal gain similar to those which had been revealed in France, Italy and Greece. In Spain, the rapid economic growth after 1986, which went hand in hand with easy money for speculators and adventurers, the continuation of one party in power for a long time, the extraordinary rise in the level of public spending, heavy state investment in massive infrastructure projects, the virtual lack of control mechanisms prior to the approval of major expenditure from the Ministry of Finance, political decentralization and the increase in sources from which expenditure was made, coupled with rising expenses of political parties, brought about generalized and widespread corruption that neither the government nor the PSOE seemed particularly anxious to curb. In fact, the control that the nucleus of power – centred around Alfonso Guerra – had come to have over the party after the 1984 congress and the absolute awe in which Felipe González was held as leader, prevented such corruption from ever coming to light.

This grim political situation got even worse after the much touted celebrations of 1992. The important legacy of the World Fair – held in Seville to commemorate the quincentennary of Columbus' arrival in America – and the Olympic Games in Barcelona, was a severe economic recession. Even though analysts had predicted that recession as much as a year earlier, the authorities went ahead with the feverish preparation of those events. In just one year, all the gains made in employment during the previous five years evaporated. Once again, the fall in GDP was accompanied by massive job losses, pushing the unemployment figure up to 24 per cent – some 3.5 million people – a

Spanish record. The vast majority of the unemployed were young people in search of their first job.

When the World Fair was closed and the Olympic torch went out, a new era began of dim lights and bleak perspectives, with more cases of corruption coming to light almost every day. Instead of being a year of splendour, as the Socialists had hoped, 1992 turned out to be, as many of the socialist leaders themselves recognized, a 'catastrophic' year. It was also a grim year for party–government relations. Alfonso Guerra, seriously weakened by the scandal involving his brother, resigned as deputy Prime Minister. The apparent triumph of the 'Guerrista' sector of the party in the 32nd PSOE congress in November 1990, had only worsened the internal wrangling between those who called themselves *'renovadores'* ('renovators'), close to the Prime Minister, and those close to Guerra who though in control of the party and in the majority in parliament, had no presence in the government. (In fact, there were few differences of substance between the two groups.) The struggle for power within the party came on the back of the cases of corruption and the economic crisis. Party unity broke over two key issues: when Felipe González decided to demand explanations from his colleagues on the executive for the Filesa affair and the very visible differences between the government and the socialist parliamentary group over a proposed new strike law. González decided to put an end to the wrangling by dissolving parliament and calling early elections. Unity had been one of the PSOE's biggest boasts, but this time the party faced the electorate divided and accused, on all sides, of corruption. They were also being held responsible for an economic situation that public opinion considered nothing short of catastrophic.

In spite of all this, the Socialists won the elections again, although it might be more accurate to say that the PP lost again. They had to be content with reducing the distance between themselves and the Socialists to a mere 4 percentage points. This fourth consecutive victory – when all the forecasts had indicated certain defeat – was due above all to Felipe González's leadership. On the night of the victory, he assured Socialist supporters that he had understood their 'message'. He had presented himself in the Madrid constituency with Baltasar Garzón – a judge who had made a name for himself in his fight against narcotics and his handling of the alleged dirty war against the Basque terrorist organization, ETA – as the number two on the Socialist list. But this time even González could not secure an absolute majority in Parliament and he had to find allies. González had always been opposed to any left coalition that might bring back memories of the Popular Front of 1936, and he chose to deal with the moderate Catalan and Basque nationalists rather than the United Left alliance led by the Communists. While he did not manage to convince them to enter his cabinet, he did get them to agree to support his government in parliament. The result was a minority government, not exactly the best situation from which to tackle the political storms that were brewing.

A long series of scandals

The fragility with which the Socialists started their new term in office did not come solely from the loss of their majority. There was also the risk of an internal breakup, given the division between 'Guerristas' and 'renovators' at the 33rd party congress, held in March 1994. González had dissolved parliament because of the lack of discipline within the socialist parliamentary group; his aim now, at least as the Guerristas saw it, was to reduce the level of control that they had within the party. Eventually, after long negotiations, many Guerristas gained important positions on the executive and this was interpreted by all as a triumph of 'integration' over 'renewal', all in an effort to divert attention from the daily corruption scandals.

With the party divided, the government had to face the worst corruption scandals of the new democratic era. The 'hundred years of honesty', the famous words of the PSOE 1982 election slogan, came tumbling down when 'the chief of the guards ran away with the money and the chief of the money was seen between two guards', as Joáquin Leguina, President of the regional government of Madrid, put it. Mariano Rubio, governor of the Bank of Spain, was accused of having an account in Ibercorp, a bank that belonged to his friend, Manuel de la Concha, a former executive of the Stock Exchange, who was also taken to court. Around the same time, Luis Roldán, the first civilian director of the 150-year old Civil Guard, was accused of having amassed a personal fortune thanks to commissions received for all sorts of contracts. Rubio was sent to prison and Roldán had fled the country, and both became symbols of how corruption had penetrated two very fundamental state institutions: the Bank of Spain and the Civil Guard. Carlos Solchaga and Jose Luis Corcuera, ex-ministers of Finance and the Interior respectively, resigned from parliament for having kept the 'delinquents' in their jobs. This was followed by the resignation of Corcuera's successor for his responsibility in allowing Roldán to slip through the hands of police and skip the country, and that of the Minister of Agriculture, accused of tax fraud. All this caused such alarm and sparked off such a crisis that the opposition, on the right and the left, as well as an important and influential part of the media, started to call on González to resign.

This situation lent special significance to the European elections held in June 1994. The defeat of the Socialists, who only managed 30.7 per cent of the vote, provided further arguments to the opposition, who continued to call for general elections, only a year after those of June 1993. Many analysts, some of them close to the Socialist party and the government, also went along with this call, taking the view that the longer the government took to do so, the worse the margin of the inevitable defeat was going to be. But for the Prime Minister, who said that a heavy defeat in the European elections would make him 'rethink things', 31 per cent of the electorate was not heavy enough. When, soon after, he once again secured the support of the Catalan nationalists, he saw no reason to dissolve parliament, reshuffle his cabinet or even consider the possibility of a vote of no confidence. So, very much against opinions vehemently expressed by the media, González chose simply to present a package of new political measures after the summer holidays, in an effort to demonstrate renewed capacity and initiative, confident that the economic recovery that was beginning was a sign of brighter times.

This was not to be. There were only more political storms. The judge who had been González's 'number two' in the Madrid constituency in the June 1993 elections, Baltasar Garzón, abandoned politics and returned to his position in the judiciary. He reopened the case on the dirty war against ETA and granted provisional freedom to two policemen who had been convicted for having belonged to the Antiterrorist Liberation Group (GAL) which, between 1983 and 1987, had killed some 28 people. These men started to point accusing fingers at their superiors and in December 1994, Garzon sent Julián Sancristóbal, former Civil Governor of Vizcaya and General Director for Security, to prison, accused of attempted murder and the wrongful arrest of a French citizen who had been mistaken for an ETA member. Two months later, the same judge ordered the imprisonment of Rafael Vera, ex-secretary of state for security, and Ricardo García Damborenea, general secretary of the Socialist party in Vizcaya during the period when the kidnapping took place. When he sent Vera to prison, the judge stated that 'a terrorist network closely linked to the Ministry of the Interior' had been organized. News of the arrests still had not died down when the bodies of José Antonio Lasa and José Ignacio Zabala, two ETA militants kidnapped by the GAL in 1983, were discovered and identified in Alicante.

At almost the same time, two leading figures in the business and financial world who had risen to prominence in the eighties and who were extremely well connected to the political establishment in Madrid and Barcelona, Mario Conde and Catalan businessman Javier de la Rosa, were also called before the courts for tax fraud and embezzlement and subsequently sent to prison. In addition to those scandals, on 20 April 1995, José María Aznar miraculously escaped unscathed from an ETA car-bomb attempt on his life. The alarm caused by this, along with the scandal that had surrounded Luis Roldán's 'capture' and subsequent handing over to Spain by authorities in Laos, coloured the political climate that preceded the municipal and regional elections called in May. The PP won another important victory, gaining 35.2 per cent of the votes, against the 30.8 per cent that went to the PSOE. Significantly, the Socialists lost in all the capitals of the country's major provinces as well as in the big cities.

What followed was absolute disaster for the government. After the Bank of Spain and Luis Roldán came the scandal of the missing documents of the CESID, the Spanish secret service. The papers in question, which were allegedly removed by the agency's subdirector, Colonel Juan A. Perote, could implicate important politicians in the creation and activities of the GAL. Those papers were put into public circulation through a network controlled by businessmen and politicians who had been arrested and it was also revealed that the papers contained important references to telephone bugging and eavesdropping on important political figures, even possibly the king. This led to the resignation of two ministers very close to Felipe González: deputy Prime Minister Narcís Serra, Minister of Defence at the time when eavesdropping and recordings allegedly took place, and his successor, Julián García Vargas.

In the face of such a scandal, Jordi Pujol, president of the regional government of Catalonia, withdrew his parliamentary support for the government and refused to vote to approve the 1997 budget. This left the government in the minority, and the Prime Minister had no choice but to call an early election as soon as Spain had finished its six month presidency of the European Union. At the beginning of 1996, Felipe González finally put an end to a very turbulent three-year term by calling elections for 3 March. Although the Spanish presidency of the Union was a success and in spite of the economic recovery which was beginning, all the forecasts pointed to a heavy Socialist defeat and it was almost taken for granted that the PP would form a majority government. Once again forecasts were proved wrong. With 9.4 million votes and 141 seats in parliament, the PSOE came a very close second to the PP, who won only 300 000 more votes and 156 seats, some way from an absolute majority.

Table 21.2 Electoral results of the major parties 1993–96 (% of the vote)

	1993 National	1994 European	1995 Municipal	1996 National
PSOE	38.8	30.8	30.8	37.5
Partido Popular	34.8	40.1	35.3	38.8
Izquierda Unida	9.2	13.4	11.7	10.6

By no means a crushing defeat, it was sufficient to remove the Socialists from power for the first time since 1982. It marked the end of a long period of 'light and darkness', during which democracy in Spain was firmly consolidated and the spectre of military coups obliterated. Spain had opened its market to the world and had become a fully-fledged member of the European Community (later Union); it had experienced great economic growth but had been unable to resolve its major problem, unemployment, which at times reached alarming proportions. It had satisfied the demands for autonomy of its different regions and nationalities, but had not resolved the problem of Basque terrorism. It had modernized a great deal of its infrastructure and customs, but had not been able to rid itself of that strange mixture of cliques and family interests which, as in so many Latin countries, informs the political culture. Successes and failures, yes, but it is still too early to make more than a provisional assessment of the Socialist era in Spain.

Chronology

1856–62	O'Donnell's 'prestige policies' lead to military expeditions to Morocco, Indochina, Mexico and Peru
1863–64	Fall of O'Donnell and return of Moderates under General Narváez
1866	Pact of Ostend unites all opposition forces against the Moderates
1868	General Prim's *pronunciamiento* in Cádiz sends Isabella II into exile. First Cuban War begins
1870	General Prim assassinated. Amadeo of Savoy becomes king
1872	Beginning of new Carlist War
1873	Amadeo abdicates and First Republic proclaimed. Revolt of the Cantons begins
1874	General Pavia's coup ends Federal Republic
1875	General Martínez Campos' coup leads to Restoration of the Bourbons under Alfonso XII
1876	Constitution of 1876 proclaimed
1878	End of First Cuban War
1879	Creation of Socialist Party (PSOE)
1881	First Liberal government under Sagasta
1885	Alfonso XII dies. Pact of the Pardo. Beginning of Sagasta's 'Long Government'
1888	Creation of Socialist union federation Unión General de Trabajadores (UGT)
1890	Universal male suffrage. End of 'Long Government' and return to power of Cánovas
1892	Bases of Manresa, first major statement of Catalan nationalism. Beginning of anarchist terrorism in Barcelona
1895	Last Cuban War begins. Basque Nationalist Party (PNV) created
1897	Cánovas assassinated
1898	Spanish–American War. Spain loses Cuba, Puerto Rico and Philippines
1899	'Regenerationist' government of Silvela. Lliga Catalana created
1902	Alfonso XIII ascends the throne
1905	'¡Cu-Cut! Incident'
1906	Law of Jurisdictions and creation of Solidaridad Catalana
1907	Antonio Maura's 'Long Government'. Creation of Solidaridad Obrera
1909	Tragic Week in Barcelona. Execution of Francisco Ferrer. Fall of Maura
1910	José Canalejas heads Liberal government. Creation of anarcosyndicalist Confederación Nacional del Trabajo (CNT)
1912	Canalejas assassinated. Declaration of Protectorate in Morocco

1913	Creation of José Ortega y Gasset's League for Political Education
1914	Spain declares neutrality in First World War
1917	Juntas militares de Defensa. Assembly of Parliamentarians in Barcelona. General strike in Asturias
1918	First 'government of concentration' headed by Maura. Beginning of 'Bolshevik triennium' in Andalucia and of *pistolerismo* in Barcelona
1921	Prime Minister Eduardo Dato assassinated. Military defeat at Annual (Morocco)
1923	Assassination of CNT leader Salvador Seguí. General Primo de Rivera's *pronunciamiento* ends constitutional government
1925	Alhucemas landing in Morocco
1930	Fall of Primo de Rivera. Failed republican uprising in Jaca
1931	Municipal elections. Proclamation of the Second Republic. National elections
1932	Failed *pronunciamiento* by General Sanjurjo. Catalan autonomy statute and Agrarian Reform Law passed
1933	Creation of CEDA. National elections
1934	Asturian revolution
1936	Creation of Popular Front. National elections. Military uprising begins Civil War. General Franco becomes leader of Nationalists. Arrival of International Brigades. Defence of Madrid. Non-Intervention Agreement signed
1937	Creation of single party (FET y de las JONS) in Nationalist zone. Nationalists conquer northern Spain. Juan Negrín becomes Republican Prime Minister
1938	Nationalists reach the Mediterranean. Battle of the Ebro
1939	Civil War ends with Nationalist victory. Franco declares 'non-belligerence' in Second World War
1940	Franco meets Hitler. Spain stays out of the war but sends Blue Division to fight against Soviet Union
1942	Fall of Serrano Suñer. Spanish policy moves towards greater neutrality
1945	Don Juan de Borbón issues Lausanne Manifesto
1946	United Nations condemns Franco regime
1947	Agreement between Franco and Don Juan sends Juan Carlos to Spain
1950	UN lifts sanctions against Spain
1951	Barcelona public transportation strike
1953	Concordat with the Vatican. Bases Treaty with United States
1955	Spain admitted into UN
1956	Student protests

1959	Visit of US President Dwight Eisenhower. New 'technocratic' cabinet with Opus Dei ministers. Stabilization Plan
1962	Miners' strikes in Asturias. Opposition groups meet in Munich
1963	First Development Plan. Julián Grimau executed
1965	Student demonstrations. Leading intellectuals expelled from university posts
1966	Referendum of Organic Law of the State
1968	Basque separatist organization ETA kills first victim
1969	Juan Carlos declared Franco's successor
1970	Burgos Trial
1973	Prime Minister Luis Carrero Blanco assassinated by ETA
1974	Renovation of PSOE under Felipe González. Creation of Junta Democrática. Franco ill and temporarily replaced as Head of State by Juan Carlos
1975	Franco dies. Juan Carlos becomes king
1976	Widespread strikes. Adolfo Suárez named Prime Minister. Law of Political Reform
1977	Communist Party legalized. First democratic elections since 1936 won by Suárez's UCD. Moncloa Pacts
1978	Democratic constitution approved
1979	National elections won by UCD. Autonomy statutes for Catalonia and Basque Provinces approved
1981	Suárez resigns. Attempted military coup. Spain joins NATO
1982	PSOE wins majority in national elections. Beginning of 'dirty war' against ETA
1985	Spain joins European Economic Community (EEC)
1986	Referendum on NATO membership. PSOE wins second majority
1988	General strike
1989	PSOE wins third election
1990	Juan Guerra case begins corruption scandals
1992	Olympics in Barcelona and World's Fair in Sevilla. Economic crisis begins
1993	PSOE wins minority in national elections. Outbreak of a series of scandals
1996	Partido Popular (PP) defeats PSOE. José María Aznar forms minority government

Further Reading

General works

Banón Martínez, Rafael and Barker, Thomas M. (eds), *Armed forces and society in Spain past and present*, New York, 1988.

Boyd, Carolyn P., *Historia patria: politics, history and national identity in Spain, 1875–1975*, Princeton, 1997.

Carr, Raymond, *Spain, 1808–1975*, 2nd edn, Oxford, 1982.

Chandler, James, (ed.), *Spain in the twentieth-century world*, London, 1980.

Enders, Victoria and Radcliff, Pamela, (eds), *Constructing Spanish womanhood: female identity in modern Spain*, Albany, 1999.

Graham, Helen and Labanyi, Jo, (eds), *Spanish cultural studies*, Oxford, 1995.

Harrison, Joseph, *An economic history of modern Spain*, Manchester, 1978.

Lannon, Frances, *Privilege, persecution and prophecy: the Catholic Church in Spain, 1875–1975*, Oxford, 1987.

Martin, Benjamin, *The agony of modernization: labor and industrialization in Spain*, Ithaca, 1990.

Payne, Stanley, *Politics and the military in modern Spain*, Stanford, 1967.

Ringrose, David R., *Spain, Europe and the 'Spanish miracle', 1700–1900*, Cambridge and New York, Cambridge University Press, 1996.

Sánchez-Albornoz, Nicolás, (ed.), *The economic modernization of Spain, 1830–1930*, New York, 1987.

Shubert, Adrian, *A social history of modern Spain*, London, 1990.

Simpson, James, *Spanish agriculture: the long siesta, 1765–1965*, Cambridge, 1995.

Part I The Travails of Liberalism, 1808–1874

Anna, Timothy, *Spain and the loss of America*, Lincoln, 1983.

Barahona, Renato, *Vizcaya on the eve of Carlism: politics and society, 1800–1833*, Reno, 1989.

Burdiel, Isabel, 'Myths of failure, myths of success: new perspectives on nineteenth-century Spanish liberalism', *Journal of Modern History*, (Dec. 1998), pp. 892–912.

Burdiel, Isabel and Romeo, María Cruz, 'Old and new liberalism: the making of the Spanish Liberal Revolution, 1808–1844', *Bulletin of Hispanic Studies*, (1998), pp. 105–20.

Callahan, William J., *Church, politics, and society in Spain, 1750–1874*, Cambridge, Mass., 1984.

Charnon-Deutsch, Lou and Labanyi, Jo, (eds), *Culture and gender in nineteenth-century Spain*, Oxford/New York, 1995.

Christiansen, E., *The origins of military power in Spain, 1800–1854*, London, 1967.

Cruz, Jesús, *Gentlemen, bourgeois and revolutionaries: political change and cultural persistence among Spanish dominant groups, 1750–1850*, Cambridge, 1996.

Kiernan, V. G., *The revolution of 1854 in Spanish history*, Oxford, 1966.

Kirkpatrick, Susan, *Las románticas: women writers and subjectivity in Spain, 1835–1850*, Berkeley, 1989.

Schmidt-Nowara, Chris, *Empire and anti-slavery: Spain, Cuba and Puerto Rico, 1833–1874*, Pittsburgh, 1999.

Tone, John, *The fatal knot: the guerrilla war in Navarre and the defeat of Napoleon in Spain*, Chapel Hill, 1994.

Tortella Casares, Gabriel, *Banking, railroads and industry in Spain, 1829–1874*, New York, 1977.

Waddell, D.A.G., 'International politics and Latin American Independence', in L. Bethell, (ed.), *The Cambridge history of Latin America*, Cambridge, 1985.

Part II The Restoration, 1875–1914

Balfour, Sebastian, *The End of the Spanish Empire, 1898–1923*, Oxford, 1997.

Cabrera, Mercedes, *Con luz y taquígrafos. El Parlamento en la Restauración*, Madrid, Taurus, 1998.

Chandler, James, 'Spain and her Moroccan Protectorate, 1898–1927', *Journal of Contemporary History*, (1975), pp. 301–23.

de la Cueva, Julio, 'The stick and the candle: clericals and anticlericals in northern Spain, 1898–1913', *European History Quarterly*, (Apr. 1996), pp. 241–65.

Esenwein, George, *Anarchist ideology and the working-class movement in Spain, 1868–1898*, Berkeley, 1989.

Glas, Eduardo Jorge, *Bilbao's modern business elite*, Reno, 1997.

González Hernández, Maria Jesús, *El universo conservador de Antonio Maura. Biografía y proyecto de Estado*. Madrid, Biblioteca Nueva, 1997.

Kern, Robert, *Liberals, reformers and caciques in Restoration Spain, 1875–1909*, Albuquerque, 1974.

Lario, Angeles, *El Rey, piloto sin brújala. La Corono sistema politico de la Restauración (1875–1902)*, Madrid, Biblioteca Nueva, 1999.

Luzón, Javier Moreno, *Romanones. Caciquismo y política liberal*, Madrid, Alianza, 1998.

Linz, Juan, 'Parties, elections and elites under the Restoration Monarchy in Spain, (1875–1923)', *Seventh World Congress of Political Science*, 9 (1967).

Moradiellos, Enrique, '1898: A colonial disaster foretold', *ACIS. Journal for the Association for Contemporary Iberian Studies*, (1993), pp. 33–8.

Nadal, Jordi, 'The failure of the industrial revolution in Spain, 1830–1914', in C. Cipolla, (ed.), *Fontana economic history of Europe*, vol. 4, part 2, London, 1973.

Offner, John, *An unwanted war: the diplomacy of the United States and Spain over Cuba, 1895–1898*, London, 1992.

Romero Maura, Joaquín, 'Caciquismo as a political system', in E. Gelner, (ed.), *Patrons and clients in Mediterranean societies*, London, 1977.

Suárez Cortina, Manuel, (ed.) *La Restauración, entre el liberalismo y la democracia*, Madrid, Alianza, 1997.

Smith, Joseph, *The Spanish–American War*, London, 1994.

Tortella, Gabriel, 'An interpretation of economic stagnation in nineteenth-century Spain', *Historia Ibérica*, (1973), pp. 121–32.

Tusell, Javier and Portero, Florentino, (eds) *Antonio Cánovas y el sistema político de la Restauración*, Madrid, Biblioteca Nueva, 1998.

Ullman, Joan C., *The Tragic Week*, Cambridge, 1969.

Varela Ortega, José, 'Aftermath of splendid disaster: Spanish politics before and after the Spanish–American War of 1898', *Journal of Contemporary History*, (1980), pp. 317–44.

Part III Spain in the interwar crisis of liberalism, 1914–1939

Alpert, Michael, *A new international history of the Spanish Civil War*, London, 1994.

Ben Ami, Shlomo, *Fascism from above*, Oxford, 1985.

Blinkhorn, Martin, *Spain in conflict, 1931–1939*, London, 1986.

Bolloten, Burnett, *The Spanish Civil War*, Chapel Hill, 1991.

Boyd, Carolyn P., *Praetorian politics in Liberal Spain*, Chapel Hill, 1979.

Carr, E.H., *The Comintern and the Spanish Civil War*, New York, 1984.

Carr, Raymond, *The Civil War in Spain*, London, 1986.

Coverdale, John, *Italian intervention in the Spanish Civil War*, Princeton, 1975.

Esenwein, George and Shubert, Adrian, *Spain at war: the Spanish Civil War in context*, London, 1995.

Horn, Gerd Rainer, *European socialists respond to fascism*, New York, 1997.

Johnson, Roberta, *Crossfire: philosophy and the novel in Spain, 1900–1934*, Lexington, Kentucky, University of Kentucky Press, 1993.

Litvak, Lily, *A dream of Arcadia: anti-industrialism in Spanish literature, 1895–1905*, Austin, Texas, University of Texas Press, 1975.

Loughran, D.K., *Federico García Lorca: the poetry of limits*, London, Tamesis, 1978.

Malefakis, Edward, *Agrarian reform and peasant revolution in Spain*, New Haven, 1970.

McGaha, Michael D., *The theatre in Madrid during the Second Republic*, London, Grant & Cutler, 1980.

Morris, C.B., *Surrealism and Spain: 1920–1936*, Cambridge, Cambridge University Press, 1972.

Nash, Mary, *Defying male civilization: women in the Spanish Civil War*, Denver, 1995.

Payne, Stanley, *Spain's first democracy: the Second Republic, 1931–1936,*·Madison, 1993.

Preston, Paul, *The Coming of the Spanish Civil War*, London, 1994.

Preston, Paul and Mackenzie, Anne, (eds), *The Republic besieged*, Edinburgh, 1996.

Radcliff, Pamela, *From mobilization to civil war: the politics of polarization in the Spanish city of Gijón, 1900–1937*, New York, 1996.

Richardson, R. Dan, *Comintern army: the International Brigades in the Spanish Civil War*, Lexington, 1982.

Romero Salvadó, Francisco, 'Spain and the First World War: the structural crisis of the liberal monarchy', *European History Quarterly*, 1995, pp. 529–54.

Shaw, Donald, *The Generation of 1898 in Spain*, London, E. Benn, 1975.

Shubert, Adrian, *The road to revolution in Spain*, Urbana, 1987.

Spires, Robert C., *Transparent simulacra: Spanish fiction from 1902–1926*, Columbia, 1988.

Townson, Nigel, *The crisis of democracy in Spain: centrist politics under the Second Republic (1931–1936)*, Brighton, 1999.

Vernon, Kathleen, (ed.), *The Spanish Civil War and the visual arts*, Ithaca, 1990.

Part IV The Franco Regime, 1939–1975

Balfour, Sebastian, *Dictatorship, workers and the city: labour in Greater Barcelona since 1939*, Oxford, 1989.

Cazorla, Antonio, 'Dictatorship from Below: *Journal of Modern History*, 1999.

Cooper, Norman B., *Catholicism and the Franco Regime*, London, Sage, 1975.

Ellwood, Sheelagh, *Spanish fascism in the Franco era*, Basingstoke, 1987.

Lieberman, Sima, *Growth and crisis in the Spanish economy, 1940–1993*, London, 1995.

Nash, Mary, 'Pronatalism and motherhood in Franco's Spain', in Gisela Bock and Pat Thane (eds) *Maternity and Gender Policies: Women and the Rise of the European Welfare States, 1880s–1950s*, London and New York, 1991.

Nash, Mary, *Defying Male Civilization: Women in the Spanish Civil War*, Denver, Arden Press, 1995.

Payne, Stanley, *Falange: a history of Spanish fascism*, Stanford, 1967.

Richards, Michael *A time of silence: Civil War and the culture of repression in Franco's Spain, 1936–1945*, Cambridge, 1998.

Preston, Paul, *Franco: a biography*, London, 1993.

Preston, Paul, (ed.), *Spain in crisis: evolution and decline of the Franco regime*, Hassocks, 1976.

Part V The Democratic Monarchy

Arbós, X., 'Central versus peripheral nationalism in building democracy: the case of Spain', *Canadian Review of Studies in Nationalism*, **14** (1987).

Barrera-González, A., *Language, collective identities and nationalism in Catalonia, and Spain in General*, European University Institute Working Paper EUF 95/6, 1995.

Carr, R. and Fusi, J.P., *Spain: from dictatorship to democracy*, London, 1979.

Clark, R., *The Basque insurgents: ETA, 1952–80*, Madison, 1980.

Clark, R., *Negotiating with ETA: obstacles to peace in the Basque Country, 1975–1988*, Reno, 1990.

Colomer, J.M., *Game theory and the transition to democracy*, Aldershot, 1995.

Conversi, D., *The Basques, the Catalans and Spain: alternative paths to nationalist mobilization*, London, 1996.

Díez Medrano, J., *Divided nations: class, politics, and nationalism in the Basque Country and Catalonia*, Ithaca, 1996.

Desfor Edles, L., *Symbol and ritual in the new Spain*, Cambridge, 1998.

Gilmour, David, *The transformation of Spain*, London, 1985.

Harrison, Joseph, *The Spanish economy: from Civil War to the European Community*, Basingstoke, 1993.

Johnston, H., *Tales of nationalism: Catalonia 1939–1979*, New Brunswick, 1991.

Keating, M., *Nations against the state: the new politics of nationalism in Quebec, Catalonia and Scotland*, London, 1996.

Lannon, Frances and Preston, Paul, (eds), *Elites and power in twentieth-century Spain*, Oxford, 1990.

Maravall, J.M., *The transition to democracy in Spain*, London, 1982.

Núñez, X.M., 'Region-building in Spain during the 19th and 20th centuries', in G. Brunn (ed.), *Region: wissenschaftliche Konzepte und politische Aufgaben*, Baden-Baden, 1996.

Pérez Díaz, V., *The return of civil society*, Cambridge, 1993.

Share, D., *The making of Spanish democracy*, New York, 1986.

Sullivan, J., *ETA and Basque nationalism: the fight for Euskadi 1890–1986*, London, 1988.

Index